Fire in the Hearth

V

Fire in the Hearth

The Radical Politics of Place in America

VOLUME FOUR OF *THE YEAR LEFT*

Edited by Mike Davis, Steven Hiatt,
Marie Kennedy, Susan Ruddick
and Michael Sprinker

VERSO

London · New York

First published by Verso 1990

Verso
UK: 6 Meard Street, London W1V 3HR
USA: 29 West 35th Street, New York, NY 10001-2291

Verso is the imprint of New Left Books

A CIP catalogue record for this book is available from the British Library

ISBN 0-86091-263-9
0-86091-976-5 (pbk)

US Library of Congress Cataloging-in-Publication Data

Fire in the Hearth : the radical politics of place in America /
edited by Mike Davis et al.
p. cm. --(The Year left ; v. 4) (The Haymarket series)
ISBN 0-86091-263-9. --ISBN 0-86091-976-5 (pbk.)
1. Municipal government--United States--Case studies.
2. Radicalism--United States--Case studies. I. Davis, Mike, 1946-
II. Series.
JS341.L38 1990
320.8'5'0973--dc20

Typeset by Northstar
San Francisco, California
Printed in USA by Courier

This volume of *The Year Left* is dedicated to

Mauricio Gastón, 1947–1986

Activist, urban theorist and planner,
Mauricio Gastón put his skills to work by
helping working-class communities like Roxbury
take control of the development of their
neighborhoods and their lives

The Haymarket Series

Editors: Mike Davis and Michael Sprinker

The Haymarket Series is a new publishing initiative by Verso offering original studies of politics, history and culture focused on North America. The series presents innovative but representative views from across the American left on a wide range of topics of current and continuing interest to socialists in North America and throughout the world. A century after the first May Day, the American left remains in the shadow of those martyrs whom this series honours and commemorates. The studies in the Haymarket Series testify to the living legacy of activism and political commitment for which they gave up their lives.

Already Published

BLACK AMERICAN POLITICS: From the Washington Marches to Jesse Jackson (Second Edition) *by Manning Marable*

PRISONERS OF THE AMERICAN DREAM: Politics and Economy in the History of the US Working Class *by Mike Davis*

MARXISM IN THE USA: Remapping the History of the American Left *by Paul Buhle*

THE LEFT AND THE DEMOCRATS: *The Year Left 1*

TOWARD A RAINBOW SOCIALISM: *The Year Left 2*

RESHAPING THE US LEFT – POPULAR STRUGGLES IN THE 1980s: *The Year Left 3*

CORRUPTIONS OF EMPIRE: Life Studies and the Reagan Era (Second Edition) *by Alexander Cockburn*

FIRE IN THE AMERICAS: Forging a Revolutionary Agenda *by Roger Burbach and Orlando Núñez*

MECHANIC ACCENTS: Dime Novels and Working-Class Culture in Nineteenth-Century America *by Michael Denning*

THE FINAL FRONTIER: The Rise and Fall of the American Rocket State *by Dale Carter*

POSTMODERNISM AND ITS DISCONTENTS: Theories, Practices *Edited by E. Ann Kaplan*

AN INJURY TO ALL: The Decline of American Unionism *by Kim Moody*

THE SOCIAL ORIGINS OF PRIVATE LIFE: A History of American Families, 1600–1900 *by Stephanie Coontz*

OUR OWN TIME: A History of American Labor and the Working Day *by David Roediger and Philip Foner*

YOUTH, IDENTITY, POWER: The Chicano Movement *by Carlos Muñoz, Jr.*

Forthcoming

CITY OF QUARTZ: Excavating the Future in L.A. *by Mike Davis*

RANK-AND-FILE REBELLION: Teamsters for a Democratic Union *by Dan LaBotz*

THE MERCURY THEATER: Orson Welles and the Popular Front *by Michael Denning*

THE POLITICS OF SOLIDARITY: Central America and the US Left *by Van Gosse*

THE HISTORY OF BLACK POLITICAL THOUGHT *by Manning Marable*

Contents

PART I

The San Francisco Bay Area

1

The Playground of US Capitalism? The Political Economy of the San Francisco Bay Area in the 1980s

Dick Walker and The Bay Area Study Group[1]

The San Francisco Bay Area has always been an anomalous enclave within US capitalism. It is too big, too rich, too left, too swish, too cosmopolitan, too weird, too much fun to live in. Can this really be part of the same country as Youngstown and Dallas? Such bold differences among regions tell us something about the varieties of capitalisms that are possible, unexpected openings for social change, and the elusiveness of forging a viable political response to the diverse situations in which people find themselves. To focus on a single region is not merely to fill in the details in the Big Picture of a world capitalism that develops evenly across the globe. It is, rather, to try to capture the workings of uneven and combined development, which is the way capitalism expands and renews itself globally.

Many of the key developments in capitalism – industrial shifts, class transformations and political struggles – begin in localized settings, from which their effects reverberate to a larger world (Storper and Walker, 1989). Because 'the local becomes the global' where key social and industrial changes are concerned, it is particularly important for the left to understand the lineaments of local economy, society and polity in those places that take a leading role in the capitalism of their time. Like Lancaster in 1830 or New York in 1920, California has been one of the key poles of capitalist development in the twentieth century; it is now the sixth largest economy in the world, having just passed Great Britain. The San Francisco Bay region forms one end of the coastal urban axis on which

California's fortunes turn.[2]

California and the San Francisco Bay Area are indicative of many of the most important developments within US and world capitalism in the late twentieth century. Among these are leading sectors such as the electronics, aerospace and biotechnology industries; 'flexible' production complexes such as Silicon Valley and Hollywood; globalized banking and investment; a 'service' economy featuring high levels of tourism, finance and retail activity; a class structure shifted towards technicians, professionals and white-collar workers and replete with nouveaux riches; new forms of 'postmodern' consumption and social life; and the massive absorption of new nationalities and women into capitalist production and the class system. In fact, California and the Bay Area in particular have been the hearth of some of these developments, particularly for the United States: new technologies, 'yuppie' culture, the new immigration, the military-industrial complex. Their roots often go back to World War II and beyond, although it is only in recent years that people have begun to speak of a new epoch of capitalism, or what is now commonly referred to as 'post-Fordism'.[3]

The Bay Area is arguably the quintessential post-Fordist city, but such a claim is both a provocation and a quandary. A provocation because it is a view to be contested in light of other local experiences and possibly proven wrong; and a quandary because it is a challenge to ourselves and our comrades, jolting us into recognizing the significance of things lying just under our noses, and therefore seemingly of less importance than those far away in the global economy or the battlefields of US imperialism. Yet the claim of significance is also hard to accept because the new and the striking are mingled with the commonplace of California urbanism and because the bold successes and emergent possiblities are no more discovered than they are thrown into doubt by economic crisis and the banalization of California life-styles.

The contradictions of the Metropolis-by-the-Bay are considerable: they include more than its summery winters and wintery summers. According to conventional economic wisdom, the Bay Area ought not to be as economically successful as it has been, because the costs of living and doing business here have always been virtually the highest of any major city in the US. Although not known as a manufacturing base, it has surpassed in size such productivist behemoths as Philadelphia and Detroit. Yet once again fears are rife of an economic decline in the face of new global economic challenges. A further contradiction is that large-scale capital has been firmly entrenched in the economy since the 1850s, yet labor has also been remarkably strong and well organized. The Bay Area has never had the kind of proletarian milieu of nineteenth-century mill towns, New York at the height of European immigration, or Detroit in the banner years of mass production; yet it has supported some exceptional examples of working-class radicalism. Certain segments of the working class of the Bay Area – chiefly white males – have been exceedingly well favored by strong demand and short supply, but others – chiefly Latinos and Asians – have suffered under some of the most oppressive working conditions in US history.

San Francisco and the Bay Area have nurtured an extraordinarily rich cultural milieu, of which the Great Yuppie Awakening is only the latest version. The region has long boasted a worldly flair, bohemian tolerance and polyglot make-up, from the adventurers of 1849 to the gay mecca of the 1970s. But this claim sits uneasily with a record of racism that makes the blood run cold, and a kind of de facto racial exclusion today that belies the liberal reputation of its white majority. The Bay Area has been a pioneer of the American way of urban life, from the mid-twentieth century suburb in all its studied plainness to the new urbanity of California cuisine. It is therefore a place oddly caught between the baroque idealism of 'alternative life-styles' and the crass materialism of rampant real estate speculation, where the latter is regularly discussed in the hot tubs of the former. Finally, nowhere else is the discourse of the left as likely to have entered the mainstream of American ideas and politics as in the Bay Area since the 1960s. Yet leftists find themselves at something of an impasse today, seriously disconnected from the blue-collar working class, the new gentry and even from each other.

The impasse of the left is doubly disturbing because the new faces being shown by capitalism in the closing decades of the century have had some dire political consequences. California has not only brought the world microelectronics and venture capital, it has sent forth the nights of Reaganism and the dark days of Nixon, and much of Carter's cabinet. This is hardly accidental, and flows from many springs of California's political-economic culture, such as dependence on military contracting, weak electoral parties and media mastery. At the same time, it suggests that we ought to look more closely at the reasons for the weakness of labor and progressive politics in a place like the Bay Area and for indications of resistance, for the city on the bay has never caved in to the New Right, from Reagan's aerial assault on Berkeley in the 1960s to the anti-gay campaigns of the Moral Majority in the 1980s.

The local left is, however, seriously constrained by narrow geographic bases focused on Berkeley, Santa Cruz and San Francisco. Spatial concentration and historic tradition have been sources of strength, of course, illustrating what Dolores Hayden calls 'the power of place' in shaping people's experience of capitalism and responses that grow out of their immediate conditions. But the places that shape most people's lives in the region lie beyond the pale as far as the left is concerned. In emphasizing a renewed attention to the local, then, we do not endorse a narrow version of community activism; instead, we argue for a 'metropolitan vision' to complement the left's relatively more developed national and international perspectives.

Our focus on place derives also from an urban vision that sees capitalism as not only the production of commodities but entire cities (Harvey, 1985a). Capitalism without urbanization is as unthinkable as capitalism without factories (Scott, 1988a). Urban areas serve as vast productive complexes and support systems for industry – and are themselves being constructed and reconstructed, piece by piece. The 'point of production' is therefore not confined to the shop floor – as important as that is – while all the rest can be relegated to the nether world of consumption or labor reproduction; it encompasses whole industrial landscapes, vast stretches of homes, multiple government jurisdictions and far-flung transport networks.

The place on which we focus is, in fact, huge: a ten-county region embracing about 7,800 square miles and 6 million people. It is now the fourth largest urban area in the United States. The City and County of San Francisco, which in the mid-nineteenth century comprised virtually the whole of the urbanized area around the bay (and over half the population of California), has long since been eclipsed in size by its 'suburban' ring. But only part of this ring consists of suburbs in the sense of bedroom communities. Rather, the outer realms of the metropolis are the mighty constructs of twentieth-century urbanism. Oakland and its East Bay suburbs grew spectacularly in the first half of the century, surpassing San Francisco by the early 1950s. San Jose and the Santa Clara Valley exploded after

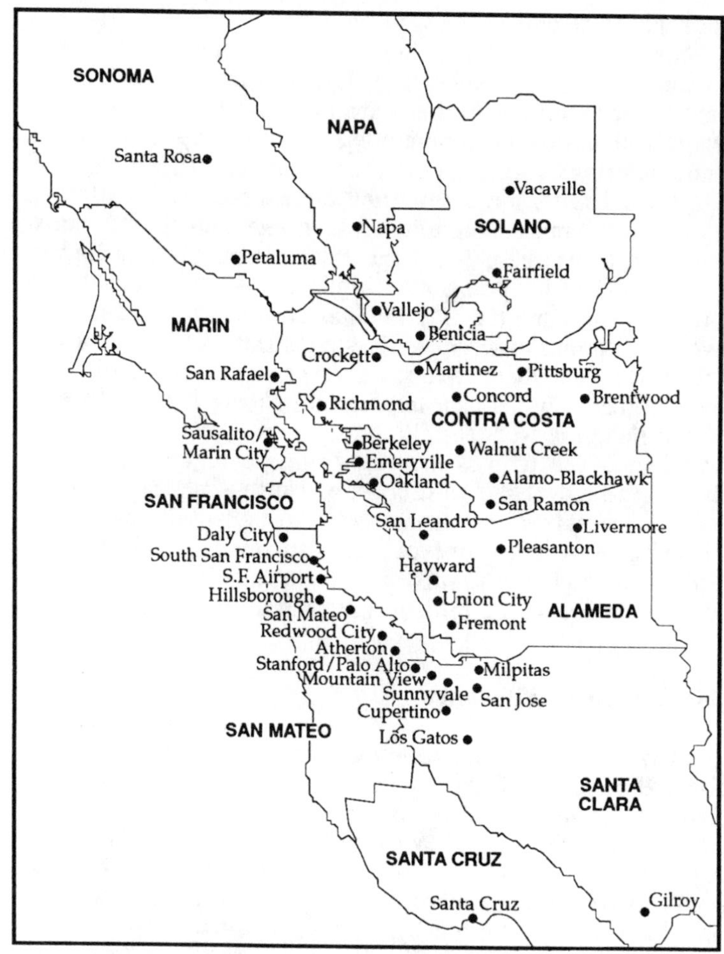

Figure 1 The ten-county San Franciso Bay Area

World War II to become the third great urban realm to be added to the metropolis, passing San Francisco by the early 1960s and Alameda County by the early 1970s. Contra Costa County overtook San Francisco in 1987.[4] There are more than four pieces to this immense urban puzzle, of course, but the important thing is to see that they fit together, despite their many differences, and that one does not leave 'San Francisco' by crossing the Golden Gate Bridge or the Bay Bridge, as one once did by stepping onto a ferryboat.

This essay serves, then, both as an introduction to a significant locale and an attempt to show that the Bay Area is distinctive and confounding in several ways. The first is the region's high-growth economic base, particularly its high-tech manufacturing, high-stakes finance and high-life recreation. The second is its upwardly tilted class structure, manifest in legions of yuppies, engorged real estate values and mass-gentrified landscapes. The third is its profoundly transformed working class, including new kinds of immigrants and new forms of work, and the way this has allowed the once-impressive fortifications of working-class organization to be breached. The fourth is the distinctive racial mix and new forms of racial division that now pervade the region, making it both the best of cities and the worst of cities for Asian, Latino and African Americans. The fifth is the vagary of the region's capitalist class, first-born of the west coast of North America and yet a perennial weakling that cannot seem to pull itself together to tackle the growing pains of an overextended and anarchic metropolis. And, lastly, we consider the state of the Bay Area left, caught between a brilliant past and a disoriented present.

The Gilt-Edged Economy

It is fitting that the main pollution threat in southern San Francisco Bay is from thousands of pounds of gold, silver, platinum, cadmium and other precious metals that pour from the sewers of Silicon Valley every year. Even waste has a gilt edge here. The economy of the region has, from its birth in the Gold Rush, been uniquely blessed. In recent years, the twin pillars of the region's economy have been high-tech electronics in Silicon Valley and high-flying finance in San Francisco.[5] Behind these giants come several other distinctive and favored sectors, such as business services, tourism and higher education, which have propelled the region's rapid growth and shaped its peculiar political economy.

The gross regional product of the ten-county Bay Area was $141 billion in 1986. If it were a country, it would rank among the fifteen largest national economies (about equal to the Netherlands). Total employment in 1987 reached 3,045,800 (CSAC, 1989); between 1962 and 1982 employment grew 116 percent compared to a US average of 71 percent and a California average of 105 percent (Brady, 1985a,b).[6] Job growth was much faster in the 1970s, when about 800,000 jobs were added at a rate of 4 percent per year. In the 1980s about 550,000 jobs were added, a rate of about 2 percent a year (Rosen and Jordan, 1988: 6).

Silicon chips and blue chip finance

The main engine of expansion in the Bay metropolis for the last thirty years has been the microelectronics industrial complex of Silicon Valley, including semiconductors, computers and instruments. Silicon Valley is the popular name for the area centered on the Santa Clara Valley, at the northern end of Santa Clara County, and spilling over into Santa Cruz, Alameda and San Mateo counties. Employment in Santa Clara County grew from 251,000 to 832,000 over the period 1964 to 1984, a 5.7 percent annual rate (State of California, 1985; CSAC, 1985). On this base, the population of Santa Clara County grew from 642,000 in 1960 to 1,421,000 in 1987, making it the largest population center in the region. Indeed, some regional planners are concerned about how thoroughly wedded the area has become to its leading sector (Brady, 1985a, 1986).

The Valley is the diversified core of the national and global microelectronics industry. It is the leading center of technical innovation in chip, computer and software design, and a major production zone for such things as microprocessors, disk drives and missile guidance systems (Siegel, 1988–89; Morgan and Sayer, 1988). Silicon Valley is the place everyone else seeks to imitate, as in Silicon Glen (Scotland), Silicon Desert (Albuquerque) and Silicon Forest (Portland), but none of the other high-tech centers in the US such as Route 128 or North Carolina's Research Triangle can match Silicon Valley's size and performance (Glasmeier, 1985). The Valley is now home to a host of new *Fortune* 500 companies: Amdahl, Hewlett-Packard, Raychem and Apple, to name a few. And it continues to generate new stars in the corporate firmament such as Sun Microsystems, Cypress Semiconductor, Weitek and Flextronics. The great strength of the Valley is its immensely rich complex of firms, skilled labor and knowledge, from which comes a stream of innovations as new design and production problems are posed and solved through a collective effort studded with individual brilliance – with a dollop of social conscience and the wallop of venture capital and lust for fame and fortune

(Saxenian, 1989; Scott, 1988b).

The microelectronics industry has had the world for its playground. Over the last twenty years, the Valley has spun off several major growth peripheries around the western US, including Sonoma County and northern Sacramento County in California, and its companies have installed plants throughout Western Europe and Southeast Asia – first assembly works and now increasingly fabrication and design facilities (Scott and Storper, 1987). It has as well deep ties through subcontracting and marketing to both areas. Indeed, electronics has been the very model of a globalizing industry and of a burgeoning Pacific Rim – although the left has often jumped to exaggerated conclusions about the New International Division of Labor based on short-term trends and certain segments of the industry (Morgan and Sayer, 1988). Its fate has, more recently, been increasingly linked to Japan, through heated competition, inward investment, subcontracting and joint ventures.

San Francisco is only slightly less representative of global financial expansion than Silicon Valley is of high-tech growth. The city has long rested among the elite of 'world cities' in the United States, along with New York, Chicago and Los Angeles (Noyelle and Stanbach, 1984). From the time of the Gold Rush until around 1980, San Francisco was the financial center of the West. It was the only significant independent pole of accumulation west of St. Louis during the nineteenth century. While challenges from Seattle, Los Angeles and other rising cities displaced San Francisco from its virtual financial and trade monopoly in the early part of this century, the city remained the preeminent business center in the West, and even rose to second place (after New York) in the amount of bank assets, surpassing Chicago sometime around 1950 (Borchert, 1978). The principal source of this continued vitality was A.P. Giannini's Bank of America, whose innovative branch-banking and liberal lending policies and, later, credit cards propelled it to become the largest bank in the world for much of the post-war era. The world headquarters of the VISA credit card operation remains in San Mateo.

San Francisco is the location for 75 major banking offices, and headquarters for 5 of the top 100 US banks (*American Banker*, 1989). B of A still ranks as the third largest bank in the United States in terms of assets, while rival Wells Fargo now ranks ninth. The Pacific coast's regional federal reserve bank is located here, and the city co-hosts the Pacific Stock Ex-

Figure 2 Principal economic zones of the Bay Area

ZONE	PLACE	IMPLANTED	ACTIVITIES
1	San Francisco/ Oakland	1850-1900	Mercantile, finance, headquarters Shipping & warehousing
2	East Bay Contra Costa Coast	1900-1940	Heavy industry Oil refining
3	West Bay Suburbs East Bay Suburbs	1870–1930	Elite residential areas
4	Silicon Valley	1950-1970	Electronics
5	I-680 corridor	1970-1990	Back Office

← Main growth corridors in the 1980s

change and is home to many brokerage houses such as Charles Schwab and Dean Witter. San Francisco also serves as headquarters to major nonfinancial corporations, including 14 *Fortune* 500 companies. Chevron is one of the ten largest industrial corporations in the world, Bechtel the world's largest engineering firm, Pacific Gas & Electric the nation's largest private utility, and Levi-Strauss the world's largest clothing manufacturer. The city's Montgomery Street shares the world's largest venture capital pool with Silicon Valley's Sharon Business Center (Florida and Kenney, 1988). San Francisco boasts one of the country's premier business services complexes, which includes major accounting, law, engineering, data processing, advertising and management consulting firms, such as Deloit and Touche and McKinsey and Company. All of the Big Eight (now Big Six) accounting firms have their regional headquarters in San Francisco.

Total employment in offices in downtown San Francisco is roughly 200,000: 180,000 in 1988 not including the staff of industrial corporations (Rosen and Jordan, 1988). Business services alone grew 425 percent from 27,000 to 142,000 jobs between 1962 and 1982 (Brady, 1985a: 5). San Francisco remains among the premier office centers in the country, and has experienced a major building boom in each of the last three decades, bringing total office space to 54 million square feet, about two-thirds of which is in the core financial district. A record 9 million square feet were added in 1985–88 in the downtown area alone (Rosen and Jordan, 1988).

The San Francisco financial, managerial and business services complex was never particularly local, having its tendrils extended throughout California and the western US. The city's mercantile empire has stretched across the Pacific for over a century. Financial growth here was part of the global financial eruption that ocurred after 1970 due to industrial sclerosis blocking former investment outlets, global outreach and 24-hour securities trading, and deregulation and fantastic rates of innovation in financial instruments (Sweezy and Magdoff, 1987; Harvey, 1982; Shapira, 1986; Thrift and Leyshon, 1988). It is the main point of entry for Chinese capital in the US, with deepening ties to the financial centers of East and Southeast Asia, and it has a healthy Japanese connection as well.

In the Bay Area as a whole, the financial-business services complex has spread outward, down the Peninsula, into Marin County, over to Emeryville, and particularly across the East

Bay hills to eastern Contra Costa and Alameda counties, in what is now called the 'I- 680 corridor', where some 20 million square feet of new office space were added in the 1980s, filled mostly by San Francisco–based companies, led by Chevron, Bank of America and Pacific Telesis. This dispersal has consisted principally of 'back office' functions that are too expensive to keep in the center city, and which draw on the ample pool of female labor in the suburbs (Nelson, 1986).

Secondary growth sectors

The Bay Area is home to some other exceptionally prosperous industries that back up its Big Two. The petroleum processing and petrochemicals complex along the Contra Costa coastline, including six major refineries, a Dow chemical and plastics plant, and a huge PG&E power plant, dates to the turn of the century, when incoming San Joaquin Valley oil made this one of the premier oil-processing sites in the world for about thirty years. The remaining food-processing and metal-working plants of Alameda County are a legacy of a time when California was the canning capital of the world (backed up by the revolutionary development of capitalist agribusiness in the interior valleys) (Cardellino, 1984) and had built up a considerable regional strength in machining, machine-making and vehicle assembly. The transport, shipping and warehousing functions along the Bay's edge go back to the beginning of San Francisco's mercantile empire, and still include four ports (Oakland, Richmond, San Francisco and Redwood City) and three major airports (San Francisco, Oakland and San Jose).[7] In both sea and air traffic, the Bay Area ranks among the top five centers in the country. The wine industry of the Napa Valley and the North Bay is world-renowned, and surprisingly well capitalized and profitable. The Bay Area is headquarters to an international construction industry, led by Bechtel, Morrison-Knudsen, Utah Construction and Kaiser Engineers, who set the standard for large-scale projects in the mid-twentieth century with such pioneering edifices as the Boulder and Grand Coulee dams, the Bay and Golden Gate bridges, and the planned city of Riyadh in Saudi Arabia. One also cannot overlook the amount of employment in government work, by local counties, municipalities and special districts, as well as in the many federal and state government regional offices, particularly in San Francisco's Civic Center.[8]

Another group of economic activities that employ large numbers of local workers deserve special mention: tourism, restaurants and retail sales. Often not considered 'industries' because they involve a greater degree of direct 'consumer contact' than traditional manufacture (but see Walker, 1985), they in fact indicate important trends in consumerism and in capitalist penetration of the realm of consumption and other areas of personal life (Harvey, 1989). Recreation and tourism have as their main form a huge hotel and entertainment complex located principally in San Francisco itself. San Francisco presently has around 19,000 hotel rooms, serving about 3 million visitors per year. San Francisco has always been a transient city and has been chock-a-block with hotels since at least the time of the Panama Pacific Exposition (Groth, 1983); much of the hotel space is still occupied by the normal flux of business travelers. But the city has also become one of the nation's leading convention centers and host to a vast flood of tourists from around the world: 28 million visitor days, $2.8 billion spent and 60,000 jobs. Another sector of note is the restaurant trade, which is extraordinarily large in San Francisco and the Bay Area as a whole: in 1986, per capita spending on prepared food was $200 higher than in any other city (*Restaurant Business*, 1987).

A further adjunct to this consumer service complex is an exceptional retail sector, with the highest per capita sales of the ten largest metropolitan areas in the US (Rosen and Jordan, 1988: 49). The Union Square–Market Street triangle does the second highest volume of retail business in the country after Midtown Manhattan (about $1.2 billion annually in sales), and is claimed to be first in sales volume per square foot (*Examiner*, 11 September 1988). Boutique shopping has also transformed Berkeley and parts of North Oakland into a gentrified playground of the East Bay middle class. So vibrant is the Bay Area shopping scene that it, too, breeds hip new retail chains with national profiles, such as Banana Republic, Williams-Sonoma, Esprit and CP Shades. The San Francisco region thrives in the new era of capitalist consumerism by virtue of its wealth and the vast expansion of consumer credit generally, but also by the modernist irony of self-promotion: the city sells itself – the capitalist playground – as a commodity to be enjoyed in measured doses, even fully packaged in plastic, as at Fishermen's Wharf (Walters, 1986). The same goes for Sausalito or the Napa Valley, and this model is being eagerly imitated by enterprising developers in whatever pockets of quaintness remain, as in Crockett or the Oakland waterfront.

A rather different group of 'industries' serving their consumers mostly on site are educational and medical complexes. The Bay Area is second only to Boston as a center for institutions of higher learning, led by the University of California and Stanford University. These are huge employers in their own right, as well as attracting thousands of students: UC Berkeley alone employs around 15,000 people and has 33,000 students. The medical schools are a major part of this complex, with their research facilities and teaching hospitals. Hospitals, nursing homes and doctors' offices are dotted throughout the region, of course, but a disproportionate number cluster around central San Francisco and Oakland's 'Pill Hill'. A prodigal offspring of the wedding of local university medical researchers and venture capitalists is, of course, the fledgling biotechnology industry. The Bay Area is the leader in this still-infant field and home to its two most famous (and heavily capitalized companies), Cetus and Genentech (Blakely, 1987). Most of the companies in that field are located in Emeryville, South San Francisco and Palo Alto.

It is impossible to ignore, lastly, the military economy of the Bay Area. During the two World Wars, the Korean and Vietnam Wars and the Cold War generally, the Bay Area was built up into one of the principal shipping and supply points for the Army, Navy and Air Force. The Navy has the greatest presence today with a half-dozen major facilities around the bay; the Air Force maintains the huge Travis Air Force Base in Solano County and its 'Blue Cube' satellite control center in Sunnyvale; the Army has cut back to its Oakland supply base, the San Francisco Presidio and Camp Parks. Total employment at local bases exceeded 40,000 in 1987 (Schutt and Siegel, 1988). A remarkable but short-lived burst of growth was generated by turning the Bay Area into the world's largest shipbuilding center during World War II, with the Kaiser and Bechtel yards hiring over 150,000 workers (Nash, 1985). Equally remarkable, and more sustained, was the link forged between scientific research and the federal government by E.O. Lawrence, which produced the atomic bomb. The Lawrence Livermore Laboratory still visits its weapons of doom on the world, and sold Reagan on the Star Wars program.

But the biggest outlet for Defense Department spending in the Bay Area is contracting for aerospace electronics systems from Silicon Valley companies. Silicon Valley was suckled on defense spending, although it has increasingly gone its own way since the 1960s (Siegel and Markoff, 1985). Total defense spending for the ten Bay Area counties in 1987 was $8.760 billion (compared with $19.733 billion for greater Los Angeles). Santa Clara County has the second largest county total for prime DOD contractsin the US, after Los Angeles County, with $4.437 billion; and the Bay Area takes in $5.792 billion as a whole, compared to $18.920 billion for greater L.A. Lockheed's plant in Sunnyvale, employing around 20,000 people, takes in over $2 billion by itself (Schutt and Siegel, 1988, 1989). The Bay Area did exceedingly well in Star Wars contracts during 1983–88, with $3 billion, or some 20.6 percent of the US total.

Competition and restructuring

'All that is solid melts into air', as Marx and Engels observed in *The Communist Manifesto*. With growth, capitalism brings change and a fearsome inconstancy in the fortunes of peoples and places (Storper and Walker, 1989). One can never be certain that prosperity will last, even in a place as blessed as the Bay Area. The 1980s were a rocky patch for the region's economy.

Workers have always been the first to know. As the Reagan depression hit in 1982, the long decline of certain heavy manufacturing sectors in California became a rout (Shapira, 1986). Job growth almost everywhere was negative except in Silicon Valley (Rosen and Jordan, 1988: 6). Virtually all steelworks, lumer mills, tire plants and vehicle assembly plants shut down, and cutbacks were severe in food processing, containers and metalworking. Yet the carnage was largely concealed by the electronics and financial booms of the same period. When the huge General Motors plant closed in 1982, the mayor of Fremont declared his indifference because that town had just been hit by the spreading wave of growth from Silicon Valley (*Chronicle*, 1 March 1982). Also overlooked were the grim facts about employment in electronics itself: very rapid turnover, frequent plant openings and closings, and long bouts of unemployment (Shapira, 1986).

By contrast, when the bourgeoisie was hit by economic turbulence in 1985–86, the public outcry was deafening. It has concentrated on three issues: Japanese competition in electronics, the financial ascendency of Southern California, and buy-outs of San Francisco–based companies. All three are indicative of important trends in global capitalism and of global restructuring. In each case the challenge is serious but the near-hysteria among some local observers is not warranted by the evidence.

When electronics went into a severe slump in the mid-1980s, leaving millions of square feet of new office space lying empty (Kroll and Kimball, 1986), the reverberations were widely felt. Indeed, the regional high tech economy has only just recovered from the 1984–85 downturn in Silicon Valley. This cyclic overproduction crisis raised fears that the Japanese had dealt the Valley a killing blow by their mastery of the production of very large memory chips (DRAMs) and associated equipment (Stowsky, 1987). Rumors of Silicon Valley's incipient death were in fact greatly exaggerated: the Valley revived smartly in the late 1980s on the basis of companies and technologies that go well beyond the now-lumbering semiconductor pioneers (Saxenian, 1989). Important doubts have been raised, however, about the Valley's reliance on new product breakthroughs in lieu of manufacturing followthrough, compared with Japanese industry. Sharp criticism has been directed at venture capital for promoting get-rich-quick schemes for new firms (often premature and at the cost of continuity in older firms), hypermobility of skilled labor and managers (highly disruptive to sustained innovation), and lack of adequate coordination among an overly fragmented set of loosely related small and medium-sized firms (Florida and Kenney, 1990; Cohen and Zysman, 1987).

The mighty economic volcano of Southern California has now raised its financial peak above that of its elder competitor to the north. Indicative of San Francisco's financial decline relative to Los Angeles was the near-collapse in the mid-1980s of the Bank of America, which *Business Week* wryly called 'the incredible shrinking bank'. Bank of America got its fingers badly burned by trying to blaze its way ahead of competitors into the international arena in the 1970s, as well as in domestic real estate, oil drilling and farming. Other harbingers of trouble have been the disappearance of the one-time eighth-largest bank in the country, Crocker Bank, and the transfer of the greater part of the Pacific Coast Stock Exchange to L.A. About 5,000 banking jobs were lost in San Francisco in the mid-1980s. To compound the problem, Japan, the capitalist Mount Fuji, has been spewing vast flows of hot money over the globe, buying local banks (for example, Mitsubishi Bank owns Bank of California and Bank of Tokyo owns California First Bank) and favoring Southern over Northern California with investments.

On the other hand, Bank of America has rebounded of late, thanks in part to an injection of about $700 million of Japanese capital, after staving off a purchase effort by L.A.'s First Interstate. Hong Kong capital favors the Bay Area over Los Angeles. San Francisco–based First Nationwide Financial Corp. has exploded to become the second largest savings and loan institution in the country, backed by cash from Ford Motor (*New York Times*, 12 Jan. 1989). The Bay Area economy has been growing at about the same rate as L.A.'s in the late 1980s, and has matched L.A. in employment growth rates since the mid-1970s (Rosen and Jordan, 1988: 6–7). But given that greater L.A. is now twice the size of the Bay Area, no one should be surprised that it has finally passed the North in the accumulation of capital.[9]

Another frightening prospect has been the purchase of many of San Francisco and Oakland's old-line companies by outside interests – for example, Crown-Zellerbach, Southern Pacific, Del Monte, Genstar, Pacific Lumber, Natomas and the various pieces of Kaiser Industries (McLaughlin, 1988). Some eighteen of the thirty-two *Fortune* 500 industrial companies headquartered in San Francisco in 1979 have been acquired by outside investors, as have many hotels, department stores and office buildings. Even newer companies have been swallowed: Saga, Shaklee and Cost Plus. In certain cases assets have been stripped, offices closed and profits diverted worldwide. At the same time, the startup of new firms in San Francisco has slowed and the growth of office centers in the South Bay and East Bay further undermines San Francisco's claim to business hegemony in the region. To make matters worse, mighty Bechtel and Chevron both fell on hard times, as the 1982 recession and the world oil bust cut deeply into their business.

Nevertheless, the economic loss due to ownership changes can easily be exaggerated. Many of the merged companies are remnants of an older regional industrial base resting on timber, canning and mining (Malone, 1986); these are no longer growth sectors. Losses are compensated for by the growth of new businesses in the city, many of them started by immigrants. Mergers do not always eliminate local office functions: for example, Del Monte and Kaiser Engineers are still here. Finally, the sword of mobile capital cuts both ways: Chevron bought Gulf Oil in the largest merger in history; California First Bank bought L.A.'s Union Bank; Southern Pacific was merged with the Denver & Rio Grande Western and headquartered again in San Francisco. San Francisco capitalists have investments nationwide and worldwide, from which they, too, siphon off profits (Pred, 1977). Calculating the net result of the crisscrossing of capital flows is impossible, and the case remains anecdotal (for example, McLaughlin, 1988).

All this highlights the grip of external forces on any local economy, even a prosperous one: deindustrialization in older sectors, intensification of geographic competition, globalization of capital investment. Nonetheless, it is rather disingenuous to fret over the loss of local ownership of capitalist enterprise and real estate, in the manner of the *Bay Guardian*, when San Francisco has been the spider in a web of distant exploitation for its entire history. We should also pause before shedding tears for the Bay Area's 'decline' relative not to the Lilliputians of the world, such as Nashville, but by the Brobdingnagian standards of Los Angeles and Tokyo. Finally, mourning over the passing of older industries leaves one grasping at the past. One should, rather, attend to the transformation and restructuring of capital and capitalist production that lies beyond the immediate crisis, and from which the Bay Area has largely benefitted, not suffered. Whether its favored economic status can be maintained by the same engines of growth is difficult to say. But clearly the conditions of labor and life in the San Francisco metropolis have been and will be for some time to come more a product of capitalist success than of capitalist crisis. This fact fundamentally sets the Bay Area political agenda in a way markedly different from talk of crisis and deindustrialization in a manner relevant to less fortunate cities such as Buffalo.

The Empire of Skilled Labor

The Bay Area is the capital of Yuppie America. It is here that the *arriviste* middle class is most disproportionate in size to the general population and has the greatest opportunity to speak in its own voice and to try to establish its own class position – in all its creative ambiguity.

The concentration of well-paid occupations and capitalist income in the Bay Area is extraordinary. The core region (not including Santa Clara County) was the fourth richest metropolitan area in 1976, with a per capita income 32 percent above the national average (Judge, 1979: 99). The 1987 per capita income for the Bay Area as a whole was $21,520, almost 20 percent higher than the average for California.[10]

But the yuppie wave rests on more than wealth: it has deep roots in the peculiar economic base and history of the region. San Francisco has been exceptionally favored from the time of the Gold Rush, both in its concentration of wealth and in the power of the populace to extract a portion of that wealth from the exclusive dominion of the capitalist class. Mike Davis calls the Gold Rush 'the only successful revolution of 1848', meaning by this that the 49ers were not a bedraggled group of n'er-do-wells, but rather a surprisingly middle-class group of fortune-seekers, with many a young lawyer, merchant and cleric among them (Dobkin, 1988). Many refused to do manual labor for hire, leaving the booming city with a labor shortage until the slump of the 1860s (Elgie, 1966). Thousands of Chinese were imported to fill the demand for common labor in agriculture, drainage and railroad construction.

Although San Francisco became the city with the highest percentage of foreign-born in the US in the late nineteenth century, it was relatively inaccessible to the most downtrodden European masses; most immigrants here had already been in the US for a time before moving west. These conditions set the stage for vigorous labor movements from the Workingmen's Party of the 1870s (with considerable petty bourgeois elements) to the Building Trades Council after 1900, many of whose members become contractors (Kazin, 1987), demanding good wages and political representation for skilled labor. This narrow but militant base of workers' power also set the white male worker against the beleaguered Chinese and their successors from Asia, Mexico and the US South in a viciously racist defense of labor scarcity (Saxton, 1971); and it omitted most of the numerous unskilled workers who were migrants in and out of the city from jobs in fields and forests throughout the West (although the equally migratory sailors and longshoremen did become well organized, the IWW was virtually absent from San Francisco). At the same time, the successful exercise of working-class power has infuriated the bourgeoisie, and the latter has struck back repeatedly: with the Vigilantes in the 1850s, the first Employers' Association in the US in the 1890s, the Union Labor Party prosecutions of the 1900s, and the American

Plan in the 1920s.

One hundred years of popular struggle – equally against capital and the excluded – have created and defended, against the backdrop of labor skill, labor scarcity, and favorable conditions of accumulation, the high-wage landscape that has been so conducive to the succession of the new empire of skilled labor. A gilded thread runs from the 49ers through the turn-of-the-century building trades to the present bearers of new forms of skill: a relatively favored position within the broad compass of the working class as a whole. This has been an ambiguous struggle, however, with an elision of class identities, a minority role for the mass production working class, and a history of racism.

The contemporary yuppie phenomenon has its class base principally among certain new and/or expanding categories of skilled labor, such as engineers, programmers, health workers, financial consultants and accountants. Their salaries run in excess of $50,000 per year, and often $100,000 or more; and they often come in two-earner households with few children, leaving huge disposal incomes. A class analysis of the contemporary yuppie is not a simple matter, and brings us back to the long-standing debate on the left over the position of the 'middle class' (Walker, 1979; Wright, 1985). The new middle class of technicians, managers and professionals is not a class in Marxist terms, but an elevated segment of the working class. This elevation rests, first, on advantages conferred by the division of labor, including skills and the scarcity wages they command, relative autonomy at work to perform unstructured tasks, high geographic mobility and wide job choice, and administrative responsibility and position in management hierarchies. These advantages are regularly levered into additional gains in money, power and prestige by means of professional monopolies, degrees and titles, and entry into the corps of upper management. Much left debate goes awry in failing to separate the division of labor (usually grouped around occupational categories) from class and ends up with a theoretical mule that has no further issue.

To say that capitalism has a two-class structure (three, if one includes individual/family proprietors) reveals much; but it can also be used to obscure things if one acts as if the problem of social difference, hierarchy and class formation ends there. Stratification studies demonstrate that social gradation involves multiple structures of difference including class, division of labor, race, gender, the state, and more. From this rich substrate various social movements and class-like phenomena can grow and assert themselves as economic, political and cultural forces. US history without its episodic eruptions of a middle class, from the Great Awakening to the Progressive era, would seem very flat indeed. Similarly, Bay Area society cannot be undertood without acknowledging the middle class as a major actor.[11] At the same time, the so-called middle class is revealed in its full ambiguity as a class force by its combination of fierce upward mobility and strong consumerism with some remarkably progressive cultural and political interventions.

Even a narrow accounting of echnical, professional and managerial occupations in the Bay Area yields an impressive figure of 565,000, made up of 322,000 managers and 243,000 technical/professional workers – 22.5 percent of the area's labor force in 1980.[12] The percentage of all white-collar workers, including those in sales and clerical jobs, in the regional job structure at the same time was 62.5 percent, indicating a classic 'service economy' skew that has always been characteristic of California and which continues despite its rank as the number one manufacturing state in the US (see Walker, 1985).

Labor markets and entrepreneurs: class divisions and elisions

The industries that have propelled the Bay Area's recent growth have also shaped its class structure. Skilled labor pools are typical of large metropolitan labor markets, but the high-tech and management-finance sectors have disproportionately high demands for technical, professional and managerial labor (Markusen et al., 1986; Noyelle and Stanback, 1984). Electronics is notorious for its bifurcated labor force, split between hoards of engineers in design and processing and large numbers of unskilled assemblers (Saxenian, 1983; Florida and Kenney, 1990).

Similarly, finance, management and business services demand huge numbers of trained managers and professionals, as well as crafty business types with a nose for money, often carrying MBA degrees. Universities and hospitals are, of course, heavily peopled with MDs and PhDs, not to mention MAs, and biotech is, at this stage, almost exclusively an employer of degree-holding research technicians. Other noteworthy contributors to the ranks of the new skilled labor force are the general governments (for example, state and federal judges, administrators of federal agencies), the military (especially the roughly 8,000 technicians in the Livermore Weapons Laboratories), construction (project engineers and corporate managers at Bechtel and Kaiser, architects), and shipping (airline pilots, port authority managers). Added to this, of course, are all the managers and bearers of 'expertise' of one sort or another connected with every other industry, in more or less normal quantities.

In the buoyant economy of the Bay Area, many technicians, professionals and managers have been able to transform themselves into capitalists, creating a strong upward elision of the middle class into the bourgeoisie. The new skills group has been busy setting up new businesses from engineering consultancies to disk-drive manufacturers, creating several thousand new millionaires (Florida and Kenney, 1990). Silicon Valley is famous for its multiplication of new firms making everything from custom chips to software, and for the get-rich-quick atmosphere this has generated (Rogers and Larsen, 1984). Indeed, the Bay Area has been held up to the world as the new model for small business and flexible production (Zysman, 1977). The business service complex of San Francisco is not so very different, for there, too, a sea of small fish swarm around the enormous pilings of the great banks and corporations. Many hope to be the next Charles Schwab (the low-margin stock brokerage king), or at least to open a law firm. Biotech is a natural extension of the entrepreneurial lusts of the American medical establishment, with its innumerable independent clinics, mini-medical corporations and psychiatric practices. The recreational activity complex contributes significantly to the spawn of entrepreneurism, with its proliferation of restaurants, shops, bed-and-breakfasts and travel agencies. A particularly self-referential form of yuppie capitalism flowers in San Francisco by turning the fashions of the middle class into widely saleable commodities, such as trendy running shoes or garden tools. Wineries, now numbering in the hundreds, are chiefly an indulgence for the previously wealthy, but have drawn entrepreneurs from all over the country. There are thousands of independent merchants and brokers who mediate the innumerable transactions of goods, labor services, money and paper titles swirling around a major mercantile shipping and financial center such as the Bay Area. Finally, there is the tried and true American road to wealth: real estate investment and landlordism.

The capitalization of skilled labor is particularly pronounced in the Bay Area, thanks to the heady entrepreneurial environment of high-tech innovation, individualism and venture capital here. The diffusion of capitalist income is striking: San Francisco–Oakland and San Jose rank number two and three nationally in stockholders per capita among the twenty-five largest metropolitan areas (Judge, 1979: 279). These nouveaux capitalists add to the general vigor of the regional economy, but their presence further elides class identities even more.

If it is true that the industrial base shapes the class structure, it is also true that the peculiar class structure of the Bay Area stimulates the growth of its industries. The more engineers pumped out by the universities, the bigger the ready labor pool for Silicon Valley to wax fat on. The more a 'middle class' haven is created along the base of the western hills, the more at home engineers, managers, doctors and their kind feel when settling into Bay Area life. The more a culture of entrepreneurism and a technical milieu is promoted by past successes and the overflowing vat of venture capital, backed up by the ideas of ingenious people, the more new companies are set up with a real chance of success (Storper and Walker, 1989). Add to this the large number of Asian immigrants who arrive with money in their pockets to invest, and the Great American Success story may be replicated a thousand times.

By comparison, the traditional working class seems relatively constricted in the Bay Area's contemporary industrialization. The older categories of skilled workers are, of course, still very much in evidence, but within the confines of the capital-intensive refinery and petrochemical belt of Contra Costa; the local construction industry, fattened on the late, great office boom; aircraft maintenance for United and other big carriers at the airports; some skilled machinists still plying their trade, as often as not making tools for electronics firms; and a host of printers in the publishing trades, putting out computer magazines or office forms in the central Bay Area. But where are the once-great armies of medium- and low-skilled mass production workers? Mostly gone, their workplaces gradually shuttered since the war or finished off in the great wave of plant closings in the late 1970s and early 1980s. In their place we find a whole new mass working-class consisting of white female office workers in San Francisco and the East Bay, Third World female assemblers in Santa Clara County, and new immigrant waiters, busboys, maids and janitors in San Francisco. Then, too, we find a whole new underclass, predominantly young, Black and male, for whom the burgeoning industries of the Bay Area seemingly have no use at all. We take up these problems further on.

The world the yuppies made

A class is not formed by economics alone, but through a full range of practices in consumption and everyday life. On the cultural front, the Bay Area's aspiring middle class has distinguished itself as a world historical force, at least gastronomically. Whoever thinks of the Yuppie Revolution, thinks of California cuisine, of hot tubs, of cafes and coffee culture, of consciousness-raising seminars, of New Age music, and new health movements such as Breema Body Work. These all flow from the artesian well of indulgence and social innovation in Bay Area culture.

The cultural sources of the modern yuppie run deep. California has a long history as a mecca for health seekers, evangelists and utopians looking for personal and social curatives, and this type of idealism still has purchase in our supposedly secular age. San Francisco, in particular, has a distinguished record as a cosmopolitan and bohemian city where people from somewhere else generate a certain electric energy just rubbing elbows, and where the odd and eccentric are tolerated and even smiled upon. This tradition can be traced back to the Gold Rush, through the original nineteenth-century Bohemian Club (before it became a ruling-class bastion), to its best-known recent manifestations, the Beat Generation of North Beach in the 1950s and the hippies of the Haight-Ashbury in the 1960s. This cultural nonconformity is reinforced by the large intellectual community, and the college town atmosphere extends well beyond the confines of Berkeley and Stanford.

The political and even radical element of this fount of cultural innovation is not to be overlooked. Much of yuppie culture got its start in self-consciously political breaks with Middle America by former New Leftists: political posters became art in the hands of David Goines, experiments with fresh foods became nouvelle cuisine at Alice Waters's Chez Panisse, alternative health care grew from the Haight-Ashbury Free Clinic to a embrace a thousand popular curatives. The countercultural call for personal liberation was answered in a hundred ways by a large cohort who came of age in the 1960s and had the economic freedom to run life-style experiments. Indeed, the energy with which the new skills group pursues its dreams of personal fulfillment can be quite astonishing. Along the way some interesting seeds of liberation have been planted, although the trail is strewn with many weeds.

Yuppie culture has spread to the bourgeoisie, especially those wishing to appear young and hip. This mobilization of social innovation as fashion for the rich to consume is of ancient lineage, of course. In wealthy Marin County counterculture threatens to become caricature, as in Werner Erhard's est seminars. This strain in local bourgeois culture also has a long history, personified by corpulent corporate frolics in the buff amongst the splendor of the redwoods at the Bohemian Grove, on the Russian River (Domhoff, 1974). The rest of the working class is affected by the dominant middle-class culture, too. This is especially so for the curiously large craftworker population of the central Bay Area, made up heavily of 'fallen' sons and daughters of the middle class who prefer honest manual labor to office work (painters with PhDs being unexceptional) and coffee from Peet's to any old cup of java.

The yuppies of the Bay Area have a more polyglot make-up than almost anywhere else in the country. Silicon Valley, San Francisco's financial district and the medical-educational complex attract a great many educated foreigners into their skilled labor forces, as well as immigrant capitalists such as Jean-Louis Gassee of Apple Computer. The most exceptional element of white skilled labor is the gay professional and managerial elite who joined the exodus to San Francisco in large numbers during the 1970s. The East Bay and San Francisco both have a respectably large Black middle class, whose social presence and 'buppie' life-style are firmly established. Also striking is the participation of growing numbers of Asian Americans, especially Chinese, in small business in San Francisco, the skilled workforce and management of Silicon Valley, and in the professions. The multinational base of the middle class adds to the cosmopolitan tastes and tolerant outlook of the yuppie, although it undermines the prevailing view of the Bay Area and its middle class as overwhelmingly made up of singles, two-professional households and childless couples. But social integration raises some unhappy questions about Bay Area culture and politics, to which we must return later.

For many, however, the exotic social experiments and cosmopolitan good life of the Big City – the cutting edge of the yuppie phenomenon – is something that only now and then touches their lives. Most of the middle class here, as elsewhere in the country, live out their nonwork lives largely in their suburban homes and in their cars during the daily commute. Beyond the 'gourmet ghettoes' of North Shattuck in Berkeley and Union Street in San Francisco stretch vast landscapes of convention embodied in tract homes and shopping centers. The Peninsula (San Mateo County) contains vast swathes of Republican virtue, awash with daily commuters to San Francisco's financial district, amid which stand a few islands of the high bourgeoisie, such as Hillsborough and Atherton. The great band of plenitude carries down through Palo Alto into the north and west of the Santa Clara Valley, where their livelihood derives from electronics. Across the Bay, the character of the middle class changes abruptly as one crosses the Oakland Hills: one leaves the Berkeley eccentrics behind in the summer fog and heads for the white heat of the interior valleys of eastern Contra Costa and Alameda counties. And beyond the greenbelts of Marin lie the burgeoning middle-class suburbs of Sonoma County around Petaluma and Santa Rosa.

The politics of an aspiring middle class are notoriously ambivalent, reflecting their middling position between labor and capital. It is wrong, however, to assume that Bay Area yuppies or even their more conventional suburban counterparts are necessarily conservative in their heart of hearts, with just a gloss of urbane trendiness. This contrasts sharply, for example, with the much more conservative milieu of Southern California (Davis, 1986).

Nor are they uniformly in close alliance with the bourgeoisie, despite the elevation of many of their number to capitalist status and the commercialization of yuppie culture. The curious thing is that the Bay Area's skilled elite is probably the most politically progressive in the country, and is notable for its high degree of social and political activism. One index is the course of presidential voting over the last few elections, which has been substantially to the left of any other region of the country. Environmentalism, gay rights, feminism, anti-imperialism, and other progressive notions are readily seized upon and developed by substantial elements of the middle class. Politics and culture merge in a heady brew of free-thinking, even though it tends toward the individualist or libertarian or even dissolute. Evidently, formation of the area's middle class is shaped by local circumstance in a way that a purely structural analysis of economic classes cannot capture. The strong Bay Area tradition of liberalism and urbanity, for which the empire of skilled labor and successful class struggles are the material base, carries on today in the progressive slant of the Yuppie Revolution.

We shall take up the relation of middle-class progressivism to the politics of the left in a concluding section, but first we must temper our insights into class formation with the difficulties of traditional labor organizing in the economic environment of the Bay region, the divisions introduced by race and urban form, and the contradictions of breakneck growth in this haven of capitalist prosperity.

Recomposition and Retreat of the Working Class

The conditions for labor organizing are in many ways propitious in the Bay Area, which has never been a reservoir of cheap labor. The Bay Area has some of the highest average wage rates in the US. While suppression of wages is always a favorite enterprise of the bourgeoisie, low wages are not always the key to growth in an advanced industrial region (Storper and Walker, 1989). Indeed, strong unions with a serious involvement in industry affairs can be salutary for industry, as shown by the postwar automation agreement in longshoring. On the other hand, vicious wage regimes are by no means foreign to California, as in agribusiness, non-union construction or the sewing trades (McWilliams, 1939).

From 1900, when the Teamsters shut down an employers' offensive, to the First World War, San Francisco was the best labor town in the world, under the suzerainty of the Building Trades Council and occasional labor governments under the Union Labor Party (Kazin, 1987). After a period of retreat in the 1920s, the stronghold of organized labor was restored in the dramatic events of the San Francisco General Strike of 1934, when the International Longshoremen's and Warehousemen's Union (ILWU) won recognition and control of the hiring hall (Mills, 1979). The industrial East Bay was also solidly organized by the 1940s, and there was even a brief General Strike in Oakland in 1946. In what was then an agricultural Santa Clara Valley, women cannery workers were organized by the CIO in the 1930s (Matthews, 1985). The role of the socialist left, and of the Communist Party in particular, in these successes was notable, and, significantly, the CP leadership was never purged from the ILWU during the McCarthy period. The result was a unionization rate of over 50 percent of nonfarm workers in 1957, and still rising – compared to 35 percent and falling in Los Angeles.[13]

The topography of a union town

A distinctive characteristic of union power in the Bay Area has been the existence of strong central labor councils in each county, providing a kind of unity among unions within the American Federation of Labor (and later AFL-CIO) that has often been sorely lacking in American history. Under the late Dick Groulx, Alameda County had for twenty years probably the strongest labor council in the United States. Santa Clara County's council was the first to break with the national AFL-CIO on foreign policy by opposing intervention in Central America. San Mateo and Contra Costa have also had quite strong councils. San Francisco's council, by comparison, fell into some disrepair under the heavy-drinking Jack Crowley of the Morticians union, now dearly departed. The central labor councils have a good deal of political clout and are part of the core of the Democratic Party at the county level.

Several important unions trace their influence from the pre–World War II period. The various building trades have ridden the crest of development waves in downtown San Francisco and the suburbs. The Retail Clerks (several locals) grew powerful on the strength of the supermarket chains, at whose head for many years stood two Bay Area corporations, Safeway (no. 1) and Lucky (no. 3). A merger with the Butchers consolidated the union's position. The Retail Clerks have been quite good at gaining job protections through the state legislature. The ILWU Locals 10 and 6 are relatively small but well organized and highly visible in local affairs in San Francisco and Oakland. The International Association of Machinists (IAM) Local 1781 (United Airlines) is the kingpin of San Mateo labor politics, and the IAM local at Lockheed is vital to Santa Clara County's council. Communication has always been close between the councils and the key independents: the ILWU, Teamsters Local 7 and the UAW (now back in the AFL-CIO), all of which have been quite progressive.

The fastest growing unions in the Bay Area over the last

thirty years have been Local 2 of the Hotel and Restaurant Employees and the public sector unions: Locals 250, 535, 715 and 790 of the Service Employees International (SEIU), various locals of the American Federation of State, County and Municipal Employees (AFSCME), the teachers' unions California Teachers Association and California Federation of Teachers, and the California State Employees Association. Local 2 is now the biggest union in San Francisco. SEIU, based among health care and county workers, has the largest membership in the Bay Area. AFSCME focuses on city workers. NEA and AFT have organized virtually all public school and college teachers. These unions have been generally quite progressive, in large part because of the sector they represent. Local 2, where an insurgency threw out a corrupt leadership in 1977, has many poorly paid Filipino and Latino workers, while the public employee unions have benefitted from a human service–oriented group of workers, a majority of them women.

But the union movement in both private industry and government is at an impasse due to the changing character of the economy and of the labor force it hopes to represent. Unfortunately, the problem is covered up by the overall growth of the Bay Area which, by generating steady increases in membership (and quickly papering over major losses), lulls union leaders into thinking all is well. This is far from the case.

Restructuring and retrenchment

The landscape of labor is in upheaval from the economic and political earthquakes of the 1980s, and the union movement is losing ground in the process. The indices are clear: unionization of the Bay Area's civilian workforce declined from 34.2 percent in 1975 to 20.4 percent in 1985 – even though San Francisco still maintains a high 36.6 percent rate.[14] The most tangible cause of the crisis of contract unionism is the onslaught on the collective bargaining system installed in the 1930s (Moody, 1989). Reaganism killed the class accord of the postwar era. Labor law and the National Labor Relations Board are now stacked against unions to such a degree than Victor Van Bourg, the leading labor lawyer on the West Coast, calls his business 'trench warfare' (Weinstein, 1989). Almost across the board, employers have been emboldened to challenge union certification, demand takebacks and keep organizers at bay (Harrison and Bluestone, 1988). A glaring example locally is the Associated Building Contractors' circumvention of unionized labor in residential construction, hugely eroding the building trades. The air traffic controllers in PATCO were wiped out at the Fremont regional traffic control center in Reagan's most direct move against organized labor.

Yet even if US labor law were suddenly rewritten on the Swedish model, the labor movement would be hard pressed by crisis and transition to a new capitalist epoch (Storper and Walker, 1989). Many of labor's long-time blue-collar bastions are gone, having been eaten away over the years as the industrial base has been transformed. Older industries such as canning, brewing and coffee roasting have dwindled or moved out of the area. American Bridge (Bethlehem Steel) was the biggest of many steel plants to close. Alameda County, the center of manufacturing locally for most of the twentieth century, was hit by a tornado of deindustrialization in the early 1980s: 122 plants closed and over 16,000 jobs were lost in 1980–84 (Shapiro, 1986). Vehicle assembly was particularly hard hit: Caterpillar, Mack Truck and Ford are gone now. Many warehouses are also moving to the Central Valley or Nevada, led by GM and Safeway. The Plant Closures Project has tried to fight back against the tide, and has achieved a couple of notable victories, but the tide has not turned (Haas, 1985).

Even those plants that remain can present a whole new set of organizing problems under new ownership, as new companies enter the area, older companies are swallowed through mergers, or joint ventures are created. The simple expansion of the hotel business in San Francisco has brought with it such non-union operators as Marriot and Portman. But the best-known instances of changing bosses are where foreign capitalists are involved. In Pittsburg, US Steel (USX) has enlisted Korea's Pohang Iron & Steel Co. to revamp its aged plant in a joint venture called USS-POSCO. United Steelworkers Union Local 1440, fearing for its life, took a pay cut, while the Koreans hired a non-union American contractor to do the actual retooling. Protests have been vigorous, but the plant is now up and running. Fremont's General Motors' plant has been reopened as New United Motors Manufacturing (NUMMI), a GM–Toyota joint venture. Many former GM workers were hired back (in much smaller numbers), and the UAW kept its representation. But these new ventures present new challenges, to which we return below.

Work has also been widely transformed through automation

and new divisions of labor. Although the great port of San Francisco was virtually shut down by containerization, the ILWU negotiated the transition and remains a viable union, but it lacks the immense vitality of the old longshore and its mass, popular way of life. The explosion in fast-food outlets, small restaurants and boutique retailing has bypassed the Retail Clerks and Hotel and Restaurant Workers, and the former are just beginning to feel the crunch from the restructuring of the grocery chains. Both Safeway and Lucky have had to pull back towards their home bases, under threat of takeover, to keep in line with the new regionalization of marketing. Product proliferation and inventory automation are making old ways of managing, and union-protected job categories increasingly obsolete. A different kind of restructuring is that felt by the Teamsters with the deregulation of trucking or the upheavals in airlines, including the closure of Oakland-based World Airways.

The restructuring of government has taken its toll on public sector unions, as well. The great wave of public employee organizing took place in the 1960s and 1970s. But the fiscal crisis of the 1970s and the right's onslaught against government social programs and taxes have meant lean years. The public unions have also learned that the taxpaying citizenry can turn a hard bargain if they feel strikes are against their interests, as the San Francisco public workers' strike in 1974 proved.

Meanwhile, whole new industries and job categories have burgeoned. The most important locus of employment growth, working class reconstitution and union failure has, of course, been Silicon Valley, which accounted for 94 percent of the 216,000 net manufacturing jobs created in the region in 1964–84. Without Silicon Valley expansion, manufacturing jobs in the region would have shrunk by 38 percent during the same period – above the national average – rather than by only 13 percent (Brady, 1987). Although Santa Clara County has over 100,000 unionized workers, the rate of unionization there is a paltry 13 percent. The absence of unions in the electronics industries is virtually complete, and the companies remain resolutely anti-union. The principal area of job growth in the East Bay has been the I-680 corridor east of the hills (mostly in Contra Costa County). The office boom has capitalized on a pool of educated, low-paid women, who remain almost completely outside the compass of union organizing (Nelson, 1986).

This is the janus mask of the precipitous decline of organized labor in America: in place of frowning deindustrialization there is the happy face of capitalist expansion into new industries and new industrial places (Scott, 1988b; Storper and Walker, 1989). These newly constituted industrial complexes, which are disproportionately located in California and the southwest, have grown, in part, by virtue of the kind of labor force and employment contracts they have been able to establish. While these are general trends in the present epoch of capitalism, they are exaggerated – because they were pioneered – in places such as Silicon Valley. As a result, the composition of the working class, the politics of work time and the conditions of employment have changed dramatically (Christopherson and Storper, 1989).

First, the labor force is flush with new entrants: Mexican and Southeast Asian immigrants (largely female), young Anglo women, and young degree-carrying (largely male) engineers and technicians from the universities. We have considered the skilled workers above; they are, it should be added, largely white and male. People of color, both US and foreign-born, are heavily concentrated in blue-collar occupations throughout California (Cabezas and Kawaguchi, 1988). The working class is also increasingly female: women have filled approximately two-thirds of the over 25 million new jobs created in the US economy since 1973 (Christopherson, 1988).

Second, the capitalist demand for 'flexibility' in the face of international competition, volatile markets, new technologies, new management systems and better safety regulations has led to greater reliance on temporary, part-time and contract employment, or what may be called the 'externalization of work' (Pfeffer and Baron, 1988; Boyer, 1987). For example, Dow Chemical's Pittsburg plant has a perfect safety record despite an explosion killing 2 and injuring 100 in 1979 because the workers at risk were on subcontract and therefore not officially employed by Dow. Workers in these categories now make up nearly one-third of the US workforce (*Wall Street Journal*, 4 May 1988). The majority of temps are female clericals, but the number of nurses, engineers, accountants and lawyers working as temps has increased, as has the percentage of men in such jobs. The Bay Area has experienced this shift very markedly (Mangum et al., 1985). In 1984 Santa Clara County had the highest concentration of temporary workers in the United States (*Mercury News*, 6 Dec. 1984). San Jose has over

100 temp agencies listed in the phone directory, and the world's second largest temp firm is the Swiss-owned Adia Services, headquartered in Menlo Park (*San Jose Business Journal*, 14 Dec. 1987). Some Silicon Valley firms rely wholly for their assembly workers on temp agencies; Hewlett-Packard has its own in-house temporary labor pool.

Finally, while some workers prefer temporary or part-time work, most of the growth in this domain is involuntary and represents a larger capitalist onslaught against the US working class, taking advantage of unorganized workers and weakened unions. The result has been an increasingly dualized labor market, for which the electronics industry and 'service' sectors are notorious (Saxenian, 1983; Freedman, 1976): on the top, a favored stratum of skilled workers, below, a much larger number of workers hired into lower tier jobs under declining conditions of employment. Worsening employment includes, besides part-time and temporary work, repeated bouts of unemployment among full-time workers: less than 50 percent of the American working class enjoys full-time, year-round employment. Furthermore, most of the new jobs created by the 'great American jobs machine' over the last twenty years have come with low wages, poor benefits and hazardous work conditions, creating what Harrison and Bluestone (1988) call 'the great U-turn' in American income distribution. The grim figures on infant mortality, malnourished children and poverty of women and immigrants in California speak darkly of the harsh underside of the California miracle.

This new working class has only just begun to fight back toward the kind of labor movement strength and level of rewards achieved by the last two generations of American workers (Davis, 1986). Until it does so, the prospects for advance in social welfare and progressive politics will be grim, and the Reaganite agenda of the New Right will remain hegemonic.

Towards a new agenda for labor

The labor movement in the Bay Area, like that across the United States, is on the defensive and has become largely reactive. Bludgeoned by the ascendent bourgeoisie of the New Right, unions are more concerned with protecting themselves from further erosion of rights than in tackling the long-term task of adjusting to altered circumstances. As a result, the economy of the region has roared past them, leaving the working class increasingly unprotected and politically outflanked. The foremost task facing the labor movement is organizing the legions of the unorganized. This means, above all, organizing electronics and clerical workers in the big factories and offices, the two leading sectors of the Bay economy. It also means reaching out to smaller sectors and workplaces, from software houses to fast-food franchises. Moreover, expanding labor organization involves reaching out to workers in new job categories, with new skills; bringing in those employed part-time and as temporaries; and responding to more 'enlightened' managerial approaches.

Yet the unions, locally as well as nationally, have no real program for mass organizing and providing leadership for a working class confronted by new forms of employment and new styles of management in the era of capitalism now opening up. Organizing success will have to go together with a reconstructed unionism.

For example, organizers working in Silicon Valley have found, to their chagrin, that employers often beat them to the punch by providing paternalistic benefits, leaving workers unconvinced of the advantages unionization might offer other than a kind of back-up insurance policy. Probably the toughest issue is responding to new management methods, which offer many workers greater freedom to exercise their judgement and responsibility in exchange for greater intensity of labor. The case of NUMMI is justly famous in this regard, though much the same thing happens throughout the electronics industry and in office work. The UAW retained its representation at NUMMI under a reconstituted labor process employing Japanese work organization (Sayer, 1986). Everyone agrees that the new labor process is more rational than the old Taylorist methods of American management, but it is much less clear how unions can respond (Brown and Reich, 1989). The answer would seem to lie in the problem: how can unions mobilize the knowledge of their members as effectively as management is doing in order to challenge the managers? In the immediate sense, one ought to appeal to workers' sense of pride in their productive skills, making mismanagement a major issue. Beyond that, however, American unions have to contest the key management prerogatives over products, technology and investment to demand at least the level of participation found among German trade unions.

Another problem requiring innovative answers is the increasing numbers of temporaries, part-timers, and contractees, as well as those suffering irregular full-time employment due to layoffs and bankruptcies. The mass production/big factory model is not well adapted to these conditions, which are more akin to the old shape-up on the longshore or building construction where workers move from job to job under various ties of subcontracting (in which Bay Area labor organizations have some expertise). Although steady full-time work may be the ideal, where it is not be possible workers need flexible protection through certification of skills to control entry, mobile pension funds, and union-certified hiring agencies. Some workers, it should be added, do not regard full-time, same-site employment as a virtue: nurses are presently doing better working through agencies. And some of these identify themselves as professionals – as is common among US skilled workers – and need to be brought into organized labor as part of a longer process of bending class formation back toward working-class hegemony.

The concerns of women workers should also be in the forefront. The union movement has never served the vast majority of female (and minority) workers relegated to secondary labor markets very well (Frank, 1989). Organized labor will have to fight for the social support systems necessary for women to work, including the ability of parents to choose part-time work. In the midst of the bleak picture in Silicon Valley one bright spot shines out: the successful fight by AFSCME Local 101 for comparable wage scales for women working for the City of San Jose in 1980–81 (Remick, 1984). The militant and widely legitimate claim for comparable worth demonstrates the potential of the new working class and new labor relations to spark new forms of labor action and lead workers into a politics of social justice, especially when they are assisted by sympathetic elected officials. This sort of initiative is crucial to organized labor's future. The situation in Silicon Valley is comparable to that of the auto, steel or trucking industries at the beginning of the 1930s: a new, leading-edge industry, with a new workforce (largely immigrants or the children of immigrants) and new kinds of labor relations, and still largely unorganized. Something like the CIO's end-run around the traditional unionism of the AFL of the time is likely to be necessary to achieve comparable results (Moody, 1989).

Divided We Grow

The American city is a marvelous machine for generating growth and subordinating class struggle to the divisive politics of residential exclusion and real estate promotion (Walker, 1981). In this the Bay Area is typical – if not archetypal. Despite its liberal practices on many fronts, the San Francisco metropolitan area has been and remains a city divided geographically, socially and politically. Indeed, the spatial form by which the city grows and transforms its parts actually helps reproduce the inequalities and contradictions of class, race and gender.

The city form that evolved in California, north and south, set the pattern for much of twentieth century urbanization in the United States, in the same way as Second Empire Paris or turn-of-the-century Chicago were models followed worldwide in earlier periods. Scott and Soja (1986) call Los Angeles 'the capital of the twentieth century', but many of the key elements of the L.A. growth machine were shared with the Bay Area. The Bay Area played an important role as incubator of many innovations in the building and organization of the modern city. For example, the cable car was developed in the 1870s to elevate the robber barons of San Francisco to Nob Hill high above the riffraff, exclusionary zoning restrictions were introduced first in San Francisco and Modesto to suppress Chinese businesses in the 1880s, and land use districting to separate housing, commerce and industry was initiated by Mason-McDuffie Realty Co. of Berkeley circa 1910 (Weiss, 1987).

San Francisco began as a city overwhelmingly made up of white men, and the Bay Area continued to have a relatively pale cast for its first century, although it did have a healthy mixture of European peoples, including Irish, Germans, Italians, Portuguese, Greeks and Scandinavians (Wollenberg, 1985). A fierce assault was visited upon Asian and Latin American settlers who might have been used to break the monopoly of white labor (Saxton, 1971). Racism became part of the lingua franca of the labor movement: Chinese immigration was cut off in 1902, and the Japanese were hit with the Alien Land Law, denying them access to farmland, in 1913 (Kazin, 1987).

Filipinos began entering after US colonization of the Philippines, but the Chinese population had ebbed to a low point of 30,000 in all of California by 1920. Japanese Americans were thrown into internment camps during World War II and their property seized. Mexicans, who had been driven out of California by the Yankee invasion in the nineteenth century, began returning in large numbers during and after the Mexican Revolution; some settled on the then agricultural margins of the Bay Area, such as San Jose and Decoto. Mexican immigration was stopped, however, by deportations, harassment and the depression of the 1930s. No more than a trickle of African Americans came west until World War II, when hundreds of thousands of Black workers were recruited from the South to work in Bay Area shipyards and war industries.

Yet in 1960 San Francisco was one of the least ethnically diverse urban areas in the country, still 83 percent white (Viviano, 1988). A sea-change began with the liberalization of Asian and Latino immigration quotas by the 1965 Immigration and Nationality Act, and has been fed by economic and political conditions here and abroad ever since. The new immigration is closely tied to the dislocations in Asia and Central America, the rural transformation and industrialization of the newly industrialized countries, the new surge of globalization in world capitalism since 1960, and the recruitment of cheap labor by US industries. Asian Americans in the Bay Area now number perhaps 1.3 million, Latinos just under 1 million, and African Americans about 600,000 (Viviano, 1988).[15] (Official Census figures are notoriously unreliable for communities of color, and do not match these figures.) In an astounding turnabout, people of color are on the verge of outnumbering people of European descent for the region as a whole.

Today, after the new mass immigration from Central America, Mexico, Southeastern Asia, and the Pacific, the Bay region boasts a cosmopolitanism few cities in the world can match. The contrast with the Midwest could not be greater. The cities of San Francisco and Oakland, in particular, have become marvelous swirls of peoples from Nicaragua, El Salvador, Guatemala, Samoa, the Philippines, China, Japan, Cambodia, Vietnam, Tonga and Thailand, among others. The outer ring of the metropolis is of fairer complexion, but not as much as the popular myth of white suburbs would have it. Five of the ten most ethnically diverse counties in the United States are to be found in the central Bay Area (Viviano, 1988).

Yet a look behind the variegated face of urban street life reveals a less pleasant reality of residential communities dappled in light and dark tones across the map of the urban area. The divided neighborhoods of the inner city have been replicated on a grand scale in the vast stretches of the new city built during the last twenty years of urban boom. The difficult fact is that neither the new immigrant bourgeoisie nor the new immigrant working class is well integrated with its white counterparts. We deal with living space here, and take up political integration later on.

Racial segregation in the metropolis

Most of the Black residential districts (read: ghettoes) of the Bay Area date to World War II, although West Oakland's African American population traces its roots to the terminus of the transcontinental railroad, finished in 1869. The largest Black concentration is to be found in the flatlands of the central East Bay, from Oakland to Richmond: roughly 60 percent of the total, or around 350,000 people. San Francisco has around 90,000 African Americans. The Black presence in Oakland and Berkeley is much stronger than in San Francisco, in part because the Hunters Point-Bayview district is so far removed from the Downtown. Yet Black and white remain far apart throughout the urban core: Hunters Point, Richmond and East Oakland are no-man's land as far as most whites are concerned. Oakland and Richmond were prime industrial zones of the first half of the century, but were largely hollowed out by the 1950s, leaving Black workers behind and economic conditions grim.

In the outer ring of the metropolis Blacks are almost invisible. A sizeable block of about 50,000 Black working-class people are found in Vallejo to the north, owing to the presence of Mare Island Naval Shipyard. On the Peninsula, about 30,000 Blacks are pressed up against the tidal flats in East Palo Alto and East Menlo Park. Around 100,000 Blacks live in Santa Clara County, chiefly in San Jose. Marin, Sonoma and Napa counties to the north are overwhelmingly white: a tiny Black enclave in Marin City is all that survives from the model integrated government housing built for Marinship's wartime shipyards (Wollenberg, 1990). Marin developed a new and unseen ghetto, however, as the Black prison population of San Quentin swelled after the War.

Even in the East Bay, Black residential areas have been kept largely within the same boundaries for fifty years. When the white working class moved out to the industrial suburbs of southern Alameda County, few Blacks were able to follow. San

Leandro, Oakland's immediate neighbor, achieved considerable notoriety for its 98 percent white population in the 1960 census, and change still comes hard, as shown by a recent incident in which KKK dolls were brought to a school by white children. The area beyond the East Bay hills might just as well be another country. One Black working-class enclave survives in industrial Pittsburg, but it is being expelled by urban renewal.

Chicano communities have grown up largely in places where Mexican immigrant farm workers and cannery laborers toiled in the 1920s and 1930s. The largest *barrio* is East San Jose, with 175,000 out of the 250,000 Chicanos in the county. The East Bay has several centers, in the former agricultural towns of Fruitvale (East Oakland), Hayward, Decoto (Union City), Fremont, and Brentwood (a total of over 200,000 people in Alameda and Contra Costa counties). San Francisco's Latino population is predominantly Central American in origin, and numbers over 100,000 people (although counts are suspect because of refugee status). Their roots go back to the coffee and fruit trade, as well as World War II, but recent arrivals are largely refugees from the revolutions and counterrevolutions in Nicaragua, El Salvador and Guatemala. Because of the politicization of Central Americans, the Mission district, where most live, has been the political and cultural center of the Bay Area left in the 1980s.

The biggest demographic change in recent years has been the influx of Asian peoples. The six counties with the highest proportion of Asian Americans in the United States are the southern counties of the Bay Area. The Chinese number almost 350,000, Filipinos almost 400,000, Vietnamese 100,000, and the Japanese and Koreans 80,000 each (Viviano, 1988; estimated 1990 populations). There are many smaller groups, including Pacific Islanders and Indochinese tribespeople. (Indeed, the term 'Asian', while preferred to 'Oriental' or various Anglo terms of derision, has itself become a barrier to understanding the rich mixture of peoples from across the Pacific). By county, Asian Americans are proportionately greatest in San Francisco (325,000), but numerically greatest in Santa Clara (350,000); an additional 260,000 reside in Alameda, 165,000 in San Mateo and 100,000 in Contra Costa.

San Francisco is the focus of the Chinese community. The old ghetto of Chinatown has the odd distinction of being both on the Grey Line Tour and the poorest neighborhood in the city, making it a kind of 'gilded ghetto' whose pathologies are disguised by tourism (Takagi and Platt, 1978). The newest arrivals crowd in looking for jobs and cheap lodging, while the better-off immigrants and American-born Chinese have been expanding their area of residence westward into the Richmond district and the Sunset.

Oakland's Chinatown – on its last legs in the 1960s – has experienced a revival due principally to the arrival of ethnic Chinese from Southeast Asia, and the community has expanded from there into central and west Oakland. Large middle-class Chinese communities have also developed in central San Mateo and northern Santa Clara counties. A long Chinese commercial strip can now be found along, ironically, Castro Street in Mountain View.

Filipinos have followed the tracks of an earlier working-class expansion along Mission Street out of San Francisco's Mission district into Daly City and South San Francisco, at the northern end of San Mateo County. It is there, rumor has it, that Cory and Benito and their friends plotted the overthrow of Ferdinand Marcos in the Aquino kitchen. Filipinos have also settled in large numbers in central Silicon Valley and Alameda County. The biggest and wealthiest enclave of Vietnamese – from the first exodus after the fall of Saigon – is in east San Jose. Most later arrivals from Indochina, including Khmers and ethnic tribes, such as the Hmung, are much poorer, and have settled in such marginal housing areas as San Francisco's Tenderloin (which has been transformed as a result), the two Chinatowns, West Oakland, and Richmond. The 50,000 or so Southeast Asians who settled in the towns of the Central Valley, where rents are cheaper but jobs scarce, were virtually unknown to the rest of the world until an AK-47 was unloaded on thirty Cambodian children in an elementary schoolyard in Stockton by a man who blamed his unemployment on Asian competition.

The assignment of peoples to different quarters of the city is not static but is instead a vigorous and often explosive process of housing growth and residential change. For example, sharp conflicts have developed in San Francisco's Richmond district over the replacement of single-family houses occupied by older whites with condominiums to house the extended families of the expanding Chinese community. Racism and class reproduction are often depicted in personal terms, as direct acts of discrimination, control or humiliation. The white working class dominates popular imagery of bigotry for this reason, because its racism (or sexism or homophobia) tends to be more blunt. And, indeed, we still find such crucial bastions of working-class racism as the San Francisco firefighters or the Oakland garbage collectors. Yet the implicit racial inequalities and barriers of American society are at work behind what often appear as the 'natural' mechanisms of the property market, and the main beneficiaries of this systematic racism are the upper classes whose money and political clout buy them the luxuries of distance, seclusion and exclusion. The resulting geography of wealth and white skin is clear to see in the Bay Area: promontories such as Pacific Heights in San Francisco, islands such as Piedmont (completely surrounded by Oakland), peninsulas such as Marin, and floods of suburban tracts sweeping across the Santa Clara Valley, eastern Contra Costa or northern Solano County.[16]

The property boom: an escape valve?

The real estate chase afflicts the Bay Area more than any other region of the United States. Housing demand has grown feverishly for the last twenty years, fed by economic growth and the upward tilt in the job market. Add to this the inevitable speculation in rent and price-appreciation by investors, landlords and owner-occupiers, the freewheeling mortgage lending of banks and savings and loans in the go-go years of deregulation in the 1980s, capitalization of low property taxes due to Proposition 13 (1978), and the rising incomes and falling taxes of the rich in the age of Reagan, and you have a formula for property inflation on a monumental scale.

Housing values roughly trebled in each of the last two decades, in a kind of feeding frenzy among buyers and financiers. House prices are consistently the highest in the country for a metropolitan region, and have been from at least the middle of the last decade. The 1978 median price was $84,300. In 1989 it was $261,500, up 32 percent from 1988. This compares with a national median of only $93,500; a California median of $200,800 and an Los Angeles County median of $215,800.[17]

The Bay Area thus had the least affordable housing area in the nation in 1989, with only 10 percent of local households being able to afford the median-priced house, compared with 48 percent nationally (and 18 percent in Los Angeles). The property boom thus further undermines the position of the working class and drives another wedge between those older workers who enjoyed postwar prosperity and access to homeownership and younger workers who cannot buy without help from their parents. It also makes living independently harder for single and divorced women, and favors immigrants with extended families over more isolated American-born workers. The bourgeoisie and middle class have become the only ones able to afford houses in large parts of San Francisco, the central East Bay, the West Bay peninsulas and western Silicon Valley, further strengthening class residential divisions.

This immense pressure-cooker has let off steam in two ways: by gentrification of older central areas and by hyper-extension of the suburban fringe. By these means, the elderly, people of color and the white working class have been rolled back from favored areas of the regional core and forced to seek housing at great distances, involving longer and longer commutes. Pressures on the land market have also generated a political response, chiefly in the form of rent control, and anti-growth and anti-densification movements. These have a significant potential for progressive political mobilization, but just as often serve as public vents for private hot air.

In the central districts of San Francisco (Noe-Eureka valleys, the Haight, Western Addition), Berkeley and North Oakland, one finds some of the most thoroughgoing gentrification of old housing and commercial strips in the country. Gentrification has also moved into the neighboring working-class areas of the Mission, Albany, El Cerrito, and central-east Oakland. It even has such outlyers as Point Richmond, Crockett and Pittsburg's Marina Bay. The good side of this process – injections of new money to restore long-neglected housing stock and to breath life into stagnant shopping streets – has been widely trumpeted, but the other side of gentrification is rising rents, housing displacement, and loss of local shops.

The response to gentrification has been bursts of citizen activism and anger. Typically, neighborhoods rally against particular conversion or densification projects, then subside. Redevelopment is frequently suppressed by throwing a blanket of downzoning over the municipality; but this also prevents well-conceived urban intensification. This energy has been channeled into progressive action in the rent-control and anti-conversion laws of Berkeley and San Francisco, and by creative demands on developers to provide quality design and restoration. But property capitalists are good at evading the cities with the greatest strictures, as evidenced by the fantastic remaking of Emeryville. Sometimes the contestation over gentrification gets ugly, like the burning of a new retail complex in the Haight. Or worse, it turns reactionary, in the festering anger of a white working class that sees its place taken in San Francisco by yuppies and gays – epitomized by assassin Dan White's seething hatred for his victims, Mayor George Moscone and Supervisor Harvey Milk – or in Black property owners crying racism over legitimate rent controls in Berkeley.

A more common response of the working class, particularly young couples just starting out, has been to seek affordable homes on the far periphery of the metropolis, where home prices are still within reach. Long-distance worker dormitories have sprung up as far away as Santa Rosa and Petaluma to the north, Benicia and Fairfield and Vacaville to the northeast, Brentwood and Tracy to the east, and Gilroy and Morgan Hill to the south. People are commuting from as far as Modesto, Santa Cruz and Vacaville, creating a new crescent of metropolitan expansion more than 100 miles from downtown San Francisco. The wave of growth spilling over the interior valleys is accentuated by the roaring property boom in the central Bay Area, but is by no means created by this alone. It is chiefly the result of the long upswing in employment and income that has propelled the region past such metropolises as Detroit and Philadelphia over the last twenty years, compounded by the skewed workforce and class structure of the Bay Area. And this growth takes the characteristic California-American form of amoebic suburban sprawl, in which the driving forces are two-sided.

On the supply side, developer profits come from land appreciation by building premium housing in more central areas and by developing cheaply acquired land at the far edge of the urban area. Better yet, double your money by doing both, as Kenneth Behring did in his nouveau riche, post-modern kitsch East Bay suburb of Blackhawk. The state happily aids the process by expanding water supplies, building roads and redrawing planning maps to fit the circumstances. A case in point, much contested by Oakland and Berkeley, is the building of a new reservoir, Buckhorn, in the East Bay hills to serve the booming area around the Bishop Ranch Business Park and Blackhawk in the southern part of the I-680 corridor.

On the demand side, the social dynamics of class, race and individualism play themselves out in the opening up of new urban space. That is, Americans cope with social needs such as housing by taking it upon themselves to buy their own single-family home – with a lot of help, again from the state (Weiss, 1990). This eats up a lot of land, and is most feasible where land is cheapest – at the suburban fringe. White Americans cope with social conflict by putting space between themselves and the less fortunate, especially people of color. They firm up these spatial barriers by erecting greenbelts, putting in large-lot zoning restrictions, and creating new micro-city governments to defend a cramped range of 'community' interests. The result is residential segregation, suburban sprawl and automobilization. This is the general drift of the Bay Area, as well, and has long been America's favored 'solution' to the urban contradictions of capitalism (Walker, 1977).

But the story of suburban growth creates a new drama that is played out in the fastest-growing reaches of the metropolis. There, the mingling of supply and demand in the birth of the built-environment is accompanied by acute labor pains. For the virtually unrestricted operation of the property market undermines the purported solution to the contradictions of urbanism. One's home-as-island is quickly swamped by a sea of identical islands; one's commute is rapidly made impassible by a flood of fellow-travelers; the nearby rural environment is soon buried under urban concrete; and a spanking new suburb is soon swept into the maelstrom of urban life. The reaction of the newly suburbanized populace is predictable: resistance to further growth (Logan and Molotch, 1986). Such 'no-growth' or 'slow-growth' movements have hit virtually every township in the Bay region, which as a result can boast the most widespread development controls of any metropolitan area in the US (Dowall, 1984). Indeed, the Bay Area had one of the earliest anti-growth movements among a broad spectrum of its citizenry of any city in the United States – due to a combination of a large middle-class, leadership in environmentalist causes nationwide, and the rapid pace of suburban growth (Greenberg, 1986).

Slow-growth movements are widely characterized, by left and right alike, in overly simplified terms, as solely representing a middle- and upper-class interest in excluding the poor and people of color (Dowall, 1984; Davis, 1989). The capitalist and middle-class base of no-growth movements is unquestionable, but the same is true of rent-control movements, which the left generally favors. Nor is racial exclusion and class-reproduction through community segregation in doubt, but no-growthers frequently target upper-income developments to oppose. Further, no-growth movements are accused of driving up housing prices throughout the urban area by restricting supply, a largely spurious charge promulgated by ideologues of the property developers (Frieden, 1979). Supply restriction has only a small effect on prices as compared with the force of high incomes, rapid population growth and the American standard of large-lot housing.

What makes the no-growth movement more contradictory, and often lends it a decidedly progressive tinge, is the element of class struggle: a middle-class, consumption-based revolt against the power of property developers (Walker and Heiman, 1981). It raises, moreover, critical questions of urban planning as more than facilitating profit-making in land. This is dangerous for capital, and is fiercely combatted by the leading bourgeoisie of every city where it strikes (Heiman, 1988). Anti-growth movements have, for example, split the Livermore power structure wide open for years (Greenberg, 1986), paved the way for a progressive city council in San Jose in the early 1980s, loosened the vice-grip of Dean Lesher's pro-growth cabal over eastern Contra Costa County (Rauber, 1987), and questioned the irrational water supply policies of local agencies such as the East Bay Municipal Utilities District. Anti-growth movements were successfully resisted by developers in Petaluma and San Jose and Concord; but the constraints on developers tighten, nonetheless. Occasionally, the no-growth struggle takes a sufficiently class-conscious form to suggest that something deeper is amiss in the way US cities are run.

The New Regionalism: Who Rules the Unruly Metropolis?

The cry is out among the opinion-makers and political leaders of the Bay Area: there is a crisis in the offing that can threaten the area' growth, jobs and the quality of life. The background to this disquiet is certainly colored by general concerns for the fate of US capitalism in a shifting global panorama of accumulation. Even California capital, perched on the Pacific Rim, has felt the new challenges of world competition and restructuring (Davis, 1986). Growing apprehension of regional unmanagability and class immobilization resonates at the state level with similar problems in Southern California (see Davis, 1989). But Northern California regionalism is very much rooted in the peculiarities of the Bay metropolis. The growing sense of crisis begins with the threats to the economic base in the form of external financial and electronics competition, as noted earlier, but it feeds on other sources within the region itself, having to do with growth, politics and class recomposition, and with the ability of the ruling class to respond creatively in the face of economic problems, strains on the urban fabric, and challenges to its hegemony.

The quest for economic leadership

Every successful locale in global capitalism must be alert to competitive challenges, and must summon new intiatives from the bowels of production and the heads of industry, often with a strong measure of collective action. The most important such initiatives for the Bay Area lie with the electronics manufacturers of Silicon Valley, who have been faced with devastating competition from Japan in memory chips, and increasingly in microprocessors and computers. US semiconductor and computer firms have responded in several ways: by moving into new product areas, such as semi-custom chips and open-system computers; by continuing to innovate in basic technologies, such as the RISC chip; and by imitating Japanese quality control methods. They have also responded collectively by creating a Santa Clara Valley Manufacturers Group; a Semiconductor Industry Association; a government-supported semiconductor research venture called Sematech; and a semiconductor-computer manufacturers' consortium to be called US Memories, Inc., for the production of 4-megabit DRAMs. The main strategy of the old-line companies has been to look to the federal government for trade relief. Semiconductor manufacturers Intel and National Semiconductor and instrument- and computer-maker Hewlett-Packard have been in the forefront of the wolf-pack crying unfair competition against the Japanese. They managed to block the sale of bankrupt Fairchild Semiconductor to Fujitsu. (At the same time, National continues to sell Hitachi computers through a subsidiary! (Siegel, 1988)). Intel founder Robert Noyce, head of Sematech, and Hewlett-Packard President John Young, former chair of the President's Commission on Industrial Competitiveness, have been particularly active. When his commission's proposals were ignored by the Reagan administration, Young formed a national Council on Competitiveness to push for a targeted policy of federal aid to specific industries (Siegel, 1989).

Signs are mixed as to the success of bolder initiatives. Silicon Valley lost the contract for Sematech to Austin, Texas, and Sematech itself has hardly gotten off the ground, even with strong Defense Department backing. The US Memories project was stillborn. The City of San Jose has been trying to fill the vacuum with its own initiatives to stimulate interaction among local small firms.

On the other hand, the new startups of the 1980s take the view that open systems, cooperation and continued technical vitality are the only road to continued growth (Saxenian, 1989) Sun Microsystems' manufacturing agreement with Toshiba for its RISC chip design has the critics aghast; but Sun's success thus far has repeatedly fooled critics of its approach to new technology. In the end it is unclear whether Silicon Valley's cluster of splintered firms can generate systematic innovation, especially in production technology, as capably as Japan's large *zaibatsu* (Florida and Kenney, 1990).

San Francisco's business community has been even more like a headless horseman. While B of A has been retrenching, Wells Fargo Bank has been quietly growing but seems content to be number 2, and not to assume a leadership position. Indeed, Wells refuses to lend in Silicon Valley, which it regards as too risky! Meanwhile, the loss or acquisition of many second-tier banks and industrial firms with a local base has left their leadership roles for the regional economy and polity uncertain. Much of the aura of dynamism and leadership emanating from the Imperial City of San Francisco, for so long 'queen city of the west', has dissipated. A vacuum has appeared at the top. There has been a passing of the old guard of bourgeois families. The postwar generation of capitalist leadership – the Swigs, Alioto, Zellerbach, Giannini – is gone.

The same is true at the other end of the Bay Bridge, where the Knowlands and Kaisers led Oakland for so long (Hayes, 1972). Some likely successors, such as Bob Lurie (real estate) and the Haas family (Levi-Strauss) have been preoccupied with the popular question of whether the Bay Area could retain two baseball teams and where a new stadium might be built. Some, such as the Bechtel family, largely opt out of public life. Some are simply not up to it: who would trust Charles Schwab, the discount brokerage king, with public leadership? And many others have been recruited to leading positions in state and national politics, especially during the Reagan regimes in Sacramento and Washington: George Schultz (Bechtel/Stanford), Cap Weinberger (Bechtel), Ed Meese (Alameda County government), Don Clausen (B of A) and David Packard (Hewlett-Packard). The Bay Area's very success may have overextended its bourgeoisie, with one leg in the Bohemian Grove and another across the Potomac (Domhoff, 1974).

A growing dilemma and opportunity for the Anglo bourgeoisie throughout the Bay Area is the delicate question of integrating their minority brethren into the regional ruling class, particularly the burgeoning Asian business community: San Francisco property developers like Leslie Tang and Vincent Tai or David Sen-Lin Lee of Qume Corp. and David Lam of Wyse Technologies. In a place where even Amadeo Giannini, founder of Bank of America, could remain a perennial 'outsider', this can pose a major problem. A strong faction of the Bay Area leadership favors integration as a necessity given the composition of the general population and ethnic ties to the greater Pacific Rim economy. This line has been pushed most strongly by the Silicon Valley-based Asian-American Manufacturers Association, founded in 1980, whose principal ethnic base lies among Chinese from Taiwan, Hong Kong and what are now called 'the nations of the South China Sea' (Viviano, 1988). They argue that more California trade emanates from that area than from Japan. San Francisco Mayor Art Agnos has picked up one of the group's themes by referring to a greater 'San Francisco family' of Asians and Asian Americans who have lived and worked in the Bay Area and now reside abroad – and who could help cement regional ties to the burgeoning economies of East Asia. Indeed, the Asian burghers probably have a greater sense of unity across the Bay Area than their Anglo counterparts.

Yet Asians pose a threat as well as an opportunity in the eyes of the Anglo business class, as both economic competitors and potential mass immigrants. Anglo ideology on the proper treatment of local Asian American minorities draws heavily on prevailing opinion about their countries of origin, and all the ambiguity that view entails. And, despite the supplications of the enlightened sectors of the bourgeoisie, equality even for the favored sons and daughters of Asia remains a solidly liberal or even radical reform that has to be fought for by people of color, as the recent fights over Asian American admissions and course requirements at Stanford and Berkeley show.

The costs of growth come due

The Bay region has been as much a victim of its own success as of outside economic forces. A great tidal wave of growth has swelled the downtown highrises and swept the city outward over hundreds of square miles of new territory. Ranchlands, hillsides and farms have disappeared under hundreds of new subdivisions, office parks, and shopping centers. Water supplies have been stretched to the breaking point in the East Bay, while the sewage load on the South Bay – even though highly treated – threatens to overwhelm the absorptive capacity of that poorly circulating basin. Air pollution has grown worse again, after a decade of improvement due to the Clean Air Act. There are virtually no sites left for garbage disposal within the built-up area of the metropolis, leaving cities to pa y exorbitant rates to truck their mountains of waste to peripheral sites, such as Altamont Pass, east of Livermore.

The touchstone of the growth bind is traffic. It is readily apparent to everyone is that growth over the last twenty years has filled the vintage 1940–60 bridges and freeways to the bursting point. Suburban expansion, combined with more two-worker households, has extended the average two-way trip from forty-three miles in 1983 to sixty miles by 1986 (Bay Area Council, 1986). Portions of Interstates 80 and 680 are in an almost continual state of traffic jam, lane additions are already in the works, but even the State Department of Transportation seems unsure what to do. One hears talk of reviving the southern crossing (a bridge south of the Bay Bridge), a second level on the Golden Gate bridge, and commuter trains from Sacramento, Gilroy and Tracy. The Bay Area Rapid Transit (BART) system is finally being extended to the San Francisco airport, but is under enormous political pressure to grow in every possible direction in order to service every possible land developer and speculator. Meanwhile, recent scandals at BART and AC Transit (the East Bay's public bus system) have added to the aura of demoralization around mass transit after years of neglect and dwindling revenues, due to Proposition 13's property tax limitations and Republican budget-cutting. The state has been frozen in its tracks for years, and regional transit improvements are being financed today mainly via local sales taxes and bridge tolls (both regressive).

The housing crunch also stimulates popular discontent and capitalist fears. While homebuyers scramble to get on the train as it pulls rapidly out of their class station, business worries that housing inflation is a cause of industrial decline in the Bay Area. (No-growth movements, it is further contended, make the problem worse.) This is much bandied about with regard to Silicon Valley, and is the position of the recently formed Bay Area Economic Forum. The argument is that expensive housing drives up wages, reducing industrial competitiveness and triggering an exodus of factories for far-away places. The evidence does not support the contention, however. While some facilities are certainly located outside the Bay Area for cost savings on land and labor, Silicon Valley continues to attract and spawn new plants faster than it spins them off (Saxenian, 1989).[18]

Industrial core areas such as Silicon Valley grow for reasons having little to do with input costs; in fact, high incomes and high house prices are more the outcome of industry growth than a barrier to it (Storper and Walker, 1989). If costs were the key issue, the Bay Area's perennially high-cost economy would have atrophied long ago. High house prices and long commutes are more a question of personal hardship on the working class than of economic survival for the region.

Behind the scenes, finance capital has also been paying a price for rampant growth. While many California banks and savings institutions have waxed fat on the property boom and the largest savings and loans are disproportionately to be found here, the casualties of speculative excess are many. Crocker Bank and Bank of America lost heavily on real estate; the largest single S & L, Financial Corporation of America (American Savings and Loan of Stockton in the Bay Area) had to be sold for salvage; Bell Savings of San Mateo went belly up in the Silicon Valley bust; Fidelity Savings of Oakland had to be sold off to Citicorp. Presently, 32 of the 189 S & L's in California are insolvent (*Chronicle*, 21 June 1989).

Political fragmentation

The question of who rules the Bay Area has been reopened by growth and a shifting economic base, both of which have left the traditional geographic centers of power, San Francisco and Oakland, in a greatly diminished position. The matter of political 'regulation' of the metro and state economy and is openly contested, or, worse, falls between several chairs. San Francisco faces a dilemma it has struggled with in the past: can the center hold? It did earlier in the century, despite greater economic growth in the East Bay. Whether it can in an even larger metro region is questionable. While the city sustains several advantages of central location and historical primacy, it also suffers from some serious difficulties of access, land costs, and jurisdictional size. Bourgeois fears over the loss of the prestigious center are regularly voiced by spokesmen from such policy centers as the Bay Area Council and the Hoover Institution (*Tribune*, 29 March 1987). Managing the relations between San Francisco and the rest of the metropolis will be crucial to whether the Bay Area region stumbles or keeps growing.

It is surprising how much the industrial realms of the metropolis go their different ways and appear to their participants as different worlds (cf. Soja, 1988). Silicon Valley's power structure evolved, like its semiconductors, rather independently of the rest of the region – despite critical areas of overlap (Traunstine, 1979). Most of Silicon Valley's leading capitalists, such as Andy Grove (Intel) and Charles Sporck (National Semiconductor), are more embroiled in electronics industry policy than in asserting a vision of the Bay Area as a whole (David Packard is a notable exception). Silicon Valley politicians also have their local base foremost in mind. Recently, San Jose has made a furious push to become the business services center and symbolic 'downtown' of Silicon Valley through a huge redevelopment effort after years of decline. To promote this project, Mayor Tom McEnery has declared San Francisco to be a has-been and San Jose to be the new heart of the metropolitan area. Such competitive chest-thumping from one of the supposed bright lights in local politics does not bode well for regional leadership from that quarter.

The independence of Silicon Valley recalls the relative autonomy of the East Bay and the long-standing rivalry between Oakland and San Francisco. This schism has nearly torn the region in two, in marked contrast to the way the feuds between Hollywood and Downtown L.A. fell within the same political jurisdiction (Davis, 1987). San Francisco lorded it over Oakland for the first fifty years, but lost much of its industry to the East Bay after the great earthquake and fire of 1906. Oakland has gotten its revenge in other ways, such as allying with Los Angeles against Bank of America's move south or to constrain San Francisco's port. It finally decimated San Francisco's once-mighty port by capturing the container business almost completely over the last thirty years (Mills, 1979). San Francisco's pet plan of the 1940s for a BART system to bring suburban commuters downtown was diverted through downtown Oakland as a condition of Alameda County joining the system (Adler, 1980). The spirit of competitive nastiness and infighting between San Francisco and Oakland lies, even now, just beneath the surface, as illustrated by the nadir of petty bickering reached by Mayors Feinstein and Wilson over the placement of a General Services Administration office building – a struggle that Oakland eventually won. Even a regional agreement among the Association of Bay Area Governments to create a biotech information center in 1988 had to be passed without stipulating any specific location – due to East Bay-West Bay rivalry (*Tribune*, 16 Dec. 1988).

Even on one side of the Bay coordination is often well-nigh impossible. The mighty and politically insular port of Oakland has been riven by dissension over whether to hold its land for port uses or to develop waterfront properties for office and retail uses. Long-time Chair Walter Abernathy resigned in disgust at the failure of Oakland leaders to support competitive infrastructure investment. The ports of Richmond and Oakland are bitter rivals, and the managers at AC Transit and BART have feuded for years. The elite of the I-680-corridor generally regard Oakland and Berkeley as foreign lands; the Oakland *Tribune*'s Black publisher-editor, Bob Maynard, tried dropping the name of Oakland from the masthead in a futile effort to garner subscribers over the hills.[19]

The challenge of popular insurgencies

Central city politics present the best-publicized challenges to business hegemony and unbridled capital accumulation in the Bay Area. Popular disenchantment with downtown interests is high in San Francisco after the largest office build-up in the city's history. A political touchstone is Proposition M, passed in 1986, which puts strict limits on downtown building – after twenty years of struggle by anti–high rise activists. The city's electorate has never been easily tamed by appeals to civic boosterism and capital flight. The sweeping victory of the liberal Art Agnos as mayor over the hand-picked successor of probusiness mayor Diane Feinstein in 1988 raised the spectre of a revived political mobilization of 'the neighborhoods' against Downtown that was cut down along with Harvey Milk and George Moscone in 1978. Yet even Agnos's support for a new downtown baseball stadium was not enough to save it from defeat in November 1989.

Rent controls instituted in the late 1970s (during the last great property boom) have put a damper on apartment speculation and rent gouging in Berkeley and San Francisco, although they have been repeatedly defeated in Oakland. Statewide drives by real estate interests have been unable to overturn existing residential rent control laws, but they succeeded in eliminating Berkeley's pioneering commercial rent control law and preventing the spread of such controls to other cities. A recently mooted proposal by Berkeley's indefatigable Marty Schiffenbauer to slow housing price inflation created a firestorm of hysteria among the Third (Real) Estate.

Popular impediments also lie in wait to derail efforts by transportation planners to solve the transit snarl. CalTrans's efforts to widen I-80 have been knocked into a cocked hat by local opposition. Much to everyone's surprise, Berkeley Mayor Loni Hancock was able to persuade the business enclave of Emeryville to join Berkeley in refusing to allow work to proceed through their jurisdictions. Emeryville's leadership is no friend of radical causes, but is worried that its recently developed yuppie consumption spaces will not be well served by the planned improvements.

At the same time, the suburbs have not been quiescent. A now-perennial disturbance to business hegemony is the eruption of opposition to rapid development. Some seventy ballot measures to control growth have been placed before local voters in the 1980s, compared with seventeen in the previous decade (*Chronicle*, 19 Oct. 1988). For example, Walnut Creek, in the heart of the Contra Costa office belt, has passed a new growth-control initiative, and most of the middle-class towns such as Palo Alto have strong downzoning. Even the conservative city of Alameda is in turmoil over the expansion of the Harbor Bay complex.

One of the curiosities of the Bay Area has been its singular resistance to military ideology despite the role of defense spending in the region. The Livermore Action Group's campaigns against the Lawrence-Livermore labs is a case in point. Another recent instance was the fight over homeporting the battleship *Missouri* in San Francisco. Cap Weinberger's Defense Department wanted to position this greying symbol of America's military prowess in an oppositional city to prove that militarism was back in vogue. After a local campaign against the plan, it was dropped by the Bush administration. An interesting fight is now shaping up over the disposal of the Presidio of San Francisco by the Army as part of the same budget cutting. Decisions concerning this last great stretch of undeveloped land will be indicative of the powers and interests at work in contemporary San Francisco.

It is unclear, as always, how much popular opposition has actually hampered capital. Most movements questioning growth get rolling after the damage is done, leaving local residents to clean up after the developers. Similarly, neighborhood politics and anti-downtown movements have probably done little real harm to business interests in San Francisco. The building booms of the 1970s and 1980s were hardly slowed by political interference. Proposition M and Agnos's victory in San Francisco signaled the passing of the office boom for economic reasons and capitalist disarray as much as a progressive resurgence.

The regionalist drive

All these issues are encompassed within a single call, from certain quarters, for a new attention to regional interests and the political suppression of 'parochial' demands and local powers. Precedent for the regionalism movement may be found in the decade or so after World War II (Scott, 1959). Then, the Bay Area Council was formed by corporate leaders, the Bechtels were planning BART, the state freeway system was being laid out, and the Blyth-Zellerbach committee was created to push for Downtown redevelopment (Hartman, 1984). That kind of coordinated capitalist effort to guide the development of the Bay Area has long been absent.

A series of conferences and reports have appeared in the last several years decrying the problems of the region, such as economic recession, overspecialization in electronics, traffic congestion, and housing inflation (Bay Area Council, 1988; Brady, 1985). A sense of urgency is being conveyed to the leading citizens of the region: 'while the world economy has grown ever more competitive, we have grown complacent' (Brady et al., 1989). Hidden amongst these dire warnings are suggestions that what is needed is more regional (or subregional) planning and more intergovernmental cooperation (*Tribune*, 29 March 1987, 6 October 1988; *Chronicle*, 19 October 1988). Education is also being singled out for its role in providing skilled labor, technical innovation and integration of new peoples into the workforce (*California Tomorrow*, 1988; Brady et al., 1989).

Leading the charge are the Bay Area Council, the main local corporate think tank, and the Association of Bay Area Governments (ABAG), a weak advisory body looking for a mission. Together they formed the Bay Area Economic Forum, chaired by Robert Parry, CEO of the Federal Reserve Bank of San Francisco. The Haas family foundations are backing a study group called Bay Vision 2020, chaired by former UC Berkeley chancellor Michael Heyman. The state has also been mobilized. Five cities in northern Santa Clara County joined together in the Golden Triangle Consortium in 1986 to coordinate planning. A Bay Area economic mission to Asia in early 1989, called 'Northern California's first regional roadshow' by the San Francisco *Examiner*, featured San Francisco Mayor Art Agnos, San Jose Mayor Tom McEnery, Oakland officials, business executives and university representatives.

In Sacramento, the California legislature is gearing up for some kinds of intervention in local governance, promising what may be a new Progressive Era of improved managerialism. Hearings have been held, statements issued and bills drawn up toward what is being called 'the new regionalism project' (Walters, 1988; California Senate, 1988). The governor has created a public/private California Economic Development Corporation to promote the state; it has issued a report covering the usual regionalist themes and calling for a 'new societal compact' for restructuring business and government (CEDC, 1988). Symbolism can be as important as substance in the effort to build a regional consciousness, and political struggles can erupt over the process of creating monuments and myths for the city (Harvey, 1985b), as in the case of the USS *Missouri* or the China Basin baseball stadium proposal in San Francisco.

Political implications of the regionalist campaign

In some ways, of course, nothing much has changed: jurisdictional fragmentation, the shift to suburbs and Silicon Valley, the lack of urban planning, housing price inflation and growing traffic have been apparent for years, even decades. Why is everyone suddenly waking up to it? Certainly, the great growth wave of 1975–85 strained the infrastructure, transformed the region and left a bitter taste in the slump of 1985–87. But the region is manifestly not in dire trouble. What is most apparent is that there is a breech in capitalist class hegemony in a top-heavy region with too many competing centers of business power, too much change in the landscape of capital, and too many unruly popular movements.

It is unlikely, furthermore, that the local bourgeoisie can ever achieve more than a loose coalition of interests and the establishment of a very general agenda: the centrifugal forces in US capitalism and US cities are just too great. There is no MITI to intervene, as in Japan in the 1950s and 1960s. Regional government has not been feasible in the US in this century (Scott, 1959).

Nonetheless, the business class needs to demonstrate some measure of unity, aggressiveness and cleverness for Bay Area fortunes to be sustained. No region can long succeed without some mobilization of and leadership from its capitalists. Regional leaders must project and protect the interests of the whole Bay Area and of its various sectors in competition with other fast-growing and innovative areas. Within the region there has to be some coordination and sustained attack on general problems such as highway building and port coordination, particularly where public funds are required to pay for solutions. There needs to be a reassertion of hegemony to head off alternative class and political agendas. Regionalism helps politically in striking back on selective fronts such as Proposition M and rent control. And, finally, regionalist ideology can be useful in recruiting new members of the bourgeoisie and the middle class to leadership roles and the inner circles of the capitalist class. Conversely, by projecting themselves as interested in the general (local) welfare, non-Anglo burghers vying for recognition can shed the stigma of having foreign or minority interests foremost in mind.

An enlightened middle class can easily be seduced by the ideological maneuvering to restore hegemony. Exemplary in this regard are the writings of Kevin Starr – the leading organic intellectual of the Bay Area renaissance – who is featured regularly in the San Francisco *Examiner*. Starr is a master at cultivating regional consciousness by blending pride of place with sense of social purpose among his readers through the clever use of historical vignettes, local curiosities, criticism of tomfoolery and touching stories of idealism. For example: the 'Oakland estuary integrates into one urban landscape the constituent elements of Bay Area culture. ... [O]ne moves into Oakland Estuary past the Alameda Naval Air Station and the Naval Supply Center. History itself thereby welcomes you'

(Starr, 1989b). At the same time, he promotes a conservative social agenda calling for less bull from below and more leadership from above, greater collective purpose and the call to duty among the better elements (Starr, 1989a).

The seductions of regionalism are particularly strong among liberals who recognize the costs of growth and understand the need for social planning – but lack a radical critique of capitalist urbanization. The California Tomorrow group has long represented a liberal tendency among the region's bourgeoisie to plan for growth while protecting some of the natural amenities that so attract people to the area. The regionalist debate touches a particularly fulsome chord with environmentalists. In the spring of 1989, People for Open Space/The Greenbelt Alliance called together a 'regional issues forum' (by invitation only) to explore the possibilities for a regulatory commission for land use, on the old Progressive Era model of an expert body above politics. But the core environmental problems of the Bay Area, which are in every way 'regional', curiously fail to make the agendas of the town-criers of regionalism, whether it is toxic wastes in Richmond or radiation wastes in Livermore, dredge spoils or the garbage pile-up (see, for example, CEDC, 1988).

There is a place, of course, for regional cooperation and planning, just as there is for industrial policy, in a progressive or socialist vision. The construction of livable cities is not something that can be left to the market and the profit motive. Metropolitan problems need metropolitan solutions, and there is always the danger after a long growth boom that the economic basis of the area may become unstuck. The cries of a ruling class in distress may actually be a favorable indicator of openings for progressive political action in the future, which the left should not ignore, just as in the past the inability of the Bay Area's leaders to forge the kind of united class front achieved by the Los Angeles Merchants and Manufacturers Association in the early years of the twentieth century was a blessing for working-class and progressive forces (Wiley and Gottlieb, 1982). But regionalism must be shorn of its capitalist allegiance to the existing class configuration of power and ways of doing business before it can be attached to a just political agenda (Heiman, 1988).

The Impasse of the Left

The Bay Area has been a center of capitalist growth, labor organization, cosmopolitan social trends, and progressive politics in the United States. These friendly currents have helped to keep the left more buoyant here than most places in this country – even though the record is unquestionably mixed. Conversely, the left has contributed immensely to the stream of social progress here, and has laid a deep foundation on which subsequent movements have been able to build. This is exactly the kind of historic legacy the left and the working class in the United States have generally found so difficult to sustain (Davis, 1986). We will now look at several of the elements that have made for a strong left and progressive presence in the Bay Area in recent years. The radical explosion of the 1960s was the jumping-off place for the present, followed by a series of vibrant social movements in the last twenty years. To these must be added the toeholds gained in electoral politics and in solidarity across racial lines. Finally, we return once more to the insinuation of the left in the ascendent middle class. In all cases, however, the legacy is a mixed blessing and presents any number of contradictions for a left politics in the region. It is thus that the left finds itself at an impasse today. We therefore turn, at the end, to some proposals outlining the direction the left ought to move, as indicated by the current political geography of the Bay Area outlined so far.

The legacy of the 1960s

The local working class and left have a string of historic victories to their credit that includes the constitutional reforms of 1879, Knights of Labor organizing in the 1880s, the Building Trades Council's political hegemony from 1901 to 1914, the San Francisco General Strike of 1934, and resistance to anticommunist hysteria in the 1950s. That legacy carried over to the New Left of the 1960s in important ways, with the New Left becoming, in turn, the inspiration for much that followed.

During the 1964–74 period loosely known as 'the Sixties', the Bay Area harbored an extraordinarily complex and vital political movement of the New Left. It became a stronghold of an anti-Vietnam War movement that, while originating among students, grew into a mass, cross-class, cross-race opposition to US war policy. Oakland was the center of the Black Panther

Party and other revolutionary national organizations of African Americans that had a base in the lower end of the Black working class and challenged racial oppression. This was the most advanced of the nationalist struggles among different minority groups, although there was significant activism also among Chinese (the Cultural Revolution), Filipinos (the International Hotel campaign) and Chicanos/Latinos (Los Siete and the United Farm Workers). Nationally, the most successful unified campus movement among people of color was the Third World strike on the San Francisco State University campus.

The Bay Area was at the cutting edge in electoral experiments, using propositions and initiatives to promote progressive goals, organizing for community control and district elections, and initiating efforts to control the police through police review boards. The region was equally a center of experiments in a counterculture that featured communal living, socially conscious rock 'n' roll and the hippies of Haight-Ashbury. Finally, out of the universities and the general milieu came a generation of politicized intellectuals who challenged the hegemony of academic conservatism, self-serving professional associations and the media through such vehicles as *Ramparts*, the *Berkeley Barb*, NACLA-West, KPFA and *Mother Jones* magazine.

New issues, new ideas and new participants give the recent past a distinctive flavor. Yet nothing quite like that breadth of common purpose and depth of militancy has occurred since the 1960s, despite continuing ferment on many fronts. Ironically, in this the left shares something with the capitalist class, whose regional impasse has left space for middle-class ascendency socially and a good bit of room for progressive and radical political movements.

Movements of 1970s and 1980s

A number of substantial movements grew out of the sixties but developed fully only after the ferment of that period was over. The 1970s and 1980s cannot be seen as a quiescent period in popular struggles. New political issues have continued to revitalize and reshape left and progressive politics in the Bay Area. Gay liberation, women's rights, environmentalism, occupational health, rights of the disabled and rent control shook up the body politic in the 1970s, and were joined in the 1980s by the peace movement, the Livermore Lab actions, divestment from South Africa, support for Palestine, and opposition to US intervention in Central America, among others. We can only touch on some of these movements here.

San Francisco's place in the emergence of a gay liberation movement is undisputed. As gay men migrated into the city in large numbers – upwards of 100,000 – they successfully coalesced into a self-proclaimed cultural and political force here (Castells, 1983). The movement took a distinctly left turn behind the leadership of Harvey Milk as it assumed the mantle of 'the neighborhoods' fighting Downtown capital as well as fighting for gay rights against the forces of reaction statewide. As a result, gay men have the curious distinction of being the only progressive constituency of white males in the US. Tolerance toward gays and lesbians is quite general in the Bay region, as shown by the recent public coming-out of Fremont's School Board chairman, although violent attacks by homophobes continue. The political potential of the gay community has been dealt two stunning body-blows with the assassination of newly elected Supervisor Harvey Milk in 1978 and the loss of so many people, including a generation of leaders, to the AIDS epidemic of the 1980s. Yet Harry Britt, political heir to Milk and a self-proclaimed democratic socialist, remains the biggest vote-getter on San Francisco's Board of Supervisors, while the mobilization for AIDS research and patient support has become a model for the rest of the country.

Environmentalism is another movement closely associated with the Bay Area and is rooted deeply in public consciousness here. While chiefly a white middle-class concern, environmentalism has spread to working-class and minority communities with the widening anger over toxic waste pollution. Bay Area environmental battles have always had important left elements and have posed radical challenges to capitalism in several ways. Property developers have been greatly constrained in certain areas: filling of Bay tidelands was halted as early as 1965, and coastal development was regulated by a state commission after an initiative in 1972. The Bay Area left has been very active in the struggles to ban pesticides such as EDB, DBCP and Alar, and to control occupational health hazards, thanks especially to occupational health activists; it has raised the issue of toxic pollution by the supposedly clean electronics industry in Silicon Valley, led by the Silicon Valley Toxics Coalition (Siegel and Markoff, 1985); and it led the ballot initiative drive to pass a sweeping statewide toxic substances control act in 1986. The titanic struggles to stop further water development, especially the referendum defeat of Peripheral Canal (a plan to expand the State Water Project) in 1982, have also had a strong left element, and have greatly discommoded agribusiness and the state (Storper and Walker, 1982).

The women's liberation movement has steadily transformed gender politics on the left, and has had a very broad impact in American society. The Bay Area was an important early center of feminist activity through such vehicles as Bay Area Women Against Rape, the Women's Health Clinics in San Francisco and Berkeley, the Center for Women's Music and the Women's Building. The East Bay has, in particular, been a focus for the alternative women's community and support for lesbian couples, single-mothers, and women moving into traditionally male occupations. San Jose was the site of a nationally pace-setting comparable worth agreement. The women's struggle has plugged into the labor movement and helped revitalize it by organizing places where women work in large numbers, such as hospitals, restaurants, schools and universities. Further, the comparable worth victory came during the administration of Mayor Janet Grey Hayes, one of many women filling electoral posts in the region, such as former Mayor Dianne Feinstein of San Francisco, Mayor Loni Hancock of Berkeley, Congresswomen Barbara Boxer and Nancy Pelosi, and San Francisco Supervisors Nancy Walker, Doris Ward and Angela Alioto. After a period of doubt and political malaise after the defeat of the Equal Rights Amendment, women are again organizing here, as they are nationally, in response to 'right-to-life' attacks on women's health clinics and around the legal defense of women's right to choose (Tax, 1989).

International solidarity movements have played an especially significant role in the Bay Area. The level of internationalism is equalled only in Washington, Boston and New York. Central America has been the focal point for organizing, no doubt due to the fertile combination of radicalized immigrants and the area's strong legacy of anti-imperialist struggles from the 1960s. The anti-intervention movement unified most of the region's left activists, who worked through Sister City declarations, medical and technical aid efforts of the most diverse kinds, ballot measures on US foreign policy, union actions and people-to-people programs. A large number of people here have a vision of the Bay Area as part of the Americas as a whole (Burbach and Núñez, 1987). The divestment movement also swept up many activists in 1985–86, stimulated by popular upheaval in South Africa, and produced the largest student protests at UC Berkeley since 1971. After significant victories at both city and state levels, however, the South Africa support movement died down again. The Palestinian cause has been an arena of contention here, as throughout the United States, due to the refusal of most American Jews, progressives and unionists to engage in any critical appraisal of Israel's policies. Important left politicians such as Harry Britt, Loni Hancock and Tom Bates have capitulated to the Israel lobby. Ballot measures on Israel/Palestine failed in both Berkeley and San Francisco in 1986.

In short, the energy of new movements over the last twenty years has been impressive, and the issues raised have undoubtedly broadened the social vision and the sophistication of the left. Yet with this growth has come a division of left and progressive forces into many streams, often with little mixing and a loss of a socialist vision about the unity, class base and anti-capitalist character of an organized left opposition. In addition, the internationalism of the Bay Area left has served as a valuable antidote to Reaganism at its high tide but has come at some cost to local political activism.

Electoral politics

The upheavals of the 1960s generated a number of politicians who owe their careers to the left: Ron Dellums, who went from the Berkeley City Council to Congress (Kelley, 1989); Gus Newport and Loni Hancock, past and present mayors of Berkeley, who ran at the head of the Berkeley Citizens' Action (BCA); Lionel Wilson, mayor of Oakland, who rode the mobilization achieved by the Black Panthers into office; the late John George, Alameda County supervisor, and his successor, Warren Widener, once the BCA-backed mayor of Berkeley; the late George Moscone, mayor of San Francisco; San Francisco Supervisors Nancy Walker, Carole Ruth Silver and Richard Hongisto (the former sheriff); Assemblyman Tom Bates of Berkeley; Oakland City Council member Wilson Riles, Jr., and several Berkeley City Council members. Experiments in electoral politics at the end of the 1960s were consolidated into a dominant party, BCA, in Berkeley, and a sustained presence in San Francisco and, to a lesser extent, Oakland.

These electoral successes represented a dramatic turnaround from the preceding decades of solid Republican control of both

Oakland and Berkeley politics and the lordship of the reactionary Knowland family (owners of the *Tribune*) over East Bay politics (Hayes, 1972; Bush, 1984). Of course, there have also been major setbacks: the betrayals of the progressive cause by Lionel Wilson, Warren Widener and Carol Ruth Silver, once in office; the assassinations of Milk and Moscone; and the loss of hard-won district elections in San Francisco and their imposition, over BCA's opposition, in Berkeley. And, it must be noted, that outside the regional core, nothing approaching a self-proclaimed left politics exists.

The left's electoral presence rides on a wider progressive current in which the Democratic Party is dominant and is itself frequently led by its most liberal elements. Democratic presidential candidates have carried San Francisco and Alameda counties in every election except 1960, in a state which has gone Republican during most of this century. Even Silicon Valley, long a Republican stronghold, is drifting into the Democratic column (*Examiner*, 11 Sept. 1988). The congressional delegation includes such consistent liberals as George Miller, Pete Stark, Norman Mineta, Barbara Boxer and Nancy Pelosi, from various corners of the Bay region. San Francisco's Phil Burton had a virtual hammerlock on state party politics and congressional redistricting for years until his death. Willie Brown, a Black Assembly member from San Francisco, controls the State Assembly from his position as Speaker. Progressive electoral politics in San Francisco continued to show a remarkable vitality at the close of the 1980s, as evidenced by the stunning election victory of Burton-protégé Art Agnos in San Francisco, accompanied by a virtual sweep of the Board of Supervisors by liberal to left candidates.

But the new Agnos regime inherited an empty cupboard from its more conservative predecessors, and was immediately forced to redirect its efforts toward fiscal solvency – hardly the way to launch a bold new social offensive. BCA has been caught in a similar squeeze for many years, trying to keep up social services and school quality in the face of Proposition 13, Reagan's social budget-slashing, and repeated deficits. It continues to hold a majority on the city council, but lost control of the school board in 1986; happily, the new school board majority is proving comparatively incompetent and is unlikely to last in the face of considerable Black community mobilization. But the limitations of running local governments and serving legislative constituencies are readily felt.

Equally apparent is the current lack of a left agenda for local government that rings true in light of the both the conservative consensus nationally (and lack of federal money for social problems), and local problems of housing cost inflation, traffic congestion and banking decline that seem quite beyond the powers of local government to deal with. BCA has done a workmanlike job of presiding over the lean years for local government in the 1980s, partly by mobilizing the citizens of Berkeley to tax themselves extra for libraries and schools. Yet the left has, in a sense, been locked into the role of an 'institutionalized opposition'. Worse, one sees in Agnos or Hancock the incipient dangers of elected officials taking on the priorities of business (for example, Agnos's interest in trade missions) or conservatives (for example, Hancock's embrace of the 'war on drugs').

In Oakland, African Americans were able to gain control of local government under Mayor Lionel Wilson, but only through an alliance with business that has created a political machine of limited social vision. The broader Wilsonian alliance has also been tainted by corruption in the administration of AC Transit and the Peralta Colleges. The Black middle-class leadership is trapped by the predominant racial stereotype of Oakland – its much talked-about 'image problem' – and the way the city has been left out of the region's growth. During the liberal administration of Governor Jerry Brown there was, briefly, a program to target state aid to Oakland, but this disappeared with the rightward shift in state politics after 1978. Rather than challenge racism and the national neglect of poverty directly, Oakland's Black politicians have fallen behind the real estate promoters' idea that downtown redevelopment/revitalization is the key to city revival, and have wasted millions of dollars on botched renewal schemes. A depressing example is the prevailing mentality is the effort to shoo the Black homeless out of Lafayette Park, just west of City Hall, to uplift a district slated for a new Bonwit-Teller department store and 'Victorian row' offices (*Tribune*, 13 March 1989). (Much the same redevelopment mentality plagues Black officeholders in industrial Richmond).

The Oakland Black left has had champions in Ron Dellums, the late John George, and Wilson Riles, Jr. Yet Dellums, who is the only avowed socialist in Congress and an invaluable thorn in the side of the military establishment (witness Ed Meese's attempt to smear him on a false charge of possession of cocaine in 1981), has not been as effective as a rallying point for local political causes as he has in serving a national left constituency (Kelley, 1989). John George was a brilliant gadfly for good causes, but was always isolated on the Alameda County Board of Supervisors (his replacement by the board with the much-despised Warren Widener was a blow to the Dellums-BCA forces). Riles, too, has been a lone voice in Oakland city government. His campaign to unseat Mayor Wilson, who is seeking a fourth term in office, is a project of the East Bay Rainbow Coalition that faces an uphill battle. Oakland remains a terrible reminder of the control that conservatives can retain on politics in a city with a nonwhite majority and desperate economic conditions.

The Rainbow Coalition and Jesse Jackson's 1988 presidential campaign raised the hopes of many Bay Area radicals for a rebirth of the Black and white electoral alliances of the past, and even a push farther into the uncharted territory of a multiracial coalition for progressive change. Jackson carried San Francisco and Alameda counties in the California Democratic primary. Unfortunately, the Rainbow has not come together as a strong organizational core here, and the promise remains unfulfilled.

Many on the left have been so infuriated by the craven behavior of the Democrats over the last decade, and so convinced that playing the loyal opposition has been a fool's quest (Davis, 1986), that they still find it hard to ally with a Rainbow or a Jackson candidacy set within the Democratic Party – despite the dramatic left turn which this represented for the party in 1988. While most people on the left locally were personally excited by Jackson's successes, they were not galvanized into action in any major way. The virtual absence of any Jackson campaign presence at the Mobilization for Peace, Jobs and Justice in April 1988 was a sad index of this inability to change directions with the shifting political tides.

Racial schisms

The left has not escaped the complex web of racism in Bay Area. As we have noted, the cosmopolitan image of Bay Area often clashes with reality of the marginalization and isolation of peoples of color. Historically, the remarkable thing is how much of the local progressive legacy is a story dominated by white men: the Workingmen's Party, the Knights of Labor, the

Building Trades Council, the 1934 General Strike, the Beats, the Free Speech Movement, the hippies, the gays. That isolation has been breached, at certain points, as in the integration of the Longshoreman's union, white radical support of the Black Panther Party, the election of Gus Newport as mayor of Berkeley, the push for divestment from South Africa, or in work with Central Americans in the solidarity movement. In these examples lies a strength and a hope for building alliances between communities. The cosmopolitan left is, unfortunately, too often unable to bridge the gulfs that exist between peoples.

For example, Berkeley seems more split today than during the school integration and insurgent politics of 1960s and 1970s. Part of this rests on the shifting social geography of the metropolis: in Berkeley, Blacks declined from 30 to 20 percent of the population from 1970 to 1980, and are likely to register less than 15 percent in the 1990 census. Even Oakland's Black middle class is having trouble holding its turf, as shown by the displacement occurring as Anglos and Asians move into the High Street corridor of central East Oakland. (Tensions between Blacks and Asians are now greater than those between Blacks and Latinos). But part of the problem is political, and lies in the inability to arrive at a common program that unites Black and white interests.

A common theme running through recent political battles is a clash between white opposition movements and African American concern with economic development of poor neighborhoods. In Berkeley, Blacks and whites split over waterfront development by the Santa Fe Corporation, and over a tax-redistribution qua redevelopment scheme to aid Black south Berkeley. In North Oakland there is a fight over tearing down the old Merritt College (a building of some architectural merit and putative starting place of the Black Panthers) and replacing it with a shopping mall in a Black neighborhood with poor access to retail shopping.

In San Francisco, environmentalist opposition to homeporting the battleship *Missouri* ran into the Navy's promise of more jobs for Blacks and unionists. That both sides have a case makes these issues intractable without a means of settling disputes and, more importantly, having greater control over the course of business planning and investment. Local political leaders have generally exacerbated the situation: in Oakland and San Francisco, Mayors Wilson and Agnos support the developers in question, and Feinstein was completely behind the Navy. In Berkeley, a weakened BCA has not been able to resolve the dispute internally. But in every case the conflict could have been ameliorated, if not resolved, by white activists showing more interest in Black problems, developing better ties to organized labor, distributing critical information on who really stands to gain, and providing a critical analysis of developer and government claims about jobs. It's not as though this situation had never arisen in the past or had never been dealt with successfully (Walker et al., 1979). A similar critique of failure to cross racial and class lines has been made of many AIDS activists (Rist, 1989).

The failure of the left to touch Asian American politics is more complete, and parallels the exclusion of those of Asian descent from electoral power in the Bay region. One Japanese American holds a congressional seat, one Chinese American a seat on the San Francisco Board of Supervisors; a Chinese, James Ho, is deputy mayor of San Francisco. Filipinos hold one seat each on the city councils of Hercules, Milpitas and Union City. (The lack of political representation of Latinos in San Jose, San Francisco, Hayward, and other cities is equally appalling.) This political isolation is due in part to the continued orientation of many Asian immigrants to politics back home and in part to a reluctance of many Asian American community leaders to seek electoral office (Viviano, 1988). Both are readily understandable in light of the recent entry of most Asians to this country and their need to cement an economic position here.The situation is likely to change under pressure from such organizations as the Chinese-American Democratic Club of San Francisco, the Chinatown Resource Center, Asian Inc., and the Filipino-American Political Association.

But Asian American community leadership is, not surprisingly, mainly upper class and far from radical. Worse, there are still sharply reactionary elements among the Vietnamese, Hong Kong Chinese, Chinatown's Six Companies and Indochinese tribespeople that make any alliance with the left impossible at this time (Takagi and Platt, 1978). For example, Tom Hayden had to cancel a talk in San Jose after a death threat by local Vietnamese rightists. The struggle with Marcos in the Philippines had some resonance among the Anglo left, and the Southeast Asian Resource Center is an important source of left analysis in the US. On the other hand, the brutal suppression of the Democracy movement in China has driven progressive Chinese into the arms of the Taiwanese and Hong Kong bourgeoisies. As it stands today there is nothing like the past levels of interest in Vietnamese or Chinese struggles, nothing comparable to the romanticization of Latin American politics, language and culture, and no La Peña of displaced Maoists or Filipinos as a left gathering place and source of popular political education.

On the whole, then, the bonds of the white left with people of color – especially the new immigrant segment of the working class – need a good deal of strengthening. Certainly the diversity of peoples in the Bay Area can be a source of support for progressive movements, owing to the obstacles of racism facing even bourgeois and middle-class minorities. A good example is the long struggle for bilingual education in the 1970s (and against the reactionary English-only state ballot initiative passed by the voters in 1986). Our guess is that a new alliance across racial barriers requires, to get off the ground, the independent mobilization of people of color as workers, citizens and professionals around the problems of their lives in the United States. This may happen with the redirection of energies of second-generation Asian Americans towards prising open opportunities in their new home country, as exemplified by the present struggles around university admissions, hiring and 'ethnic studies' course requirements. It may happen through increased unionization of Asian American workers, as in the case Local 2 of the Hotel and Restaurant Workers. It may happen through a revived African American struggle for justice after the years of Reaganite depravity. It has not yet happened here via the Rainbow Coalition, despite hopeful signs.

The gentrification of politics?

The continued liberalism of the political culture of the Bay Area is quite remarkable. For example, the disastrous Dukakis run for the presidency in 1988 was a triumph locally, carrying eight of the area's nine counties by substantial margins. A wider spectrum of the citizenry here readily embraces such things as environmentalism, tolerance about sexual preference, women's rights, and racial equality here than almost anywhere else in the country. These attitudes compare favorably with the ideological conservatism of so much of southern and rural California, which regularly favors conservative initiatives such as Proposition 13, the Victims' Bill of Rights, and efforts to restrict the rights of people with AIDS.

That the progressive legacy is so widely diffused here rests in not inconsiderable measure on the favored status of the Bay Area as the Playground of Capitalism, and of the yuppies drawn to the high-tech sandbox. It may be hard for many on the left to swallow the idea of a putatative middle class as a progressive force, but in the political context of the Bay Area, the yuppie tide has lifted many boats. This is our puzzle: one simply cannot sustain the thesis that the left current here over the last thirty years rests solely on the traditional working-class and trade-union base, as vital as that has been. The gentrification of the Bay Area runs even to the heart of the left itself, and its many middle-aging professionals. One cannot gainsay the attractions of the good life in the Playground, and here leftists can resist proletarianization in the same way the 49ers did. Indeed, an irony of the New Left is that many of its ideas, proponents and followers have 'gentrified', and in so doing strengthened the middle-class base for progressive politics.

This is not exactly a 'bourgeoisification' of the left, however, and here our conception of changing class and industry structure in contemporary capitalism matters. The left's model for political struggle has long been the CIO and the left parties of the 1930s – a good model but not the only one to draw on (Davis, 1986; Moody, 1989). It is worth considering the parallels between a place such as the Bay Area and nineteenth-century Paris, with its legions of skilled workers, small merchants, bohemians, internationalists and leisured classes, and with a long tradition of revolutionary upheaval (Harvey, 1985b). Such a comparison is certainly as strong as comparisons of the Bay Area with Detroit in the high tide of Fordist mass production. To say this is not to embrace the Prudhonist ideal of a socialism of workshops, nor to denigrate the role of less skilled mass production workers (and mass consumers) in progressive and left politics, past and future. This is, after all, a modern industrial metropolis experiencing the contradictions of growth and change in a new era of capitalist development; it is not a reversion to an earlier path long forgotten, as some would have it (for example, Piore and Sabel, 1984).

But the Fordist model, for all its importance, was never universal across industries or places, and is under assault throughout the capitalist world today. It is not just to the big factories, heavy industries and manual workers that one should look for a base for left politics. In the ranks of the 'middle class' lie many modern skilled workers who are open to liberal and even radical appeals, and whose skills can be invaluable to any political mobilization.

Nonetheless, middle-class liberality can easily fade when pressed by direct challenge to class pretensions and libertarian proclivities. As Berkeley's electoral left has discovered, the town's growing gentry is more conservative on local issues than on national and international ones; even many Democrats who vote loyally for Ron Dellums will oppose Berkeley Citizens' Action on city issues. And there is remarkably little sympathy for the practices necessary to maintain a ruling political party such as BCA: individualistic voters are suspicious of 'machine' politics (a laughable accusation given BCA's threadbare infrastructure), and individual activists such as John Denton or Myron Moskowitz readily break off to form their own tendencies or join the opposition.

Moreover, it is all too easy for a gentrified left to lose contact with the bulk of the working class, who are not yuppies and do not live in gentrified communities, and who still form the indispensable foundation for progressive and socialist advance in the United States. The many middle-class intellectuals among us do not always relate well to folks who live in Hayward, shop at K-Mart and listen to country music. It can be even harder to connect with a working class that is shunted off to far suburbia, or has different national or racial roots. It is harder yet where unionization has diminished and the old workplaces and firms have disappeared.

This is not to say that all leftists are yuppies, by any means: the presence of the traditional working-class left in older unions such as the ILWU and newly burgeoning ones such as SEIU remains substantial. Also, many New Leftists, hopeful of becoming the new workers' vanguard, went into factories and unions to do the hard work of day-to-day organizing. Some are still there, although the vanguard parties are largely gone. More important, the restructuring of industry and work, and the recomposition of the working class and of the spatial organization of production and community life have eroded past achievements and linkages forged by the left.

There remains a sizable socialist left in the Bay Area, which, though checked by the conservatism of the 1980s, has not become anticommunist or withdrawn from politics. While some fellow-travelers in the movements of the 1960s have thrown in their lot with the bourgeoisie and are now happily engaged in real estate investment, on the whole the true 'Contras' of the

Bay Area left, such as Eldridge Cleaver, David Horowitz and Peter Collier, are few in number. What role the remaining left can play in revitalizing a broad progressive movement in the area, and for the country as a whole, remains to be seen.

Whither the left?

The review of the political economy of the Bay Area presented here can help provide a few pointers for future efforts by the left, although we mean to be indicative rather than rhetorical. To begin with, this look at the Bay region is premised on a view of the importance of becoming rooted in local affairs, even while maintaining a national and internationalist outlook. The vitality of the issues raised – and the number of unanswered questions – should sustain that premise for those of us with local roots. More than this, however, an important laboratory for present and future capitalism is to be found here under our noses – a grand experiment in new forms of industrial production, labor relations and class construction. The Bay Area is not just peculiar – in the way that New Orleans is an American oddity – but is central to the contemporary dynamics of capitalist production, consumption and class formation.

We have argued that the economy has changed as it has grown, and that it rests on new forms of industrialization, in the widest sense of the term. This does not make it in any way 'post-industrial', much less 'post-capitalist'. But the new era of capitalism represented so vividly here does require new kinds of responses. The labor movement is hard-pressed to come to grips with altered terms of employment, revamped working conditions, and a constantly shifting division of labor. In general, what is wanted is, above all, a new mass mobilization of the working class – comparable to the CIO organizing drivesof the 1930s – in the new industries and expanding sectors, including electronics, banking and hotels. The Bay Area is part of an emergent heartland of the new industries, in the same way that the Midwest was the heartland of early twentieth-century US industrialization.

But this new mass mobilization will have to be different from that of the 1930s in several respects. It cannot be other than a rainbow movement, if it is to reflect accurately the new social composition of the working class and of the peoples of the region. An immense and vital potpourri of peoples mix here, but they do not easily combine in fruitful ways. The left has a crucial responsibility to find avenues for them to work together for social change. Racial unity, gender equality and sexual tolerance are the basis for the new California we seek. A vision that makes race and gender central does not represent a retreat from class analysis and a socialist movement based in the working class (Navarro, 1989). On the contrary, the increasingly cosmopolitan nature of the working class and the Bay Area in general is a vibrant and potentially explosive substratum on which to galvanize the future class struggle.

At the same time, the left has to cope with the upward skew of the class structure in the Bay Area, and with the advantages and disadvantages that come with the very favorable lot drawn by so many who work here. From our place-based perspective, it is a mistake to write off the yuppies too quickly as legions of the right waiting for their marching orders. The progressive elements of new skilled workers can provide a source of support to the left in addition to the traditional working class and labor unions – something much less in evidence in, say, Detroit or Cleveland. Further, it should be admitted that many of the issues raised in the pursuit of the gentrified life in the Playground have been absorbed into a wider progressive and even socialist agenda: healthy food, recycling, historical preservation, and so forth. But the left has to work continually to focus middle-class projects on claims against capital and to strip them of self-indulgent faddishness and denial of just redistribution towards working people and the poor. This is not a call for a 'historic compromise' with centrists in which the left takes a moderate position to appear more reasonable to the middle class; it is, instead, an assessment of the possibilities inherent in the ongoing process of class formation for constructing a left agenda that appeals to the broadest definition of the working class, including its most skilled and least class-conscious elements.

Finally, the left must have a metropolitan vision that recognizes that the ways of the city are fundamental to the ways of working, the ways of life and the political formation of working people. The left needs a vision that extends beyond the city limits of San Francisco and Berkeley to encompass the factories of Silicon Valley and the refineries of Contra Costa. It must look into the wide belt of working-class suburbs, whose ambivalent interests so often divide workers and races against one another. It needs to come to grips with the debate over the growth of the whole urban area – when major development issues arise, most activists have no sense of the regional scope of the problem – in order to turn dissent toward the growth machine into a critique of unbridled capitalist accumulation. The left can unite with the widespread popular revulsion against hazardous substances in the urban environment. And it must take care not to be sucked into the conservative agenda of bourgeois regionalism, however, as the costs of unplanned urban growth mount. Perhaps what is needed is a left counterpart to the Bay Area Council that can put forth a vision of the regional political economy that goes beyond opposition to challenge the power of capital to say where development occurs.

Despite considerable achievement by the local left, there is no denying the malaise induced by Reaganism and the rightward swing of American politics in the 1980s. The organized left has atrophied, from the implosion of the Democratic Workers Party to the tiredness of the Democratic Socialists of America. A great deal of energy went into party building in the Bay Area during the 1970s, but it has been a failed project. Large demonstrations can still be periodically mounted, as shown by the Spring Mobilizations for Peace, Jobs and Justice circa 1985–88 or the Women's Day march of 1989, but there is no sustained presence in the streets. On the other hand, the Bay Area remains a vital center of what may be called 'left political interest groups', often very well organized around particular issues, and able to publish valuable newsletters or books, as in the case of the Central America Research Institute, the Center for the Study of the Americas or the Food First Institute, or to provide essential services, as at the Center for Independent Living, the Worker's Clinic, or the Haight-Ashbury Free Clinic. After New York City, the Bay Area probably offers the richest kaleidoscope of left groups and institutions in the US, from KPFA radio to the Data Center. Yet one senses a fragmentation of effort and failure to sustain the kind of cross-fertilization that existed in the 1960s. What is needed is a new basis for unity and mutual affirmation without sectarian purposes. It will take a newly constituted left to help lead the way out of the impasse.

If the 'era of new thinking' unleashed in the Soviet Union and spilling over the world is to resonate here, it means that some new thinking is required about our own circumstances and the challenges facing us. One can adapt to the times in thinking about what constitutes industry, the working class, progressive movements and constructive political work without falling prey to the absurd revisionism that denounces hard-won Marxist insights and the achievements of previous socialist struggles as bunk (for example, Laclau and Mouffe, 1985). It is also necessary to think anew about what it means to have a socialist future. It is no longer clear that we have a good answer: what would a future socialist city, a humane and democratic Bay Area metropolis look like? There is a new world to win, but what would we do with it if we won?

Notes

1. The Bay Area Study Group – Dick Walker, Roger Burbach, Steven Hiatt, Phil Hutchings, Elizabeth Martinez and Tony Platt – came together at the urging of Roger Burbach to take a fresh look at regional political and economic issues. We greatly appreciate the extensive input of those who read and commented on the manuscript: Andy Barlow, Tom Brom, Bill Domhoff, David Harvey, Bob Heifetz, Jeff Lustig, Vicente Navarro, Lenny Siegel and Charles Wollenberg. Thanks, too, to Marty Manley and John Trinkl for valuable information freely given, to Tim Sturgeon, Liz Vasile and Rod Newmann for research assistance, and to Sheryl Freeman for cartography.

Special thanks are due Mike Davis for his encouragement and input, and for his love of the well-turned phrase.

2. For discussions of amazing Los Angeles, see the work of E. Soja, 1986, 1987; A. Scott, 1986, 1988a; and M. Davis, 1987, 1989.

3. A much-debated term. For an entry into the debate, see Piore and Sabel, 1984; Scott, 1988b; Williams et al., 1987; Storper and Scott, 1988; Walker, 1989; and Storper and Walker, 1989.

4. The population of the nine-county area (excluding Santa Cruz County) has grown as follows: 1940, 1,734,000; 1950, 2,681,000; 1960, 3,639,000; 1970, 4,628,000; 1980, 5,180,000; 1990 5,911,000 (est.)

5. 'San Francisco' refers to the city and county of that name. 'San Francisco Bay Area', 'San Francisco region', 'Bay Area', and 'Bay region' all refer to the metropolitan area. The US Census now includes ten counties in the metro area: San Francisco, Alameda, Contra Costa, Marin, San Mateo, Sonoma, Napa, Santa Clara, Solano and Santa Cruz. Occasionally figures will refer to the nine-county area, less Santa Cruz, or to smaller parts of the region, as indicated.

6. Employment growth based on the nine-county area. For comparison, the Houston metropolitan area in the same period grew 295 percent; Los Angeles, 95 percent; and Chicago, 29 percent. Based on data from the US Department of Commerce, *County Business Patterns*.

7. For the ten-county area in 1983, wholesaling employed 145,000 workers, transport, 160,000 (CDC, 1985).

8. Total government employment in the ten counties was 487,000 in 1985 (CDC, 1985).

9. San Francisco has long benefitted by having its banking tentacles deep in the surplus value of booming Southern California – as well as Silicon Valley and Central Valley agribusiness. Ironically, L.A.'s growth was heavily funded by

San Francisco capitalists such as Henry Huntington – a classic example of capital overflowing ('switching') into new geographic areas (Harvey, 1982).

10. Marin and San Mateo counties ranked first and second in per capita income among counties on the Pacific Coast, Santa Clara sixth, Contra Costa eighth, Alameda eighteenth. However, rural Northern California has eight of the twenty poorest counties in the Pacific Coast Region (US Department of Commerce, 1988).

11. We therefore retain the terms *middle class* and *yuppie* because of their general currency in American political discourse, but in full awareness of the difficulties inherent in using the terms too freely. Would it really help matters if we used the term *labor aristocracy*? Surely not.

12. Defined as architects, engineers, physical and social scientists, doctors, dentists, planners, lawyers, judges, and health and engineering technicians – that is, excluding all teachers, librarians and counselors, all nurses and therapsists, social, recreation and religious workers, and writers, artists, entertainers and athletes – and all managers except self-employed retail owners. Numbers taken from US Department of Labor, Employment and Training Administration, Run No. 831119 on 1980 US Census sample estimate, Lawrence Berkeley Laboratory.

13. Figures are for the five-county central Bay Area and the county of Los Angeles.

14. Comparable figures for all of California are 41 percent of all workers unionized in 1951, falling to below 20 percent by 1985. Unionization of manufacturing workers fell from 27.6 percent to 21.5 percent, 1979–85; and all workers from 22.1 percent to 19.2 percent, 1979–85.

15. By contrast, the percentages of Latino and Asian-Pacific peoples among the 8 million people in Los Angeles County are nearly reversed: 27 and 12 percent, respectively.

16. On residential segregation by class in the Bay Area, see Feldman (1981). Significantly, however, class segregation is frequently overridden by racial divisions and gender-mixing across class in the same household.

17. Figures from the Federal Home Loan Bank Board and California Association of Realtors.

18. Note that Annalee Saxenian, whose research was the main evidence for the self-destruction view of Silicon Valley's growth (1983), has changed her views on the matter.

19. The fracture of the region is well indicated by the closed realms within which its newpapers circulate: the *Examiner* in the city, the *Times-Tribune* on the Peninsula, the *Mercury* in San Jose, the *Tribune* in Oakland/Berkeley, the Lesher papers in Contra Costa, and so forth. Only the *San Francisco Chronicle* has a wide circulation, but its persistent mediocrity is a good index of the decrepit state of San Francisco's ruling class. The best paper is now the *San Jose Mercury*, as might be expected from the rising star of Silicon Valley.

References

Adler, S. 1980. 'The Political Economy of Transit in the San Francisco Bay Area, 1945–63'. Unpublished doctoral dissertation, Department of City and Regional Planning, University of California, Berkeley.

American Banker. 1989. 'Top Numbers 1989'. New York: *American Banker*.

Bay Area Council. 1986. *Bulletin*. 2(2), Summer.

Bay Area Council. 1988. *Making Sense of the Region's Growth*. San Francisco: Bay Area Council.

Blakely, E. 1987. 'Prospects for Development of the Biotechnology Industry in the Oakland-East Bay Area'. Working Paper No. 87-123. Berkeley: Center for Real Estate and Urban Economics.

Bluestone, B., and Harrison, B. 1982. *The Deindustrialization of America*. New York: Basic Books.

Borchert, J. 1978. 'Major Control Points in American Economic Geography. *Annals of the Association of American Geographers* 68 (2): 214–32.

Boyer, R. 1987. 'Labor Flexibilities: Many Forms, Uncertain Effects'. *Labour & Society* 12(6): 107–29.

Brady, R. 1985a. 'Perspectives on a Region's Growth: Maintaining the San Francisco Bay Area Economy'. ABAG Working Paper No. 1. Oakland: Association of Bay Area Governments.

Brady, R. 1985b. 'Economic Competitiveness of the San Francisco Bay Area'. ABAG Working Paper No. 3. Oakland: Association of Bay Area Governments.

Brady, R. 1985c. 'Economic Growth and Wealth: Looking at the San Francisco Bay Area'. ABAG Working Paper No. 2. Oakland: Association of Bay Area Governments.

Brady, R. 1987. 'The Changing Structure of the Bay Area Economy'. Oakland: Association of Bay Area Governments.

Brady, R., Kroll, C., and Munroe, T. 1989. 'The Bay Area Economy: A Region at Risk'. San Francico: Bay Area Economic Forum.

Brown, C., and Reich, M. 1989. 'When Does Labor-Management Cooperation Make Sense?' *California Management Journal* (Summer).

Burbach, R., and Núñez, O. 1987. *Fire in the Americas*. New York: Verso.

Bush, R. 1984. 'Oakland: Grassroots Organizing Against Reagan'. In R. Bush, ed. *The New Black Vote*, 317–74. San Francisco: Synthesis Publications.

Cabezas, O., and Kawaguchi, G. 1988. 'The Continuing Significance of Race/Ethnicity, Gender and Nativity in an Empirical Study of Industrial Sectorization in California in 1980'. In Chan, S., ed. *Persistent Inequality in the United States*. Lewiston, N.Y.: Edwin Mellen Press.

Cagan, L., Albert, M., Chomsky, N., Hahnel, R., King, M., Sargent, L. and Sklar, H. 1986. *Liberating Theory*. Boston: South End Press.

California Department of Commerce. 1985. *County Profiles*. Sacramento: State of California.

California Economic Development Corporation. 1988. *Vision: California 2010*. Sacramento: CEDC.

California Senate. 1988. *Challenge and Opportunity: A Working Paper for the New Regionalism Project*. Select Committee on Planning for California Growth. September.

California Tomorrow. 1988. *Crossing the Schoolhouse Border*. San Francisco: California Tomorrow.

Cardellino, J. 1984. 'Industrial Location: A Case Study of the California Fruit and Vegetable Canning Industry'. Unpublished master's thesis, Department of Geography, University of California, Berkeley.

Castells, M. 1983. *The City and the Grassroots*. Berkeley: University of California Press.

Christopherson, S. 1988. 'Overworked and Underemployed: The Redistribution of Work in the US Economy'. Unpublished MS, Department of City and Regional Planning, Cornell University.

Christopherson, S., and Storper, M. 1989. 'The Effects of Flexible Specialization on Industrial Politics and the Labor Market: The Motion Picture Industry'. *Industrial and Labor Relations Review* 42(3): 331–47.

Cohen, S., and Zyman, J. 1987. *Manufacturing Matters*. New York: Basic Books.

County Supervisors Association of California. 1985–1989. *California County Fact Book*. Sacramento: County Supervisors Association of California.

Davis, M. 1986. *Prisoners of the American Dream*. London: Verso.

Davis, M. 1987. 'Chinatown, Part Two: The Internationalization of Downtown Los Angeles'. *New Left Review* 164: 65–86.

Davis, M. 1989. 'Homegrown Revolution'. Unpublished MS.

Dobkin, M. 1988. 'Biography Formation and Daily Life in a Frontier City: The Joint Constitution of Society and Subjects in San Francisco, 1848–58'. Unpublished doctoral dissertation, Department of Geography, University of California, Berkeley.

Domhoff, W. 1974. *The Bohemian Grove and Other Retreats*. New York: Harper and Row.

Dowall, D. 1984. *The Suburban Squeeze: Land Conversion and Regulation in the San Francisco Bay Area*. Berkeley: University of California Press.

Elgie, R. 1966. 'The Development of San Francisco Manufacturing, 1848–1880'. Unpublished master's thesis, Department of Geography, University of California, Berkeley.

Feldman, M. 1981. 'The Political Economy of Class and the Journey to Work: The Case of the San Francisco Bay Area'. Unpublished doctoral dissertation, University of California, Los Angeles.

Florida, R., and Kenney, D. 1988. 'Venture Capital, High Technology and Regional Development'. *Regional Studies* 22(1): 33–48.

Florida, R., and Kenney, D. 1990. *The Breakthrough Economy*. New York: Basic Books.

Frank, D. 1989. 'Labor's Decline'. *Monthly Review* 41(5):48–55.

Freedman, M. 1976. *Labor Markets: Segments and Shelters*. Montclair, N.J.: Allanheld, Osmun and Co.

Frieden, B. 1979. *The Environmental Protection Hustle*. Cambridge: MIT Press.

Glasmeier, A. 1985. 'The Structure, Location and Role of High Technology Industries in US Regional Development'. Unpublished doctoral dissertation: University of California.

Greenberg, D. 1986. 'Growth and Conflict at the Suburban Fringe: the Case of the Livermore-Amador Valley, California'. Unpublished doctoral dissertation, Dept. of City Planning, University of California, Berkeley.

Groth, P. 1983. 'Forbidden Housing'. Unpublished doctoral dissertation, Department of Geography, University of California, Berkeley.

Haas, G. 1985. *Plant Closures: Myths, Rights and Responses*. Boston: South End Press.

Harrison, B., and Bluestone, B. 1988. *The Great U-Turn: Corporate Restructuring, Laissez Faire and the Rise of Inequality in America*. New York: Basic Books.

Hartman, C. 1984. *The Transformation of San Francisco*. Totowa, N.J.: Rowman and Allenheld.

Harvey, D. 1982. *The Limits to Capital*. Oxford: Basil Blackwell.

Harvey, D. 1985a. *The Urbanization of Capital*. Baltimore: Johns Hopkins University Press.

Harvey, D. 1985b. *Consciousness and the Urban Experience*. Baltimore: Johns

Hopkins University Press.

Harvey, D. 1989. *The Condition of Postmodernity*. Oxford: Basil Blackwell.

Hayes, E. 1972. *Power Structure and Urban Policy: Who Rules in Oakland?* New York: McGraw-Hill.

Heiman, M. 1988. *The Quiet Evolution: Power, Planning and Profits in New York State*. New York: Praeger.

Judge, C. 1979. *The Book of American Rankings*. New York: Facts on File.

Kazin, M. 1987. *Barons of Labor: The San Francisco Building Trades and Union Power in the Progressive Era*. Urbana and Chicago: University of Illinois Press.

Kelley, K. 1989. 'Dellums'. *East Bay Express* 26 May: 1–27.

Kothin, J. 1989. 'The Innovation Upstarts'. *Inc.* (January):70–76.

Kroll, C., and Kimball, L. 1986. 'The Santa Clara Valley Research and Development Dilemma: The Real Estate Industry and High-Tech Growth'. Working Paper 86–116. Berkeley: Center for Real Esate and Urban Economics.

Laclau, E., and Mouffe, C. 1985. *Hegemony and Socialist Strategy: Towards a Radical Democratic Politics*. London: Verso.

LeGates, R., and Hartman, C. 1986. 'The Anatomy of Displacement in the US'. In Smith, N., and Williams, P., eds, *Gentrification of the City*, 178–203. Boston: Allan and Unwin.

Lipietz, A. 1987. *Mirages and Miracles*. London: Verso.

Logan, J., and Molotch, H. 1986. *Urban Fortunes*. Berkeley: University of California Press.

Lustig, J. 1985. 'The Crisis of Contract Unionism'. Unpublished manuscript, Political Science Department, Humboldt State University.

Malone, 1986. 'The Collapse of Western Metal Mining: An Historical Epitaph'. *Pacific Historical Review* 3:27–31.

Mangum, G., Mayall, D., and Nelson, K. 1985. 'The Temporary Help Industry'. *Industrial and Labor Relations Review* 38: 599–611.

Markusen, A., Hall, P., and Glasmeier, A. 1986. *High Tech America*. Boston: Allen and Unwin.

Marlin, J., and Avery, J. 1983. *The Best of American City Rankings*. New York: Facts on File Publications.

Matthews, G. 1985. 'The Fruit Workers of the Santa Clara Valley: Alternative Paths to Union Organization in the 1930s'. *Pacific Historical Review* 40: 51–70.

McLaughlin, C. 1988. 'The Corporate Conveyor Belt: Branch Office by the Bay'. *The Bay Guardian* 5 October: 11–39.

McWilliams, C. 1939. *Factories in the Fields*. Boston: Little, Brown.

Mills, H. 1979. 'The San Francisco Waterfront: The Social Consequences of Industrial Modernization'. In A. Zimbalist, ed., *Case Studies on the Labor Process*, 127–55. New York: Monthly Review Press.

Moody, K. 1989. *An Injury to All: The Decline of American Unionism*. London: Verso.

Morgan, K., and Sayer, A. 1988. *Micro-circuits of Capital*. Cambridge: Polity Press.

Nash, G. 1985. *The American West Transformed: The Impact of the Second World War*. Bloomington: Indiana University Press.

Nathan, H., and Scott, E., eds. 1978. *Experiment and Change in Berkeley*. Berkeley: Institute of Governmental Relations.

Navarro, V. 1985. The 1980 and 1984 US Elections and the New Deal'. In Milliband, R., Saville, J., Liebman, M. and Panitch, L. *The Socialist Register, 1985–86*. London: Merlin Press.

Navarro, V. 1987. 'The Rainbow Coalition and the Challenge of Class'. *Monthly Review* 39 (2): 19–27.

Nelson, K. 1986. 'Labor Demand, Labor Supply and the Suburbanization of Low-Wage Office Work'. In Scott, A.J., and Storper, M., eds. *Work, Production, Territory*, 149–71. Boston: Allen and Unwin.

Noyelle, T., and Stanback, T. 1984. *The Economic Transformation of American Cities*. Totowa, N.J.: Rowman and Allenheld.

Pfeffer, J., and Baron, J. 1988. 'Taking the Workers Back Out: Recent Trends in the Structuring of Employment'. *Research in Organizational Behavior* 10: 257–303.

Piore, M., and Sabel, C. 1984. *The Second Industrial Divide*. New York: Basic Books.

Pred, A. 1977. *City-Systems in Advanced Economies*. London: Hutchinson.

Pred, A. 1990. 'Outsider in and Insiders out: South Korean Capital and Local Struggle in a California Industrial Suburb'. Unpublished MS.

Rauber, R. 1987. 'Citizen Lesher and the Battle of Walnut Creek'. *East Bay Express* 22 May: 1–20.

Rist, D. 1989. 'AIDS as Apocalypse: The Deadly Costs of an Obsession'. *The Nation* 13 February.

Remick, H., ed. 1984. *Comparable Worth and Wage Discrimination*. Philadelphia: Temple University Press.

Rogers, E., and Larsen, J. 1984. *Silicon Valley Fever*. New York: Basic Books.

Rosen, K., and Jordan, S. 1988. 'San Francisco Real Estate Market: The City, the Peninsula, and the East Bay'. Berkeley: Center for Real Estate and Urban Economics. Working Paper No. 88–152.

Sassen, S. 1988. *The Mobility of Labor and Capital*. New York: Cambridge University Press.

Saxenian, A. 1980. *Silicon Chips and Spatial Structure: The Industrial Basis of Urbanization in Santa Clara County, California*. Unpublished master's thesis, Department of City and Regional Planning. University of California, Berkeley.

Saxenian, A. 1983. 'The Urban Contradictions of Silicon Valley: Regional Growth and the Restructuring of the Semiconductor Industry'. *International Journal of Urban and Regional Research* 7(2): 237–62.

Saxenian, A. 1989. 'The Political Economy of Industrial Adaptation in Silicon Valley'. Unpublished doctoral dissertation, Political Science Department, Massachusetts Institute of Technology.

Saxton, A. 1971. *The Indispensible Enemy: Labor and the Anti-Chinese Movement in California*. Berkeley: University of California Press.

Sayer, A. 1986. 'New Developments in Manufacturing: The Just-In-Time System'. *Capital and Class* 30: 43–72.

Schutt, R., and Siegel, L., eds. 1988–89. California Military Monitor 1988–89, nos. 2, 3 and 5. Mountain View, Calif.: Pacific Studies Center.

Scott, A. 1988a. *Metropolis: From the Division of Labor to Urban Form*. Berkeley: University of California Press.

Scott, A. 1988b. *New Industrial Spaces*. London: Pion, Ltd.

Scott, A., and Soja, E. 1986. 'Los Angeles: The Capital of the Late Twentieth Century'. *Society and Space* 4(3): 249–54.

Scott, A., and Storper, M. 1987. 'High Technology Industry and Regional Development: A Theoretical Critique and Reconstruction'. *International Social Science Journal* 1(12): 215–32.

Scott, M. 1959. *The San Francisco Bay Area: A Metropolis in Perspective*. Berkeley: University of California Press.

Shapira, P. 1986. 'Industry and Jobs in Transition: A Study of Industrial Restructuring and Worker Displacement in California'. Unpublished doctoral dissertation, Department of City and Regional Planning, University of California, Berkeley.

Siegel, L., and Markoff, J. 1985. *The High Cost of High Tech.* New York: Harper and Row.

Siegel, L., ed. 1988–89. *Global Electronics.* Mountain View, Calif.: Pacific Studies Center.

Soja, E. 1988. *Post-Modern Geographies.* London: Verso.

Starr, K. 1989a. 'Rebirth of a Neighborhood'. *Image* 26 March, 24–25.

Starr, K. 1989b. 'Oakland's Busy Estuary'. *Image* 18 June, 26–29.

State of California. 1965. *California Statistical Abstract.* Sacramento: State of California.

Storper, M., and Scott, A. 1988. 'The Geographical Foundations and Social Regulation of Flexible Production Complexes' In Wolch, J., and Dear, M., eds. *The Power of Geography 21–40*. Boston: Allen and Unwin.

Storper, M., and Walker, R. 1982. 'The Expanding California Water System'. In Kockelman, W., Conomos, T., and Leviton, A., eds. *Use and Protection of the San Francisco Bay System,* 171–90. San Francisco: Pacific Division, AAAS.

Storper, M., and Walker, R. 1989. *The Capitalist Imperative: Territory, Technology and Industrial Growth.* New York: Basil Blackwell.

Stowsky, J. 1987. 'The Weakest Link: Semicondutor Production Equipment, Linages and the Limits to International Trade'. Working Paper No. 27. Berkeley Roundtable on the International Economy, University of California, Berkeley.

Strange, S. 1986. *Casino Capitalism.* Oxford: Basil Blackwell.

Sweezy, P., and Magdoff, H. 1987. *Stagnation and the Financial Explosion.* New York: Monthly Review Press.

Takagi, P., and Platt, T. 1978. 'Behind the Gilded Ghetto: An Analysis of Race, Class and Crime in Chinatown'. *Crime and Social Justice* 9: 2–25.

Tax, M. 1989. 'March to a Crossroads on Abortion'. *The Nation* 8 May: 613–33.

Thrift, N., and Leyshon, A. 1988. 'The Gambling Propensity: Banks Developing Country Debt Exposures and the New Industrial Financial System'. *Geoforum* 19 55–69.

Traunstine, P. 1979. 'Who Are the City's Most Influential and Interlocking Memberships Tell a Story of City's Power Elite'. *San Jose Mercury News* 12 August.

United States Department of Commerce, Bureau of the Census. 1986. *State and Metropolitan Area Data Book.* Washington, D.C.: US Government Printing Office.

United States Department of Commerce. 1988. *Local Area Personal Income, 1981–86.* Washington, D.C.: US Government Printing Office.

Viviano, F. 1988. 'Asian Growth in the 1990s'. *San Francisco Chronicle* 5–12 December. (Available as a *Chronicle* reprint.)

Walker, P., ed. 1979. *Between Capital and Labor*. Boston: South End Press.

Walker, R. 1977. *The Suburban Solution: Capitalism and the Construction of Urban Space in the United States.* Unpublished doctoral dissertation, Johns Hopkins University.

Walker, R. 1981. 'A Theory of Suburbanization: Capitalism and the Construction of Urban Space in the United States'. In Dear, M., and Scott, A., eds. *Urbanization and Urban Planning in Capitalist Societies,* 383–430. New York: Methuen.

Walker, R. 1985. 'Is There a Service Economy? The Changing Capitalist Division of Labor'. *Science and Society* 49: 42–83.

Walker, R. 1989. 'Regulation, Flexible Specialization and Capitalist Development'. Paper presented at Cardiff Symposium on Regulation, Innovation, and Spatial Development, Cardiff, Wales, 13 September 1989.

Walker, R., and Heiman, M. 1981. 'Quiet Revolution for Whom?' *Annals of the Association of American Geographers. 71: 67–83*

Walker, R., Storper, M., and Widess, E. 1979. 'The Limits of Environmental Control: The Saga of Dow in the Delta'. *Antipode* 11(2): 1–16.

Walters, D. 1986. *The New California*. Sacramento: *California Journal* Press.

Walters, D. 1988. 'The Renewed Regionalism'. *Sacramento Bee* 29 November

Weinstein, H. 1989. 'Guerrilla Labor Law'. *California Lawyer* 9(4): 50–55.

Weiss, M. 1987. *The Rise of the Community Builders: The American Real Estate Industry and Urban Land Planning*. New York: Columbia University Press.

Weiss, M. 1990. *Own Your Own Home*. Unpublished MS, MIT, Boston.

Wiley, P. and Gottlieb, R. 1982. *Empires in the Sun*. New York: Putnam.

Williams, K., Cutter, T., Williams, J., and Haslam, C. 1987. 'The End of Mass Production?' *Economy and Society* 16(3): 405–39.

Wollenberg, C. 1985. *Golden Gate Metropolis*. Berkeley: Institute of Governmental Studies, University of California.

Wollenberg, C. 1989. *Marinship at War: Shipbuilding and Social Change in Wartime Sausalito*. Berkeley: Western Heritage

Wright, E. 1985. *Classes*. London: Verso.

Zysman, J. 1977. *Political Strategies for Industrial Order: State, Market and Industry in France*. Berkeley: University of California Press.

2

Berkeley: From the April Coalition to the Clean Underwear Gang

Gus Newport

Berkeley, California has a national reputation: the People's Republic of Berkeley, home of the Free Speech Movement and People's Park. This image projects so brightly that the media often ignores Berkeley itself in favor of a 'better story', the Berkeley of legend. Yet the struggles in Berkeley politics over the past twenty years are worth reviewing for what they suggest about the realities of progressive coalition politics in urban America – realities that are sometimes at odds with what people think they know about the city.

Berkeley is a city of 100,000 on the eastern shore of San Francisco Bay; like Oakland to its south, Berkeley flows down from the affluent hills that rim the bay to the working-class flatlands along the bayshore. The city is built around the University of California at the foot of the Berkeley Hills and around an industrial sector that is part of the long industrial belt extending along the bay's east shore from Hayward north to Richmond. Berkeley has a diverse population that is approximately 65 percent white, 19 percent Black, 8 percent Latino and 8 percent Asian.

In the early 1950s, Berkeley was a Republican town, controlled by business and the Chamber of Commerce. In the late 1950s and early 1960s moderate Democrats took control (although elections are officially nonpartisan) and with the change of leadership came greater support for social programs. Berkeley's shift toward more radical politics began in response to the Civil Rights Movement; Berkeley has a long tradition of

Blacks participating in electoral politics as well organizing around issues. Immediately after the Second World War, Blacks formed about 25 percent of the population, most of them living in the working-class flatlands; up until the 1970s Blacks could not live east of Grove Street, often referred to as Berkeley's Mason-Dixon line (but now renamed Martin Luther King, Jr. Boulevard). The schools were segregated, and until Wilmont Sweeney was elected to the City Council in 1961 no Black had ever held elected office. But in 1964, Berkeley became one of the first school districts to initiate busing to foster integration of its schools, leading to a campaign to recall four of its liberal school board members. Two resigned – but the others won the recall election by wide margins, 22,000 and 14,000, due in large part to an exceptionally heavy Black voter turnout. Several Black precincts recorded 100 percent or nearly 100 percent turnouts in support of these candidates. Support for integration in white liberal neighborhoods was also very high.

Berkeley politics continued to move left in the late 1960s and early 1970s, influenced by the Free Speech Movement, the Black Liberation Movement, the anti–Vietnam War Movement, and various countercultural movements. The coalition that eventually became Berkeley Citizens' Action came together in 1967–68 as the April Coalition, put together by Ron Dellums when he first ran for Congress from the 8th Congressional District (Oakland-Berkeley). Dellums was the first progressive to be elected to the Berkeley City Council, taking office with Warren Widener and Loni Hancock, both of whom subsequently became mayor. The April Coalition candidates ran on issues like community control of the police and the need for rent control.

Berkeley Citizens' Action was organized in 1974 by the more left or progressive forces in the April Coalition to offer a broader populist alternative and to include those sectors that had not been well represented in the April Coalition: the working class, disabled, people of color, gays and lesbians – all the forces which, when combined, supposedly represent a progressive coalition. But BCA remained mostly white, and some activists tried to maintain control of the organization through their domination of a steering committee, which in turn hired BCA's executive director.

BCA did have formal procedures to encourage democratic participation. Every election year the BCA adopted a platform, voted on by members who had paid their dues by a certain deadline. BCA then invited other organizations to send representatives to participate on panels to screen potential candidates; this screening was based in part on the candidates' support for the BCA platform. These candidates would be presented at a BCA convention and had to receive two-thirds of the votes cast to receive BCA's endorsement. This endorsement assured a candidate of a position on the BCA slate, assistance in raising money for literature, the collective support of an issues committee, and volunteers to write campaign literature as well as the support of members and friends to carry the candidates' literature into every neighborhood of the city. This process took a great deal of time, and the most active members continued to be white middle-class people whose lives permitted them to spend long hours at political meetings.

In 1975, BCA came out of its convention better organized than previously, but somewhat bruised because of the difficult decision it had had to make about whether to run a candidate against incumbent Black Mayor Warren Widener. Widener had been elected in 1971, largely through the efforts of the April Coalition, but had abandoned the coalition's program once in office. The convention chose Ying Lee Kelley, an Asian City Council member who had proven to be a consistent progressive voice and a principled advocate of social change as well as an ardent peace activist. Ron Dellums, a former member of the Berkeley City Council and by this time a consistent and eloquent voice for peace and justice in Congress, endorsed Kelley, although he had backed Widener four years earlier. I believe that BCA was right to take on Widener, who had joined forces with the middle-of-the-road Berkeley Democratic Club, which in turn later joined with the Republicans to form the All Berkeley Coalition. Widener won the election in 1975, but by only 700 votes, and it is my judgment that this election proved his vulnerability since I was able to defeat him four years later in my first run for elective office.

In 1977 BCA suffered a stunning defeat in the City Council races, as it ran only three candidates, all of whom lost. BCA did not choose a candidate for the fourth council seat because the convention was divided over the candidacy of Mark Allen, a Black and a member of the Communist Party who had played a vital role in the development of the left's platform and who had brought many Blacks to support BCA activities. Despite Allen's effective work, the liberal forces, or the Clean Underwear Gang, as we later came to call them, allowed anti-communism to weaken our forces. This opposition was led by supposed progressives such as Tom Hayden, who was the founder and leader of the Campaign for Economic Democracy, and Tom Bates, the state assemblyman from Berkeley. I had been asked to run for the fourth City Council seat, but because of the opposition to Mark Allen, I requested time to consult with the BCA's Third World Caucus to discuss the situation. I decided to withdraw my candidacy, and the Third World Caucus threw its support to Mark Allen, but he did not win a place on the BCA slate.

I did not realize it at the time, but BCA was establishing a framework for relating to people of color, communists, and the working class in general. The Clean Underwear Gang was more concerned that Allen might harm its image than with the results that he could help them achieve, or with educating working people to demand structural change and economic justice. Politically speaking, as a Black person, I have often said that it is not the Communist Party that has hurt my people, but that both the Democratic and Republican parties are responsible for the structures and policies that have kept this country from reaching its full potential through full participation of all its people.

After its 1977 defeat, BCA held several community meetings to assess what had gone wrong. Out of these meetings, retreats and hours of discussion came a decision to turn BCA into a membership organization and reorganize the steering committee to reflect the diversity of the population, including women, minorities, gays and the disabled. BCA also decided to include all the pertinent issues of the base community in its platform, which could then be a working document by which to initiate and measure change.

This program laid out concerns and programmatic ideas around alternative economic development, which included attempting to lure labor-intensive, clean industries to the city to provide jobs for the unemployed. It advocated assisting worker collectives and cooperatives. Berkeley already had a fair number of these. Many were succeeding but others were floundering; with city assistance they could become a viable part of the city. We realized that such kinds of businesses are more neighborly, more concerned about environmental impacts, and are sure to recycle their earnings in the community.

We also supported commercial rent control to protect long-term small businesses from being pushed out by spiralling rent increases that allow an influx of chain store operations that do not recycle money locally, pay low wages, and usually produce more litter than local small businesses do. The BCA program also dealt with affirmative action, child-care needs, the status of women, youth needs, alternative energy policies, public safety regulations, the need for rent control and development of low-income housing, local peace policies and many other issues relevant to the quality of life.

The 1979 Mayoral Campaign

In 1979 I ran against Warren Widener, the incumbent mayor who in 1971 had been endorsed by many of the same forces who eight years later endorsed me. They abandoned Widener because I represented their program and because they felt that only another Black could effectively oppose Widener. Widener had been seen as an up-and-coming politician in the Bay Area. He was a lawyer who presented a fairly smooth front and appeared to be a nice team player. In other words, he seemed to be the model Black candidate to appeal to both moderates and liberals. However, Widener had sided with the opposition forces soon after becoming mayor, abandoning the more progressive positions and moving to the center. In addition, he could not stand on his own; it appeared to all that Sue Hone, the vice mayor, controlled his every move.

I presented a different image. I had been a confidant of Malcom X and knew government programs well, having worked at the city, county and federal levels as well as having directed community nonprofit programs. I had served on the BCA steering committee, the City Planning Commission, the Police Review Commission, the county revenue sharing commission, the executive committee of County Supervisor John George, and the executive committee of Congressman Ron Dellums. Just before running for mayor, I had put in place a Youth Employment Services program for Berkeley and I had worked in the city's Recreation and Parks Department overseeing federally funded programs.

These positions had put me in touch with a lot of people, especially community groups that were vying for resources to successfully operate their programs and to develop long-term strategies. I therefore had an idea of some of the problems confronting Berkeley, although I was well-known by activists and not by average citizens, Black or white. I had moved to Berkeley only at the end of 1974, so I had not yet been in Berkeley five years when I became mayor. Perhaps because I was a relative newcomer, I was not endorsed by Berkeley's established Black leadership, although Ron Dellums both supported me and urged me to run because of the role I had played within Berkeley Citizens' Action.

I was also urged to run by John George, the County Supervisor, who played a very active role in our coalition and was its soul and spirit as no one before him and certainly no one after him has been. John George died in 1987, but the role that he played in the East Bay was vital to whatever success that the progressive forces have had in recent years.

The BCA nomination process indicated some of the fissures in the coalition that later widened when we took office. My opponent in the convention process was John Denton, an incumbent white male on the City Council; Denton was a lawyer who was twenty years my elder. I was asked if I would run for a City Council seat if Denton were nominated for mayor, and I replied no. My refusal upset some people in BCA, who publicly accused me of arrogance and not being a team player. I reminded them that I had never aspired to run for office, that at the urging of many of them I had agreed to run for mayor, and that if I was not nominated to run for mayor I would support the ticket – but that I would not run on a ticket headed by John Denton.

Fundamentally, Denton represented the narrowly focused neighborhood forces who did not respect or support the rest of the coalition's agenda. His faction in BCA also thought that white males had the best chance of being elected and should therefore have prominent positions on any ticket. I was also approached by an older white woman who had lived in Phoenix when Denton was a professor there. She claimed to have proof that Denton had fingered her husband for the McCarthy hearings of the House Un-American Activities Committee. Taking all these things into consideration, I refused to run on a ticket headed by John Denton.

After six ballots, neither Denton nor I had the necessary two-thirds vote for nomination. It was decided that we would recess for one week to allow both camps to organize and work out a process that all could accept. The procedure agreed upon was that there would be only two ballots, and that whoever was leading on the second ballot would become the candidate, even if he did not have two-thirds of the vote. I led on both ballots and received the nomination. But during that week many of the BCA forces asked me to soften my presentation because my presence scared a lot of them. I come out of the Civil Rights Movement, and I say what's on my mind; I don't try to sugar-coat it. For example, some people in BCA tried to get me to talk about 'rent stabilization' rather than rent control. They also wanted me to tone down my criticism of Warren Widener; I had said that he was a representative of the corporate power structure – which shouldn't have surprised anybody, because he had been a corporate lawyer. What I learned from this experience and others that came later is that liberals often will support safe Blacks with little substance over ones who are not necessarily controllable, who are committed to a progressive program, and who will fight for what they believe is correct.

In November 1979, I won election as mayor, and three other BCA members were elected to the City Council. Our grass-roots campaign was very effective. We were able to write our own literature, develop our own newspaper, which we put out twice during the campaign, and take our message door-to-door in every neighborhood. Candidates participated in seventy to eighty campaign discussion meetings before different groups. We got very good at teaching people to master the one-minute speech, the three-minute speech, and so on. So our organizing skills made for broad participation within the campaign itself and set the stage for broad participation when we took office.

In 1981, two years after I was first elected mayor, and before the city changed the dates of elections to coincide with congressional elections in even-numbered years, BCA's four City Council candidates were defeated. Following this defeat, BCA held a membership retreat to assess our mistakes. During the discussions, Hardy Frye, who served as my executive assistant for a year, gave a comparison of the different factions in BCA. He broke them down into three groups: the Clean Underwear Gang, the No Underwear Gang, and the Dirty Underwear Gang. The Clean Underwear Gang consisted of those liberals who were very concerned about their image and unwilling to take any risks. The No Underwear Gang was the left flank of the organization; and the Dirty Underwear Gang included the more undisciplined, single-issue factions in BCA.

In 1982 I was reelected by a wide margin, and four other BCA candidates won seats on the City Council. I gained almost 90 percent of the Black vote, and the other BCA candidates were also heavily supported by the Black community. I made it known to members of BCA that I was going to hire Mark Allen as one of my two executive assistants, and was soon threatened by members of the steering committee that they would quit the organization if I did so. Loni Hancock also asked me not to hire Mark. I reminded them that I was not hiring Mark Allen because he was a member of the Communist Party, but because he was a highly committed, intelligent activist who had continuously played an important role in the transformation of Berkeley politics and that I greatly needed his skills. I hired Mark, he performed excellently, and his analysis was sought by all who had to deal with community problems.

The BCA in Office

What did we accomplish while I was mayor? I was available to all citizens of Berkeley, which made them feel that they had a voice in City Hall; this included people in the opposition, some of whom ended up supporting me in my second term. While I was in Berkeley, more rental housing was built in the city that in the previous thirty to forty years, even with strong rent control. This housing included both government- and private-financed projects as well as limited equity co-ops. I was one of the pioneers in developing local foreign policy initiatives, recognizing that we cannot leave that responsibility to the federal government and the transnational corporations. I attempted alternative economic development and encouraged expansion of existing businesses when I thought it would benefit the city's tax base and create jobs. I endorsed use of alternative methods of producing energy, and hosted a committee of small entrepreneurs involved in methods of alternative energy. I supported and worked to put in solid waste management facilities.

However, much of the BCA's program was never implemented because we were never able to prioritize the most essential parts of it, especially as they related to the needs of working-class people and people of color. Usually a few issues bring a coalition together, and when you expand on that original basis of unity to build a long-term progressive program, it takes discipline and a deep understanding of the big picture to avoid losing political focus. Many who call themselves 'progressive' are only interested in a single issue. They will participate in a coalition to gain its support for their position, but they may in fact oppose other items on the agenda of the coalition, especially if they have conflicting class interests. We found this to be true in Berkeley when we attempted to push neighborhood issues such as affordable housing or use the city's redevelopment authority to take advantage of tax increments and special zoning to redevelop depressed areas. I will never forget the day that Anna Rabkin, the city auditor and a member of BCA, came to me and said, 'Why don't you forget all this talk about working-class needs. Berkeley is not a working-class city.' She was voicing the class interests of the Clean Underwear Gang rather than the interests of the working-class people who had labored for BCA's success, including her own election.

Their caution extended to international and peace issues. On my birthday in April 1982, Anna Rabkin and Loni Hancock invited me out to lunch. We had a general discussion about politics, but at one point they asked me to assure the citizens of Berkeley that if reelected I would not continue to participate in the World Peace Council or continue my trips to countries such as Cuba and the Soviet Union. I listened carefully; however, when I put my reelection team together, I directed them to highlight in my campaign literature my involvement in the World Peace Council and other disarmament and solidarity groups. I wanted to make this type of work a positive point of my campaign and indeed emphasize it as a responsibility of a local elected official. As a result of being forthright about this work in my literature, these activities never became an issue in the 1982 campaign, contrary to the fears of the Clean Underwear Gang.

The issue of gentrification also illustrates the problem of maintaining the unity of a coalition around a progressive agenda. In 1970, Berkeley's Blacks were 25 percent of the population. Today, Blacks are probably around 17 percent. Many Blacks and white working-class people have been pushed out of town by gentrification. Berkeley's rent control program has helped to some extent, and support for rent control has tended to unite the BCA coalition overall. However, broader efforts to fight gentrification through community-oriented economic development and construction of low-income housing have met a great deal of resistance from some elements within the coalition, often under the banner of environmentalism.

For example, I had gotten Colgate-Palmolive to convey an

old plant to us – 683,000 square feet on twelve acres of land. We wanted to use that building as a small business incubator to help replace some of the industrial jobs that were leaving the East Bay. The project would have had child care, computers to assist small businesses, training programs, and so on. We could have brought twenty or thirty co-ops, worker collectives, and small businesses into town through this project, found a way to write down their rent payments until they got on their feet, and then benefitted from the taxes they would pay and the jobs they would create. 'Environmentalists' and liberals, some of them in the BCA, stopped that from happening – and the building is still vacant. They wanted to put into place industrial zone restrictions to stop development and fight traffic congestion. Many of these people, even people well on the left of the coalition, like Florence McDonald, thought that talk about any kind of development made me sound like a basic for-profit developer. They would not or could not distinguish between community-oriented projects for development like this and large-scale corporate projects.

The attitude of the Clean Underwear Gang was clear. They saw Berkeley as their own haven and wanted to maintain the city just as it was. There were at one time 120,000 people in Berkeley, and they always felt there shouldn't be more than 100,000 people in town. It doesn't take much imagination to figure out what kinds of people they thought were expendable. They therefore opposed new affordable housing or job creation. They could relate to international issues, like El Salvador or South Africa, but 'don't touch a god-damned thing in my neighborhood or anywhere near me, because I want it to stay just as it is.' These people did not have the depth or the concern to look at broader and longer term needs of the community.

Berkeley's rent control program also illustrates this split within the coalition. Berkeley started out by exempting two- and four-unit buildings, mostly because many of them were owned by small landlords, working-class people. Many of them were in the Black community, people who had bought these buildings to use the income from them for their retirement. Average rents for these units were significantly lower than in larger buildings – as much as $100 or $150 a month lower. But the BCA-dominated Rent Control Board ended the exemption for these small landlords; that move organized the small landlords to join the big real estate outfits, alienating a part of the coalition's base. Behind the Rent Control Board's action were a lot of professionals making $50,000 or $60,000 a year living in these houses, and they would do anything so as not to pay reasonable rents, not taking into consideration the long haul, that these small landlords needed enough of a return to maintain the buildings and provide a decent income.

The fact is that a local progressive coalition faces considerable difficulties. It faces obstruction from its opponents, and from their allies. For example, real estate interests around California have poured money into Berkeley elections to try to defeat BCA candidates for City Council and the Rent Control Board, and the same interests succeeded in getting the California state legislature to ban commerical rent control laws like the one we instituted in Berkeley to aid local small businesses. More important, the coalition faces powerful local opposition that is sometimes able to split off the coalition's right wing, particularly on 'not-in-my-backyard' neighborhood issues. For example, BCA was opposed by a number of previous supporters, like John Denton and Milton Moskowitz, when we decided to put in a few low-income housing units on the site of an abandoned gas station on north Berkeley.

Broad participation is important if a coalition like BCA is to resist rightward pressure and keep on track implementing a progressive program. BCA did have annual and monthly meetings to elicit directions and comment from the coalition's base. A lot of people did participate; you had about thirty-two committees to give advice and develop ideas for legislation on different issues, each with nine people or so; that's 270 to 300 people giving input regularly. But of course a lot of working-class people, single mothers and others don't have the kind of time, energy, transportaion and childcare to be able to participate regularly, so it was hard to get broad input from the full range of people in Berkeley.

We therefore did some other things to encourage participation and dialogue. At City Hall, ropes between poles separated the Council from people attending the meetings. At the very first meeting I presided over as mayor, I took some big old shears and just cut that rope and said, 'Look, there ain't going to be no separation any more.' And people loved that. We used to have an open microphone at the beginning of each Council meeting; people could come up and say what they wanted for three minutes. We found the open mike was sometimes a way of getting an emergency situation out in the open, because the city bureaucracy sometimes wouldn't respond.

We were also able to respond to citizens' concerns about crime in a positive way. Through the Police Review Commission we determined under what circumstances police officers could use a weapon, we did away with police dogs and helicopters, we determined the kinds of training sessions officers could go to – they couldn't go to FBI training sessions – and we even prioritized what kinds of crimes they should go after: hard crimes like rape, robbery, mugging; we gave marijuana possession a lower priority. After Proposition 13 passed in California in June 1978, I had to cut the city budget. We took $1 million out of the police budget, and put $900,000 into social services. Far from being 'soft on crime', this made good sense: statistics from the National Police Institute show that for every 1 percent increase in unemployment there is 4 percent increase in crime. And we worked with the Police Officers Association to figure out where to patrol to be most effective.

We were able to show that in the very first year crime went down by 22 percent. That's understandable. Social services include things like mental health services, and if people aren't receiving the care they need, they may not be hardened criminals but because of their situation they may get involved in crime. Under Loni Hancock, this approach has been abandoned in favor of conventional law enforcement strategies. Berkeley is now experimenting with the use of a mobile surveillance system to stop drugs. I understand the need to curtail drug traffic, but who would have thought Berkeley would be putting all of its resources into such programs when they have not even dealt with root causes of drug dependency, such as poverty and unemployment.

If my assessment of BCA seems critical, I mean to be. If I appear to be saying that I will never again participate in a coalition such as the BCA, I am not. I believe that multi-ethnic, multi-class coalitions can be successful, but whites and especially liberals cannot assume that only they have the intellect to make such coalitions work. Without the full participation of all the classes and ethnic groups in such coalitions, they are unlikely to make the structural changes that are needed to make this a more just society. The divisions I have described in Berkeley's BCA-led coalition are not unique to Berkeley; they flow from the stagnation of the progressive forces in this country, and failure to address them soon means that we progressives are at fault for not doing all we can to halt the continued decay of this society.

PART II

The Rustbelt

3

Roxbury: Capital Investment or Community Development?

Marie Kennedy, Mauricio Gastón and Chris Tilly

The story of Boston's Roxbury could be the story of almost any inner-city minority neighborhood around the United States. Roxbury has been the center of Boston's Black community since World War II, and is increasingly the center of the city's Latino community. Located only ten minutes by rapid transit south of the city's growing downtown, it has suffered from disinvestment, abuse and neglect, both benign and malign. The people of Roxbury have experienced enormous disruption and loss of housing and industry at the hands of the market, and injustice at the hands of the state through urban renewal and highway clearance. Roxbury has all the signs of intense poverty – high unemployment, low participation in the labor force, low educational levels, a high crime rate, flourishing drug traffic, and indicators like a high drop-out rate from school, a high rate of teenage pregnancy, and a high infant mortality rate. Some of the census tracts in Roxbury are in fact among the poorest in the country, on a par with the poorest counties in Mississippi or Indian reservations in the West. In one area of the community locally known as the 'Bermuda Triangle', 70 percent of the housing stock has been lost to abandonment and arson in less than two decades. In the context of this massive disinvestment, and in resistance to it, the people of Roxbury have an impressive and creative history of organization, struggle and development.

Yet the biggest threat to Roxbury today is the danger of new investment bringing gentrification and massive displacement. This threat is eliciting from the community new forms of struggle and organizing, which may become a model for other urban communities confronting a similar situation.

An Analytical Framework

Two facts stand out about the recent history of Roxbury. First, after World War II, while the Boston area economy was transforming, reviving and finally booming, Roxbury became a community of color in a majority white city and went into a drastic physical and economic decline. Second, realization of the presently enhanced value of Roxbury's land seems to require the removal of the Black and Latino people and businesses that currently occupy the land. To understand these facts, it is helpful first to consider the concepts of *uneven development* and the distinction between *neighborhood* and *community*, paying particular attention to the role of racism in these concepts.

Understanding of the first concept, uneven development, begins with the fact that capital flows to those places where conditions are more favorable for accumulation. Capitalist development and underdevelopment are two sides of the same coin, since investment in one area generally depends on draining of capital from other areas (Smith and LeFaivre, 1984: 47). This process of uneven development, often cited in an international context, also takes place regionally and within a metropolitan area like Boston as well. Uneven development does not occur, as some would have it, 'naturally', or simply as a result of the actions of the 'invisible hand' of the market. Rather, it is the combined actions of specific investors, bankers and politicians, all of which can be identified and analyzed; in essence, the result of the capitalist production of space (Smith, 1984: 67–96). It is facilitated by various branches of the state, which ensure that conditions are favorable to the accumulation process. In the case of development within the city, urban planning is often the process by which accumulation is facilitated and legitimated (O'Connor, 1973).

In particular, communities of color are prevented from developing, in part by racism. Discrimination in economic life, education, housing, political activity, culture, the media, all militate against the efforts of Blacks and Latinos to develop their communities. The national and local state intervene in this situation in various capacities. The state can enact reforms that legitimate the status quo, or, as under the Reagan administration, the federal government can take measures to reinforce the structures of discrimination.

The second concept, the distinction between *neighborhood* and *community*, is much debated in sociological literature. As planners, we find it useful to maintain such a distinction and define the terms in a particular way. Roxbury can be analyzed in two ways, both of which are important to an understanding of its unique role in the current transformation of Boston. It is a neighborhood, meaning that it has a particular location, is made up of buildings and other supporting structures, and occupies a piece of land. It is also a community, specifically a Black and Latino community, which means that it has a social and political as well as a physical reality.

As a neighborhood, Roxbury is a commodity, or rather a collection of commodities. Its land and buildings are bought and sold on the market for profit. As a commodity, a neighborhood goes through cycles in which it is developed, decays, and is rebuilt, cycles that occur in the context of cycles of accumulation for the city and the economy as a whole. The fate of a neighborhood, viewed as a commodity, at a particular time depends on the flow of capital to the built environment, which is regulated by financial institutions, and on the ground rent structure, which determines the location of investment. As the larger economy and city go through downturns in accumulation, the neighborhood goes through a devalorization cycle, from new construction to landlord control, to blockbusting, to redlining, to abandonment. This results in a rent gap: 'the gap between the ground rent actually capitalized with a given land use at a specific location, and the ground rent that could potentially be capitalized under a [different] use at that location' (Smith and Lefaivre, 1984: 50). When a rent gap exists, a neighborhood is ripe for a major transformation: gentrification and displacement.

But the neighborhood is also a place where people live; organize themselves; study; reproduce themselves, their culture and ideas; sometimes work; and generally make themselves into a community. The needs of people in communities and the needs of capital do not always coincide, and when they do not a struggle ensues. The community struggles to survive, to reproduce itself, to develop, to gain power over events affecting it. From the point of view of capital, a community has a social function, mainly to reproduce labor power and social relations. Black and Latino communities in particular are subject to pressures that maintain significant parts of these communities as cheap labor (or part of a secondary labor market) and as a reserve army of labor, in more or less permanent unemployment. Indeed, discriminatory pressures shape almost every aspect of life in communities like Roxbury, from choice of residence, to access to education and training, to relations between the police and the community. This makes Roxbury, like the dozens of other Roxburies in US cities, a ghetto.

On the one hand, it is desirable for capital that these communities function smoothly without upsetting the established order of things, and certainly without disrupting the basic labor market. On the other hand, such a stable community tends to generate consciousness of its own oppressed condition, a sense of collective self, networks of social support, creative ideas, solidarity and political power, all of which may contradict the needs of capital to maintain the neighborhood as a pliable 'free' commodity for the market (Smith and Lefaivre, 1984: 46). In sum, a community is a subject as well as an object.

Boston Rises, Roxbury Declines

Using these concepts, it is possible to analyze the recent history of Roxbury and Boston. Economic changes that have transformed and revived the Boston metropolitan area in recent decades have simultaneously devastated Roxbury. Boston emerged from World War II with problems that came to be typical of northern industrial cities. In Boston, however, these problems surfaced twenty years earlier than in other 'frostbelt' cities. When Detroit and Cleveland were still prospering, industries were tripping over each other to leave Boston, either for the suburbs or out of the region entirely. Although Boston had never been a purely industrial city, it possessed a physical structure built largely for industry and a working class shaped and tempered by industrial production. Between 1947 and 1975, the number of manufacturing jobs in Boston fell from about 112,000 to about 50,000; concomitantly, the number of wholesale and retail trade jobs declined from about 150,000 to about 91,000. The loss of jobs was accompanied by falling municipal revenues, declining city services, deteriorating building stock and infrastructure, and other signs of urban crisis.

While Boston itself languished, its suburbs boomed. The old pillars of Brahmin Boston, the financial institutions and elite universities, pushed the development of high-tech research and production, fueled by federal military spending. New industrial parks dotted Boston's postwar circumferential highway, Route 128. As the suburbs boomed and whites left the city in droves, the migration of people of color to the central city, particularly Blacks from the southern United States, increased dramatically; but the suburbs were closed to them.

The return of investment to Boston itself came with the recognition that its future lay in administration and finance rather than in manufacturing and trade. The central management of large enterprises required constant interaction among managers, financiers and such outside experts as accountants, lawyers and advertisers. The suburbs were not well suited for this kind of infrastructure. The central city, if it could be reshaped to meet the emerging needs of industry, was the only place where the regional economy could be effectively coordinated. Besides, permanent capital investment in the city was too important to abandon.

New investment in Boston was facilitated by major highway construction and by one of the most vigorous urban renewal programs in the US between 1952 and 1979. The state, through federally and locally financed urban renewal, gave away enormous benefits to corporations willing to locate offices downtown and cleared away large areas of 'blight', meaning obsolete building structures and working-class residential areas situated where other functions had become more desirable to capital.

After about twenty-five years of these actions, enough public funds had been spent to create conditions for profitable private investment. Capital began to flow back to the city in the late 1970s. In charge of this process was the Boston Redevelopment Authority (BRA), given a peculiar dual function recommended by the Boston Chamber of Commerce: the BRA was the planning *and* redevelopment arm of city government (King, 1981: 22). The agency's centralized power, wielded with gusto in the 1960s by director Ed Logue, symbolized the changing nature of Boston politics. Long known for its confrontations between Irish populists and Brahmins, with the advent of urban renewal, the city entered a period of professionalized management under a series of avidly prodevelopment mayors, John Hynes (1952–60), John F. Collins (1960–68), and Kevin White (1968–82).

While the postwar transformation revived the Boston region, it crippled Roxbury. As a low-income community of color, Roxbury experienced fully the negative side of uneven development. The 'invisible hand' of the private sector led the assault with massive disinvestment, redlining, arson and abandonment. Between 1950 and 1980, Roxbury's population fell by 57 percent (Roxbury Technical Assistance Project, 1986). Roxbury's housing stock, by now mostly seventy-five to one hundred years old, was generally in need of serious repair, but as far as banks were concerned Roxbury property provided no equity. Not only were tenants forced out by landlords who milked and then burned buildings, but even many homeowners – typically with fully paid-off mortgages – were forced to abandon their homes because they could not finance necessary repairs (Kennedy, 1978).

Part of the economic pressure on the housing stock took the form of a tax squeeze by the city government. Proportionately higher property taxes were levied in Roxbury than in any other part of the city. A 1974 study evaluating the impact of a proposed (now enacted) market value reassessment throughout Boston showed that while reassessment would increase Boston's overall tax liability by 20 percent, Roxbury's liability would *drop* by 27 percent (Holland and Oldman, 1974: 15). In return for higher taxes, Roxbury got strikingly poor services: 'Whole areas, particularly in Lower Roxbury, were allowed by the city government to deteriorate. Vacant buildings were torn down, dumping garbage was permitted in Madison Park...' ('Moving in Boston', 1980: 5). This did not happen by accident. It was deliberate public policy to 'triage' neighborhoods, concentrating services in middle-class areas and particularly neglecting those neighborhoods occupied by people of color – specifically Roxbury, Dorchester and Mattapan (McDonough, 1975).

The state contributed to the devalorization of the neighborhood with plans to extend the interstate highway system into Roxbury from two directions. Before a popular movement stopped the roads, early demolition of the Southwest Corridor cut a broad swath through Lower Roxbury and along Columbus Avenue (Gastón, 1981; Geiser, 1980). Major urban renewal programs in Madison Park and Washington Park (recently renamed Malcolm X Park) also resulted in massive demolition of housing and industry. The BRA promised that 'substantial benefits would accrue to the community and the city in general by replacement of badly deteriorated conditions' (Boston Redevelopment Authority, 1982), but the community saw something different:

> And so urban renewal in those days was done by the subtle means of a bulldozer. And so a lot of these intersting little streets with the little wooden houses, all of them were wiped out, practically.... Then I started to realize – I said gee – these houses aren't here any more. Then I walked through acres and acres of open lots. They haven't done a darn thing to it. (Alan Crite, as quoted in 'Moving in Boston', 1980: 6)

Today, over 30 percent of Roxbury's population is below the poverty line, and more than one quarter of Roxbury's families have *no* worker, despite large family size and relatively few elderly. Roxbury has a home ownership ratio of only 20 percent, while 53 percent of all housing and 73 percent of rental housing is subsidized (Gastón and Kennedy, 1985: 13, 21–22). Of the land parcels, 'a little more than half is tax exempt, largely publicly held, and of this, half is vacant' (Boston Redevelopment Authority, 1984).

The Community Organizes

Thus, Roxbury the neighborhood – a collection of land and buildings, housing and businesses – declined sharply between the 1950s and the 1980s. What of Roxbury the community? Over the last thirty years a rich legacy of struggle, organizing, leadership and organizational development and consciousness raising has been built in Roxbury. The same forces that oppressed and damaged the community influenced the forms of resistance that Roxbury developed to defend itself. The process of self-defense included struggle for civil rights, particularly against school segregation, for housing, jobs and services, against highway and urban renewal displacement and for political representation and power.

The forms of expression of this political development have been diverse, forming what Black leader Mel King has called a 'chain of change'. Different struggles have followed each other, leaving behind more developed leadership, consciousness, organizations and institutions. The state's efforts to cope with struggles through repression and reform have also helped to generate a minority of community leaders and organizations who have a stake in keeping struggles within bounds convenient to the system. Given the key role played by education in reproducing social relations and the peculiar character of the

Boston School Department (the last patronage stronghold of the old Irish populist machine) the struggle for equal and high-quality education has evolved over decades and has been central to the recent development of Black politics in Boston. Activities in the decades-long campaign to desegregate Boston's schools have ranged from the unsuccessful School Committee candidacy of Black woman Ruth Batson in 1959, to the 'Stay Out for Freedom' boycott in 1963, to the lawsuit that resulted in a desegregation court order in 1974, to massive demonstrations to defend desegregation from physical as well as political attacks by organized racist groups.

Efforts by Blacks (and later, Latinos and Asians) to gain access to jobs included boycotts of lily-white employers organized in the early 1960s, attempts to build Black-controlled businesses such as Freedom Industries and the Unity Bank in the late 1960s, picketing of construction sites by the United Community Construction Workers in the early 1970s, and in the late 1970s lobbying for the 'Boston Jobs for Boston Residents' executive order and ordinance, which set aside shares of jobs for Boston residents, people of color and women on development projects that receive city assistance (King, 1981, provides the best summary of these movements).

An important component of these struggles was the Black community's increased capacity to generate coalitions, including interracial coalitions, with other forces in the city and metropolitan area. The struggle against highways is a particularly impressive example of this new strength. In the late sixties, as mentioned above, demolition began in Roxbury for two new major highways, Interstate 95 and an inner-city circumferential road called the Inner Belt. Led partly by Chuck Turner, who represented the Black United Front's Operation STOP, a coalition of metropolitan scope, the Southwest Corridor Coalition, was formed. This formation included inner-city Black neighborhoods and white working-class suburban neighborhoods, both concerned about loss of jobs and housing, along with wealthy suburban residents worried about preserving 'suburban tone' and environmentalists concerned about the loss of wetlands. This somewhat unlikely coalition became powerful enough to force Republican Governor Sargent to declare a moritorium in 1970 on state highway construction in the metropolitan area and eventually to redefine the region's transportation plans entirely. This struggle even had a national impact; the coalition was intrumental in the release of Federal

Highway Trust Funds (financed from gasoline taxes) to finance public transit (Gastón, 1981).

The Southwest Corridor Project, a coalition of city, state and metropolitan agencies, was formed to develop the land originally cleared for the highway for a new rapid transit line. The Orange Line, until recently running through the heart of Roxbury, was relocated to the Southwest Corridor in 1988. Under pressure of groups originally organized to stop the highway, an elaborate participatory planning process was developed for the huge project. Ongoing movements have wrested considerable reforms from the Southwest Corridor Project (for example, affordable housing and a new campus for Roxbury Community College).

Other struggles over the years, especially around tenant, education and welfare issues, have linked Roxbury groups, not only with others in the city, but also with national networks. Through coalition building, Roxbury successfully fought against efforts to isolate the Black community politically and in the process developed the experience, skills and contacts for future struggles that would more clearly strengthen the political power of the Black community. The Rainbow Coalition, the multiracial electoral coalition that powered Jesse Jackson's presidential campaigns, originated in Boston with the participation of activists who had earned their political wings in the Southwest Corridor battle and other coalition efforts. In fact, in 1985, the first annual Martin Luther King Leadership Award of the Boston Rainbow Coalition was given to Chuck Turner for his efforts in leading the struggle for community control in Roxbury.

Until several years ago, Blacks and Latinos accomplished little in Boston's electoral arena. While some Blacks were elected to represent Boston districts in the state legislature, the 'at-large' municipal election system and the grip of a series of machines dominated by Irish and Italian ethnic groups served to block Blacks from municipal office. Throughout the 1960s and 1970s, Black activists ran candidate after candidate, but with meager results. The NAACP's Tom Atkins, elected to the City Council for one term in 1971, was the first Black elected to a Boston municipal office in this century; no other Black was to follow until 1977. No Latino even ran for office until 1979, and to date only one has been elected (to the Boston School Committee). But in the years since 1977, significant achievements have been made in electoral politics. The Black

Political Task Force, formed in 1978, has become a powerful organization whose endorsement is sought by white candidates as well as by Black ones. Bostonians voted in 1981 to reform municipal government, instituting representation by districts in the School Committee and City Council, and half a dozen Black candidates have made the breakthrough into elected office. Most significant, a Black progressive, Mel King, was propelled into a runoff election for mayor in 1983.

The 1983 mayoral election was unusual in ways that have a direct bearing on the situation Roxbury faces today. After decades of openly progrowth, probusiness mayors, both Mel King and his adversary Ray Flynn ran on left-of-center campaigns with similar platforms, with King clearly on the left flank. A major difference centered on King's antiracist campaign and Flynn's refusal to confront the issue of racism. Flynn won the runoff by a two-to-one margin with a platform billed as populist, representing the interests of 'the poor', and fighting for the 'neighborhoods' against the greedy 'downtown'. The final election and the voting were highly polarized along racial lines, although King succeeded in winning over 20 percent of the white vote.

Because of the populist rhetoric and racial overtones of the election, Flynn has been compelled to at least make the appearance of accomodating the wishes of Roxbury. Particularly important was Flynn's campaign promise to redress the balance between a glittery new downtown and the city's decaying neighborhoods by funneling some of the development money away from the center of the city. Despite King's large margin of defeat, Boston's Black and Latino communities emerged from the election with increased political clout.

In summary, the period since the World War II has been a trying one for the city. For the dominant groups in the city, who tend to speak in the name of 'Boston', the period was a difficult transition from an outdated and obsolete city to one that is 'modernized' to the point where Stephen Coyle, the Boston Redevelopment Authority director appointed by Flynn, boosts Boston as the 'best performing economy, not just in the country, but in the whole world' (Menzies, 1985). The combined result of a series of transformations and policies has been a prosperous economy, but one tending towards a more uneven distribution of income and wealth, with racial disparities increasing (Boston Redevelopment Authority, 1984: 5). The city has a changing labor force, a downtown investment boom, and a growing population of yuppies who are gentrifying its neighborhoods.

Roxbury, on the other hand, has had 'the short end of the stick' in the transformation of Boston. As a community, it suffered a disproportionate part of the loss in old industrial jobs, while gaining access to only the worst among the new ones. As a neighborhood, it was scarred by demolition for highways and urban renewal. It suffered through forty years of disinvestment with the accompanying abandonment and arson. It fought very hard, defending itself on all fronts. It won concessions such as housing and services from the state, developed its own institutions, strengthened its culture and identity, and began to build a serious political base.

New Pressures for Development in Roxbury

Over the past several years, the combination of continued pressures for investment in Boston with limits to downtown growth has led to consideration of Roxbury as a new target for business and upscale residential development. Here we focus on events in 1984–86, the years in which battle lines were drawn between community forces, determined that Boston's Black community would not be displaced yet one more time, and a city whose development policy, despite rhetoric to the contrary, works inexorably towards the twin patterns of gentrification and displacement.

Despite urban renewal, Boston is an old city. The downtown building boom has strained the infrastructure and physical capacity of the central city to its limits and threatened its historical legacy. Traffic jams are legendary in the two harbor-crossing tunnels and the Central Artery, an elevated limited access highway which runs through the downtown. A decades-old effort to build a third harbor tunnel and to modernize the Artery is finally bearing fruit - construction is scheduled to begin in 1990 but is expected to take twelve years to complete. Parking capacity is woefully inadequate for current demands. There is little prospect for large amounts of additional development downtown.

Simultaneously, there is an ongoing fiscal crisis of the local state. In 1979, a statewide plebiscite passed Proposition 2 1/2, modeled after California's Proposition 13. This law limits growth in real estate taxes to 2.5 percent of the assessed value of property, the major source of municipal revenue. Boston has been kept afloat financially through carefully negotiated assistance packages from the state legislature, and by selling valuable downtown property such as parking garages to developers – practices that have only exacerbated the inadequacy of the infrastructure. There are, however, no more publicly owned garages and few other properties left downtown to sell for premium prices. The state legislature, faced now with its own budget crisis, is unlikely to provide assistance except for emergencies.

The city administration has to continue to promote new investment to generate municipal revenues. In short, the pressure to invest is enormous, and the downtown is approaching its limits. BRA director Coyle's strategy has been to continue attracting investment, but to cap development downtown, funneling it instead into existing open land nearest to downtown (Menzies, 1985). The situation can be compared to the controlled explosion of an internal combustion engine: there is a sudden violent expansion of the activities now concentrated downtown, but there are strong constraints against the expansion. The energy has to be directed somewhere.

Roxbury is located minutes away from the central business district, with easy access to public transportation and major regional highways. This, along with Roxbury's large amount of publicly held (and largely vacant) land, would seem to make an ideal new turf for capital. The Flynn administration hoped that extending downtown-type development to Roxbury would also be seen as meeting Flynn's campaign commitment to narrow the gap between downtown and the neighborhoods, Roxbury in particular. The city also thought it could portray its development agenda in Roxbury as a gesture to the Black community, something that Flynn sorely needed in the aftermath of the 1983 election.

In this context, in early 1985 the BRA released a 'Dudley Square Plan' and BRA director Stephen Coyle announced that he had lined up twenty-one developers with $750 million to invest in the Dudley Station area, the commercial, transportation and cultural center of Roxbury. Although specifics of this plan have since been abandoned in the face of community opposition, it still symbolizes the main direction of city development policy in Roxbury. For this reason, it is useful to look at this initial plan in some detail.

Implications of the Boston Redevelopment Authority Plan

The Boston Redevelopment Authority plan, produced with virtually no community involvement and kept secret until its release, had several major components:

1. Development of Dudley Square into a historical town center, with the station renovated into a commercial 'galeria' (the prototype for this type of enclosed shopping and eating area is the Galeria in Milan, Italy).

2. A high-rise 'business park', with an initial 750,000 square feet of space for offices, shops and a 500-car garage.

3. Converting the Orchard Park public housing development into tenant-owned cooperatives.

4. Construction of new single-family housing affordable for families earning 'as little as $20,000 a year' (BRA, 1984).

The BRA claimed that this proposed development in Roxbury would not cause displacement since new construction was to be mostly restricted to already vacant land. Although this policy would limit the immediate *direct* displacement, *indirect*, or off-site, displacement of such a development, if not controlled, would be drastic. And displacement began almost immediately after the plan was announced.

Mere talk of a $750 million dollar wave of investment immediately accelerated speculation in the private housing market as well as arson in the area. In 1986 the Boston Arson Prevention Commission released a report showing an alarming increase in the number of suspicious fires near Dudley since the BRA announcement. Within weeks of the release of the BRA plan, homeowners in the area were reporting the almost daily receipt of slips under the door from real estate agents urging them to sell; in classic blockbusting fashion, some of these slips alluded to the threat of an influx of Latinos in traditionally Black neighborhoods. Almost daily, one began hearing of one after another dilapidated triple-decker selling for an enormous sum of money. An eighteen-unit block of appartments was auctioned in 1980 for $15,000, and renovated and sold in 1985 for $400,000. The manager said at that time that within two years he expected it to be worth twice that (Kaufman,

1985). By mid-1987, condominiums in Roxbury's Fort Hill area listed for $109,000 to $215,000; the average sale price for a house in this area in 1969 was $8,000 (Malaspina, 1987). Given the low rate of homeownership, the displacement of tenants in this area began immediately, before major corporate investment even started. For awhile, some commercial property in the area of Dudley Station jumped in value by 50 percent every few months.

While displacement in the open private market is most difficult to control under current laws and conditions, the semi-public market of subsidized units fares little better. These units make up a large percentage of housing in the neighborhood, and a substantial portion of them are in financial trouble, as they are throughout the country. The Department of Housing and Urban Development (HUD) is under contract to continue subsidies for fifteen years, but HUD has already requested Congress to change the regulations to allow the federal government to strip foreclosed properties of the subsidies, and to permit their disposition in the open market with no guarantee of affordability or security of tenure. Although observers believe it is unlikely that Congress will grant HUD this request, potentially 10,000 people could be displaced in the short run, almost all of them people of color, into a housing market with a vacancy rate of less than 1 percent and in a city with the lowest income-to-rent ratio in the country. Longer range displacement would be far worse, since many subsidized units not currently on the auction block are in financial trouble and could expect a similar fate in a few years. Given Boston's recent history of racial strife and housing discrimination, the impact of this development could be devastating.

Displacement in public housing is a somewhat different problem. There are nearly 2,000 units of public family housing in Roxbury; over 200 of these units are currently vacant, awaiting repairs. Overall, the condition of most of Boston's public housing is so deplorable and the federal attitude towards increased, or even continued, subsidies so negative that what has traditionally been the most secure stock of low-income housing is now in jeopardy. The BRA plan suggested that the 700-plus units in the Orchard Park public housing development be turned into tenant cooperatives. Unless the option includes limited equity, it would be difficult for the current low-income residents to resist selling in a lucrative market.

The housing component of the BRA plan, called 'Building the American Dream', addressed the construction of only 1,200 new units, besides the conversion of public housing to homeownership. By totally writing down the cost of the land, using factory-built construction methods and piggy-backing every available subsidy, the BRA argued that the units could be affordable by households earning 'as little as $20,000 a year'(Boston Redevelopment Authority, 1984). According to the BRA's own figures, median household income in Roxbury was only $4,515 in 1980. And the number of Black households in the entire metropolitan area with an annual income in the $20,000 range is relatively small. According to the 1980 Census, only 20,545 Black households earned over $15,000 a year in the metropolitan area. If, as the BRA plan suggests, Roxbury is to be repopulated to 1960 levels (over twice the present population), it is questionable whether it will remain primarily a community of color.

The problem of job creation through development in Roxbury has been a primary concern of Roxbury's leaders for years and is perhaps the single most important issue facing the community. The proposed BRA plan purports to create the kinds of workplaces which have been the staple of Boston's growth in this decade: hotels and office towers. While the community has vocally preferred industrial jobs in the past, the city and business authorities promoting the plan and its more recent variants have argued that such jobs are not feasible. Little research has been done exploring alternatives for job creation.

For a neighborhood like Roxbury, which has been suffering from disinvestment for decades, the prospect of investment, especially on the scale proposed, may appear to some like relief from a drought. Certainly, the BRA's Dudley Square Plan, the formalized mechanism for publicly greasing the wheels for private investment in Roxbury, was billed in such terms. But working-class communities of color have accumulated a vast experience in confronting the siren song of capital, and their insistence on gaining some control of the process has a firm basis in popular understanding of current conditions. The current investment wave has the potential to displace enormous numbers of people, destroying the community in order to 'save' the neighborhood.

The Struggle for Roxbury and Community Power

The image of David and Goliath often comes to mind when analyzing the struggle for Roxbury. Goliath – downtown developers and the BRA – at first looms all-powerful and invincible. But the community, with its demonstrated capacity to fight successfully, may be David in the story. The efforts of the Roxbury community to become actors in the process are remarkable in their effectiveness, vision and creativity. They draw on three decades of experience in Boston's communities of color in fighting against the BRA in particular, but also against the larger forces behind urban transformation.

People involved in the fightback include many who successfully led the fight against extension of Interstate 95 through the city, displacees of the South End urban renewal program, and residents of the Madison Park and Washington Park urban renewal projects in Roxbury, all of them with a rich experience fighting the Boston Redevelopment Agency with at least partial success. Fightback forces include people who pioneered the Mel King campaign and the Rainbow Coalition, who have developed experience in using newly acquired political strength. In addition, a group of young activists, for whom this struggle represents a political baptism, are showing a refreshing new energy and leadership. The city's Black and Latino communities and the larger progressive movement have developed highly skilled professional planners, architects, lawyers and other technicians. Little David is getting very good at the sling and has been landing a few good-sized rocks on target – and David now looks poised to win a decisive battle.

The process by which the BRA plan entered the public discourse is itself a lesson in the politics of urban development. The BRA's Dudley Square Plan, which few in the community even knew was being prepared, was deliberately leaked in early 1985, only days before the first meeting of a community coalition that was organizing to begin developing the community's own plan and consensus for the development of Roxbury.

In late summer 1984, it was common knowledge in the community that the BRA was conducting a study of conditions in Roxbury, particularly the Dudley Station area. People also assumed that some development in the area would accompany the removal of the Washington Street Elevated (effected in 1988, when the new Orange Line along the Southwest Corridor began operation). The El was a blighting influence in the neighborhood and many felt that its removal would stimulate development along Washington Street.

In early fall 1984, Mel King and other community leaders began to organize to build a broad-based community coalition within the Roxbury/North Dorchester area to promote and guide development of jobs and housing that would benefit the current community and poor and working-class people, particularly in the Black community.

At the same time, two of the authors, Maurico Gastón and Marie Kennedy, were completing *Dudley in 2001: After the El, Center for Whom?*, working with the Roxbury Action Program, a community development corporation active in the Highland Park section of Roxbury for over fifteen years. This study assessed the likely impact on the economic life of the Dudley area of proposed alternative replacement transit systems for the Washington Street Corridor after the El was removed. Signs such as an alarming increase in development-related arson along the Southwest Corridor and property speculation in the Highland Park section of Roxbury (which lies between Dudley Station and the Southwest Corridor and had earlier suffered great loss through arson) combined with an assessment of the physical character of the area itself (especially its proximity to downtown and large amounts of publicly owned vacant land), led us to view gentrification, rather than continued decay, the most likely outcome in Roxbury. Our conclusion was that community development rather than gentrification could be promoted only if popular control could be won over impending development decisions. The major recommendation of this study was the establishment of a neighborhood development authority that would have many of the powers and resources traditionally held by the BRA (Gastón and Kennedy, 1984).

The first mass meeting of the community coalition was called for 12 January 1985, and the discussion of what would constitute real community control over neighborhood development was launched. A fairly careful and necessarily slow process of coalition building was foreseen; this was to be only the first meeting in that process. Ideally, the process of building community unity would proceed simultaneously with the provision of technical assistance that would help the community to set goals and develop knowledge of what trade-offs are involved in different development decisions. In this way, community-based planning would have real meaning. It was hoped that the expected BRA study, along with *Dudley in 2001*, would begin to build the data base necessary for the community to make informed decisions. Instead, in the week prior to the 12 January community meeting, the BRA leaked its Dudley Square Plan for the development of the major commercial and transportation center in Roxbury. This was not the fact-finding study that had been anticipated, but rather an alarmingly concrete plan that had been developed in the traditional 'closed door' fashion typical of the BRA in the past, and contradictory to the rhetoric of the new 'populist' administration. As of the second community meeting, the BRA representatives were talking of a specific twenty-one developers with $750 million to invest. If they could not move quickly, if the community was not accommodating, said the BRA, these investors would go elsewhere.

Community power and inclusiveness: the Greater Roxbury Neighborhood Authority

Community activists responded to this BRA threat by intensifying their efforts to build a broad-based community coalition that could control development in Greater Roxbury. At a press conference held on Frederick Douglass Day, 14 February 1985, the Greater Roxbury Neighborhood Authority (GRNA) was formally launched.

The GRNA demanded a moratorium on land disposition until a degree of popular participation and control could be established. In fact, the publicity generated by this press conference embarrassed the City into a de facto moratorium on land disposition for a short period. Veto power over land disposition has continued as a community demand. At this initial press conference, the GRNA refused to be drawn into specific criticisms of the BRA's Dudley Square Plan. While welcoming reinvestment and community development in Roxbury, they insisted that the question,'Development for whom, and by whom?' be answered first.

The GRNA's position was based on several factors. First, the fact that the planning process had been undemocratic meant that the questions posed for the plan to answer were so narrow that various alternatives dealing with job creation, housing and financing were never even explored. Second, and building on the first point, focusing on a specific plan at this point in the planning process would have meant narrowing the debate to the level of nitpicking – necessary prior questions would never be posed; GRNA refused to get trapped into an agenda set by the BRA which would have effectively derailed a truly inclusionary process and would have channeled all energy to crafting compromises about unessential disagreements (for example, whether office buildings would be fifteen or twenty stories – not whether there would be any office buildings; whether owner-occupied housing would be detached or duplex, not whether more cooperative forms of ownership might be appropriate). Third, the BRA plan only addressed development in a small part of the Greater Roxbury area, whereas the community faces crucial community development and political issues in many areas of Greater Roxbury.

GRNA recognized that specific development decisions in one area would affect – positively or negatively – the development possibilities of the broader community and therefore should not be taken in isolation. GRNA called for a geographically more integrated, coordinated and community-controlled planning process, with powers of decision-making placed in the hands of the various sectors in the numerous Greater Roxbury neighborhoods. The area that GRNA defines as its 'turf' is home to 95 percent of Boston's African American population – approximately 160,000 people reside in these 12+ square miles.

The GRNA has built an extremely broad coalition, embracing Blacks and Latinos, merchants and ministers, politicians and community organizers, public housing tenants and small landlords. The planning and control process they envision can be likened to a spider plant – decentralized but coordinated with formalized lines of communication. The Project Advisory Committee (PAC) that GRNA organized in the Dudley area and the Dudley Street Neighborhood Initiative (also see below), with whom they are allied, are examples of the type of neighborhood-controlled planning groups that GRNA has been working to develop in other Roxbury neighborhoods, such as Grove Hall, Blue Hill Avenue and Mattapan Square.

GRNA has balanced its efforts between concrete planning, grass-roots organizing and coalition building. Particular care has been taken with leadership building and consciousness raising in general, but using and improving technical skills and expertise have also been an important part of the agenda. General policy decisions are taken by an elected Steering Committee composed of both long-time and experienced community activists and younger people who have grown up politically in recent electoral and community struggles. Both standing and ad-hoc committees take up the actual work of the organization. A list of the initial subcommittees of the Planning Committee gives an idea of the breadth of planning concerns addressed: Housing, Transportation, Commercial/Retail, Light Industry, Historic Preservation and Parcel 18 (this last is a specific parcel targeted for redevelopment – see below).

From the beginning, GRNA took on a leadership role in a number of community coalitions. It is not a competitive organization but rather has sought to augment the overall capacity of the community to make knowledgeable decisions about its future and to build political power. Working with City Life (a multi-issue, socialist community organization based primarily in the neighboring Jamaica Plain neighborhood), the Dudley Street Neighborhood Initiative, Massachusetts Fair Share, and the Legal Service Center (the primary legal aid resource in Boston), GRNA established an 'Eviction Free Zone' in the areas of Roxbury and Jamaica Plain currently most susceptible to gentrification. In this area, anti-eviction and public benefit legal service work is targeted in order to keep people in their homes; the long-range goal is to convert housing to various forms of nonspeculative social ownership, including limited-equity coops and nonspeculative homeownership.

GRNA also worked with a network of HUD tenants' organizations concerned with upgrading subsidized housing and most specifically with HUD foreclosed developments to ensure that they were not turned over to the private market and that current tenants were not evicted. Most of the HUD projects foreclosed in Boston are in Greater Roxbury – approximately 3,000 units. Although this struggle is far from over, the mayor, under pressure from tenant and community organizations and housing activists, negotiated with HUD to ensure continued subsidies (for fifteen years) for most of the Roxbury units. Most recently (1989), GRNA has worked with a wide array of Roxbury groups to expose racist lending patterns in the area.

Advice or control: the Dudley Project Advisory Committee and the Coalition for Community Control of Development

Perhaps the most significant for neighborhoods across the city of GRNA's early organizing and coalition-building efforts were the negotiations over control of development around Dudley Station. The BRA, impressed by the level of popular support harnessed by the GRNA, floated a proposal to create a Project

Advisory Committee with members appointed by the mayor and only advisory power over development. The GRNA countered by organizing constituency caucuses of small merchants, clergy, tenants, neighborhood associations, community development corporations and other groups, identifying representatives from each sector and presenting them for ratification at a Roxbury 'town meeting' of over 500 people, as a popularly elected 'interim PAC' that would serve until broader elections could be held. This interim PAC was presented to the mayor as an unavoidable presence, and he was unable to create his own appointed front.

The 'interim PAC' won the grudging recognition of city officials and entered into negotiations with the BRA and the mayor. The city accepted the thirteen people whom the community had elected as legitimate members of the PAC but insisted on the appointment by the mayor of eight additional people. Perhaps the greatest initial victory for GRNA was that the publicity achieved in the process of electing the 'interim PAC' threw a spotlight on the city's land give-away, embarrassing the city into reinstating the de facto moratorium on land disposition, although the city, in principle, continued to refuse to agree to it.

Although the PAC was not accorded veto power over plans or final say on the selection of developers, it did negotiate impressive powers. Twelve 'Agreed Upon Principles' emerged from the negotiations, including the right to elect the PAC; PAC approval of all BRA requests for proposals prior to issuance; PAC approval of any zoning changes; and a PAC budget from the BRA. Mayor Flynn was politically pressured into public support for the agreement – announcing in October 1985, in front of television and more than 500 people convened by the GRNA, that 'we have a deal'. Speedy implementation of the agreement was expected.

In the meantime, the BRA continued to plan and to negotiate with developers, and BRA Director Coyle kept refusing to put the agreement to a vote of his Board. It became clear to the PAC that the BRA had no intention of honoring the agreement, so the PAC determined to directly lobby and pressure the BRA Board to vote on the agreement. This effort yielded a negative vote of the Board, largely because the PAC refused to cut the controversial Parcel 18 out of their planning district. The BRA had now officially reneged on the agreement. Although Flynn had publicly supported the agreement, neither he nor Coyle delivered the vote of the BRA Board, and Flynn's credibility as the 'neighborhood' mayor was damaged. Speculation in the media was that a subsequent 40 percent cut in the BRA budget was Flynn's response to Coyle's inability to control his board on this issue.

Another town meeting was called by the PAC to present the situation to the community and to explore alternatives for action. In the week before this town meeting, Flynn exercised his option to appoint the eight new PAC members in an attempt to manipulate the situation. The PAC countered by inviting the mayoral appointees to participate with other PAC members in a lawsuit to demand that the BRA cease its redevelopment efforts until certain legal requirements were met. In a spirit of community solidarity, most of the mayor's appointees agreed to join the suit against the BRA.

The lawsuit itself is based on requirements, amended into the BRA's enabling legislation of the early 1960s, for a master plan to be approved by the City Council and the State before any redevelopment can proceed. The BRA claims that a master plan is meaningless given the current planning environment where there are few public funds available to promote development. BRA spokespeople also claim that the BRA is acting in its capacity as the city planning agency, not as the redevelopment authority, the latter being the only role that requires a publicly approved master plan.

The lawsuit and related organizing activities forced the BRA back into negotiations with the PAC. But GRNA and its lawyers recognized from the beginning that the real importance of the lawsuit was its use as an organizing tool, especially in building links with other city neighborhoods. They began to draw other neighborhoods into support of the principles of the lawsuit – that there should be community control of development. This organizing led to the creation in 1986 of the Coalition for Community Control of Development, which includes neighborhood groups from all but two of Boston's historically divided neighborhoods. The fact that initial organizing and much of the ongoing leadership in the CCCD comes from the Black community is particularly significant in racially divided Boston. In 1988 the CCCD submitted a Home Rule Petition to the Boston City Council, which, if successful, will assure considerable control over development to affected neighborhoods. Already, the principle of elected neighborhood PACs has been won for most Boston neighborhoods, and BRA-sponsored development is being subjected to much more public scrutiny than it has ever had before.

Parcel 18: Development for whom?

The controversy over Parcel 18 provides an interesting case study, further illuminating aspects of the struggle over development in Roxbury. Parcel 18, the largest development parcel of the Southwest Corridor, enjoys a strategic location, adjacent to a new Orange Line rapid transit station (Ruggles Street) and near the current Dudley Station. For ten years, the Parcel 18 Task Force, a coalition of tenants, community development corporations, Black developers, agencies and abutting institutions, researched, planned and explored development alternatives for the site. After ten years, considerable work had been done.

In the meantime, the Flynn administration began to implement various 'linkage' policies, akin to policies first developed in San Francisco. In addition to requiring from developers a contribution of $5 per square foot of new office construction over 100,000 square feet for a fund to promote housing in the neighborhoods, the BRA introduced 'parcel-to-parcel linkage'. Under this policy, development parcels in downtown Boston are 'linked' to less desirable neighborhood parcels and offered to developers who would develop them simultaneously.

The first parcel-to-parcel linkage project linked Parcel 18 to the downtown-Chinatown Kingston/Bedford site. In the opinion of many urban planners, Parcel 18 didn't need linkage. Given the parcel's location, the public funds already spent on land improvement, and skyrocketing land values along the Southwest Corridor, it is unlikely that a modestly scaled development of Parcel 18 would have required the leverage offered by parcel-to-parcel linkage.

However, the type of development the BRA had in mind presumably did require linkage. Due largely to GRNA organizing, the BRA was unable to move directly, and in the short term, on the Dudley Square Plan. As a result, developing Parcel 18 as an extension of downtown became a primary focus and enormous leverage was exerted to this end.

After analyzing the various proposals for development articulated by the Parcel 18 Task Force, the BRA representatives literally said, 'Thank you for your input' and proceeded to unveil a fully developed plan, quite different from anything the Task Force had had in mind. This plan consisted of two 30-

story towers, 600,000 square feet of office space with adjacent commercial space, parking and related uses (Boston Redevelopment Authority, 1986: 95, 96). With minor alterations, this is the plan that is being built. When challenged about the lack of community input, the Deputy Director of the BRA, Ricardo Millett, responded that 'process' is irrelevant as long as the 'development content' benefits the community (who determines what is a benefit was not addressed).

In addition to denying the validity of ten years of 'process' the BRA quickly moved to co-opt members of the Parcel 18 Task Force by offering various of them equity in the project in return for acceptance of the BRA plan. It was against this backdrop that the PAC refused to eliminate Parcel 18 from its own planning process; as a result the BRA's Board refused to ratify the agreement that the mayor had made with the PAC.

The 'development content' that the BRA proposes to benefit the community immediately raises the question, 'What community?' The BRA's parcel design is based on an extension of the city's new service economy of office towers into the neighborhood. While the BRA planned significant minority equity and participation in jobs, the PAC argued that the parcel should be conceived as an extension of the economy of Roxbury, not of downtown and that something other than towers of 'back-office' space must be built. Light industry, small commercial space and student housing are some of the proposals that they feel bear investigation.

Still encountering resistance from the Dudley PAC and having not yet won agreement from the Chinatown PAC (Kingston/Bedford is in its planning district), the BRA extended promises of equity participation to various additional Black, Latino and Asian developers. For minority developers in Boston this was a first chance to have a piece of the downtown development action, and the 30 percent minority development share eventually arranged was a sufficient wedge to disarm community opposition. Although it was clear to many that creating a few millionaires of color would not solve the problems of most Roxbury residents, this particular battle was lost.

Evidence of development-related arson and the BRA denial

An even more chilling example of how far the BRA is prepared to go in defending its role and prerogatives in the redevelopment of Roxbury is offered by the response of the BRA to the

1986 report of the Boston Arson Prevention Commission, which found an alarming increase in arson in Roxbury following the announcement of the BRA's Dudley Square Plan. BRA Director Stephen Coyle led a virulent attack on the credibility of the commission's work, calling them 'bozos' and insisting that the commission 'improve its methodology or resign'. He was particularly adamant in opposition to the report's finding of a connection between arson and development, because exposing such a connection would 'endanger planned redevelopment' and 'hamper potential financing' (Frisby, 1986). Besides pressuring the commission's director to resign, the mayor has proceeded to stack the commission itself with appointees expected to be more pliable to the mayor's and the BRA's position. Although no one justifies arson, the BRA, in pretending that arson is simply a law enforcement problem, has acted to undermine a vigorous opposition to it, particularly in trying to discredit the statistical data that indicate a connection between arson, speculation and development.

Uniting diverse ethnic groups: the Dudley Street Neighborhood Initiative

Some of the most creative energy generated by the fightback in Roxbury is taking shape with less relative visibility in various smaller neighborhoods. Of these localized efforts, the Dudley Street Neighborhood Initiative (DSNI) stands out as a particularly interesting example and an indication of trends in local efforts. In fact, GRNA considers DSNI a good example of the type of planning effort it hopes will evolve in every district of Roxbury.

The neighborhood concerned is located just west of Dudley Station. It has a population of about 15,000, including African Americans, Cape Verdeans, Puerto Ricans, Dominicans and other Latinos. It's probably the poorest neighborhood in Roxbury aside from public housing developments such as Orchard Park (which it borders). The infamous 'Bermuda Triangle' lies within the DSNI area, as does much other land cleared through arson and disinvestment. In fact, in the area's 1 1/2 square miles there are over 1,000 parcels of vacant land, most of it owned by the City of Boston (Dudley Street Neighborhood Initiative, 1986).

The DSNI grew out of a series of meetings held in 1984 of the area's various human service agencies, including the Roxbury Multiservice Center (the nation's first multiservice center), La Alianza Hispana, Cape Verdean House, and religious centers such as WAITT House. Although there was a long history of communication and good relations among these agencies, there was little work in collective long-range strategizing and planning. Each of the ethnic groups, while getting along with others, was rowing its own boat.

According to Melvyn Colón, director of Nuestra Comunidad Development Corporation and a founder and board member of the DSNI, the formation of the Rainbow Coalition and the 1983 Mel King mayoral campaign qualitatively changed the situation and laid the basis for groups to move beyond willingness to cooperate to developing the trust necessary to plan joint strategy. Because of this inclusiveness, skillful political and technical leadership, and the fact that the DSNI area has been the focus of much recent struggle in Roxbury, the DSNI has managed to obtain significant resources from business-supported foundations.

An initial campaign to stop dumping of garbage and hazardous waste on the neighborhood's vacant lots proved a good 'down-to-earth' issue around which to organize the community. From the start, much of DSNI's organizing and planning work has been done in cooperation with other groups in the area. DSNI worked with the Orchard Park United Tenants Association to oppose plans for a new prison and a waste-to-energy plant proposed for location in the industrial zone adjacent to the neighborhood. DSNI organizers are among the most active in the Eviction Free Zone Coalition. And two DSNI leaders, Melvyn Colón and Fadilah Muhammad, were amongst the originally elected members of the Dudley PAC (the PAC area includes part of the DSNI neighborhood).

DSNI was able to attract enough foundation money to hire its own consultants to develop a comprehensive revitalization plan for the neighborhood. The process involved a multitude of community meetings and resulted in a strategy that 'aims at revitalizing the community to the benefit of current residents, while fighting speculative pressures that cause displacment' (DSNI, 1987). It is now working to implement its plan while continuing to advocate generally in the interests of the people who live in the area.

A City Called Mandela: The Greater Roxbury Incorporation Project

Although not the most significant epsiode in the development of Roxbury, the Mandela campaign threw into stark relief issues delineated earlier: the problems of segregation and disinvestment, and the questions of self-determination, political leadership, the role of the media, and community control of development and resources. We therefore analyze this campaign in some detail.

On 4 November 1986, close to 50,000 citizens of Boston living in or near the predominantly Black area of Greater Roxbury voted on whether the area should leave Boston and incorporate as a separate municipality to be called Mandela, in honor of South African Black leaders Nelson and Winnie Mandela. The separation proposal – technically a nonbinding proposal to 'de-annex and reincorporate' Roxbury, which was until 1868 an independent town – whipped up a storm of controversy.[1] Boston city officials damned it as 'economically preposterous and at worst, a program of racial separation.' The Greater Roxbury Incorporation Project (GRIP), sponsors of the Mandela initiative, maintained, 'We want land control because land control is the key to self-determination.'

The Mandela referendum was defeated, 75 percent to 25 percent. However, the proposal rekindled a debate that has simmered in US Black communities for over a hundred years: can the Black community (or any other community of color) better achieve well-being by assimilation into white society, or by establishing community control over development? The arguments that rocked Boston in the month before the vote on Mandela hold lessons for communities of color across the country.

The actors

Three groups of actors played the most important roles in the drama of the Mandela referendum: the originators of the Mandela idea; the Boston establishment, which sharply attacked the concept; and the Black leaders and activists who ended up taking different sides on the issue.

Two people, public television producer Andrew Jones and architect/urban planner Curtis Davis, founded the Greater Roxbury Incorporation Project. Inspired by the incorporation of mainly Black East Palo Alto, California, which became a town in 1983, they called on Mayor Flynn in 1985 to hold a plebiscite in Roxbury over the question of forming a separate city. When Flynn refused, they gathered the 5,000 signatures necessary to put the question on the ballot as a nonbinding referendum instructing the state legislators from affected districts to begin the process of reincorporation. Jones noted, 'We didn't create this area, we just described it. The city of Boston is so incredibly segregated, it was easy to divide.'[2]

Jones and Davis played something of a maverick role in Boston's Black community. They had not been leaders in other community struggles and hewed to a narrow and sometimes idiosyncratic agenda. At one point, they even disrupted a Greater Roxbury Neighborhood Authority 'town meeting', called to discuss a draft housing plan, by insisting that it was pointless to further develop the community planning process since control over development could be gained most effectively through incorporation of Roxbury as a separate city. GRNA leaders countered that even in Mandela a neighborhood authority would be necessary to ensure maximum participation.

GRIP appealed for votes based on several rationales: reversing the decades of racist neglect experienced by Roxbury, controlling the impending flood of investment, and simply gaining accountable government. Although the reincorporation strategy clearly draws on Black nationalism, GRIP often adopted moderate and even 'all-American' rhetoric: GRIP's main position paper begins, 'Independence. It is as much a part of the Massachusetts spirit as it is the American one, if not more so.' GRIP's literature emphasized, 'Our community is integrated and our city will be, too' (GRIP, 1986).

The second group of actors, the Boston white establishment, reacted with a self-righteous anger born of wounded liberalism. Boston's leading daily newspaper, the *Globe*, in an almost hysterical outpouring unprecedented since the 1974 racial violence associated with busing, published by our count at least twelve negative articles on Mandela in the three weeks preceding the election. The articles included two editorials and two signed columns, charging Mandela advocates with 'deceitfulness', 'negativism, untruths, and confusion', making 'loud, angry charges', and 'promot[ing] racial segregation'. The *Globe*, along with other opponents of Mandela, persisted in calling the reincorporation proposal *secession*, a term that GRIP rejected. The *Phoenix*, Boston's leading 'alternative' weekly, joined the *Globe* in deploring Mandela.

City officials were not to be outdone in the rush to denounce reincorporation for Roxbury. A typical comment from Flynn was, 'We should not slam the door on the future to make up for the problems of the past.' Flynn's administration released a report projecting that Mandela would run an annual deficit of over $135 million. In the month before the election, city workers were instructed to assume that any inquiries about Roxbury (for example, about assessments and land disposition) came from Mandela supporters and that they were to withhold information until after the election. Flynn's political organization was mobilized to stop Mandela at the polls; city workers were seen at many polling places during normal business hours.

Flynn and the *Globe* did their best to present the image of Black progress in Boston. For example, the Flynn administration issued figures showing that the number of Blacks holding construction jobs in Boston had increased – while neglecting to mention that the *percentage* of such jobs held by Blacks had decreased. Apparently in response to the heat from the Mandela issue, Flynn reappointed a Black political figure to the Boston Redevelopment Authority Board of Directors, restored police cooperation with the Black-organized Drop-a-Dime anticrime group, and increased the powers of Black members of his administration. Perhaps most important, Flynn made a deal giving minority developers 30 percent of Parcel 18. The last action was also aimed at defusing widespread community opposition to the type of development being proposed.

The *Globe* and the Flynn administration made three main criticisms of GRIP's separation proposal: it would pull Blacks out of Boston just when they were starting to make progress; it would be fiscally infeasible; and even if the proposal were not adopted it served to inflame racial divisions. But why was the reaction of Boston's powers-that-be so violent? Three motivations lay behind the rhetoric.

First, city officials and the liberal corporate interests represented by the *Globe* have staked their political and development agenda on the image of a Boston that has healed its racial divisions. That image is required to attract further development necessary to shore up Boston's shaky fiscal base and to assure Flynn's reelection. The *Globe*'s stake is also significant; for over thirty years the *Globe* has been connected with Boston-based financial and development interests concerned with rebuilding Boston's economic power. Mandela threatened to shatter that image.

Second, they wanted to block initiatives for grass-roots community control over development – not only in Roxbury, but in communities across Boston – and to perpetuate the 'democracy' that depends on the exclusion and demobilization of the many, or at best their subordinate participation in initiatives crafted by the reformers in City Hall. A vote for Mandela would have represented a public mandate for community control by a large fraction of Boston's population.

Third, as pointed out by James Jennings of the University of Massachusetts, the white powerholders of Boston are doing their best to control Black leadership in the city – to suppress insurgent Black leaders and to facilitate the emergence of 'cooperative' Black leaders (Jennings, 1986). In particular, Mel King, who endorsed the referendum, remains a key figure for independent Black and progressive politics in the city. And indeed, King was singled out for particularly vicious criticism in articles that predicted that support for Mandela would end his political career. Even after the defeat of the referendum, Flynn and the *Globe* blasted politicians who supported Mandela as well as, in the *Globe*'s words, 'politicians who counseled "maybe" on this important issue.'

Meanwhile, the Black figures who voiced opposition to the referendum were catapulted to prominence by the media as 'reasonable' spokespeople for the community. The *Globe* hailed the new Black leadership that 'prefers working quietly within the system, rather than confronting it.'

It is interesting that both the *Globe* and Flynn waited until three weeks before the vote to launch an all-out attack on the referendum. Most likely, they were waiting to see the reaction of the Black community, meanwhile working behind the scenes to organize a Black opposition to the Mandela initiative.

By three weeks before the November election, the lines had been drawn in the Black community: there was a broad group of community activists supporting Mandela, and there was a well-publicized opposition group, the One Boston Campaign, spearheaded by a few Black ministers. But in the period immediately following August 1986, when Jones and Davis announced to everyone's surprise that they had the signatures necessary to put the measure on the ballot, there was much confusion and debate among Black activists.

Leaders like Mel King and State Representative Byron Rushing, who had supported and in some cases helped to initiate earlier proposals for a separate Roxbury, quickly supported

GRIP. Grass-roots groups such as the Greater Roxbury Neighborhood Authority hesitated longer, put off by GRIP's single-minded and sometimes sectarian insistence that incorporation was the only way to solve Roxbury's problems. But the GRNA, as well as progressive multiracial groups such as the Rainbow Coalition (a spinoff of Mel King's 1983 mayoral campaign) eventually endorsed the Mandela referendum as one strategy for community control and self-determination.

The sharpness and implicit racism of the public attacks on Mandela by the *Globe* and the Flynn administration motivated many Black activists and other progressives to defend the initiative even more strongly. Some other supporters faded under fire, however. Black state senatorial candidate Bill Owens told a *Globe* columnist that while he 'philosophically' supported the reincorporation and would vote for it, 'I'm not encouraging people to vote for it because I don't have all the information.'

The One Boston Campaign, the organized group opposing Mandela, surfaced just about three weeks before the election, and was described by the the *Globe* as 'made up largely of minority clergymen and business and political leaders'. Its two most visible spokespeople were Bruce Wall and Charles Stith, two relatively young Black ministers. Ironically, Wall had even joined the call for a Roxbury plebiscite on separation in 1985. Wall pronounced that 'a number of us have planted the seeds of opportunity over the last seven years or so, and we intend to stay here', but also acknowledged that he had in the past used the separation proposal as a source of leverage over Flynn. GRIP had botched the opportunities for such leverage, he argued, by taking itself too seriously.

Black business owners interviewed by the *Globe* complained that reincorporation had little to offer them. Richard Taylor, president of the Minority Developer's Association, stated, 'I don't really believe much of the basis of the Mandela proposal is grounded in trying to solve business problems. I think its root is based in trying to gain political self-determination. ... There has been no discussion on how it will affect the overall business climate.' Some businessmen stood to lose directly – for example, the minority developers who had a piece of Flynn's $400 million Roxbury redevelopment project. John Cruz, a minority contractor who was part of that deal, observed, 'Roxbury only recently has begun to attract outside capital. ... Secession would put it even farther behind.'

Although Wall and Stith echoed some of the Flynn administration's claims of new opportunities for Blacks in Boston, most Black leaders who opposed Mandela took a more independent position. State Senator Royal Bolling, Sr., patriarch of Boston's mainstream Black political dynasty, supported the effort to put the question on the ballot but opposed the content of the proposal, saying, 'We have the swing vote to determine any election. So why give up the whole pie for just a slice?' Bolling's son Bruce, currently City Council president, initially backed the referendum, but his press statements showed him being slowly dragged into opposition.

The arguments

While many arguments flew in the brawl over Mandela, we focus on three central claims made by the opponents of separation: 1) To the extent that the separation proposal appealed to people in the Black community, it was because they felt that they received an inadequate amount of services from the city; 2) Formation of a separate city would not be fiscally feasible, because Roxbury could not be self-sufficient; 3) Mandela supporters were peddling the illusory promise of separation as a panacea for Black problems.

It's true that Roxbury residents complained loudly about deficiencies in city services – city-assisted jobs and housing, schools, police and fire protection, even snow removal. As one Black hairdresser interviewed by the Boston *Herald* commented, 'How do I feel about the services? What services?' But the Flynn administration responded that the Greater Roxbury area has more police officers (and arrests), more weekly street sweepings and trash collections, and sends more students to the public schools and to Boston's city hospital than any other neighborhood. Are Roxbury residents just too greedy?

Part of the answer, of course, is that they're just too *needy*. Roxbury suffers from more crime, has more kids (and particularly more kids whose parents can't afford private or parochial school), has more health problems and fewer people covered by health insurance than other neighborhoods.

But the story doesn't end there. Another part of the problem is that regardless of the level of service, the City of Boston doesn't deliver the services in a way that is sensitive and responsive to the specific needs of the Black community. An example illustrates the point: during the 1970s, the city decided to construct a clinic in Mattapan, a mainly Black area that is located within the boundaries of Mandela. Health experts carefully studied the census data to determine the number of children, women of child-bearing age, elderly, and other groups with special health care needs. They reviewed income levels to estimate how many families would be unable to afford a private doctor, and noted that few Mattapan residents used Boston City Hospital or other city-supported health centers, which were all fairly distant from Mattapan. They planned screening programs for health problems that are prevalent in poor Black populations – lead paint, sickle cell anemia, hypertension. Finally, they opened the doors and ... few came. What the city's experts had neglected to notice was that many of the Blacks in this part of Mattapan were not African Americans but West Indians. The West Indians brought with them cultural differences that affect delivery of health care, often including language differences and a distrust of institutionalized medicine. As a result, many were simply unwilling to visit the clinic.

Most likely, a Mandela city government would not have made the same mistake. And surely a Mandela cop would do a better job of community protection than the average cop from the Boston police force, on which people of color are still severely underrepresented.

Taking the question of city services one step further, the underlying issue is not just the quantity *or* quality of services, but *who controls the services*. This issue lies beyond the boundaries of the avowed populism of Flynn's administration: despite their genuine commitment to redistribution of resources, they have been unwilling to push for or even support redistribution of power. But without movement toward community empowerment, a reform government lacks the popular mobilization necessary to carry out substantial, lasting redistribution. The government remains hemmed in by 'not enough money', unable to make more aggressive demands on capital or to stimulate self-help initiatives. The 'gifts' from the city to the disadvantaged neighborhoods turn out to be small, poorly planned and delivered and, most likely, temporary.

GRIP and its allies emphasized the issue of community control. GRIP cofounder Davis told us that, 'The primary issue is self-determination. ...This political strategy will put people who live in the area in control of the resources that they need.' We don't know how widely this view was shared in Roxbury. However, we saw GRNA activists winning over Roxbury residents with this argument, and we suspect that many others – such as the person-on-the-street who told the Boston *Herald* that 'Roxbury has always been a separate city' – also agreed with it.

The second claim of Mandela's opponents was that Mandela would quickly go broke. As noted earlier, Mayor Flynn's staff projected a $135 million annual operating deficit for Mandela. GRIP, on the other hand, projected a surplus of $8 million. Both analyses were flawed. For example, the city's study assumed that Mandela would receive state aid in proportion to its share of Boston's population, while in fact state aid is based on need as well. GRIP's study included revenue sources like the one-time sale of downtown parking garages – which could not be repeated by Mandela – and seemed to omit significant expenditures. As a 'business-as-usual' projection, the city's figure is probably closer to the mark.

But Mandela might be able to break away from business as usual, in a process akin to decolonization. In the late 1960s and early 1970s, militant Black leaders – including Malcolm X, Roy Innis and Stokely Carmichael – compared the Black liberation struggle in the United States with anticolonial struggles around the world. A number of radical economists developed the analogy. William Tabb, writing in 1970, pointed out that 'the economic relations of the ghetto to white America closely parallel [the relations] between third world nations and the industrially advanced countries' (Tabb, 1970).

Tabb explained that like the typical developing country, the Black community has low per-capita income; has a small middle class, limited entrepreneurship, and an internal market too underdeveloped to support much local business; faces a low price and limited demand for its chief 'export' – unskilled and semi-skilled labor; shows high internal demand for expensive 'imports' – consumer goods such as cars, televisions, designer clothes; and experiences low rates of savings, investment and productivity growth. Tabb concluded that 'internal colonialism is an apt description of the place Blacks have held and continue to hold in our country.' All of these characteristics describe Roxbury, whose per capita income in 1979 was less than two-thirds that of Boston as a whole.

If community control can help poor Blacks empower themselves and alter some of the 'colonial' economic mechanisms that marginalize them, then in the long run the community control strategy may offer a great deal of promise for economic development – a promise that projections from last year's budget cannot reveal. Advocates of community control such as Bob Terrell of the GRNA and Curtis Davis suggested a long list of economic development strategies that an independent Greater Roxbury could use. These strategies range from direct negotiations with Japanese businesses that are thinking of locating plants in the Boston area to passage of a real estate speculation tax to control speculation and also to reclaim windfall profits. Other strategies include establishing consumer cooperatives for the distribution of food, clothing and housing. Mel King has also suggested a form of community-based economic planning through a 'community scoreboard' that would keep track of skills and resources and their allocation (King, 1986). This range of strategies seems more likely to succeed given the current hot investment environment in Greater Roxbury. As GRIP cofounder Andrew Jones put it, 'We're sitting on gold.'

Tanzania's Julius Nyerere has made a number of observations that seem relevant to the struggle to develop Roxbury. 'A country, or a village, or a community cannot *be* developed,' Nyerere argued, 'It can only develop itself. For real development means the development, the growth, of people' (Nyerere, 1974). Mel King made similar points in arguing that Mandela 'would mean making a break from a dependency model to work on what would ultimately be an interdependency model' (King, 1986). We think that the only prospect for development without displacement in Greater Roxbury lies along these lines.

The third claim of Mandela's foes was that separation was being sold as a cure-all for the Black community. But GRIP's literature was quite clear on this point: 'Q: Will incorporation solve all our problems? A: No. By incorporating as an independent city, we will acquire the tools necessary to solve our social, political, and economic problems.' GRIP's Davis explained, 'Democracy doesn't provide any guarantees. It just gives us an opportunity, with a government that's more accountable.'

In fact, by focusing on the narrow issue of separation, Mandela's critics obscured the most important choice for the Black community, between strategies of assimilation and community control. Advocates of assimilation argue that Blacks can get a 'piece of the action' by pushing their way into the dominant economic and political system. In practice, assimilation has meant building Black political machines and Black businesses and pushing for Black access to jobs. In some cities, the 'piece of the action' obtained by Blacks in this way has brought political gains for at least part of the Black community. Cities such as Detroit, Chicago and Atlanta, for example, have elected Black mayors. In Boston, where Blacks remain a minority, they have made some gains through assimilation: a Black City Council president and superintendent of schools; the 30 percent share for Black and other minority developers in the $400 million development deal mentioned earlier; a specified 25 percent share of construction jobs for people of color. The security of these limited concessions remains in question. As Mel King told reporter Vince Valvano of *City Life*, 'The question is, how did we get a Black president of the Council? How did we get a Black person to head the schools? They were not put there by the Black community. They can be taken out by the power of the people who put them in.'

The second strategy is community control over development and services – whether through reincorporation or other forms of local autonomy. Advocates of community control hope not just to break into the system, but in one corner of the system to actually change the rules of the game. Commented Bob Terrell of the Greater Roxbury Neighborhood Authority, 'It's nice that individuals have mobility from Boston's investment boom, but the masses of Black folks don't. ... To move everybody forward, we need community control.'

Terrell holds that incorporation of Mandela would only be one step toward such control: 'In itself, having a Black majority doesn't change the nature of the capitalist state. We need a form of democracy that deals with collectivities rather than just with individuals.' Terrell, Davis, King and many other activists struggled during the Mandela campaign (as well as before and since) to build an alternative vision of governance and community development for Roxbury.

If the advocates of Mandela saw incorporation as one tool in a broader strategy, why did the *Globe* and the City choose to cast the referendum as a single-issue vote? Mel King opined, 'It is my belief that they purposefully focused on racial divisiveness and separation as a way of keeping people from focusing on the real issue, and that is the control of the land' (King, 1986:2).

The outcome

On election day, the Mandela initiative went down to defeat by 75 percent to 25 percent. What are we to conclude from this lopsided margin?

The answer is not simple. For one thing, because of the shape of Boston's voter districts, 65 percent of those who voted on the Mandela question were white, although 74 percent of those living in Mandela are Black and 10 percent were Latino. But the margin of defeat was similar in all the wards involved, those with a mainly Black population as well as mainly white wards, so we don't believe that this was the key factor.

To some extent, it is appropriate to compare the referendum to the Puerto Rican vote for the pro-independence parties (which is consistently small) or the Québec plebiscite on independence (which was defeated). Like these other groups, Roxbury residents would take the risk of political and economic retaliation and isolation if they actually opted for separation. Dependency dies hard. The dominant ideology constantly drives home the notion that oppressed populations are incapable of handling their own affairs. On the face of it, the evidence – poverty, unemployment, high crime – seems to reinforce this notion. Thus, many of the 12,000 people who voted yes on Mandela were taking a step that required courage and consciousness.

It must be added that Mandela's advocates did not succeed in building broad support for or even understanding of the proposed change. GRIP started out with a narrow agenda, campaigned for only a few months, and did not build a grass-roots campaign. Groups like the GRNA came around late to support for Mandela, and although they integrated incorporation into a broader vision, they had limited success in communicating that vision to the Black community. Despite the hysteria of the *Globe* and Mayor Flynn, the Black community did not get excited about the issue: voter turnout was low, and there was nothing like the buzz of organizing and voter registration that accompanied Mel King's mayoral campaign.

Nonetheless, the referendum had a concrete political effect that constituted a positive opening in Boston politics. It highlighted the continuing problems of the Black community, revealing that racism is more than just racial epithets or physical attacks on Blacks. It placed the issue of community control – of land, development, services – squarely on the agenda. Although the *Globe* and city government spokespeople harped on the racial divisiveness of Mandela, *every* Black leader who spoke on the issue – including Wall and Stith – acknowledged the importance of increasing community control. As Mel King told *City Life*, 'I think that both sides [of the Black leadership] agree on the need to change the existing relationship [with City Hall]'; the disagreement was over what strategy to use.

Groups like the Greater Roxbury Neighborhood Authority and the Coalition for Community Control of Development continue to organize for community control in a variety of arenas. Boston's powers-that-be tried to use the Mandela referendum to discredit the GRNA and other Black groups and leaders that seek to pursue a community control strategy. We believe that instead, the debate over incorporation gave new visibility and a political boost to that strategy.

Lessons for Other Cities

The current situation of Roxbury may have some peculiarities, but it is in many ways symptomatic of the current situation of working-class communities of color in major US cities. Chief among these similarities is the problem of racism. It is a central determinant of the condition of life for neighborhoods like Roxbury, permeating every aspect of their economy, demographic structure, institutional environment, political situation. It created the ghetto, and rendered its occupants vulnerable to the abuses of the market and the state. When conditions determine that the ghetto is no longer desirable to the powers that be, its dissolution is facilitated, or perhaps more likely, its atomization and dispersal into separate smaller concentrations less likely to generate resistance and political power. Since racism has gained in strength in recent years, it is more likely that other centers of Black and Latino concentrations will find themselves under more vigorous attack in the near future.

Roxbury's location and its proximity to the growing central business district is also no anomaly. Black and Latino migrants to northern cities moved into locations abandoned by a labor force that had fled the city in similar conditions throughout the country. Disinvestment, whether planned (as in Roxbury's history of redlining) or market driven, is a common condition among Black and Latino neighborhoods. The majority of vacant land in Roxbury was in fact created through national, not local, programs of 'blight removal', urban renewal and highway construction. The 'triaging' of services is a national practice. The concentration of publicly subsidized housing now in danger of losing subsidies is a national problem.

But if new forms of abuse are taking shape in Boston and Roxbury, so are new forms of resistance and struggle. Central to the recent effort has been the Greater Roxbury Neighborhood Authority. In its vision of class alliances, its call for representation by 'sector' (tenants, homeowners, clergy, agencies, small business owners), and its attention to building broad, multi-ethnic coalitions, it reflects the lessons in the importance of unity of past struggles and political campaigns. In its effort to think in terms of neighborhood and local organizing, the GRNA reflects a growing trend by oppressed groups in this country to 'localize' their efforts in order to mobilize their bases. And in its potential for delivering some popular victories, it is a fountain of hope.

Notes

This is a September 1989 revision of an article published in *Antipode*, vol. 19, no. 2. Parts of this article appeared previously in *The North Star* 2, Fall 1985, and in 'Mandela, Massachusetts', which appeared in *Dollars and Sense*, March 1987. Much of our analysis is also based on conversations with Bob Terrell, Mel King and Curtis Davis.

1. Supporters of Roxbury's reincorporation have chosen *not* to use the word *secession*, although all the major media used that term. Secession is technically illegal under the Massachusetts Constitution, while the majority of the cities and towns of Massachusetts were formed by de-annexation and incorporation.

2. Quotations excerpted from press accounts (the *Boston Globe*, the *Guardian*, 29 October 1986, and *City Life*, Jan./Feb. 1987) and from interviews with Curtis Davis and Bob Terrell are not referenced separately.

References

Ball, J. 1986. 'From Tenants to Future Homeowners'. *Boston Globe*, 3 August.

Boston Arson Prevention Commission. 1986. 'Report to the Boston Redevelopment Authority on the Status of Arson in Dudley Square'. Boston: Boston Redevelopment Authority.

Boston Redevelopment Authority. 1982. 'District Profile of Roxbury'. Boston: Boston Redevelopment Authority.

Boston Redevelopment Authority. 1984. 'Dudley Square Plan: A Strategy for Neighborhood Revitalization'. Boston: Boston Redevelopment Authority.

Boston Redevelopment Authority. 1986. 'Parcel to Parcel Linkage Program; Interim Report; Project 1; Kingston/Bedford-Parcel 18'. Boston: Boston Redevelopment Authority.

Colón, M. 1984. Interview with the Executive Director of Nuestra Communidad Development Corporation. Unpublished.

Frisby, M.K. 1986. 'City Hall Declares Arson Study Flawed: Report Seen as Threat to Rehab Plans'. *Boston Globe*, 13 March.

Gastón, M. 1981. 'Community Participation in Boston's Southwest Corridor Project'. Unpublished Masters of Community Planning Thesis, Massachusetts Institute of Technology.

Gastón, M., and M. Kennedy, with B. Gomes-Beach, B. Kanter, J. Lescault. 1984. *Dudley in 2001: After the El, Center for Whom? Boston: University of Massachusetts at Boston.*

Gastón, M., and M. Kennedy 1985. *From Disinvestment to Displacement: The Redevelopment of Boston's Roxbury as a Case Study*. Boston: University of Massachusetts at Boston.

Geiser, K. 1970. *Urban Transportation Decision Making: Political Process of Urban Freeway Controversies*. Cambridge: Massachusetts Institute of Technology, .

Goldsmith, W. 1974. 'The Ghetto as a Resource for Black America'. *Journal of the American Institute of Planners*, January.

Greater Roxbury Incorporation Project. 1986. 'Greater Roxbury Incorporation Project: A New Municipality'.

Holland, D., and O. Oldman 1974. 'Estimating the Impact of 100% of Market Value Property Tax Assessments of Boston Real Estate'. Boston: Boston Urban Observatory.

Howard, M., and K. S. Rodrigues-Taylor. 1986. 'The Move to Secede: "Mandela" Supporters Say the Time to Part Has Come'. *Boston Herald*, 19 January.

Jennings, J. 1986. 'Towards Black Empowerment: The Question of Secession in Boston'. Unpublished MS, University of Massachusetts at Boston.

Kaufman, J. 1985. 'Roxbury Boom Troubling to Some'. *Boston Globe*, 12 April.

Kennedy, M. 1978. 'Why Roxbury Participation in the Housing Improvement Program is Minimal', Boston: Mayor's Office of Housing.

King, M. 1981. *Chain of Change: Struggles for Black Community Development*. Boston: South End Press.

King, M. 1986. 'Mandela'. Unpublished MS.

Malaspina, Ann. 1987. 'Roxbury: A Brighter Chapter Unfolds', *Boston Globe*, 18 April.

McDonough, J. 1975. 'Kevin White's Neighborhood Triage'. *Real Paper*, 20 November.

Menzies, I. 1985. 'A Clash over Dudley Square', *Boston Globe*, 12 March.

'Moving in Boston'. 1980. 'Moving in Boston: The Black Experience', Slide-tape show available from Museum of Afro-American History in Boston.

Nyerere, J. 1974. *Man and Development*. London.

O'Connor, J. 1973. *The Fiscal Crisis of the State*. New York: St. Martin's.

Roxbury Technical Assistance Project. 1986. '20-Year Projection of Residential Displacement in Roxbury', Unpublished MS, University of Massachusetts at Boston.

Smith, N. 1984. *Uneven Development*. New York: Basil Blackwell.

Smith, N., and M. LeFaivre 1984. 'A Class Analysis of Gentrification', in J. Palen and B. London (eds), *Gentrification, Displacement, and Neighborhood Revitalization*. Albany, N.Y.: State University of New York Press.

Tabb, W. 1970. *The Political Economy of the Black Ghetto*. New York: Norton.

4

Bernie Sanders and the Rainbow in Vermont

Ellen David-Friedman

The electoral landscape in Vermont has seen some dramatic changes in recent years. These include the Democratic takeover of all branches of state government and the landslide reelection of prominent liberal US Senator Patrick Leahy in 1986. To the left, there have been the nationally unparalleled four-term mayorality of socialist Bernie Sanders in Burlington, the succession of this seat of independent progressive Peter Clavelle in March 1989, and Sanders's near-miss run for Vermont's single US House seat in November 1988. There is also the surprising strength of Jesse Jackson's performance in 1984 and 1988 and the continuing activity of the Rainbow Coalition of Vermont (RCV) in supporting progressive legislative candidates. Both the mainstream and left press have found this transformation of the 'rock-ribbed Republican' backwater state into a liberal/progressive bastion an interesting phenomenon.

But for American socialists, the lessons to be learned from these developments are far from simple or definitive. There are, as in any situation, important local features (such as, in this case, the racial uniformity of the population, the lack of a developed industrial base and working class, and the historical absence of organized labor interests) that make our experience different from those outside Vermont.

But there are also some aspects of our experience that should be useful to anyone experimenting with left electoral strategies. Most important, there are some sharp questions that our experience allows us to examine from the basis of actual practice: what can the left take from its experience in mass-based issue organizing to the electoral arena? Can a strategy of working inside and outside the Democratic Party (proposed by Jesse Jackson and tested nowhere else so thoroughly as by the Rainbow Coalition of Vermont) really work?

Unlike some other states, Vermont has never had a strong left presence in the Democratic Party. For fifteen years there has been a consistent string of third party efforts – beginning with the Liberty Union Party in the early 1970s (with Bernie Sanders as one of its founders and regular candidates), to the Citizens Party (which had its first electoral success in Vermont when Terry Bouricius was elected to the Burlington City Council in 1981), and, currently, through the Progressive Coalition in Burlington (the organization, though only recently constituting itself as a party with caucus and nomination mechanisms, that has supported Sanders and the independent City Council members for the last seven years). These efforts have been propelled by progressive activists, generally operating with a class analysis, but not affiliated with national left parties. Their disdain for the Democratic Party was generally unequivocal.

The early impetus for and continuing strength of this trend drew on the migration of East Coast student radicals and counterculturalists to Vermont, beginning in the mid-1960s and not slacking until the late 1970s. There was a natural draw to this pristine, rugged and wide-open rural state for young people who gathered in their hands the various threads of environmentalism, 'back-to-the-land' self-sufficiency, antiauthoritarianism, mysticism and hedonism, and – in strong measure – a social utopianism fueled by rejection of the corrupt imperialist infrastructure that seemed, at the time, about to collapse. The busyness and fervor with which new structures were created at this time can barely be measured: collectives and communal farms, food cooperatives and health food stores, day care centers and alternative newspapers, and above all, political study groups and activist organizations and political parties that took their energetic charge from the antiwar movement and acted on the powerful impulse of the time to build a progressive alternative in the 'belly of the beast'.

The Liberty Union Party, successful even at a time when electoral politics was distinctly out of vogue with radicals, gained major party status in 1974 (this status is granted and retained in Vermont to parties that capture at least 5 percent of the vote for any statewide candidate), and maintained it until 1988. A party of explicitly anticapitalist ideology and addressing itself to the survival issues of poor people (utility rates, health care, housing), it supported the candidacies of some superbly smart and articulate radicals. But by the beginning of the 1980s it had lost its leadership (including Bernie Sanders), and ultimately its ability to mobilize to its base of support.

Independent Politics

By comparison with the rest of the country, an independent left approach to electoral politics in Vermont has recently found extraordinary success. This has been particularly true since Sanders's dramatic upset in 1981, when he won the Burlington mayoral race by ten votes. Since then, he has had considerable success in pursuing his program and evidenced great popularity in three subsequent elections. The Progressive Coalition has been able to find and field excellent candidates to the City Council (falling just short of a majority, but securing the ability to maintain a Sanders veto). Finally, Sanders made a credible showing in the governor's race in 1986 – where he won 15 percent of the vote as an independent socialist, although he was outspent ten to one by his opponents.

The base which, in other parts of the US, had constituted itself as the left wing of the Democratic Party (labor, progressive Blacks and Latinos, feminists) does not really exist in Vermont, and so the strategy of left infiltration of the Democratic Party – articulated in this period by the Democratic Socialists of America (DSA) – had not historically found many adherents on the left. Not until, that is, the dramatic effects of Jesse Jackson's 1984 presidential campaign began to have an impact on Vermont's left. The Jackson campaign galvanized that sector of activists who had been devoting themselves to issue organizing (tenant, anti-nuke, anti-intervention, civil rights) but not electoral work during the long post–Vietnam War period. With a late start, no budget, no minority base, and the debilitating effects of the 'Hymie' incident hitting just prior to the March 1984 Vermont primary, Jackson won only 8 percent of the vote at that early stage in the campaign.

However, a strategy of using Jackson's campaign to knit together and publicize a progressive issues program proved very dynamic. By the time the Democratic town caucuses were held in April, Jackson's share of the vote had risen to 14 percent; at the State Democratic Convention in June he captured

20 percent of Vermont's delegation to the National Convention. A swell of excitement about being able to defend a progressive program within the mainstream electoral arena also fueled the election of leftists to party posts. A publicly visible socialist, with no previous relationship to the Democratic Party, won the post of Democratic National Committeewoman at the State Convention. Rainbow activists were elected to posts in town, county and state Democratic committees.

The crafting of the state party platform was commandeered by the Rainbow, resulting in an outspoken – even radical – document. Many of the state's most seasoned issue leaders were drawn into this arena, incited by Jackson's audacious challenge to conservative Democratic policies. Despite Jackson's routing by center/reactionary national Democrats at the 1984 Democratic Convention, or perhaps because of his dignified and principled response, the forces that had comprised his Vermont campaign were eager to stay together.

The next stage of development began immediately without a period of consolidation or strategizing. Events overtook the moment as several leading progressive activists decided to run for state legislative office, publicly upholding their Rainbow identification while running as Democrats. Five out of seven Rainbow Democrats were elected to the state legislature. A long-time Central America activist with no previous electoral experience won the Democratic primary for Vermont's single congressional seat, and went on to run a dynamic and issue-oriented race against five-term incumbent Representative Jim Jeffords.

The election period was a time when progressives were bringing to bear their considerable expertise in grass-roots organizing and issue development in a more mainstream setting than most had ever operated in before. What in other states are absolutely necessary skills for an election campaign (voter identification, phone polling, major fundraising events, expensive media campaigns) could more easily be glossed over in Vermont – at least the first time out – because local elections are still generally amateur events.

Consequently, the lack of experience in traditional electoral techniques did not set progressives back, at least at this juncture. There were fresh working alliances with Democratic Party stalwarts, which lent the progressives – who had long operated on the margins of political life – a sense of new opportunity. Party Democrats welcomed the energy and tenacity of the 'newcomers', and responded in a variety of ways to indicate their openness to the left forces. One telling example was the willingness of the State Compliance Committee (overseeing the rules for delegate selection to the Democratic National Convention) to defy the Democratic National Committee and reduce the threshold for delegate selection from 20 percent to 10 percent, the position advocated by the Jackson campaign. To all appearances, the Jackson campaign was the spark for reinvigoration of the state Democratic Party.

Inside/Outside the Democratic Party

The honeymoon between the Rainbow left and the Democratic Party was, however, short-lived. One of the Rainbow's first considered acts in statewide electoral politics (after Jackson's elimination from the presidential race) was to decline to endorse the Democratic nominee for governor, Madeline Kunin, on the principled ground of not supporting 'lesser of two evilism' politics. Kunin, though she was a woman and though she had been a liberal at the start of her political career, then strongly supported by feminists and labor, was not a progressive in the left-tilted context of Vermont in 1984. Rainbow leadership (including the Rainbow Co-Chair, who had been elected to the Democratic National Committee) often pointed publicly to this nonendorsement as evidence of their inside/outside relationship to the Democratic Party – a theme that would only become more pronounced as time went on.

The debate ignited by the spark of the Rainbow's refusal to endorse Kunin has continued for the last four years. On the Rainbow side, the spectrum of positions has run from 'We should become an independent political party' to 'We should function as the left wing of the Democratic Party', with the strength of the former position considerably outweighing that of the latter.

The Democrats' reaction was predictably ambivalent. Liberal Democrats at first believed that an active 'progressive wing' would strengthen their influence within the party, but quickly saw that this particular group was not interested in being a tame left wing. When it became clear that Rainbow activists intended to maintain political independence, angry denunciations of the Rainbow's refusal to endorse Kunin mounted. An unsuccessful effort was made to remove the errant Democratic

National Committeewoman from her seat.

Conflicting tendencies within the party came to the fore, and those who did not want to lose the new activists argued for tolerance – the position which, more or less, ended up carrying the day. The Democratic State Party Chair, who led the purge efforts, was not supported by his own Executive Committee and resigned shortly thereafter.

The arguments in favor of not alienating the Rainbow forces drew their rationale from the recent political history of Burlington. The lesson that far-sighted Democrats drew in 1984 was that they should do anything they could to avoid creating a 'Burlington situation' throughout Vermont.

Burlington: Progressives versus Democrats

Bernie Sanders's razor-thin victory in the 1981 mayoral race came over an old-line 'machine' Democrat (insofar as a city of 35,000 in an all-Republican state can claim machine politics). The city seemed nearly uniformly excited that a boring, increasingly complacent era was being swept away by new winds. Sanders fought tough and exhausting battles to make the new city administration effective in creative and audacious ways. His popularity zoomed among progressives (who had initially taken a stand-off attitude toward his campaign), unions and poor people.

With the support of several talented progressives elected to the Burlington City Council (some as independents, some on a Progressive Coalition slate, and one as a Citizens Party candidate), as well as an extraordinarily talented cadre of progressives in city administration appointments, many policy initiatives were undertaken. The Sanders administration found ways to fight the private utilities, including imposing fees, challenging monopoly franchises, and redesigning rate structures to benefit residential customers and reassign the burden to commercial users. Sanders worked to greatly enlarge the available stock of moderate-income housing in the city through creative grant work, the development of a land trust, and restrictions on condominium conversion.

The administration sought to promote alternative – as well as more mainstream – economic development, to fight for and win important changes in local taxing authority to reduce reliance the regressive property tax, and to initiate innovative programs primarily affecting women and children. These last included the state's only municipally funded day care center and a shelter for battered women (both of which spun successfully off into independent enterprises), an afterschool program for the children of working parents, a Women's Council, a city ordinance requiring the employment of a set percentage of women on any construction work contracted by the city, and women's self-defense classes. Sanders's mundane, but equally impressive, exercises of public authority also won adherents – including housecleaning of deadwood in the government, a move to institute competitive bidding for public contracts, and an upgrading of street repair and public services in general.

More controversial was Sanders' unwavering commitment to having a 'foreign policy', one, not surprisingly, characterized by outspoken anti-imperialism and public activism. Burlington City Hall became host to every major demonstration, and the site of regular speaking engagements. The city divested itself early of South African investments and established an extremely important Sister City relationship with the Nicaraguan city of Puerto Cabezas, which has been the springboard for some of the most effective material aid campaigns in the entire state. Sanders used every opportunity to link conditions and issues within Burlington to the national and international economic context, and to challenge Reaganism and imperialism in its every manifestation. This tenacious refusal to allow any false isolation of 'local' politics from global politics has been one of the most heated points of dispute among Sanders' critics – and one of his highlights for the left.

Overarching these specific policy initiatives has been a single accomplishment, probably unmatched anywhere in the US: Burlington has become a politicized town, with an uniquely informed and motivated electorate, with passionate contests waged for virtually every modest public post, and with debate proceeding on the true issues of political life: who has power and how are they using it. And this happened in the context of the only town in the country that has a three-party political system. For its extraordinary ability to take a fluke electoral win and turn it into the most powerful progressive political entity in the nation, the Progressive Coalition earned deep enmity in some quarters.

Perhaps not surprisingly, the most unyielding opponents of the Progressive Coalition in Burlington were the Democrats, who had been summarily knocked down to 'third party' status and found themselves abandoned by their own most forward-thinking supporters. On the Board of Aldermen, where pitched battles were regularly fought out, Democrats consistently sought alliances with the Republicans rather than the Progressive Coalition. In part because of this antagonistic relationship (and in part because of Sanders's personal disgust for bourgeois parties and their hold on American politics), the Progressive Coalition came to embody an institutional anti–Democratic Party pole – expressed most dogmatically by Sanders himself.

When Jesse Jackson made his single Vermont campaign visit in 1984 and went to pay a call on Sanders in City Hall (having been incorrectly led to believe that he would find a warm welcome), Sanders gave him the cold shoulder. In like fashion, Sanders upbraided any members of his administration – and there were many – who worked on the Congressional campaign of Rainbow Democrat Anthony Pollina. (It should be noted that this very inflexibility on Sanders's part, exposed as it was in the popular campaigns of Jackson and Pollina, became the source of later estrangement for a number of his chief political aides, who argued that progressives should not engage in doctrinaire posturing during this period. Several of them have become staff members and organizers in progressive – not necessarily Rainbow – Democratic electoral campaigns.)

This atmosphere of hostility to the Democrats created a situation in which Rainbow leaders in Burlington, pursuing a strategy of working with the Democrats when appropriate, were held in suspicion by the Progressive Coalition. Several members of the State Legislature who had been elected as Rainbow Democrats were viewed with disdain (despite their willingness to support Sanders's agenda in the Legislature) until they publicly endorsed a Progressive Coalition candidate in an aldermanic run-off race against a Republican in 1986. In this episode, the Democratic candidate had been knocked out of the contest, and Democratic Party leaders, to avoid giving any aid at all to the Progressive Coalition, threw their support behind the right-wing (Citizens for America) Republican contender.

When the Rainbow legislators endorsed the Progressive Coalition candidate, city Democratic leaders freely threatened that they would never win another election in Burlington. They tried to make good on this threat in the 1986 legislative elections by writing in several old-line Democrats on the Republican line to challenge the Rainbow Democrat incumbents.

These Republican/Democrats were handily defeated, signaling a realignment process in Burlington the dimensions of which are broad and possibly enduring. Another and crucially indicative event in this realignment trend was the nomination of a conservative Democrat to go head-to-head with Sanders in his January 1987 bid for a fourth term as mayor, with agreement from the Republicans to stay out of the race. Burlington, after six years, was once again having a two-party election contest: the Progressives against the Republicrats. The Progressives won again; the fusion Republican/Democrat candidate was routed.

The Sanders Wild Card

It could be argued that, were it not for Bernie Sanders and his central position in any progressive electoral strategy for Vermont, the Rainbow Coalition could well have devolved into a left wing of the Democratic Party. Certainly the individual decisions taken by many Rainbow activists to run for legislative office in 1986 as Democrats rather than independents would have logically led to close functional relationships – the sharing of lists, resources, money and expertise. And even were this trend actively struggled against on the theoretical front by proponents of a third party within the Rainbow, the material realities of campaigning as a Democrat tend to move candidates towards the party's center.

This slide towards the comfortable middle was not an option for the Rainbow, because Sanders was, and is, a reality to be reckoned with by all of Vermont's progressives. And it was his long-nurtured desire to compete seriously in the governor's race that came to shape the Rainbow strategy in 1986 more than any other single factor. Beginning with the debate over whether he should run in 1986, advancing through the question of the Rainbow Coalition's relationship to his campaign, and continuing still through the postelectoral analysis and projected game plan for 1988, the features of Bernie Sanders's own political style and strategy have dominated the discussion.

Sanders is a complicated player in a complicated game, yet his favorite summary statement for any political conundrum is 'Look, it's really not all that complicated,' meaning, almost invariably, 'We are acting out the class struggle, and any situation can be analyzed in that light.' That he has often been out of step with the times in his life-long quest to resist bourgeois cooptation, while at the same time competing for public power, is demonstrable (although some of his left critics – notably the grouping of Greens coalesced around anarchist philosopher Murray Bookchin – argue that he has sold out the working class on various issues). That he is a difficult personality is universally agreed – driven, demanding, and unlikely to take the time to build trust or consensus with allies.

But it remains that the most important thing to say about Bernie Sanders is that he is one of the only major officeholders in the United States in this decade to fight for a radical, class-based political program as a socialist. If he has not built a powerful independent party, if he has not advanced socialist goals sufficiently through his municipal government, if he has alienated key supporters through personal arrogance and failed to create alliances that could have been made (the categories of criticism most frequently leveled at him from the left), these are the difficult features of his style of leadership. And while the problems that flow from his style have been burdensome in Burlington politics, they surged to the fore when Sanders began discussing a race for governor.

The Progressive Coalition members of the Burlington Board of Aldermen and the city administration, as well as street-level activists throughout Burlington, were nearly unanimous in opposing a Sanders campaign for governor in 1986. Their reasons covered a range of opinion: many did not want to risk losing the gains made in Burlington; others feared that Sanders lacked a sufficient base and contacts outside Burlington and that he would suffer ignominious defeat; some argued that a race against an incumbent woman Democrat was an illogical splitting of the progressive vote.

But another, more uniform sentiment also bound the Progressive Coalition forces in their view of Sanders's plan. Nearly everyone agreed that Sanders would not seek input from his supporters, and that he would not respond to ideas that differed from his own judgement. It has become a given among Progressive Coalition activists that Sanders makes up his own mind – a feature of his leadership that is sometimes brilliant (when a seemingly cockeyed intuition proves to be just right) but is almost always deeply disturbing to progressives who value democratic processes. As, one by one, the stalwarts of previous mayoral campaigns indicated their unwillingness to be drawn into what they considered an ill-conceived campaign, Sanders turned deliberately to the Rainbow Coalition, which was organized statewide.

The Rainbow and the Sanders Campaign

The tendencies within the Rainbow that had kept it floating for several years both inside and outside the Democratic Party were set at furious odds against one another when the question of supporting Sanders for governor came up. It was not a question of people actually coming to Governor Kunin's defense; far from it. Kunin had managed, in her two years in office, to disappoint most progressives in all sectors – labor, social services, teachers and environmentalists – with an infuriatingly cautious, often neo-liberal approach to public policy. Rather, it was the prospect of having to defy both the Democratic Party and the hegemony of the two-party system by opposing Kunin, that seemed to create panic.

These arguments came wrapped in pragmatism ('Sanders can't win anyway, and we will burn our bridges to Kunin') or veered off into irrelevance ('Why doesn't he run for Congress' against – it should be noted – the Republican incumbent who had been unbeatable for six terms, and who even the Democrats did not challenge in 1986). Nor were people explicitly defending the Democratic Party, but rather the access to the party that progressives had secured over the previous three years. Those who argued that support for Sanders would cause a definitive break with the party generally took themselves out of active Rainbow participation as the campaign proceeded. This, if it were to be labeled, would have to be called the 'right' opposition position.

The 'left' opposition within the Rainbow was qualitatively quite different. Here the concern was focused on Sanders and his own history – one that is characterized by a clear lack of emphasis on organization building and democratic processes. For those Vermont progressives with a commitment to left independent politics, there is a strong appetite for bottom-up, grass-roots democracy. Sanders is widely understood to be – by his own choice and description – outside this trend, leaving him oddly isolated from his best natural base of progressive issue activists. But at the same time and almost in spite of themselves, it was these same activists who were most compelled by his program, his powerful rhetoric and his unique ability to reach poor and working-class people with the zeal of a class fighter.

This group – representing, ultimately, the dominant position within the Rainbow – came to believe, perhaps with some degree of wishful thinking, that Sanders's own anti-organization stance could be overcome by the Rainbow's plan for base-building. The Sanders campaign, which the Rainbow eventually supported both formally and through the transplanting of its central administrative staff to the campaign, was to be run along a grass-roots organizing model. It hoped that the same sort of disenfranchised constituencies that came into the Jackson campaign and ended up mingling with progressive organizers would also be galvanized by Sanders and stick around to constitute a broad community base for ongoing progressive activity.

Initial chaos mingled with euphoria characterized the beginning of the Sanders campaign. A faint air of conspiracy attended those who, early on, called the office or asked for campaign buttons. Some Democratic officeholders, angry at Kunin and glad to have a way to put her on notice, made some guarded overtures to Sanders. People stopped at campaign events to say that they had never voted in their lives, but that they would vote for Bernie. But rather quickly, these isolated incidents gave way to the harsh realities of an independent challenge.

There were three natural constituencies that progressives could expect to carry the weight of such an ambitious campaign: the unequivocally independent left (whose most highly experienced forces were concentrated in Burlington); the inside/outside Rainbow cadre (centered in Montpelier); and the natural – but often unformed – leaders among poor and working-class networks. If all these elements had enthusiastically and harmoniously come together in the campaign, perhaps the most formidable obstacles (fundraising, media and political organization) could have been overcome. As it was, the earliest – and perhaps most debilitating – reality the campaign had to face was the withholding of energies by all of these groups.

Attempts to draw some Progressive Coalition strategists, fundraisers and organizers into the early parts of the campaign were largely, though not entirely, unsuccessful. The pervasive attitude of members of the Sanders administration in Burlington and Progressive Coalition leaders was guarded. People felt, justifiably, that since they had not advocated a gubernatorial campaign, they could not be expected to drop everything to work on it once Bernie made his own decision. A consensus instead emerged that the city administration, and the Progressive Coalition as a political organization, needed to work on surviving Sanders's departure (even if only for the duration of a campaign).

The questions of maintaining a vigorous city government, of developing a new generation of popular and effective leaders, and of maturing past the stage of being a Sanders phenomenon, were very much in people's minds. The result of these attitudes was a tremendous loss of needed talent and experience from the early campaign work. Since this group included the closest of Sanders's colleagues, friends and supporters from his mayoral tenure, he also suffered from a personal isolation in this endeavor that took its own toll. It is, however, difficult to consider this problem of support from the Burlington forces as broadly instructive for the left elsewhere in the country. For one thing, it was Sanders's style of highly individual decision-making that created the atmosphere of reserve among his supporters – and not any disapproval among them for his ultimate goal of higher political office. In fact, it was the wide support for him as a public leader that eventually brought many of these forces into the campaign towards its conclusion.

Equally problematic was the response or, rather, lack of it, from left/progressive activists outside Burlington. From the start a nucleus of experienced organizers, located primarily within the Rainbow Coalition, committed themselves to the Sanders campaign as their central task for a six-month period. This group was characterized both by its years of involvement in many issue constituencies in the state, and also by its limited investment in the Democratic Party. It is probably fair to describe the view of the Democratic Party held by this group as tactical, not strategic. (One Rainbow leader argued this way: we need to view the Democratic Party as a community organizing target, and not as the community organization itself.)

Central to any success that this group could achieve in supporting Sanders would be the response from other issue leaders. Since Sanders pulled no punches on his positions on the issues (calling for the shutdown of Vermont's only nuclear power plant, progressive tax reform, a major reemphasis on social services, aggressive targeting of corporate polluters, support for the struggling family farm economy, etc.), the campaign generally believed that leaders in these issue areas would energetically rally behind his candidacy. Further, there was little concern that loyalty to the Democratic Party would be a problem because neither Kunin nor the Democratic Party in the state had actively courted or aided these issue leaders in any consistent way. This assessment proved to be profoundly naive, however. As the campaign unfolded, the struggle with the liberal/progressive center forces more and more dominated strategy.

The unexpected dynamic that displayed itself from the outset and that was not resolved until perhaps the last two weeks of the campaign (and only then because of a mini-scandal that erupted in the Kunin administration), was the state of frozen ambivalence in which many progressives found themselves. People who had no trouble engaging in civil disobedience to protest the *contra* war in Nicaragua, who organized in their churches for nuclear freeze resolutions, who lobbied their legislators for divestment – in short, people who saw their lives as dedicated to political activism – were entirely unwilling to face the implications of an independent electoral challenge.

Rather than fight for a bourgeois politician (although, to be sure, there were those who offered a defense of Kunin because she was a woman and 'not bad' on many issues), the majority simply opted to sit out this historic race. People did not even want to debate the issue but rather consigned it to some highly personal, almost moral, sphere and kept their thoughts private. Energies flowed instead toward the much cleaner race between incumbent Democratic Senator Patrick Leahy and his rich businessman opponent, Republican Dick Snelling. Leahy had a wealth of volunteers and a campaign infrastructure that was extraordinary. His staff included many leaders of progressive issue groups (such as one of Sanders's most talented former administration members). Money poured into the Leahy campaign, with the surplus so substantial that Leahy was able to donate money to the struggling Kunin campaign. This was the way for many to displace their disquiet over the Sanders-Kunin choice by simply avoiding it.

Without this stratum of support – its organizing expertise, its contacts and ability to influence networks, and, most definitely, its ability to raise money – there was hardly a realistic possibility of organizing the third natural constituent base. Without knowledgeable organizers to build the structure, those Sanders supporters with no ambivalence towards the campaign (poor and working-class Vermonters) could not be effectively moved.

The requirements of voter registration, voter identification and voter mobilization among the disenfranchised constituencies are, minimally, enough money and enough volunteers to beat the bushes in the trailer parks, backwoods, and tenements to produce a noticeable vote. The Sanders campaign was not able to muster these resources. When Sanders, facing these severe limitations and unwilling to withdraw from the campaign, decided to forge ahead, the entire staff was laid off and reorganized with volunteers. The headquarters was relocated from Montpelier to Burlington and the strategy entirely redrafted to reflect the limited financial and human resources.

Fundraising for the Sanders campaign was, not surprisingly, extremely difficult. Institutional sources that historically had supported the progressive wing of the Democratic Party were generally entirely hostile to a third-party candidate. Even those labor unions whose national leadership was linked to Jesse Jackson and the Rainbow Coalition (such as the International Association of Machinists and its social democratic president William Winpisinger) would not break ranks with a Democratic incumbent. Sanders won support from only a few union locals, including the small but outspoken United Electrical Workers Council in Vermont. This lack of union support was particularly galling in light of Sanders's outstanding track record on labor and class-based issues.

Women's organizations were keenly antagonistic, despite Sanders's far more aggressive support for the state ERA referendum (which shared the November ballot), and his generally stronger record on feminist issues than Kunin. The state's environmental groups, long a conduit of significant campaign funds from national sources, snubbed Sanders entirely. In fact, so thorough was the financial blacklisting by Vermont and Washington-based liberal organizations that even a nonpartisan voter registration project, organized by an assortment of Vermont groups including the Rainbow Coalition of Vermont (RCV) and entirely separate from the Sanders campaign, was boycotted by half a dozen foundations.

In all quarters the rationale was the same: 'There is a Democrat in office. Let's not risk splitting the vote and electing a Republican.' Decades of 'two partyism' have left deep instincts of habit and fear, so that even progressive donors who fund left-issue organizations of every sort shrink from the terror of 'risking Republicanism'. This is an ironic feature of our political landscape that will continue to hobble serious third party efforts, while leaving intact the issue organizations from which these parties often spring.

Sanders turned to a small core of very committed supporters in Burlington to continue his campaign – relying more on public appearances, free media and debates (all arenas in which he excels and could use effectively to promote a superb platform) than on grass-roots organizing and voter registration. Although the problem of money was never overcome, Sanders maintained a broad and serious presence in the governor's race. Sanders was not dismissed as marginal, and, in fact, exerted leftward pressure around issues that many had hoped for – moving both the Democrat and Republican candidates along in areas of taxes, utilities and nuclear power. His campaign did not ignite, but neither was it ignored, and he received a credible 15 percent of the vote in November, enough to rob Kunin of her required 50 percent majority by 2 percentage points and bring the election to the Legislature for formal ratification.

Rainbow/Democratic Legislative Campaigns

In addition to Sanders's independent campaign for governor, 1986 saw a raft of Rainbow/Democratic legislative campaigns in Vermont. The issues Sanders ran on, and even the principle of his independent candidacy, were central to many of the Rainbow/Democratic legislative campaigns. This is not surprising since the RCV had determined to support (through recruitment, fundraising and technical campaign work) candidates – both Democrat and independent – based on their demonstrated commitment to the RCV platform. Sanders met this criterion, as did about a dozen legislative candidates (including half a dozen from the RCV Steering Committee, of whom half were elected).

The inside/outside strategy flowered in all its complexity during a protracted period when these legislative candidates, running as Democrats with clear RCV identification, were debating whether to support Sanders publicly. The question was never whether to support Kunin, but whether to remain studiously neutral on the question. The price of endorsing Sanders, it was felt, would be to risk sabotage from the party and/or the media for betraying the 'top of the ticket'. As the campaigns unfolded, individual choices were made by candidates – with those who were most deeply committed to the RCV openly endorsing Sanders and often, consequently, fighting brushfires on both the right and the left. Andrew Christiansen, the co-chair of the RCV and a native Vermonter who still lives on his parents' dairy farm, was attacked in a newspaper display ad taken out by a Republican town official one day before the election: 'Andrew Christiansen is running for State Representative from East Montpelier. He belongs to the Rainbow Coalition of Vermont and he supports Bernie Sanders for Governor.' Christiansen was elected. On the other hand, Liz Blum, a RCV leader and long-time progressive activist and Rainbow/Democratic candidate for State Senate, was actively undermined by liberal Democrats in her home county for publicly campaigning with Sanders. She, unfortunately, lost.

While the incontrovertible evidence is that the Vermont Democratic Party as a whole has moved leftward while achieving majority status, and specifically that its elected officeholders in the State House and Senate are increasingly liberal, the role of the RCV within it was constricted by its alignment with Sanders. As long as the RCV played a gadfly role, as long as it proclaimed political independence without actualizing it, to that degree liberal elements within the party could identify with its 'loyal opposition' role. However, the Sanders campaign – and the RCV's public support – polarized those elements into a dramatically anti–third party stance.

Repeatedly, these party liberals advocated Sanders's entry into a Democratic primary. This, they argued, would make it possible for them to support him and his progressive program. Otherwise, he would need to be punished for not playing by the rules, and suffer the consequences of losing liberal support and financing. (Since Sanders himself disdained this liberal element and did not look to them for support, he was unmoved by their arguments and undaunted by their rejection.) And, if anything, this rupture between the RCV and the Democratic Party did not surprise the leadership: its goal had been to move the party to the left on issues, while simultaneously challenging the party internally and externally by support of third-party candidates. The aim, at this stage, was not to initiate an independent political party, but to draw constituents to a specific independent candidate as an achievable step in the direction of building a third party. Although the number of party Democrats who supported Sanders was, apparently, quite small, the credibility and seriousness of an independent candidate became a matter of record, not theory. This, by itself, contributed to the forward movement of independent electoral politics and the erosion of two-party hegemony in a tangible way.

The 1988 Races

In 1988 Vermont's only US House seat came open after twelve years of incumbancy by Republican Jim Jeffords. Sanders entered the race as an independent. He immediately drew more support than he had two years earlier in his run for governor, partly because the seat was open (with no incumbent Democrat to dump), as well as because of some general sense that Sanders's powerful identification with foreign and national policy concerns coincided more clearly with a national office. This open congressional seat – more and more a rarity in US politics these days – also had an intoxicating effect on the Democrats, and a crowded primary season ensued. The effects of the party being pulled leftward were evident in this unusual primary, which pitted two of the party's leading liberals against a prominent labor Democrat of increasingly liberal tendencies and a progressive Black female university professor. Progressive activists around the state, as in the 1986 campaign, were somewhat divided among these choices – although much more energy coalesced around Sanders from the start.

The RCV, already in high gear for Jesse Jackson's presidential campaign, was approached by Sanders and all four Democratic candidates for an endorsement. A decision to endorse Sanders again alienated certain elements within the Rainbow who had favored one of the more convincing liberal Democrats, Presdient Pro Tem of the Vermont Senate Peter Welch. But when Welch was narrowly defeated in the primary by more moderate House Majority Leader Paul Poirier, labor's choice, the progressive consensus firmly reestablished itself around Sanders.

In this campaign, Sanders was both a source and beneficiary of a tremendously strong campaign for Jesse Jackson in the state. The maturity and organizational capacity developed by the RCV in the four years since Jackson's last campaign paid off with an energetic and broad effort – this in spite of the fact that virtually every Democratic office-holder came out early for Dukakis, and that Vermont's next-door-neighbor relation to Massachusetts was counted on to deliver the state for him.

Compared with his hands-off apporach to Jackson in 1984, this time around Sanders was a visible and enthusiastic supporter and appeared with him during one of Jackson's two campaign visits to Vermont. When Jackson won the presidential primary in May 1988, it gave an enormous psychological boost to progressives and was particularly felt as it rippled back through Sanders's campaign. A dynamic of reinforcing excitement was palpable between the two campaigns, causing Democratic regulars to comment with increasing frequency in the press that the 'technical' organizing skills that progressives were wielding didn't necessarily reflect the political views of Vermonters.

The 'authentic' political views of a population are always hard to interpret – particularly when the indicators are electoral results. The facts of the 1988 elections in Vermont were these: Jesse Jackson won the Democratic presidential primary and George Bush carried the state in the general election. A Republican won the race for US Congress, but Bernie Sanders lost it by a mere 3 percentage points. Both the Jackson and Sanders victories (it cannot be called less when an independent socialist comes that close to being elected to the US Congress) must reflect not only good effort on the part of progressives, but the tapping of some well of populism that is, minimally, neither racist nor reactionary (as some tendencies of American populism have been).

The Succession in Burlington

In March 1989, another crucial test was waiting for Vermont progressives. Burlington's Progressive Coalition activists, hardly recovered from the rigors of the November election, had to face a race for mayor, as Sanders definitively declined to run for a fifth term. Sanders's director of economic development for the last six years, a native Vermonter of working-class and 'regular' Democratic background, Peter Clavelle, was nominated by the Progressive Coalition. Opponents of all stripes were waiting for this moment of vulnerability. The Democrats and Republicans (perhaps the name 'Conservative Coalition' would be apt here) ran a fusion candidate who they hoped would break the progressive winning streak in the city. From another direction came a challenge by the Burlington Greens, who ran attorney and long-time left activist Sandra Baird for mayor and two other Greens for City Council seats. This move didn't herald, but rather capped, a long and bitter split between the Greens and the Progressive Coalition – an antipathy that periodically flamed over issues of development and the environment, the two areas on which the Greens most consistently attacked Sanders and his administration. But the regular bouts of verbal bashing and occasional hostile campaigns (as during a still-controversial epsode in which the Sanders administration attempted to pass a public referendum for development of Burlington's waterfront, while the Greens successfully organized against it, claiming that it represented gentrification), accelerated precipitously during the mayoral race into ideological warfare.

Until this moment, the Greens' public statements (accurately reflecting the anarchist perspective of their leader Murray Bookchin), had showed distain for an electoral strategy and instead had emphasized building a broad-based grass-roots movement that could sweep before it massive structural and economic change. Running for office was a distinct change of strategy for the Burlington Greens, and left Progressive Coalition leaders feeling, and charging, that the Green electoral challenges were not serious but merely spiteful. In Progressive Coalition circles, it was common to hear the analysis that the Greens had been unwilling to mount a campaign against the wildly popular Sanders, and that they were running at this moment to exploit the perceived weakness of an open mayoral seat.

Other standard charges emerged on both sides: the Progressive Coalition argued that this split of votes would cost the city its progressive administration; the Greens responded that the Progressive Coalition was in fact no different from the Democrats and Republicans, so that such an outcome wouldn't matter. Publicly, Clavelle ran on the strong record of accomplishment during Sanders's tenure, and publicly, Baird said that any economic prosperity in this period in Burlington had accrued to the affluent, while class stratification and homelessness grew. Privately, the Progressive Coalition activists were furious over the refusal of Greens to work with them and even angrier that the Greens seemed willing to turn the mayoral race into a PC–Green fight and leave the Democrat/Republican entirely unchallenged in public statements and debates.

Both the bourgeois and the left press of course found this a compelling story. The possibility that one of the most important independent-progressive city administrations in the country might be seriously threatened both alerted and activated progressives beyond Burlington. Drawing on the base from the Rainbow Coalition and the Jackson campaign, Clavelle was able to raise money and volunteers in abundance, while the skill and experience of Progressive Coalition workers, who had been mounting campaigns for eight years, shaped an efficient effort.

The outcome was not really close: Clavelle won handily, and Baird drew only about 3 percent of the vote. The two Green candidates for City Council fared better (winning between 15 and 20 percent of the vote in the races), but neither was elected. As a footnote, Progressive Coalition City Council member Erhard Mahnke was unexpectedly elected President of the Council, which still lacked a Progressive Coalition majority. The succession from Sanders to another PC mayor was profoundly reassuring to progressives in Burlington and elsewhere, and Clavelle's first six months in office have been marked by a consistency of progressive character.

Next ...

The left in Vermont has just had an anniversary party: on 13 and 14 June 1989, five hundred people attended the Second Vermont Solidarity Conference, the first having coincided with both Reagan's and Sanders's elections in 1981. Sanders, Clavelle and other PC activists were on hand to debate the Greens, but this was just one theme against a background of evaluation and planning among the hundreds of activists who attended. Other discussions focused on the reaction to recent changes in the National Rainbow Coalition made by Jesse Jackson, and the implications of those changes for the Vermont Rainbow, the linking of environmental work (ever more imperative) with other progressive activism, and the tremendous ferment in the communist world. An extraordinary decade of activity in Vermont was reviewed, and the movement continues.

5

New York: David Dinkins Opens the Door

Barbara Day

When Manhattan Borough President David Dinkins, a native son of Harlem, made history in September 1989 by becoming the first African-American to win New York City's Democratic mayoral nomination, the left, too, emerged victorious. That loosely aligned network of politically progressive, grass-roots and social action groups had been in eclipse for more than a decade but successfully reasserted itself and coalesced around the Dinkins primary campaign to stop Mayor Ed Koch's bid for a fourth term.

Dinkins won by a margin that surprised his supporters – 51 percent to 42 percent. The coalition that gave him victory prominently and productively included labor, the Black church, women, gays and lesbians, Black nationalists and white activists in the city's anti-racist movement, and made the most of voters' disenchantment with the Koch administration. In many ways the coalition marshalled a quiet revolution against the forces that swept Koch to power in 1977 and that kept him there for twelve years.

Two other Democrats in the race, City Comptroller Harrison Goldin and former Metropolitan Transportation Authority Chair Richard Ravitch, ran campaigns that never caught fire, making the primary a race between Koch and Dinkins. Goldin and Ravitch, despite informative campaigns, garnered only 7 percent of the vote between them.

Election results showed that Dinkins carried 96 percent of the Black vote, his main base of support, and capitalized on a well-run campaign of fusion politics, capturing 56 percent of the Latino vote, 56 percent of the city's growing Asian vote and

30 percent of the white vote – confounding claims that a Black candidate can never get more than 22 percent of the white vote the first time around.

Primary night newspaper and network exit polls profiled an electorate fed up with racial tension, corruption, homelessness, drugs and crime. Post-election figures indicated that Dinkins also did well with women, besting Koch by more than a 5 to 4 margin. City workers supported Dinkins 2 to 1, and he won the union household vote by more than 3 to 2.

In addition, Dinkins was endorsed at strategic points during the primary campaign by former New York mayors Abraham Beam, the city's first Jewish mayor, and John Lindsay, the city's last Republican chief executive; he also had the solid backing of a labor coalition that included the largely Black and Latino District Council 37, the United Federation of Teachers and the Hospital Workers of 1199.

Union support and independent grass-roots mobilization, along with Democratic Party endorsements in Manhattan and the Bronx and backing from rebellious Black and Latino Democrats in Brooklyn and Queens, gave Dinkins the edge in getting out the primary vote. While Koch had the support of the police union, the Democratic Party apparatus in Staten Island and at the eleventh hour, white Democrats in Queens, his campaign never matched Dinkins' reserve of about 10,000 volunteer campaign workers.

'On primary night, the left won a major victory,' said David Lerner of Riptide Communications, a public relations firm providing media advice, skills and strategy to the progressive community. 'Just look at the broad sweep of progressives who supported him. He didn't shrink from identification with the Rainbow.' While some leftists argue that Dinkins is really little more than a left-leaning centrist, Lerner countered that 'in the context of New York City politics, and the issues which affect people here, like the relationship between the real estate lobby to the issue of homelessness, Dinkins is not in the center on that issue. His intentions are good.' On the feminist issue of choice and the rights of lesbians and gays, representatives of both communities said that he has acted honorably. But Lerner, like other members of the coalition that supported Dinkins, cautioned that progressives must be mindful of the enormous pressure he will be subject to from the status quo. 'Part of the role the left must now play', according to Lerner, 'involves keeping their candidate on track.'

Many activists involved in the Dinkins campaign had also taken part in earlier, unsuccessful attempts to recall or unseat the volatile Koch, but in 1989 the spiralling decline of the city, corruption that weakened the Democratic Party, and a stronger-than-usual candidate provided a different outcome. By the early months of 1989, New York was perceived in the local press and public opinion polls as a 'city in crisis'. While some of its 8 million citizens lived high-visibility lives of incredible wealth and privilege, many more were seen in daily newspapers and on nightly TV news living on the streets and in the subways in states of abysmal wretchedness. During the last decade the city's infrastructure, subject to well-documented corruption and neglect, had been crumbling unattended; its local economy was swamped with minimum-wage service jobs while manufacturing, which in 1950 accounted for one of every three private sector jobs, had shrunk by half; and its communal fabric was ripped to rags by nerve-shredding racial tension and the debilitating effects of poverty and drugs in the neighborhoods.

Grass-roots activists and social agencies had long criticized Koch's footdragging on problems such as the city's sordid child welfare bureaucracy, healthcare, AIDS and the homeless. Even as Koch attended the annual mayors' 1989 mid-wintercon-ference in Washington, which focused on hunger and homelessness, police in Pennsylvania Station were ordered to keep some of New York's estimated 75,000 homeless moving between the upper Amtrak and lower Long Island Rail Road levels of the station until they tired and chose another place away from the warm, well-lit station to settle.

While many of the homeless migrate between New York City's Grand Central Terminal, Pennsylvania Station and the Port Authority Bus Terminal, only Penn Station remains open all night. The city now houses more than 10,000 people nightly in often dangerous and disease-spreading shelters: this in addition to 5,000 homeless families, including more than 9,000 children sheltered in dangerous welfare hotels.

Koch's back-of-the-hand treatment of the homeless was highlighted last December, when the Community Service Society (CSS) reported that the city failed to seek available federal and state funding for the homeless. According to CSS, thousands of dollars in potential cash benefits from government programs for homeless people who are unemployed, mentally ill, physically disabled or Vietnam veterans go untapped.

Ironically, despite this deterioration in its social and physical fabric, New York City remains a world-class metropolis: a cosmopolitan center of high finance and the world capital of culture, education, fashion and communications. But prominence in these areas was not able to shield the city from the disastrous consequences of a national recession, eight years of federally mandated fiscal retrenchment, a steady loss of unionized unskilled and semi-skilled jobs, nor from a decade marked by extraordinary social decay and divisively short-sighted local leadership.

Its people, nearly half of whom reported being crime victims during the past year, complained of having to be 'afraid and careful all the time', and they, in turn, bear the burden of providing care for the nation's largest number of people without homes and people with AIDS. Besieged by the violence that attends a thriving illegal drug economy and the virulently destabilizing effects of a vicious crack epidemic now spilling beyond the confines of inner-city neighborhoods, they had also by late 1989 become cynical in the face of a recurrent backwash of morally enervating municipal corruption and ineptitude. Most people surveyed in the last months of 1988 and early 1989 said that they were equally upset by corruption in the Koch administration and by the mayor's public behavior.

Koch's Polarization Strategy

In this city of varied ethnic groups and interests, Koch made contention part of his style, managing, at one time or another during his twelve-year tenure to alienate just about everyone. He unabashedly admitted to enjoying 'a good fight'. Critics, however, charged the mayor with targeting the weak and those he perceived to be without retaliatory power for abuse.

He baited the city's mainly Black transit workers' union, refusing to make any attempt at conciliation during their 1980 strike; he used a nationally published interview to gratuitously declare that Blacks were 'basically anti-semitic'; and upset the Irish while junketing in the south of that country by declaring the British army in the north 'a peacekeeping force'.

Perestroika and *glasnost* were not yet household words when Koch, hosting a group of Soviet schoolchildren on a ceremonial visit to City Hall, told them that their system of government was 'the pits'. Occasionally, however, Koch misjudged his opponent, as was the case with the Canadian chain that raised prices at its Manhattan movie theaters. Mayor Koch, positioning himself in front of lines of ticket-buyers to protest the price increase, provided good weekend copy for a slow day for local TV news, but failed to stem the tide of grumbling, yet steady, movie-goers. Corporate heads at the chain ignored Koch, and, after two or three weekends, he quietly dropped the issue.

One issue that Koch and many of his more vocal opponents have not dropped quietly, however, has been the issue of race – an issue that marked his first run for mayor and dogged his final effort. The racial composition of New York City, according to the 1980 census, is nearly half minority and the projection for 1990 is that whites will make up 41 percent of the population, Blacks 28 percent, Hispanics 24 percent and other minorities 7 percent. The drive for minority empowerment in New York City has been no less intense than in other cities, and, as in other cities, it resulted in bruising battles with an entrenched white power structure.

When Congressman Ed Koch shed his liberal skin and entered the pit of New York City politics in the late 1970s, he became a leading spokesperson for the white backlash movement and its opposition to proposed low-income scatter-site housing in Forest Hills, a middle-class Jewish community. (The enclave, noted chiefly for its tennis facility, was the center of controversy in the 1960s, when the son of United Nations diplomat Ralph Bunche was denied admission because of his race.) Bitter battles, engaging the enormous resources of the status quo to beat back minority challenges around the issues of school decentralization and police brutality, had already been fought when Koch emerged as the leader of whites frightened by the changing racial make-up of the city.

Koch's calculated cynicism toward New York City's minorities continued throughout his tenure as mayor – for example, in the operation of his City Hall–based Talent Bank. The program, created during Koch's second term to stem criticism of his administration's dismal minority hiring record, was designed to place minorities and women in city jobs. Instead, in January 1989, the state Commission on Government Integrity heard corroborated testimony that the mayor's functionaries perverted the program for patronage purposes – dispensing the well-paying jobs to mostly white, politically connected males – and destroyed files to hide the fact. Later the same month, the Mayoral Commission on Black New Yorkers concluded that Blacks in New York City 'constitute a community in crisis' that has been shut out of the city's economic mainstream and whose economic vitality is sapped by institutionalized prejudice.

Fiscal Crisis and Polarization

Koch often takes credit for saving the city's finances. During the 1989 primary he campaigned on his fiscal prowess, warning voters that hard times were again at hand, and that not to re-elect him to a fourth term meant losing the management maven who steered the city through its earlier crisis. Felix Rohatyn, chairman of the Municipal Assistance Corporation, while avowedly 'undecided' as to which candidate to back in the primary, reinforced the mayor's message late in the campaign. 'I think we're in for some difficult times', Rohatyn told the *New York Times*, 'which means the Mayor and the Governor are going to have to ask people who depend on government the most to accept some sacrifices.' However, despite Koch's claims, he did not save the city single-handedly. It is true that he took office in 1977 needing to fashion a budget for the 'financially strapped city', but he has yet to publicly acknowledge that many of the measures responsible for the city's recovery were designed during the last two years of the Beam administration. Meanwhile, citywide anger and prideful resolve, in the face of Washington's rebuff – President Gerald Ford had, in effect, told New Yorkers to 'Drop Dead' – united New Yorkers around the new mayor and a program of municipal fiscal reform.

Koch had the financial support and goodwill of the city's union, Gov. Hugh Carey and the city's power elite, represented by high-profile banker Rohatyn. And while the package to save the city included federal loans, union pension funds and private investment, the overwhelming effect of fiscal restructuring was borne mostly by the poor in the form of severely reduced social services: hospitals were closed in areas designated as 'medically underserved' by the federal government, and among a host of other draconian measures, funding to the City University and its network of community colleges slashed.

In the early months of his first term, Koch set the tone toward the city's minorities and the poor that he would take consistently during his twelve-year stewardship. His demonstrated constituency, the middle class, like the city's poor and working class, was increasingly feeling the fiscal pinch, and

Koch, pitting one class against the others, targeted an easy opponent.

As Charles Green and Basil Wilson contend in their essay 'Contemporary Black Politics', the election of Ed Koch as mayor in 1977 must be understood not only in the light of the fiscal crisis but from the perceived state of 'white ethnics disturbed by the changing racial and ethnic demographics of the city. Koch's task was not just to preside over retrenchment and restore the fiscal well-being of the state sector, but to ensure white hegemony of state power.'[3]

'Poverty pimps', some of the people running the federally initiated Model Cities and anti-poverty programs and the 'Little City Halls' that proliferated during the liberal Lindsay administration, furnished Koch with a target and helped him score points with white middle-class voters. There are signs that Koch attempted to accommodate the Black and Hispanic middle class and enlist their silence in his effort to isolate the city's poor and working class, but this design, after some initial success in his first term in office, ultimately failed.

Poverty program administrators and the people they served were mainly Black and Latino and poor. The programs, with lots of storefront neighborhood offices in the 'outer' boroughs, provided concrete contact with City Hall. They were an invaluable source of feedback concerning neighborhood needs and the efficiency of city services. Staffed as they were by many former 1960s activists, the offices helped clients with housing problems, notified them of tests for civil service jobs, directed them to legal and medical services, and in many ways contributed to the politicalization of New York City's poor.

Perhaps equally important, the storefront anti-poverty offices provided a positive counterweight to the city government's primary neighborhood presence, the police. Koch never honestly proposed reforming the programs. He instead alienated their staff and clients by insisting on their elimination. His crusading self-righteousness stemmed from 'the accepted convention that the poverty programs were the special bailiwick of the Black political establishment, and in quest of efficiency and competence, he was willing to eliminate that source of patronage.' Thus, at the start of the Koch era, the Democratic Party clubhouse became City Hall's major source of neighborhood intelligence.

School for Scandal

Many of the city's poverty programs were fiscally mismanaged, mostly due to overwork or ineptitude, a few feloniously so. But the amount the so-called poverty pimps may have stolen never amounted to a fraction of the wealth Koch's clubhouse cronies subsequently pimped New York City for – a point never alluded to by political commentators during the 1989 primary.

Koch began his third term flanked in various newspaper photos by Queens borough president and Democratic boss Donald Manes, Bronx Democratic boss Stanley Friedman and Brooklyn Democratic boss Meade Esposito. By year's end, Manes, faced with revelation of his role in looting millions from the city's Parking Violation Bureau, had taken his life; Friedman and Esposito had been indicted for corruption.

The subsequent wave of municipal corruption scandals and trials – which saw nearly a hundred members of the Koch administration leave office under a cloud, if not under indictment, the swelling ranks of homeless people coupled with Koch's highly publicized pandering to the city's powerfully aggressive real estate lobby, crumbling bridges, dangerous and dirty subways, grossly inept school and social service bureaucracies, drugs and their attendant violence and social decay – fueled opposition to Koch, supporting the growing perception that he brought more rhetoric than substance to his job.

A November 1988 *Newsday* poll registered rising disapproval ratings for the Koch administration and a February 1989 *Daily News*/Eyewitness News opinion sample continued the trend: 77 percent of the people surveyed said that drugs, homelessness and crime were the city's major problems; 72 percent noted a 'decline in the quality of their lives' since Koch had become mayor; and 73 percent said it was time for someone else to run the show.

As Manhattan borough president, David Dinkins was noted for a 'personal warmth and gentlemanly style', and struck many voters as a calming elixir for a city reeling from physical rot, administrative corruption and Koch's grating combativeness. But in the quarters where Koch was most criticized for a needlessly abrasive style, Dinkins also faced criticism. With little more than a month before the primary, activists in the Black community argued that the Dinkins campaign was missing a major opportunity. 'Dinkins is campaigning not to lose', said Roger Wareham of the Medgar Evers Center for Law and Social Justice. 'He's running a colorless, non-threatening campaign', Wareham complained in a late mid-July interview with the *Guardian,* while noting that Dinkins had recently ignored the opportunity to address more than 700 activists attending a grass-roots conference on housing, healthcare, criminal justice, education and economic development. He wondered if campaign strategists might not be taking Dinkins's Black support for granted. The same sentiment was voiced by the *City Sun* in an editorial: 'In the city's Black neighborhoods, the Dinkins campaign apparatus is hardly active or visible,' said the Black Brooklyn weekly. 'No people working the streets. No voter registration. No presence.' Meanwhile, longtime Brooklyn activist Sonny Carson reported registering more than a thousand young voters in four hours at a borough rap concert. 'Dinkins is missing an important chance to get out into the neighborhoods and inspire our young people', complained activist Elombe Brath, late in July. 'Now is the time for him to talk to them, to make them feel connected to the city with a stake in its future.' While Wareham, Carson and Brath lamented Dinkins's failure to identify more openly with grass-roots leadership, all actively supported him as the candidate most likely to be attentive to the needs of the city's minorities and the poor. 'We certainly don't advocate sitting this election out', Brath told the *Guardian,* adding that 'New York City is not Chicago. Our first Black mayor is not likely to be a firebrand.'

But Dinkins had other problems too: former Congressman and three-time Democratic mayoral candidate Herman Badillo still bore a grudge against Harlem politicians for blocking his 1985 mayoral endorsement by a citywide coalition of Black leaders. During the campaign Badillo had, despite reported appeals, refused to meet with Dinkins, and even as local columnists dredged up personally embarrassing comments made by Koch about Badillo in Koch's best-selling book *Mayor,* the long-time Latino leader endorsed him for a fourth term on the steps of City Hall, less than two weeks before the election.

Daily News columnist Miguel Perez, describing primary night in the winner's headquarters, reported that 'among the Latino leaders in Dinkins' camp, there was a special reason for celebration. They had delivered the vote from a community that was considered pivotal for winning the Democratic primary. And so while white political analysts kept talking about how "it was the white vote that put Dinkins over the top", Latinos were taking credit for giving Dinkins perhaps even more support than they gave Koch four years ago.' According to Perez, 'In Badillo's case there was general consensus' among Dinkins' Latino supporters: 'He committed suicide the day he endorsed Koch, but today [primary day] we hammered the last nail in his coffin.'

The Dinkins forces were also on the alert for the clownish antics of another spoiler, Rev. Al Sharpton. Sharpton, according to July newspaper reports, expected momentarily to be charged with federal income tax evasion. The pulpitless preacher told the New York *Village Voice* that if he came to trial during the mayoral campaign, he intended to 'remind everyone that Dave Dinkins never was charged with any crime for not filing his taxes.'

The issue of Dinkins's tax problem had been rehashed earlier in a front page *New York Times* article that offered readers no new information. Addressing a New Democratic Coalition breakfast days after the *Times*'s 'expose', Dinkins said the tax issue had first come up in 1973, when the question was raised by the city Department of Investigation. At the time Dinkins was head of the city Board of Election and had been tapped by newly elected Mayor Abraham Beam to be the city's first Black Deputy Mayor. His failure to file, however, ended that possibility. Dinkins told the breakfast forum that he borrowed money and paid all the taxes and interest for the four years in question, and said that he was never contacted by the Internal Revenue Service or State Tax Department.

Koch: Doing the Wrong Thing

The mayor's behavior following the cold-blooded, racially inspired murder of a Black teenager by a mob of thirty white males in Brooklyn's Bensonhurst neighborhood three weeks before primary day was as dismal as his performance following a similar racial incident in 1986 that resulted in a Black man's death in Howard Beach, Queens.

Sam Roberts, in a *New York Times* analysis, wrote with veracity of the killing and by extension of the city itself. 'Blacks', he said 'will always be singled out by their skin color. They are reflexively identified in some neighborhoods as outsiders. In those same neighborhoods, when they are young or casually dressed, many are perceived as potential criminals.' Continuing the essay, he argued that that was true of Yusuf

Hawkins, who ventured into Bensonhurst to answer an advertisement for a used car, and it was true of Michael Griffith, who was chased to his death in Howard Beach after the car in which he was riding had broken down.

Koch used a City Hall press conference to chastise the coalition of Blacks and whites planning a protest march through Bensonhurst, telling reporters, 'I am talking about what is helpful to the city – lowering the passions, lowering the rhetoric, and you don't do that by marching into a community and getting that community to feel that they are the culprit, as opposed to five or thirty people who live in the community who are the culprits.' Rev. Timothy Mitchell of Queens likened Koch to Bull Connor, the police commissioner of Birmingham, Alabama, who used cattle prods, dogs and water hoses on civil rights marchers in the 1960s. Dinkins, who had made low-key statements after the killing, joined the city's Black religious leadership in declaring that city streets were open to all citizens, and noting that, as yet, Bensonhurst was still part of New York City.

Koch and the Rainbow

Koch had committed a major faux pas during New York City's 1988 Democratic presidential primary when he savaged the nation's first African American Democratic party contender – who was then leading in national polls – insisting that Jews 'would be crazy to vote for Jesse Jackson.' Koch so offended liberal Democrats and national journalists covering the primary that he was unwelcome at their July mediafest in Atlanta. True, superdelegate spots were hard to come by and Koch's candidate, Tennessee Sen. Albert Gore, did lose the primary that Jackson won. But New York Governor Mario Cuomo's son Andrew warranted a seat with the state delegation, room surely could have been found at the National Democratic Convention for the mayor of the state's largest and most Democratic city – had party leadership wanted him there. Instead, Koch captured local headlines during convention week, by travelling to Ireland, where he again choked on his boot over comments endorsing British army behavior in Northern Ireland.

Koch's rabid anti-Jackson rhetoric and embarrassing performance damaged him, forcing a later admission that maybe he had missed the symbolic significance of the Jackson campaign.

But by that time he already convinced enough voters that he had also missed the symbolic significance of the office of the mayor of New York City.

In December 1988, as the mayoral contest was coming into focus and polls showed Dinkins with a 52 to 37 percent lead in a two-candidate primary, Koch telegraphed his concern about the race issue and the role Jackson might play in the Dinkins campaign. The mayor's pollsters put two questions to Democratic respondents. First, 'How do you feel about a ticket of Koch for mayor and Police Commissioner Benjamin Ward for council president?'

Ward, the city's first Black Police Commissioner, identified himself adhesively with Koch – so much so, that when he resigned two weeks after Koch's primary loss, the *Amsterdam*, a Black city weekly, in a wry editorial noted that the mayor 'appointed Ben in order to save his own hind parts politically when this city was about to explode over the issue of police brutality, and the murder of innocent Black males while in police custody.' The editorial went on to criticize Ward for 'his undying loyalty, and unshakable faith' in his boss, and Koch for having 'used Ben cynically'. The second question in the mayor's poll asked: 'What about mayor Koch's statements on Jesse Jackson – do you think they demonstrate he is a racist, or just speaking out forcefully on the subject?'

'We are all together now', said Dinkins, from the ballroom podium during his primary night celebration. Flanked by representatives of the coalition that earned him victory, and with the statesman-like demeanor he wore throughout the campaign still in place, he told supporters, 'You voted your hopes and not your fears – and in doing so, you said something profound about the soul and character of this town.'

Several local commentators have labelled Dinkins's primary win as Jesse Jackson's revenge. It certainly might have been that, but it had a further significance. It signaled a victory for Rev. Herbert Daughtry and the city's grass-roots leadership; it was a step in the direction of good governance for Black and Hispanic progressive politicians and a source of pride for the city's embattled but growing community of white anti-racist activists. It is a triumph belonging to the people who manned the barricades and often went to jail at the site of Koch's hospital closings and sustenance for those parents and education activists who continued to struggle for legitimate community school control of schools from Oceanhill-Brownsville to the coming battle over the Board of Education, and it was vindication for all of those anti-poverty program workers whose reputations were unfairly tarnished over a decade ago.

The Race to November

Dinkins's primary victory was only one of several firsts in this election. Two-term Brooklyn District Attorney Elizabeth Holtzman vanquished three male opponents to win the Democratic nomination for city comptroller. Holtzman, a former New York City member of Congress whose intelligence won her wide respect during the Nixon impeachment hearings, is likely to become the first woman to hold the second spot in city government.

Former city councilwoman Ruth Messinger won the race for Manhattan borough president by a landslide. A veteran of progressive-liberal politics, Messinger will be the first woman to hold that post. For Holtzman and Messinger, a Democratic primary victory was tantamount to election in this city where Democrats outnumber Republicans 5 to 1. Race as the factor that threatened to negate that usual truth for David Dinkins.

Republicans, heartened by the 'mess at City Hall', fielded two primary candidates: former US Attorney Rudolph Giuliani and Ronald Lauder, former US ambassador to Austria and heir to the Este Lauder cosmetics fortune. New York City is not generally hospitable territory for Republicans. The party won its last mayoral election in 1965 with John Lindsay, who switched to the Democrats before his term ended.

President George Bush got only 33.3 percent of the city vote in 1988, running 20 points worse here than in the rest of the country. But flushed with victory from the presidential contest, Republicans were sure that they had a chance. Just as New York City's primary contest was getting under way last June, Bush, addressing a posh Manhattan fund-raising dinner, plied his audience with praise for Giuliani while ignoring Lauder.

Bush had great difficulty pronouncing Giuliani's name, but his message was clear: the government gangbuster could capture 'the most powerful local office in America' for the Republicans. Later in the campaign, *Village Voice* columnist Doug Ireland was less kind, describing Giuliani as 'a prosecutorial opportunist who ran for mayor because polls showed he couldn't beat incumbent [Democrat] Patrick Moynihan in a senate race.'

As a former federal prosecutor, Giuliani's strong suit is attacking the corruption of the Koch administration. About a month before the primary, he pledged that as mayor he would establish an anti-corruption commission to recommend changes in 'city practices and policies which currently make institutional corruption possible.' Noting that 'New York City is known throughout the country as a city for sale,' Giuliani told reporters that corruption robbed the city of money for human services. *City for Sale* is the title of a best-selling book by New York political writers Jack Newfield and Wayne Barrett that details Koch administration corruption.

Giuliani un-self-consciously billed himself as 'the only candidate who knows firsthand how to find corruption and root it out of the system' and claimed that 'if the Mayor had not turned over the Parking Violations Bureau to two of the biggest crooks in the city's history, there would have been $200 million to $250 million more in revenues' – though how Giuliani came up with those figures is a mystery. When city comptroller Harrison Goldin, also a candidate strongly critical of Koch, was contacted and asked for an estimate of what was stolen by the mayor's cronies, he said an accurate estimate would be difficult to determine without the candid cooperation of the felonious parties involved.

As rumors that President George Bush might come to the city to campaign for the Republican nominee circulated at Giuliani's primary night celebration, just a few blocks away Dinkins told cheering supporters, 'There will be no Republican beachhead in New York City.' Meanwhile, Giuliani campaign manager Peter Powers, claiming that issues took precedence over race, disputed reporters' primary night suggestions that the November contest would be racially polarized because Dinkins could become the city's first Black mayor.

Trading on a strong 'crimefighter' image, Giuliani trounced the reactionary Lauder by 67 percent to 33 percent, despite the fact that the right-winger waged the costliest campaign in city history in an attempt to convince voters that he was the 'real Republican' in the race. Even though Lauder lost the Republican nomination, he still held a spot on the November ballot as the Conservative Party standard bearer. Giuliani, having negotiated the Liberal Party nomination months ago, appeared on two ballot lines. Meanwhile, the Lauder primary campaign posed a major problem for Rudolph Giuliani, forcing him to convince the large conservative faction of his party that he was a 'Reagan Republican', while simultaneously persuading the city's overwhelmingly Democratic electorate that he was not.

Now Comes the Hard Part ...

Giuliani was unsuccessful. On 7 November, David Dinkins won New York City's mayoral election, becoming the first Black man to fill that office. Celebration of Dinkins's breakthrough was tempered, however, by the ugly nature of Giuliani's campaign and the unpredicted closeness of the results – clear evidence, if any was needed, that racism retains a central political role.

In a city where registered Democrats outnumber Republicans 5 to 1, the race that many thought would be an easy Democratic victory was in fact a 'dogfight' that saw Dinkins savaged personally in a media campaign directed by veteran Republican strategist Roger Ailes and labelled a 'fancy schwartze' by Giuliani campaign aide Jackie Mason.

The two-month-long battle engaged the attention and aid of prominent national Democrats, as the White House lent its considerable political clout to Giuliani's effort, with President George Bush actively fundraising, while putting an end to Conservative Ronald Lauder's campaign and forcing New York state's highest elected Republican and Giuliani's arch enemy, Sen. Alphonse D'Amato, to deliver a grudging endorsement of the party standard bearer.

The contest, marked by little discussion of substantive issues, was decided by less than 50,000 votes out of 1.7 million cast. Dinkins's four-point winning margin was slighter than public opinion pollsters led their editorial paymasters and the public to believe it would be, and surely warrants a closer look at some common, and perhaps faulty, assumptions in the field.

It is naive not to expect that in a contest between a Black candidate and a white – in a city with a racial history as turbulent as New York's has been over the last two decades – that some voters would be disinclined to reveal their racism to a stranger on the phone or outside a polling station.

However, Dinkins's win (and this too should have surprised no one) grew from soil ploughed by Rev. Jesse Jackson during the 1988 presidential campaign – an assessment with which Jackson proudly agreed in separate postelection news conferences and that Dinkins wisely acknowledged.

The 1989 mayoral election marked the final demise of the long-ailing voting coalition of Blacks and Jews (previous Koch strongholds voted solidly Republican), and signaled a new era in New York City. The Democratic establishment coalition that made Edward Koch mayor for over a decade – dominated by business and real estate interests and supported by middle-class white liberals – was supplanted by the most progressive grouping to influence City Hall in forty years.

Dinkins's victory was earned by an alliance of organized labor, African Americans, Latinos, prochoice women, lesbians and gays. With this poor and working-class base of support, the claims on the new mayor's attention will differ from those of his predecessor, even as he tries to make his peace with the powers that be (the mayor-elect is after all a centrist Democrat with progressive leanings).

Over the course of the next four years, however, Dinkins must be as solicitous and mindful of the poor and working class as Koch, for the past twelve years, has been of those who are not. Granted, this difficult task will probably be made even more so by the looming fiscal crisis and the running commentary of the new WCBS pundit and *New York Post* columnist Ed Koch.

Wasting little time, the day after the election, Koch assumed the posture of ex-officio shill for the status quo, warning Dinkins against a host of humane measures including commercial rent control, racial set-asides in city hiring and paid benefits to unmarried partners of city employees – in short, telling Dinkins not to attempt the very programs that supporters expect him to implement.

As Manhattan borough president, Dinkins demonstrated a talent for attracting intelligent, imaginative progressives to his staff. A fresh set of creative and compassionate answers to New York City's problems is sorely needed now. Fiscal resources are severely limited and grave challenges lie ahead. Given Dinkins's base of support, any attempt to mimic the former mayor and balance the budget solely on the backs of the poor would be unconscionable.

Meanwhile, the election of New York City's first African American mayor certainly does not mean that the walls of racism have come tumbling down, but it does seem to indicate that they have weakened a little.

Notes

1. 'City on the Brink: Crime', *New York Newsday,* 13 August 1989.
2. Shere Hite, 'What Makes New Yorkers Angriest? Life in the City', *New York Observer,* 5 June 1989.
3. Charles Green and Basil Wilson, 'Contemporary Black Politics', in *The Struggle for Black Empowerment in New York City,* New York 1987, p. 27.
4. Ibid., p. 95.
5. 'Once Again, Racism Proves to be Fatal in New York City', *New York Times,* 3 September 1989. Roberts continues: 'Mayor Edward I. Koch has boasted that there have been no race riots during his tenure. But despite gains in employment and a growing middle class, life for many Black and Hispanic New Yorkers remains a daily riot of poverty and discrimination.'

6

Youngstown, Ohio: Rebuilding the Labor Movement from Below

Staughton Lynd

The Meaning of Local Organizing

In *Reunion*, Tom Hayden describes a meeting outside Chicago in March 1968 at which the idea of a protest at the Democratic Convention in August was presented to about two hundred movement activists. 'Staughton Lynd', he writes, 'who was now active in an ERAP-type project among industrial workers, thought I was risking the movement's resources on a "one-shot" national fantasy.'[1]

In that discussion, those who raised questions about a convention demonstration believed that local organizing requires the temperament of a long-distance runner. By contrast, it seemed to us, apocalyptic actions like that in Chicago in 1968, their many virtues notwithstanding, encouraged the hope of quick results, and, when these don't fully materialize, cause participants to drop out altogether. I was thinking of the effect on SNCC work in the South of the protest at the 1964 Democratic Party Convention. It seemed to me that after the 1964 convention many SNCC field workers never made it back to their local projects. Somehow, the trip to Atlantic City, and the congressional challenge that followed, broke the rhythm of local organizing in the South. I feared that this might also happen in the North in the aftermath of the 1968 Democratic Convention.

We who were trying to articulate a rationale for local organizing in that period made certain key assumptions. First, I think we viewed local organizing as a Movement equivalent of the scientific method. Already in 1968 there were groups who felt that the way to be scientific was to derive strategy and tactics deductively from received texts. I considered this scholasticism, not science. It seemed to me that organizing strategies should be understood as alternative hypotheses, and that the way to decide between them was to try them out. In expounding this approach I often found myself using the Biblical parable of the sower: we organizers were like those who scatter seed, and the fruitfulness of our work would depend on the seed and on the soils where we planted. I instanced Bob Moses's work in Mississippi. Bob arrived there in 1961, and within three years more resources were flowing into Mississippi than to the SNCC national headquarters in Atlanta. This was an instance, I argued, of the Movement reorganizing itself around a successful experiment.

Second, I was determined to organize among industrial workers. My impression in 1968 was that the Movement had painted itself into a corner. It remained, as it had begun, a student movement. As these students used more and more radical tactics on their campuses, middle Americans who had never been to college and whose children might be the first in their family to have such an opportunity denounced the crazy kids who were throwing theirs away. In response, students escalated their tactics even more to make up for their lack of mass support, and hardhats watching TV were thus further alienated. Much as I disliked the Progressive Labor Party, its members seemed to me correct in insisting on the need for outreach to industrial workers. I resolved that I would find a way to carry on that outreach without sacrificing the vision and values of the early New Left.

Finally, I reluctantly decided that I would come on as a professional, not as a worker. A friend told me, 'Staughton, you could be in the mill twenty years, and if a problem arose, people would say, "Let's ask the professor."' At the time my only professional skill was history. My wife Alice and I approached a series of Chicago-area steelworkers, tape recorder in hand. Our thought was: Many young people are now getting jobs in factories or working-class communities; what can they learn from those who organized in the 1930s? Sometimes the interviews were at kitchen tables. Most exciting were times when older workers shared their memories at community occasions, like a forum at St. Joseph's Community College in Hammond, Indiana on 'Labor History from the Viewpoint of the Rank and File'. These interviews became our book, *Rank and File: Personal History by Working-Class Organizers.*[2]

More and more frequently the workers whom we interviewed asked about legal problems, too. We tried to find them legal assistance. Their difficulties were as often with unions as with employers, but especially at that time lawyers who knew something about labor law but were beholden neither to unions nor companies were hard to find.

At last Alice and I decided to become lawyers ourselves. This would give us, I foresaw, not only a useful skill but also a recognizable identity. If a question arose at a gathering of workers, 'Who is this guy?' the answer could be, 'He's our lawyer.' Everyone would then relax, and I could stay in the meeting.

More than a decade later, on trips to revolutionary Nicaragua, we encountered priests and nuns whose organizing strategy was the same. Inspired by Vatican II and the Medillín Conference of 1968, they practiced a 'preferential option for the poor' by moving into poverty-striken *barrios* and villages. They did not pretend to be anything other than priests and nuns. And they stayed for a long time.

How Do Workers Become Radicals?

In order to learn from experience one must articulate a theory that the experience is used to test. This is as true for the organizer as the historian. An organizing venture can serve as an experiment that tests the validity of alternative hypotheses about social change in working-class communities, but only if the hypotheses are made explicit. Similarly, research into a patch of labor history can stretch our understanding of the variables involved in working-class radicalization, provided we have the courage to put into words some preliminary notion of how such radicalization happens before embarking on the research.

For all of us engaged in the encounter with working-class reality in the United States, the underlying question is this: Why in the seventy-five years since World War I has there not been the sort of generalized sense of class grievance and class mission that there was among workers in the United States during the half-century 1865–1915? And the explanatory scheme explicitly or implicitly at issue in the encounter is the model of working-class radicalization – what I believe it is now fashionable to call the 'essentialist' model – to be found in traditional Marxist texts. The fact that there is not, or is not yet, a widespread radical consciousness among American workers or a mass socialist party contending for power, has led many to conclude that the traditional Marxist model is, simply, wrong.

The traditional Marxist model as set forth in, for instance, *The Communist Manifesto* posited two steps or stages in working-class radicalization. The first stage was the formation of industrial unions, which, it was assumed, were inherently more disposed to radicalism than were craft unions, because industrial unions would reach out to include the unskilled, Blacks and women – those whose stake in the system was least – and because as large aggregations of working people they seemed destined for radicalizing confrontation between the class as a whole and the state. That confrontation with the state would be the second phase of radicalization, according to the model, bringing with it recognition that government is not neutral but is an executive committee of the capitalist class, and that labor, to advance its interests, must form its own political party.

So much has been written deriding the traditional Marxist paradigm that it seems important to observe that this explanatory model corresponds perfectly to the step-by-step radicalization of the most celebrated socialist in American history, Eugene Debs. Debs entered the labor movement as a local lodge officer for a craft union, the Brotherhood of Locomotive Firemen. Experience convinced him that all railroad workers should join together in a single industrial union, and he organized the American Railway Union. In the Pullman Strike of 1894, he led this industrial union into battle, only to see it crushed by the national government, acting through a Democratic president and an attorney general who was a former lawyer for the railroads. At Woodstock jail or soon thereafter, Debs's consciousness was permanently raised to the second stage, and on 1 January 1897 he told the members of the ARU in an open letter, 'The issue is Socialism versus Capitalism. I am for Socialism. ...[3]

The Marxist paradigm that works so well in explaining Eugene Debs (and, I conjecture, many other radicalized workers in the period 1865–1915) has fallen into disfavor because it seems to explain so little about the years since World War I. Industrial unionism reasserted itself dramatically in the 1930s, of course, but by and large, at least in the half-dozen years before World War II, it did not lead to political radicalism. Why, it is asked, did workers disregard the counsel of trusted leaders like John L. Lewis and Harry Bridges to vote overwhelmingly for Franklin Roosevelt in 1940? Why were local labor parties unsuccessful in CIO strongholds like San Francisco, Detroit, Akron and Aliquippa, Pennsylvania? Why, during the 1960s, did rank-and-file workers so long and so vehemently support the Vietnam War?

I don't believe that the 1940 Roosevelt landslide proves anything at all about labor radicalism. Had FDR been running against a national Farmer-Labor Party headed by John L. Lewis, and if in that situation workers had opted for Roosevelt rather than Lewis, then some doom-and-gloom about working-class radicalism might be in order. As it was, workers simply showed the good sense or even the class consciousness to vote for Roosevelt rather than for a corporate lawyer who attacked the TVA.

The failure of local labor parties based on the CIO to emerge in the years 1935–40 presents a more complex question.[4] Proposals for local and/or national labor or farmer-labor parties bubbled to the surface of the labor movement more or less continuously during the period 1932–48. Between the years 1932 and 1936, such parties fielded their own candidates for local office in Cambridge, New Bedford and Springfield, Massachusetts; Berlin and Lincoln, New Hampshire; Danbury and Hartford, Connecticut; Buffalo and New York City; Allentown and Philadelphia, Pennsylvania; Akron, Canton and Toledo, Ohio; Detroit, Hamtramck, and Port Huron, Michigan; Chicago and Hillsboro, Illinois; Sioux Falls, South Dakota; Everett and Goldbar, Washington; and San Francisco, California. In 1934 the Labor Party of Berlin, New Hampshire, a timber town with a population of about 20,000, was elected to power. In at least ten other communities, central labor unions endorsed the idea of a labor party, as did the state federations of labor of Rhode Island, Connecticut, Vermont, New Jersey and Wisconsin. And at the 1935 AFL convention, a resolution endorsing a labor party lost narrowly, 104 to 108.

To say, in the face of this evidence, that labor parties in the late thirties were doomed by the unevenness of working-class consciousness or the fragmentation of the class itself, seems less than persuasive. The fact is that the nascent CIO leadership did its best to prevent such parties from materializing. Sidney Hillman persuaded the Amalgamated Clothing Workers union to renounce its traditional commitment to a labor party and to endorse Roosevelt in 1936. At the UAW convention that same year, delegates first voted unanimously for a resolution calling for the formation of a national labor party and defeated a resolution to back FDR. Only when Lewis made a personal plea to the convention and Adolf Germer, one of his lieutenants, issued a private warning to UAW president Homer Martin did the delegates reverse themselves. Overall, the formation of Labor's Nonpartisan League in April 1936 by Hillman, Lewis and their associates, supporting a popular president of the United States, led by a popular president of the CIO, and bankrolled by half a million dollars from the UMW alone, was the kiss of death for independent labor politics for the remainder of the decade.

Even so, there was no necessary conflict between work for a local labor party in communities like Berlin, New Hampshire and support for Roosevelt in national elections. CIO activists could have supported or acquiesced to Roosevelt's candidacies in 1936 and 1940 while putting their main energies into building local political movements independent of the Democratic Party. The critical reason why they did not was that no national grouping on the left – not the CIO, not the Socialist Party, not the Communist Party – provided sustained leadership, as distinct from occasional rhetoric or tactical posturing. During the war there continued to be labor party talk, for example in the Michigan UAW. After the war at least one local labor party *was* formed, the United Labor Party of Akron. To use the failure of workers to do more along these lines as a critique of the Marxist model or as evidence for the inherently nonideological or fragmented character of the American working class, to find in these events support for what might be termed an essentialism of the right, seems to me unreasonable. There is abundant evidence from the early 1930s to suggest that American workers, given different leadership, might have pursued more radical strategies with respect both to the kind of union they formed and to the way they voted.[5]

Workers' relation to the Vietnam War raises even more fundamental issues. Let me suggest an approach to them, again by way of traditional Marxist theory. If the absence of revolutionary consciousness among industrial workers in the advanced capitalist countries is a problem for labor history, it is even more of one for practitioners of Marxism working as organizers within the culture of traditional Marxist theory. Marx's leading disciple struggled with the question, for instance in *What Is to*

Be Done? At the outbreak of World War I, appalled by the failure of the international socialist movement to take a stand against the war, Lenin retreated to the libraries of Zurich and wrote his booklet on imperialism. Whereas in *What Is to Be Done?* Lenin blamed lack of socialist consciousness on the betrayals by the leadership of the existing socialist parties, in *Imperialism* he suggested more systemic causes of the problem. Very roughly, he argued that capitalism had entered a new phase characterized by export of capital and recurrent war for control of overseas territories; that the tendency of imperialism was 'to divide the workers, to encourage opportunism among them and to cause temporary decay in the working-class movement'; so that until the contradictions of imperialism itself had ripened, it might very well be that revolution would occur in low-wage, superexploited, colonial or neocolonial nations, rather than in the nations that were economically and technologically most advanced.[6]

Let me try to extract from this familiar rhetoric some related hypotheses for testing. First, has the recurrence of war in the period since 1915 served to disrupt and disorient the growth of native American labor radicalism? I think the answer is patently Yes. The half-century from 1865 to 1915, during which a homegrown American radicalism grew and flourished, was a time of, relatively speaking, almost uninterrupted peace. Compare the smashing of both the Socialist Party and IWW during World War I and the years following; the domestication of the new CIO unions during World War II by means of the no-strike pledge and the institutionalization of grievance arbitration and the dues check-off; the effect of the permanent war economy after World War II in making an anticommunist foreign policy economically advantageous to many American workers; the impact of the Korean and Vietnam wars in cutting short social experimentation in the late 1940s and early 1960s. For example, Youngstown steelworker John Barbero described the effect of the Korean War on the United Labor Party of Akron:

> The United Labor Party functioned until the first Eisenhower administration. [Its candidates for Congress and City Council] got a vote of about 10,000 in Akron until 1950 or so. But after that, it just became impossible. We had an antiwar pamphlet on the Korean War that we wanted to distribute at the mill gates but [the atmosphere] was just too hostile. It never got out.[7]

Second, has the periodic smothering of domestic discontent in patriotic frenzy specifically encouraged workers to distrust their own experience, to devalue their own traditions, and to participate in a 'false consciousness'? (I have noticed, by the way, that although it is no longer hip to speak about 'false consciousness', one can discuss the same thing in academic circles if it is called 'hegemony'.) Again, the answer is Yes. Let me give an example of this false consciousness, or rather, its transcendence, from my own experience as an organizer. In the late 1960s, I was invited to speak about the Vietnam War at a community college on the south side of Chicago. The student body was predominantly white and almost entirely working class. When I walked into the class I knew at once that they were laying for me. Marked copies of *Time* magazine, with stories about the radical professor who had been to Hanoi, were everywhere. So I said, 'We all know that we can't trust the media. In this class we will believe only those of you who have been to Vietnam and whom you personally trust. I will write on the blackboard what you tell me.' For an hour or an hour and a half I wrote: The Vietnamese don't want us there. The soldiers on the other side care more about this war than we do. The South Vietnamese government is corrupt .... When the class time had elapsed, I said that I too believed what had been written on the blackboard, and left.

Finally, it is possible that the Vietnam War was the *Aufhebung*, the beginning of the end for United States imperialism, and as a consequence, the start of a new season of opportunity for American working-class radicalism. This longest war in American history ended in defeat for the United States government at the hands of a small third world nation, and left behind a tangible resistance throughout all sectors of American society to fighting another such endless and meaningless war. At roughly the same time, other capitalist economies began to invade the American market, and the real standard of living of workers in the United States began to decline.

These changes were reflected in the mood of working-class communities. The new feeling was one of a dream betrayed. There was a feeling that working-class America had done everything asked of it, but that society had not kept its side of the bargain. Young men and women in working-class communities, like their parents and grandparents before them, had gone to work after high school, labored in unsafe and dirty jobs, gone off to war when called, met their bills and paid off their mortgages, deferred to their superiors in family, church, school, the armed forces, and the plant, and looked forward to a secure retirement.

What these people experienced was not the American Dream, but plant closings in which people and their communities were thrown away like orange peels; low-wage, non-union jobs stripped of the protections won by a generation of struggle; pension promises dishonored; medical insurance modified or cancelled. Youngstown, John Barbero wrote, was like a leper colony: the government would have done more to help had it been hit by a tornado. When LTV Steel closed the Brier Hill mill, where John had worked for more than thirty years, he was asked to burn the accumulated production records. 'They have made us non-persons', he remarked.[8] All this lay just ahead when Alice and I arrived in Youngstown.

Death of a Steel Industry

During the summer of 1971, when Alice and I were still living in Chicago, the Basic Steel Contract came up for renegotiation. We were doing oral history at a storefront in Gary, Indiana under the auspices of a group of young working-class intellectuals who called themselves The Writers' Workshop. The Workshop undertook to collect the most far-out proposals of the various rank-and-file caucuses in the Calumet Region and combine them in an imagined ideal basic steel contract. The pamphlet was duly printed, and at the suggestion of a long-time activist at Inland Steel, I mailed a copy to the address of something in Youngstown, Ohio called the Rank and File Team (RAFT).

A few evenings later, the phone rang.

'Hello!', bellowed a voice over the wire. (I later learned that the speaker had been partially deafened by work in the mill.) 'This is Litch, in Youngstown. What mill do you work in?'

I had to explain that I was a mere historian.

'That doesn't matter!', said the voice. 'We liked your pamphlet.'

It transpired that the RAFT group was planning to picket outside a hotel in Washington, DC where the union and steel companies were to begin negotiations. I was planning to be in Washington that same day and met them on the picket line. After picketing for a time, we adjourned to a nearby coffee shop and got to know each other.

Two of the most remarkable members of this remarkable group were John Barbero and Ed Mann.[9] Both were then in their forties. They had gone to work in the Youngstown mills after getting out of the army at the end of World War II. Each had gone most of the way through Youngstown State University, taking classes at night with the help of the G.I. Bill. Both joined a local labor party based in nearby Akron called the United Labor Party, which permanently influenced their view of the world.[10]

I had never met workers like John and Ed. They were outspoken advocates of racial equality, in the community and in the mill. They opposed not only the Vietnam War but had opposed the Korean War as well. They were comfortable with the idea of socialism, and sophisticated about the various left groups. (Ed regularly introduces himself as a member of the IWW.) I concluded that on this rock I would try to build my church. When I graduated from law school in 1976, the Lynds moved to Youngstown.

We arrived in what was once the second steel-producing city in the nation just as the bottom dropped out of the steel industry. In September 1977 Youngstown Sheet & Tube announced the closure of its Campbell Works. Five thousand workers were terminated. In October 1978, workers at Sheet & Tube's Brier Hill Works (where Ed Mann and John Barbero were officers of the local) learned from a shareholders' proxy statement that their mill was to be closed. Another 1,500 workers lost their jobs. In November 1979, US Steel announced the closing of its Youngstown Works, putting another 3,500 workers on the street.

I have told the story of the fight against these shutdowns elsewhere.[11] Here I mention only certain aspects of the struggle that influenced what came later. First, the small group of activists who took part in all three shutdown struggles developed a more and more radical analysis of what caused the mills to be closed. We came to reject populist notions (the problem arises when conglomerates acquire steel companies), conservative notions (government causes the problem by over-regulation), liberal notions (plant closings are the inevitable price of progress). Slowly it became clear that those who make the decisions to close steel mills do not ask themselves, 'Where should we put our new steel mill?' but 'Where can we put our investment capital (inside or outside the steel industry) so as to make the most profit?' At the same time we learned that to prove a plant is profitable is not enough to save it. The issue for capitalist decision-makers is always, 'How can we use our money so as to maximize profit?' Marx's emphasis on the *rate* of profit as the cornerstone of capitalist calculation was borne out by our experience.

Second, we found the national Steelworkers' union consistently unsupportive or worse. Local unions, notably Local 1462 (Brier Hill Works) and Local 1330 (US Steel's Ohio Works), provided natural leadership in the Youngstown campaigns. But the national ('international') union red-baited us, bad-mouthed our tactical decisions in the press, and dragged its heels over supporting our requests for government aid. On balance, the national union would have helped us more had it not existed.

Third, the mill-closing struggles crystallized *direct action* as the preferred tactical option for Youngstown activists, with Ed Mann as its most eloquent exponent. On 28 January 1980, there was a rally at the hall of Local 1330, USWA, just up the hill from US Steel's Youngstown administration building. After speeches by many politicians, Bob Vasquez, president of the local, introduced Ed Mann.

His own mill down, his own local union all but disbanded, Ed Mann could speak for himself in a way that had been difficult when he was representing the many interests within Local 1462. He began by saying, 'You know we've heard a lot about benefits this morning, but I thought we were here to save some jobs.' He went on:

> And I'm not interested in calling a lot of people together and just talking to them and going home. I think we've got a job to do today. [Responsive noises from the crowd] And that job is to let US Steel know that this is the end of the line. No more jobs are going to be shut down in Youngstown.
>
> You've got men here, you've got women here, you've got children here, and we're here for one purpose. Not to be talked to about what's going to happen in Congress two years from now. What's going to happen today? There's a building two blocks from here. That's the US Steel headquarters. [Laughter] You know the whole country is looking at the voters, the citizens. What are you going to do? Are you going to make an action, or are you going to sit and talk and be talked to?
>
> The action is today. We're going down that hill, and we're going to let the politicians know, we're going to let US Steel know, we're going to let the whole country know that steelworkers in Youngstown got guts,

> and we want to fight for our jobs. We're not going to fight for welfare! [Cheers]
>
> In 1919 the fight was on for the eight-hour day and they lost that struggle and they burned East Youngstown, which is Campbell. Now I'm not saying burn anything down, but you got the eight-hour day.
>
> In 1937 you wanted a union and people got shot in Youngstown because they wanted a union. And everything hasn't been that great since you got that union. Every day you put your life on the line when you went into that iron house. Every day you sucked up the dirt and took a chance on breaking your legs or breaking your back. And anyone who's worked in there knows what I'm talking about.

Then came the most remarkable part of Ed's speech. Addressing an audience that included many Blacks but was primarily made up of white middle Americans, he read an extended excerpt from Frederick Douglass's 1857 speech: 'Power concedes nothing without a demand. It never did and it never will.' Finally, Mann concluded, 'Now, I'm going down that hill and I'm going into that building ... and ... we're going to stay there until they meet with Bob Vasquez.' The crowd surged out of the union hall, moved down the hill, smashed the front door of US Steel's administration building, and occupied the building until the company agreed to talk.[12]

The Workers' Solidarity Club of Youngstown

The network of friends that had formed in the campaigns against steel mill shutdowns (and through the first five years of my representation of discharged workers) needed a vehicle for its further expression. We wanted a place where rank-and-file workers could go to get strike support without a lot of hassle and delay. We were disillusioned with big national unions that encourage their members to 'pay your dues and leave the rest to us.' We were called rebels and dissidents, but we believed in solidarity, and we wanted a way to see each other regularly, share experiences, laugh at each other's jokes, and dream up plans to change the world.

The Workers' Solidarity Club grew out of classes at the hall of Utility Workers Local 118, where the club still meets. Local 118 had been through a long stike a couple of years earlier. There was a core of members who were eager to give tangible strike support to other workers on strike. In the fall of 1981, we held a series of discussions at the hall on the topic What Has Gone Wrong with the Labor Movement? We talked about all kinds of things – for instance, the encyclical by the Pope called 'On Human Labor'. As the discussions drew to a close, we realized we didn't want to disband. We gave ourselves a name and started to meet monthly.

From the beginning, the club has been extremely informal. There are no officers except a treasurer. Two members put out a monthly notice describing what is expected to happen at the next meeting. Individuals volunteer (or are drafted at the last minute) to chair meetings. If there is a speaker scheduled, the person who invited the speaker is likely to become chairperson. There are no dues, but by passing the hat we have raised hundreds of dollars for legal defense, publications and travel expenses. We also raise money by selling bright red suspenders with the words 'Workers' Solidarity' silk-screened in black. Beer at the end of every meeting and annual Christmas parties keep us cheerful.

The Workers' Solidarity Club is like a Wobbly 'mixed local', or a local branch of Polish Solidarity, in that its members come from many different trades and unions. A recent leaflet was signed by twenty-five people. Of these, seventeen are current employees; they work for Ohio Edison, Schwebel Baking Company, LTV Steel, and other enterprises. Six of the seventeen are stewards or local union officers. The remaining signers are retired or unemployed. The signers include present or former members of the Utility Workers, the Laborers, the Steelworkers, the Bakery Workers, the Teamsters, the Mine Workers, the Ohio Education Association and the Amalgamated Clothing Workers.

Out first big action came in the summer of 1982.[14] Service and maintenance workers at Trumbull Memorial Hospital in Warren, Ohio organized in an AFSCME local, went on strike. Two members of the club visited the picket line. The club put out a series of leaflets that appealed to strikebreakers not to cross the picket line: 'THINK before you cross a picket line. Think before you take your neighbor's job.'

The leaflets also invited members of other unions to rally every Wednesday afternoon in front of the hospital. The rallies grew larger and larger. People brought homemade banners and signs, and chanted slogans like 'Warren is a union town, we won't let you tear it down.'

On 13 October 1982, there was a confrontation with the Warren police. Thirteen demonstrators were arrested, including three members of the club: Ed Mann; Greg Yarwick, a member of Local 118; and Ken Porter, laid off from a local cement company. The other arrestees entered agreed-on pleas for lesser offenses and paid a fine. Ed, Greg and Ken pled not guilty and were convicted of conspiracy to riot and resisting arrest. With the help of the ACLU they appealed to the Court of Appeals and Supreme Court of Ohio. In the end, not only were they acquitted, but the club recovered $1,000 in court costs from the City of Warren.

As a result of all this mass activity, the AFSCME local survived the strike. Afterwards the club conducted classes for sixty to eighty members of the AFSCME local at the hall of Local 1375, USWA.

Other club activities have included weekly picketing at the Bessemer Cement Company, which closed and cut off benefits (only to reopen as a non-union shop under a different owner), and strike support for the United Food and Commerical Workers. Although there are three lawyers in the club, we all agree that legal acitivity should reinforce mass activity, not the other way around. For example, when a local bakery became notorious for its many firings, club members were involved in picketing, NLRB charges, and a lawsuit. The number of firings has since decreased dramatically. In another instance, executives of one of the very few businesses to move to Youngstown since the steel mills closed, Avanti Motors, told the local media that if a union were organized they might leave town. The Workers' Solidarity Club filed a charge with the National Labor Relations Board. Avanti Motors was obliged to post a notice promising not to threaten a shutdown, and the UAW is now organizing the plant.

In evaluating the Trumbull Hospital strike, many club members felt that our role had been essentially reactive. Union leaders made decisions about strategy. Rank-and-file members and strike supporters had to live with these decisions whether or not they agreed with them. The sentiment was expressed that the club should seek ways to do its own organizing.

This has been a long process, and of course we are still learning. Club members have been involved in three attempts to organize unions. One was successful. A small group of visiting nurses and home health aides formed an independent union for which they (not we!) chose the name Visiting Nurses Solidarity. Two other organizing drives, at medium-sized metal fabricators, have failed.

The most dramatically successful organizing in which club members have taken part involves retirees from LTV Steel and other steel companies, and workers disabled by exposure to toxic chemicals at the Lordstown General Motors plant. These people are not union members but they are directly affected by union decisions. In the case of LTV Steel, for example, contracts affecting the pensions and medical benefits of over 40,000 hourly retirees are ratified by 20,000–25,000 active workers. By organizing independently, retirees have been able to bring some pressure to bear on union decision-makers, although retirees still have no formal voice. At GM, chemically disabled former workers and the relatives of deceased workers have joined forces with current rank-and-file employees to do something about occupational hazards.

In all this activity, a solidarity-building process is at work. Youngstown-area LTV retirees, organized as Soldarity USA (again a name chosen wholly by those involved), have reached out to other LTV retirees in Canton, Ohio and Aliquippa, Pennsylvania, and to retirees from other, smaller steel companies. The group from General Motors, known as Workers Against Toxic Chemical Hazards (WATCH), has been sought out by employees of other companies who are exposed to similar hazards. Some of the leaders of both Solidarity USA and WATCH have become new and valued participants in the Workers' Solidarity Club.

What is the purpose of the Workers' Solidarity Club? What is its long-range contribution to rebuilding the labor movement in Youngstown? There may be as many legitimate answers to these questions as there are members of the club. At a recent meeting, one member characterized the club as the local labor movement's SWAT team. One of the club's founders remarked, 'We don't fit in. We shouldn't. We're free-flowing.' Another long-time participant commented on the hundreds of people who have passed through meetings of the club during its eight-year history: 'What we've shown is that you have to get people involved; you just can't throw money at problems, but must be able to build a mass movement in your own backyard.'

Recently, the club has seemed on its way to building that mass movement. The first 1989 meeting of Solidarity USA attracted an estimated 400 persons. The Mahoning County AFL-CIO Council has invited Solidarity USA to send a delegate to its meetings on behalf of retirees, and Ed Mann attends.

There are a couple of things we would like to share with others who might want to try something similar. First, from the outset, a majority of those present have been rank-and-file workers or retirees. Rather than fast-speaking professionals or academics setting the tone, it's been the other way around. While lawyers and academics (including the director of labor studies at the local university) take part, they are minority voices.

Second, we have discouraged lecturing, and rarely make long written presentations. We think that a broader consciousness has grown naturally from the experience of talking and acting together. Having lived through the way big corporations trampled on people's lives in Youngstown, we find it easy to relate to corporations doing the same thing to Indians in the Southwest or to Nicaragua. In April 1988, four members of the club went to Nicaragua for two weeks with steelworkers from Aliquippa and Pittsburgh. Most of the group worked at the Metasa steel mill near Managua. In February 1989 one of the group, an electric lineman, returned with a fellow worker and helped string electric lines bringing power to a hospital in northern Nicaragua.

Third, we don't feel the need to come to a group decision about the correctness of a proposed action before a member does something. Instead, the member will say, 'I'm planning to do so-and-so. I need help. Any one who wants to give me a hand, meet me at such-and-such a time and place.' Acting in this way gives us a chance to try out things in practice. It's like the experimental method in science. We're able to draw conclusions from what works and what doesn't.

Personally, I think that the Workers' Solidarity Club of Youngstown is doing what the line in 'Solidarity Forever' talks about: in its small way, it is bringing to birth a new world from the ashes of the old. All around us is a capitalist society that believes in dog-eat-dog. We in the labor movement know that at its best our movement is bound to a higher ethic: that an injury to one is an injury to all. But we have to live that ethic, not just talk about it. The basic idea is simply that if we believe in solidarity, we should start living that way here and now.

What Have We Proved?

It's more than twenty years since 1968, when different people chose such differnt ways to try to move forward. At a reunion of SDS people in the summer of 1988, I said I felt like those Japanese soldiers who were found on Pacific islands in the 1950s, still thinking there was a war on. I feel I am still trying to carry out the assignment I undertook in the late 1960s (to be sure, in the manner of that Movement, it was an assignment I gave myself). But there is no headquarters to which I can report my results, no general staff to evaluate my experiment.

The work in Youngstown has reached the point that, if there were a national movement to join, we might appropriately become a local chapter. But if that movement exists, we are not aware of it. The available national organizations all seem premature, top-down, focused on national election happenings rather than on building a vigorous local movement. Specifically with regard to labor, these organizations tend to approach workers from the top, through the national bureaucracies of various unions. And I'll confess frankly that I am still so shell-shocked by the way the Movement of the 1960s ended that I am frightened to try again.

Nevertheless, we in Youngstown have proved certain things to be possible. In a community with no organized left presence, a growing number of workers have come to identify with the left's most fundamental perspectives: anti-imperialism, acted out by workers who use their vacactions to do skilled labor in Nicaragua; anti-racism and feminism (the chairpersons of Solidarity USA and WATCH are women); and, most important, a thoroughgoing anti-capitalism, together with unblinking openness to what amount to socialist alternatives. At a recent meeting of the steering committee of Solidarity USA, the evening came alive around discussion of an endorsement of socialized medicine.

These experimental findings tend to rebut, not just the naive disregard of workers characteristic of the 1960s, but the sophisticated premise of much of the new labor history that the Marxist model for how workers become radicals is 'essentialist' and wrong. The two-step process of radicalization posited in *The Communist Manifesto* is more or less the process I have seen unfold with my own eyes in Youngstown. And 'if two and two and fifty make a million, we'll see that day come round.'

Notes

1. Tom Hayden, *Reunion: A Memoir*, New York 1986, p. 263.
2. Staughton Lynd and Alice Lynd, *Rank and File: Personal History by Working-Class Organizers*, 3d edn, New York 1988.
3. Nick Salvatore, *Eugene V. Debs: Citizen and Socialist*, Urbana, Ill. 1982, p. 161.
4. The following three paragraphs are drawn from Eric Leif Davin and Staughton Lynd, 'Picket Line and Ballot Box: The Forgotten Legacy of the Local Labor Party Movement, 1932–1936', Radical History Review, vol. 22, Winter 1979–80, pp. 43–63.
5. See Staughton Lynd, 'The Possibility of Radicalism in the Early 1930s: The Case of Steel', in James Green, ed., *Workers' Struggles, Past and Present: A* Radical America *Reader*, Philadelphia 1983, pp. 190–208, and 'The United Front in America: A Note', *Radical America*, vol. 8, July–August 1974, pp. 29–38.
6. V.I. Lenin, *Imperialism: The Highest Stage of Capitalism*, New York 1939, p. 106.
7. Lynd and Lynd, *Rank and File*, p. 268.
8. The 'leper colony' image for an abandoned steel town occurs both in the papers John Barbero left at his death in 1981 and in the words of another Youngstown retiree, Mike Bibich, quoted in Teresa Anderson, 'Mike Bibich and Youngstown, Ohio', *The Mill Hunk Herald*, Winter 1985–86, p. 14. Barbero made his remark about 'non-persons' in the audiovisual tape *Shout Youngstown!* by Dorie Kraus and Carol Greenwald.
9. Barbero and Mann together with others in the RAFT group tell their stories in 'A Common Bond', *Rank and File*, pp. 259–78. The Workers' Solidarity Club will publish a pamphlet biography of Ed Mann at the end of 1989, which may be ordered from the Lynds, 1694 Timbers Court, Niles, Ohio 44446.
10. See Lynd and Lynd, *Rank and File*, pp. 267–68, where Barbero comments, 'It seems to me that the United Labor Party was the SDS of its day, very democratic, very free in attitude .... All of them looked to Trotsky. ... It was the one group in my life where everybody seemed to trust each other. ... In fact, they had a slogan in the United Labor Party, "The only left party that treats a member as well as a non-member".' See also Staughton Lynd, 'A Chapter from History: The United Labor Party, 1946–1952', *Liberation*, Dec. 1973, which draws on the papers of several former members.
11. Staughton Lynd, *The Fight Against Shutdowns: Youngstown's Steel Mill Closings*, San Pedro, Calif. 1983, and 'The Genesis of the Idea of a Community Right to Industrial Property in Youngstown and Pittsburgh, 1977–1987, *Journal of American History*, vol. 74, no. 3, pp. 266–98.
12. Lynd, *The Fight Against Shutdowns*, pp. 153–55.
13. This description of the Workers' Solidarity Club of Youngstown appeared in a slightly different form in *Labor Notes*, March 1989.
14. A Workers' Solidarity Club pamphlet, 'The Trumbull Memorial Hospital Strike', can be obtained by sending $1 to Ed Mann, 6078 Richards Ave. SE, Hubbard, Ohio 44425.

7

Bank Hegemony and Class Struggle in Cleveland, 1978–79

Davita Silfen Glasberg

We have just passed the tenth anniversary of Cleveland's infamous 1978 default. It is rare for a city to actually default; banks usually renegotiate municipal debt to avoid this outcome, and Cleveland's experience is thus noteworthy. We are entering the 1990s with a murky economic outlook made more complicated by a restructuring of the banking community as a result of deregulation. What lessons can we learn from Cleveland's case, as cities approach the next decade facing a watershed period that could yield either growth or decline?

What factors influence urban decline and fiscal crises in American cities? This question increasingly concerns social scientists and politicians alike, and has generated considerable debate. While some observers point to bureaucratic inefficiency and corruption, normal economic cycles, or market politics as the sources of municipal fiscal crises, others blame capital mobility.

Along these lines, critics have recently begun to emphasize the role of relocation of the means of production as a major factor in urban decline and fiscal crises (Bluestone and Harrison, 1982; Stillman, 1983; Kennedy, 1984; Yago et al., 1984). The ability of corporations to change production sites at will can and often does precipitate urban economic depressions due to job loss. However, this analysis is incomplete, ignoring the impact of those corporations that remain in the city. What influence do they have in shaping urban policy? Moreover, what is the role of an organized banking community in influencing urban processes and policy? What is the effect on urban policy and decision-making processes when the business and banking communities coalesce? Capital mobility decisions can be motivated by political/economic concerns, such as capital accumulation and the control of labor (Gordon, 1977). When the state fails in its role to assist capital accumulation, fiscal crises of the state ensue, as firms leave in search of greater state assistance, including subsidies, tax breaks, low-interest loans, and money for training. Banks encourage the state to stimulate capital accumulation by extending short-term municipal loans and by influencing how the state spends borrowed capital. Loans will not be extended for municipal activities that compete with private enterprise (O'Connor, 1973:193). Finance capital flows have been pivotal in determining both development (Beveridge, 1985) and decline in US cities (Ratcliff, 1979; 1980a; 1980b; Lichten, 1980; 1986; Tabb, 1982; 1984; Newfield, 1983), but what motivates finance capital mobility into and out of cities?

The process of Cleveland's default highlights an important distinction between mobility of productive capital and finance capital mobility. Whereas urban decline produced by runaway shops results from the actions of individual corporations, the effect of finance capital mobility results from the collective control of capital flows by an organized banking community. Cities victimized by runaway shops can attract new or competing corporations or industries to replace the lost ones. It is not possible, however, to attract alternative sources of finance capital because of banking's hegemonic position, particularly among the lending consortia and the bond market community. The inaccessibility of alternative sources of finance capital empowers banks to interfere in and influence urban policy formation. Hence, in order to understand urban crises, we must appreciate the political power of organized finance capital and its ability to shape urban policy. Cleveland's experience in 1978–79 provides an instructive example of how this power is exercised.

Cleveland is an older industrial city in the northern Midwest, where unions have historically been strong. Iron and steel manufacturing and Great Lakes shipping once dominated the city's economy. Like many other industrial cities in hte Midwest, Cleveland's economy began to erode in the late 1940s because of recession, foreign competition, mechanization, and perhaps most important, plant closings (Swanstrom, 1985:72). Cleveland's decline reached a crisis in 1978 and 1979, when a hostile banking community locked horns with City Hall, resulting in Cleveland's default on $15 million in loans.

What caused the city to reach the point of default, and why was the banking community so intransigent in its refusal to rollover or renegotiate the loans? What provoked the banking community's antagonism and provided a basis for its power over Cleveland? What role did the banking community play in shaping local policy making in Cleveland?

Public Interest vs. Private Interest: Populating the Barricades

National attention focused on Cleveland in 1977 when the city's voters sent Dennis Kucinich to the mayor's office. The youngest mayor of a major US city, he was elected on the conviction that the city needed to maintain public control of the municipal power system (US Congress, House: 1979a:6). Kucinich had preserved his working-class life-style and loyalties as the son of a Croatian-American truck driver, a self-proclaimed populist maverick and advocate of the interests of the city's working class, which formed the base of his political power. For some analysts, this populist activism produced the business and banking communities' animosity to his administration, as the city's economic leaders (with Cleveland Trust Company, Cleveland's largest bank in the forefront) tried ' ... to capsize it [the populist activism] through default' (Branfman, 1979:44). Others point to Kucinich's belligerent personality for much of the city's combative relations with the banks. Kucinich did indeed engage in several highly publicized clashes throughout his term, often reported as personal squabbles sparked by his abrasive style. However, evidence suggests that the hostilities and battles were more fundamentally politically and economically motivated by powerful interests in the city.

Tenacious attempts to place a special recall election on the ballot to remove Kucinich from office were largely financed by the city's banks and the Greater Cleveland Growth Association (GCGA) and by the personal resources of the banks' officers and directors. Four of the city's six banks and the GCGA together provided $20,228 to the campaign and the officers and directors (and their families) of four of the six banks individually contributed at least $8,750 more (US Congress: House, 1979a:772–73). A congressional report concluded that 'when an effort to recall the Mayor [in the summer of 1978] was underway. ... Much of the banking fraternity – from which the Mayor was seeking an extension of the city's credit – lined up to support his ouster' (US Congress: House, 1979a:4).

These contributors were Cleveland's corporate elite, with strong ties to Cleveland Electric Illuminating Corporation (CEI) and the banking community. For example, White Consolidated Industries had officers who sat on CEI's board of directors. Squires, Sanders and Dempsey was the legal representative for CEI in its defense against Cleveland in an antitrust suit. One partner of this law firm was a former chairman of CEI and an advisory director of Cleveland Trust. Another partner sat on Central National Bank's board, and yet another on CEI's board (US Congress: House, 1979a:207). Jones, Day, Reavis and Pogue were the legal representatives of Ohio Edison (codefendents with CEI in Cleveland's antitrust suit). Partners of this law firm sat on the boards of the Central National, National City, and Cleveland Trust banks (US Congress: House, 1979a:207). These major business interests, along with the city's banks and GCGA, contributed 31.3 percent of the total $128,681 in recall campaign funds. Suburbanites, prominent members of the business community, and other corporations supplied the remainder of the recall campaign contributions (*Cleveland Plain Dealer*, 22 April 1979).

The city's working class and its unions, together with Cleveland's legal representatives, provided most of the $102,000 raised to defend Kucinich's mayoralty). These included the United Auto Workers, Cleveland city workers, the American Federation of State, County and Municipal Employees, and Hahn, Loeser, Freedheim, Dean and Wellman, the city's legal representatives in its antitrust suit against the utilities (*Plain Dealer*, 28 September 1978); these organizations contributed 71.6 percent of the campaign funds raised to support Kucinich. The recall election was not, as commonly believed, a grass-roots movement of the city's voters. Rather, the city's working class and their representatives rallied to Kucinich's defense against the city's corporate elite.

The city's dominating force was Cleveland Trust Company (CTC). CTC was the lead bank in Cleveland's lending consortium, which comprised the city's six major banks. In addition to its intricate network of interlocking directorate relationships, all but two of its twenty-six directors were executives of firms whose single largest stockholder or principal stockholder was CTC. A 1968 congressional investigation identified CTC and

Cleveland's other major banks as 'probably the single most influential element in the entire economy of the area' (US Congress: House, 1979a:195a). The dominating influence of CTC on corporate boards was widely acknowledged by other bankers, one of whom noted that 'no one can ignore the voting power they hold' on corporate boards (US Congress: House, 1979a:196). One businessman complained that CTC's domination was 'one of the greatest deterrents to the growth of Cleveland.' CTC and its chief executive officer and chairman, Brock Weir, were not reluctant to exercise this power to influence the electoral process, as was noted during congressional hearings:

> There's enough conviction in the financial community of Cleveland and enough resources to fill the short-term need with their own resources, provided we have *confidence in whom we're dealing with.* [Emphasis added] ... I have said I would personally undertake a program to develop an enthusiasm for the banks to recognize the possibility in the right circumstances of putting together a consortium that could provide up to $50 million. (*Financier*, April 1979; cf US Congress, House: 1979a:196–97)

The banking and business communities clearly suported the recall effort. Yet, in spite of their opposition to the mayor, Kucinich retained his position by a narrow margin (*New York Times*, 15 August 1978; 18 August 1978).

While Kucinich's energies focused on defending his political position, Cleveland's economic problems grew more serious. Part of the city's difficulties derived from a national trend in capital mobility. Many industries and manufacturing plants in the upper Midwest and Northeast were relocating to the US South and Southwest and overseas, largely in search of cheaper labor. Since 1969, the trend of runaway shops left Cleveland with an annual loss of 17,000 jobs, and an annual population drain of 20,000 (*New York Times*, 13 November 1978).

Although these indicators of economic decline were indeed quite serious, the city's default was not inevitable. Nor were these economic problems caused by Kucinich or his personality. The most devastating blows to the city were delivered by the spending habits of the administration of Mayor Ralph Perk (1971–77). Perk's solution to the city's revenue loss was to meet daily operating costs with money from bonds for capital improvement projects (Marschall, 1979:54). The Kucinich administration came to City Hall faced with having to restore $52 million in misspent bond funds. City Council President George Forbes conceded that the Council could have 'brought the city to a halt then [in 1978] instead of today' (*Cleveland Plain Dealer*, 3 August 1978).

In addition to the inappropriate use of bond funds, Perk also increased Cleveland's short-term debt fourfold, from $22 million to $88 million (Marschall, 1979:54). Perk's short-sighted attempt to raise the city's revenues contributed to Cleveland's cash flow shortage in 1978. This was because of the legal stipulation that the short-term notes issued in 1972 and 1973 be transferred to bonds in 1978 and 1979. The bill for Perk's highly questionable fiscal management thus came due during Kucinich's administration.

Perk also burdened the city's fiscal position when he granted almost $35 million in tax abatements for the construction of two new office towers, one of them for National City Bank (Marschall, 1979:26; Clavel, 1986:78). Thus, while Ralph Perk's incompetent fiscal management planted the seeds of Cleveland's financial crisis in 1978, Cleveland's banks neither supervised nor questioned Perk's spending and accounting practices.

By December 1978 the city was veering toward default on $15.5 million in notes due that month. Kucinich responded by asking voters to support a 50 percent increase in city income taxes. The City Council, however, fiercely opposed this proposal. In fact, the Council had consistently opposed all proposals except the sale of the city-owned electric utility (Municipal Electric Lighting Corporation, or MUNY). These efforts to avoid Cleveland's default had already galvanized the financial community: Moody's, Standard and Poor's, and The Dreyfus Tax Exempt Fund had downgraded Cleveland's bond rating to BAA by June 1978. One month later, Standard and Poor's simply suspended the city's rating (US Congress: House, 1979b:507; *New York Times*, 7 December 1978). This forced the city out of the national bond market, and meant that its only alternative was loans from its banks. Moreover, Cleveland's lead bank, Cleveland Trust Co. (which held $5 million in loans due that December) opposed Kucinich's fiscal rehabilitation and recovery proposals. CTC chief executive officer Brock Weir announced that the banks would renegotiate Cleveland's debts to avoid default only if the city sold MUNY. Kucinich flatly refused. The stalemate between the mayor, the City

Council and the banks meant default on $15.5 million in loans by mid-December 1978.

Cleveland's problems were aggravated when the Carter administration denied Kucinich's petition for an advance on the city's revenue sharing funds (*New York Times*, 17 December 1978). Federal officials asserted that the city's fiscal crisis was of its own making because its expenditures exceeded its revenues. The Carter administration believed that municipal fiscal crises are best resolved on the local level. Moreover, Ohio law abandoned Cleveland because of the stipulation that the state may not intervene in the affairs of chartered cities 'without formal invitation'. Cleveland's officials did not want Ohio's state government to intervene because they anticipated losing local control of the city (*New York Times*, 24 December 1978). Cleveland was thus isolated in a direct confrontation with an antagonistic banking community.

The Banks, CEI and MUNY Light: Power to the People?

Harvey Molotch has argued that land-based elites use the authority of the government to secure growth-producing resources in their city: 'Conditions of community life are largely a consequence of the social, economic, and political forces embodied in this growth machine' (Molotch, 1976:309). Municipal Electric Light Corporation, a growth-producing resource, became the focus of struggles between the city government and city elites in the battle to resolve Cleveland's fiscal crisis. MUNY, a publicly owned electric system that provided relatively cheap electricity to 20 percent of the city's residents (and to all municipal buildings and streets), posed unwanted competition to Cleveland Electric Illuminating Company, a private utility.

Cleveland had created its own power system in 1905 instead of depending on existing private systems. From the beginning, demand for MUNY power was greater than its capacity (particularly during peak hours). MUNY was thus faced with the choice of purchasing power from its private competitor CEI or obtaining it from other utilities outside CEI's customer area. The problem increased over the years as demand surged and the condition of MUNY's operating plants declined. No matter which option MUNY chose to obtain power, an interconnection with CEI was imperative: the cost of constructing its own transmission lines was prohibitive.

CEI did not warmly greet the request for interconnection by its competitor, but it could not legally deny it. CEI's response, rather than the city's corrupt or inefficient expenditure policies, was a major factor in causing Cleveland's cash flow shortage. CEI formed an interconnection with MUNY only after years of protracted and bitter negotiations. And CEI supplied MUNY with insufficient power, causing regular power outages (US Congress: House, 1979a:205). The US Nuclear Regulatory Commission accused CEI of delaying restoration of service after power outages and of providing inadequate work crews for repairs and restorations (Bartimole, 1977). The result was a decline in MUNY's reputation as a reliable utility. 'CEI took advantage [of this situation] ... through its aggressive campaign to take customers away from MUNY' (US Congress: House, 1979a:205). When this campaign failed, CEI tried to eliminate competition from the public utility by simply buying it. In response, Cleveland filed an antitrust suit against CEI and other regional utilities in 1975 (US Congress: House, 1979a:205). However, the city lost its case and was forced to pay the entire bill for CEI-supplied power that had accumulated under the Perk administration. The requirement to pay these bills in full became one of the most important drains on the city's budget.

Supporters of the sale of MUNY to CEI, like the Greater Cleveland Growth Association, argued that the public utility's deteriorating physical plant was a financial drain on Cleveland. GCGA's position was predictable, since CEI had been one of the founders of the association in 1962 (Clavel, 1986:61). Kucinich vehemently opposed the sale of any city assets (particularly MUNY) to raise revenues, and challenged the GCGA's description of MUNY as a fiscal drain on the city:

> The operation of MUNY has been stabilized. It is no longer draining the city treasury. In fact, with the MUNY Light debt [to CEI] paid off, we can expect MUNY to earn several million dollars a year for the city, as well as continuing to furnish us with low-cost street lighting, which saves Cleveland's taxpayers hundreds of thousands of dollars yearly. (US Congress: House, 1979a:209)

This analysis was corroborated by the American Public Power Association, a trade association of public utilities.

The struggle to maintain MUNY as a viable public utility crystalized into what some observers called Cleveland's 'class war' (Branfman, 1979:43). Where Kucinich and his working-class supporters fought to preserve the publicly owned utility, the business and banking communities waged a rancorous campaign to force the sale of MUNY to CEI. Such a sale would leave CEI with a monopoly on Cleveland's electricity supplies. Kucinich appealed to Congress, charging the banking community with deliberately pushing the city into default to benefit its business allies by demanding the sale of MUNY to CEI as a precondition for renegotiation of Cleveland's debts (US Congress: House, 1979a:2–3; 1979b:5–13). Kucinich insisted that 'the decisions of the banks concerning extension of credit to the city [were] ... influenced by massive conflicts between the banks' loan-making functions and their direct and indirect ties to other interests in the Cleveland area' (US Congress: House, 1979a:1).

Why would Cleveland's banking community care about the ownership of MUNY Light? Congressional investigations identified a strong relationship between the city's six major banks (all of whom participated in Cleveland's lending consortium) and CEI, based on loans and lines of credit to CEI, shares of CEI stock held in trust and pension accounts administered by the banks, voting rights of shares of CEI stocks, interlocks between CEI and the banks (including direct representation of the banks on CEI's board), management of CEI pension funds by banks, and substantial CEI deposits at the banks. For example, four of the six banks provided a total of $74 million in lines of credit to CEI, and the two largest banks (CTC and National City) provided a total of $79 million in actual loans to CEI between 1974 and 1978 (US Congress: House, 1979a:372–74).

Furthermore, CEI maintained almost $2.8 million in compensating balances at four of the six banks (US Congress: House, 1979a:375). At least five of the six banks held almost 1.8 million shares in CEI (Capital National Bank did not provide its figures), holding voting rights for more than 1 million shares (US Congress: House, 1979a:50). Cleveland Trust and National City combined held almost 4.5 percent of CEI's stock (US Congress: House, 1979a:46) and 2.9 percent of its voting stock (US Congress: House, 1979a:47). These six banks shared 205 interlocking directorates with CEI and sent a total of 10 bank representatives to sit on CEI's board (US Congress: House, 1979a:183). Cleveland Trust was the sole manager of $70 million of a total of $130 million of CEI pension funds managed by the banks (US Congress: House, 1979b:10). In addition to these common links and interests between the banking community and CEI, the law firms representing the defendants named in Cleveland's antitrust suit against the utility provided indirect connections:

> The firm representing CEI is Squire, Sanders and Dempsey, a major law firm in Cleveland with 78 members and 95 associates. One of the Cleveland partners is Ralph Besse, former chairman of CEI and an advisory director of Cleveland Trust Company. Squire, Sanders and Dempsey also has a partner sitting on the board of Central National Bank and another on CEI's board. Representing Toledo Edison in the case was Jones, Day, Reavis and Pogue. That firm has 60 members and 58 associates in Cleveland and 63 members and associates in its Washington office. Partners of Jones, Day, Reavis and Pogue sit on the boards of Central National Bank, National City Bank, and Cleveland Trust Company. (US Congress: House, 1979a:207)

These structural arrangements unified CEI and Cleveland's banking community in their battle against the city over the sale of MUNY Light. Because of their enormous investments in CEI, it was in the banks' collective interest to eliminate any cost competition from its publicly owned rival.

Interlocks between banks and local nonfinancial corporations, moreover, tend to deprive the local community of finance capital (Ratcliff, Oehler, and Gallops, 1979). Banks give lending priority to their interlocked corporations over residential mortgage business, the availability of which is a key factor in urban development, such that lack of these funds produces urban decline, lower property values, and ultimately lower city revenues. Cleveland did, indeed, experience this problem of disinvestment and 'redlining' (US Congress: Senate, 1975; 1980). This disinvestment was significant in the face of the banks' investments and interlocks with CEI and other capital accumulation interests in Cleveland.

The investor-owned utilities around Cleveland had also become seriously interested in nuclear power generation. MUNY emphasized the cost inefficiencies of nuclear power compared to fossil fuels. This is because economies of scale are a critical factor in electric utility rates. The larger a plant and a system, the lower the kilowatt per hour costs (McGuire, 1986; Morgan, 1979; Doyle and Reinemer, 1979). That MUNY was the only large plant serving a large number of customers and that it had economies of scale comparable to the investor-owned utilities (such as CEI) was an important factor in the utility's and the banks' decision to act against it. By absorbing MUNY, CEI could expand its rate base and raise the revenues needed to build its nuclear power plant, while fending off the unpleasant possibility of a public inquiry into the desirability of nuclear power, the capital-intensive nature of which would have been plainly evident because of the markedly lower rates associated with MUNY's fossil fuel power generation.

But why would the banks care so much about such details of the utility industry? Investor-owned utilities' bonds are protected both indirectly and directly. Indirectly, the precedent set in 1898 by *Smyth* v. *Ames* (which is the basis of the industry's regulation) stipulates a 'reasonable return' on capital 'used and useful in the public's service' (Bonbright and Means, 1969:163; see also Metcalf and Reinemer, 1967:21–23, and Bonbright, 1972). The Supreme Court ruled in *Smyth* v. *Ames* that rates could not be set so low that it forced a private utility into bankruptcy (see Glaeser, 1957). Failure to pay a bond would do just that, especially since the utility's board could choose to use this as a form of leverage on public service commissions to secure the rates wanted. The phrase 'reasonable rate of return' soon 'became a de facto guarantee of income sufficient to cover operating costs of fixed and variable capital plus debt service and profits' (McGuire, 1986:258).

Sometimes, state guarantees of a bond can be applied directly in order to raise capital and stimulate bond sales during crises, or to support joint utility–state participation in a project. These bonds tend to be tax-free (Metcalf and Reinemer, 1967; Olson, 1976; Wasserman, 1979; Hertsgaard, 1983). Banks therefore obtain a guaranteed return at rates typically 2 percent to 3 percent above those issued by the state (McGuire, 1986). The total capital costs of the investor-owned utility industry swelled more than 600 percent between 1969 and 1979 (Munson, 1979:349), a significant increase in the bond market when other industries were suffering recession and contraction. Banks, then, had a clear interest in supporting the investor-owned utilities in Cleveland (particularly CEI) and in the utilities' growing interest in nuclear power investments. Costs of such investments would be routinely passed on to consumers and supported by state-guaranteed bonds. They therefore represented a risk-free and highly profitable venture for the banks.

In addition to the ample evidence of the fusion of the banks' interests with those of CEI and the business community, there was a political dispute between Kucinich and National City

Bank, a member of Cleveland's lending consortium that held $4 million of the city's notes. National City had been given a $14 million tax abatement from Mayor Perk to support construction of the bank's new headquarters. Kucinich vehemently opposed this abatement. The banks' willingness to thrust the city into default to further their own political agenda was best expressed when National City's Chairman Claude MacClary Blair pronounced that 'default, with all its problems, might be the best thing that could happen to Cleveland if it meant the defeat of Dennis Kucinich' (US Congress: House, 1979a:830).

The banks' frustration with their inability to win a recall election to unseat Kucinich apparently led them to resort to forcing default as their next best strategy. Cleveland Trust's Chairman and CEO M. Brock Weir blithely observed that the banks were not seriously worried about the city's fiscal difficulties: 'The business climate remains healthy'. Rather, the banks perceived Kucinich and his political perspectives to be at issue: 'The only problem is the little canker downtown' (US Congress: House, 1979a:830).

Although the city's financial picture was bleak, the banks could easily have rolled over Cleveland's loans (as is usually done when municipalities are in danger of default). But the sanctity and security of a favorable political climate to support the elimination of MUNY Light as a source of cost competition for CEI and the reinstatement of the banks' tax breaks were more important. Said Weir, 'We [the banks] had been kicked in the teeth for six months. On December 15 [1978], we decided to kick back ... ' (US Congress: House, 1979a:829).

The banks were joined by the Greater Cleveland Growth Association in their efforts to pressure the city to sell MUNY Light. GCGA's Taxation Committee had advocated the sale of MUNY Light as early as 1977. GCGA's position was to be expected, given the strong relationships between GCGA, the banking community and CEI. These interconnections put the banks and CEI in a unique position to influence the organization. The GCGA is governed by a chairperson, nine vice-chairs, a treasurer and a secretary-general. The chair and three of the nine vice-chairs were officers or directors of the banks in Cleveland's lending consortium. Nine of GCGA's 25-member executive committee were officers or directors of the banks, and 2 were officers or directors of CEI. Ten of GCGA's 51-member board of directors were officers or directors of the banks, and 2 were officers or directors of CEI. Five of GCGA's

10-member ex-officio executive committee were officers or directors of the banks (US Congress: House, 1979a:211–13). The significance of this strong representation of banks at GCGA underscores the political (rather than fiscal) motivation of the banks' actions against the city: evidence indicates that as early as 1975, GCGA was aware that Cleveland's budget and accounting reports did not provide an accurate assessment of the city's fiscal condition. A report from the association advised Cleveland against reliance on short-term notes and recommended instead that the city sell some of its assets to raise operating revenues (US Congress: House, 1979a:214). Yet the banks continued to lend short-term money to Cleveland until 1978 without insisting on greater accountability or improved ledger management by City Hall.

Both the banks and the GCGA continued to insist on the sale of MUNY Light. The failure to press for improved fiscal management and the continued extension of loans beyond the GCGA's estimation of prudence placed the city in the banks' control three years later, forcing the sale of MUNY Light, which Cleveland Trust demanded as a precondition for renewal of the loans necessary to avoid the city's default.

Cleveland's quickly eroding economy forced Kucinich to soften his opposition to the sale of MUNY Light, and to float a proposal that provided for an increase in the city income tax from 1 percent to 1.5 percent. The City Council approved Kucinich's referendum proposal after a contentious debate. The sale of the public utility, however, was never completed. The voters agreed to raise the city's income tax but refused to sell MUNY.

Kucinich then appealed to the City Council to approve an ordinance to get the city's lending consortium to refinance Cleveland's defaulted loans. Cleveland Trust Company eventually agreed not to demand repayment of $5 million on which Cleveland had defaulted until after 27 February 1979. At this point, business and civic leaders agreed to develop 'new cooperative efforts to rescue the city from default' (*New York Times*, 30 December 1978).

Throughout these struggles and negotiations, Cleveland Electric Illuminating Company tried to tighten the vise around the city with a request for a 25 percent rate increase for the power it sold to Cleveland: Kucinich strongly protested the request. Despite all protestations, however, Cleveland suffered another setback in its dispute with Cleveland Electric when the city was denied review by the US Supreme Court of its appeal in a 'dispute over its authority to pay off some electric bills' . The Ohio Supreme Court's ruling stood unchallenged: the city could not issue bonds to pay its debts to Cleveland Electric. That decision confirmed Cleveland's inability to tap the national bond market and tightened the grip of the lending consortium. After nearly destroying the city financially with its prolonged squabbling, the City Council and the Kucinich administration devised a fiscal rehabilitation plan to offer the banks, requiring 'an escrow account for income tax money from about 20 of Cleveland's biggest companies' (*New York Times,* 10 June 1979). Monies from the account were to be designated for payments to the banks in Cleveland's lending consortium.

The City Council steered Cleveland clear of a second default in July 1979 when it unanimously passed a provision giving the city another year to repay $7.6 million it had borrowed from its own agencies (*New York Times,* 7 July 1979). Kucinich also asked the council to repeal the legal requirement of a bond lawyer's approval to refinance the city's notes. Bond lawyers had previously denied that approval to the city.

Although the city avoided default on loans from its own agencies, it faced another default on 31 August. Following further clashes, Kucinich and the City Council finally agreed on a proposal to begin overdue repayments of loans to Cleveland's lending consortium. Later the Council agreed to refinance $14.4 million in municipal debts, which helped prevent a third default for Cleveland in less than a year.

Kucinich suffered the political fallout from Cleveland's struggles when he lost his bid for reelection. Republican Lt. Governor George V. Voinovich, who was strongly favored by business interests, defeated Kucinich in the acrimonious 1979 election. Voinovich's victory opened the door to the governor's mansion in Columbus and facilitated the city's access to finance capital: 'with Kucinich turned out of office, Governor James A. Rhodes, State Senate leadership, and the City Council [were] prepared to enact legislation that would allow the city to enter the debt market and gain some relief from a series of defaults that [had] plagued it for the last year' (*New York Times,* 8 November 1979). However, this effort was too late to turn around the city's economic prospects. Cleveland's officials conceded that even the 50 percent increase in the city's income tax rate did not prevent Cleveland from closing 1979 with an even larger deficit ($111 million) than in 1978.

Cleveland then hired Lazard-Frères and Company, the Wall Street banking firm and investment company, as its financial advisor. Among its partners was Felix G. Rohatyn, renowned for his success in rehabilitating New York City's finances. The mayor submitted a financial bail-out plan, which was approved by Cleveland's Financial Planning and Supervision Commission. By June 1980, Cleveland and the banks agreed to refinance $36.2 million in debt. This included the more than $10.5 million on which the city had already defaulted. The City Council also approved Voinovich's proposal to issue $36.2 million in 14-year bonds to the banks, thereby converting Cleveland's debts from short-term notes to long-term bonds.

Ironically, Voinovich found himself asking voters to increase the city income tax again, from 1.5 percent to 2 percent. Taken together, these measures worked: Cleveland balanced its budget 'for the first time in years' in 1980, with a $3.9 million surplus. Standard and Poor's resumed the city's previously suspended bond rating in August 1981 with a rating of BBB (*New York Times*, 16 August 1981). This gave Cleveland access once again to the national bond market, thereby loosening its tethers to the banks. By 1982 Cleveland began to enjoy downtown revitalization, reflecting 'growth of the skilled service industry' (*New York Times*, 5 February 1982). But expansion in the service sector had been well under way before 1982, and was vigorous during the Kucinich administration, suggesting that Cleveland's economy was relatively healthy during Kucinich's term as mayor. More important, the trend also suggests that the cause of the city's crisis and eventual default was not simple fiscal mismangement, but rather the politically motivated machinations of the banks and their allies.

Cleveland's struggles with the banking community and its default in 1978 revealed the role of finance capital in the development of urban crisis and in local policymaking processes. The banking and business communities never did achieve their goal of selling MUNY Light to CEI, primarily because Kucinich had succeeded in raising the issue as a symbol of class struggle, resulting in the voters' rejection of the sale. The ability of the banking community to push the city into default, however, unseated the populist Kucinich in an election that brought to power a mayor far more sympathetic to business interests. Indeed, Voinovich's bailout plan included an 8 percent increase in MUNY's rates to support CEI's increasingly expensive interconnection service. Voinovich also rectified Cleveland's accounting practices, made the city's books available to the banks, fired 650 municipal workers, and froze the wages of the remaining city employees. The upshot of Voinovich's program was that the working class, which had defeated the banking and business communities' grab at MUNY, was made to pay for the city's bailout through lost jobs, lower pay and higher income taxes. Adding insult to injury, the city used the revenues raised from increased income taxes to pay back the banks rather than to preserve jobs and services. The organized power of the banks was not absolute, but was strong enough to intrude into the electoral process. It was also sufficiently powerful to force reprisals against the working class by forcing the city into default and then eliciting a recovery program that hurt labor more than any other group.

Nor was the struggle over a municipal utility unique to Cleveland. Brock Weir was a seasoned warrior in municipal battles over such utilities. He had been a major opponent of the creation of San Francisco's public power system and the proposal for the city to take over part of Pacific Gas and Electric Co. in the early 1970s. An executive with the Bank of California (and now its president), Weir was Pacific Gas and Electric's largest stockholder (Rudolph and Ridley, 1986:254). Bruce Brugmann, editor of the San Francisco *Bay Guardian*, argued that Weir was specifically selected to head Cleveland Trust Company in 1973 because of his successful opposition to San Francisco's public takeover of the private utility (Rudolph and Ridley, 1986:255).

The prevalent media explanation for Cleveland's struggle with its banks cited Mayor Kucinich's confrontational style and aggressive personality. Such a monocausal and personalist explanation cannot be sustained. Cleveland's politics have historically been dominated by business interests. However, the city also has a long (although somewhat erratic) tradition of populist politics, with various community action organizations, unions and City Hall periodically mounting serious challenges to business interests (Clavel, 1986). In fact, Kucinich was not alone in the fight to preserve MUNY and to resist the banking and business communities. Those efforts were supported by the United Auto Workers, the American Federation of State, County and Municipal Employees, the Cleveland City Planning Commission, the Ohio Public Interest Campaign, and many local community organizations (Clavel, 1986; *Cleveland Plain*

Dealer, 28 September 1978).

Far from being a tale of one man's hubris, Cleveland's battle with the banks instanced something incomparably more significant: genuine class struggle. This view has been explicitly challenged by Todd Swanstrom in his *Crisis of Growth Politics* (1985). He contends that Kucinich's thin support among lower income voters and Blacks demonstrates the mayor's incapacity to represent working-class interests. Swanstrom points specifically to the numerous public confrontations between Kucinich and George Forbes, Cleveland's leading Black councilman. But while the limits of Kucinich's ethnic politics were revealed in these clashes, this by no means argues for the non-class basis of Kucinich's policies. The Forces–Kucinich struggle was, in fact, less about intra-class rivalry across a racial divide than about the distinctive class political programs of the two figures. Forbes consistently supported the interests of capital accumulation, precisely that which Kucinich stridently opposed. One could argue, of course, that the interests of the working class as a whole might better have been served by Forbes's program, but this was clearly not the view of many of the unions and community organizations that consistently supported Kucinich. The difference between Forbes and Kucinich was precisely that between reformist and class-struggle politics.

Municipal cash flow shortages do not inevitably result in default, as they did in Cleveland. New York City endured a similar crisis in 1976; but the banks collectively bailed out the city and averted fiscal collapse. The difference between Cleveland and New York City was the extent of cooperation by each city's respective mayors with the banks' perceptions of acceptable fiscal rehabilitation approaches. Kucinich stubbornly rebuffed the banks' insistence on the sale of MUNY Light. By contrast, New York City Mayor Ed Koch agreed to sell valuable city property to private interests, laid off a significant proportion of the municipal work force and severely cut the city's social welfare expenditures. He also insisted that the municipal workers' pension funds contribute to the city's bailout by purchasing the Big Mac bonds (see Lichten, 1980; 1986; Tabb, 1982). Koch's Emergency Financial Control Board also enabled a 'significant transfer of public power to the private sector' by creating an institutional mechanism through which 'the major banks and corporations were granted a direct veto over government decisions' (Berkman and Swanstrom, 1979:297), including the business and banking communities' participation in the negotiation of municipal workers' contracts. Whereas Kucinich refused to bail out the city on the backs of his working-class constituents, Koch implemented an austerity plan that disproportionately hurt labor. The results in each case depended on the banking community's definition of each city's situation and the consequent social construction of municipal reality: New York City was bailed out, and Cleveland was pushed into default. Noteworthy, too, is the fact that Cleveland was once again in danger of defaulting on its loans in June 1980; but instead of repeating the process of struggle with the city's mayor, the banks were quick to refinance its debt. The difference between Cleveland in 1978–79 and Cleveland in 1980 was that by the latter date the city was run by George Voinovich. In June 1980 the business community did not need to engage in struggle with the mayor, since 'their man' was already running the city instead of 'that little canker downtown'.

Conclusion

Urban decline and fiscal crises are often presumed to result from excessive city spending, coupled with declining revenues, or simply from poor fiscal management. This analysis is not supported by the case presented here. Cleveland's fiscal problems were not caused by extraordinarily low revenues or excessively high expenditures compared to other US cities (Beck, 1982:216). The cause was the banking community's collective control of the city's access to critical capital flows. Political/economic concerns and interests in the business and banking communities took precedence over the needs and interests of the city and its working-class citizens.

Bureaucratic and fiscal inefficiency in the Perk administration helped set the stage for fiscal crisis later, but by itself did not produce the city's default. CEI's behavior in opposing MUNY and its legal struggles with the city resulted in serious cash flow shortages for Cleveland, but again, these need not have inevitably produced default. Normal economic cycles, market-oriented investment, and capital mobility contributed to erosion of the city's economic base by shrinking its population, employment, property values, and tax revenues; but these were not sufficient to cause the city's default either. Other cities around the nation suffered similar problems but did not go into default. The critical factor here was the political/economic power of an organized banking community to pull its collective pursestrings and label Cleveland's cash flow shortage a crisis. Once the banks applied this definition to the economic situation, the mechanisms for producing default were set in motion (see Glasberg 1985 for a discussion of the social construction of crisis). The political/economic power of organized finance capital thus effectively defined the limits of Cleveland's policy options.

Cleveland's case is consistent with Whitt's (1979; 1980; 1982) assessment that urban elites strongly influence municipal policy formation and expenditure decisions. Although conflicts and antagonisms within the business and banking communities exist, these urban elites generally can achieve consensus on specific issues. Cleveland's case highlights the structural bases of this process of consensus formation. Elite consensus there developed through the structural mechanisms of the lending consortium, the GCGA, and interlocking directorates and stockholding between the banks and the business community. These structural bases of elite consensus do not necessarily ensure absolute domination of municipal decision-making. They do, however, provide the basis for the critical influence over urban policy by certain economic actors.

Urban decline and fiscal crises can be the result of the resolution of both corporate and finance capital accumulation problems. The problems of class struggle and class control in the capital accumulation process were evident in Cleveland, particularly in the issue of the sale of MUNY Light to CEI. The city's frequent and bitter labor strikes showed an increasingly militant labor force, and the sale of MUNY Light became the embodiment of the problem of labor control over capital accumulation. Bringing the city to default helped unseat a populist mayor and justified budget cuts that reinstituted greater control over labor.

Cleveland's default suggests the need for cities to develop alternative sources of financing to mitigate the influence of the business and banking communities on urban policy formation. Although this is clearly not an easy option to realize, an alternative capital source would offer cities an opportunity to counter the power of banks.

One possible avenue to explore is the use of pension funds. These represent the single largest pool of private capital in the world, topping $1 trillion and growing by approximately 10 percent annually (Rifkin and Barber, 1978; Born, 1980). Pension funds are currently managed by financial institutions as 'prudent investors', yet they have consistently underperformed the Standard and Poor's averages for at least twenty years (*Business Week*, 13 August 1984:86–93). In order for a cooperative partnership to develop between cities and their working-class citizens, labor must first regain control over these deferred wages. Such a cooperative partnership between labor and urban leaders can mean a greater role for labor in urban policy formation, and less dependence on the business and banking communities. New York's unions reluctantly bailed out the city by purchasing Big Mac bonds with their pensions. But they never insisted on power-sharing and participation in the city's decision-making. The unions took great risks without gaining benefits or power (in fact, they suffered pay and benefit cuts and lost jobs). Alternatively, municipal unions might offer to purchase bonds or lend their cities money from pension funds in exchange for meaningful participation in decision making and policy formation. This arrangement not only gives the working class an active function in creating urban policy, but also provides an alternative source of finance capital.

Indeed, lack of access to finance capital became an important barrier to progressive urban politics in Cleveland. As such, issues concerning capital flows should be given serious consideration when cities attempt to implement progressive policies. Swanstrom (1988:247) has contended that 'it was not just the banks who killed [Kucinich's populist] experiment; Kucinich made crucial political errors on questions of race, coalitional politics, and neighborhood empowerment.' No doubt. Does that invalidate the class character and the power of collective pursestrings in defining Cleveland's political economic reality? Hardly. Kucinich's political errors and his abrasive style simply made him (and therefore his agenda) an easier, bigger target for the banks. His style and his political mistakes drew attention away from the class basis of the populist issues he tried to raise. The banks' collective ability to throw the city into default also forced the city to focus on crisis management, thereby obscuring long-term class issues.

Kucinich's manifest deficiency in political savvy cannot erase the basic facts in the case: to wit, that the political/economic power of the banks acting in concert was simply too great at that moment for the local working class to overcome. As always, the outcome of such struggles depends not only on the tactical skills of the combatants, but on the balance of forces on each side. One cannot avoid the suspicion that even the cleverest of political maneuvers could not have mounted a more successful challenge to the banks' power.

In the intervening years since Cleveland's fiscal crisis, federal deregulation of the banking industry has significantly augmented the banks' collective power by concentrating greater capital resources in ever fewer hands. Reversing the mania for deregulation that overtook the Carter administration in its later years and continued under Reagan could, in principle, help to limit the collective strength of banks in relation to municipalities. In addition, the reinstitution of federal revenue sharing could increase the financial resources to which cities have access, thereby reducing their reliance on bank loans.

Barring such shifts in policy on the federal level – most unlikely in the current political climate – cities will perforce have to rethink their relation to sources of financing. As Todd Swanstrom has recently argued, 'Almost all cities have access to an impersonal national bond market, and most municipal lending today is not done by banks' (1988:246).

But if we are to draw any lesson from the experience of Cleveland ten years after the Kucinich experiment, it is surely that cities remain precariously perched atop a pile of soft financing that can vanish virtually overnight, leaving the city clinging by its fingertips to the ledge of solvancy, while the banks, like the Joker at the end of *Batman*, stomp on them mercilessly. Deprived of the high-tech gadgetry that ultimately delivers Bruce Wayne and Vicki Vaughn to safety (and, not incidentally, does in the Joker), cities must consider the more sober and realistic course of responsible fiscal administration, reasonable, nonregressive taxation, and integration of the working class in the political process beyond election day. Confronted by the legacy of mismanagement and ovespending of previous administrations and by the collective resolve of the local financial and business communities to resist at all costs any infringement on their prerogatives, Kucinich hardly stood a chance.

But not every municipal government faces such insurmountable obstacles to replacing the stranglehold of capitalist finance over its political life. As cities recover their economic viability, the potential for successful resistance grows. If the Kucinich administration was doomed by the bad fortune of arriving at the wrong historical moment, one need not conclude that it now represents an opportunity lost forever.

References

Bartimole, R. 1977. 'US Ruling Puts CEI in Jeopardy of Losing $325 Million Antitrust Suit to MUNY Light'. *Point of View* 9(14):11–14.

Beck, John H. 1982. 'Is Cleveland Another New York?' *Urban Affairs Quarterly* 18(2):207–16.

Bell, Daniel. 1973. *The Coming of Post-Industrial Society*. New York: Basic Books.

Berkman, Ronald, and Swanstrom, Todd. 1979. 'Koch vs. Kucinich: A Tale of Two Cities.' *Nation* 24 March: 297–99.

Beveridge, Andrew A. 1985. 'Credit and Community Change: A Case Study During Early United States Industrialization'. Paper presented at the annual meeting of the American Sociological Association, Washington DC.

Block, Fred. 1977. 'The Ruling Class Does Not Rule'. *Socialist Revolution* 7(3):6–28.

Bluestone, Barry, and Harrison, Bennett. 1982. *The Deindustrialization of America*. New York: Basic Books.

Born, Roscoe C. 1980. 'Pension Power: Organized Labor Seeks to Wield It More Aggressively'. *Barron's* December: 4–6ff.

Bonbright, James. 1972. *Public Utilities and National Power Politics*. New York: DaCapo Press.

Bonbright, James, and Means, Gardiner. 1969. *The Holding Company*. New York: August Kelley Publishing.

Branfman, Fred. 1979. 'The Cleveland Story: How the Banks Foreclosed Dennis Kucinich'. *Nation* 20 January: 43–46.

Breckenfeld, Gurney. 1977. 'Refilling the Metropolitan Doughnut'. In David C. Perry and Alfred J. Watkins, eds, *The Rise of the Sunbelt Cities*. Beverly Hills: Sage.

Business Week. 1984. 'Will Money Managers Wreck the Economy?' 13 August.

Clavel, P. 1986. *The Progessive City*. New Brunswick, NJ: Rutgers University Press.

Cleveland Plain Dealer. 1978–79; various issues, as noted.

Cook, Earl. 1971. 'The Flow of Energy in an Industrial Society'. *Scientific American* September: 135–43.

Doyle, Jack, and Reinemer, Vic. 1979. *Lines Across the Land*. Washington, DC: Environmental Policy Institute.

Glaeser, Martin. 1957. *Public Utilities in American Capitalism*. New York: Macmillan.

Glasberg, Davita Silfen. 1985. 'Corporate Crisis and the Role of Finance Capital in the Social Construction of Corporate Reality'. *Insurgent Sociologist* 13(1):39–51.

Gordon, David. 1977. 'Capitalism and the Roots of Urban Crisis', in Roger E. Alcaly and David Mermelstein, eds, *The Fiscal Crisis of American Cities*. New York: Vintage Books.

Hertsgaard, Mark. 1983. *Nuclear, Inc*. New York: Pantheon Books.

Kennedy, Michael D. 1984. 'The Fiscal Crisis of the City', in Michael Peter Smith (ed.) *Cities in Transformation: Class, Capital, and the State*, Beverly Hills: Sage.

Lichten, Eric. 1980. 'The Development of Austerity: Fiscal Crisis of New York City', in G. William Domhoff, ed., *Power Structure Research*. Beverly Hills: Sage.

Lichten, Eric. 1986. *Class, Power and Austerity: The New York City Fiscal Crisis*. Boston: Bergin and Garvey.

Magnet, Myron. 1989. 'How Business Bosses Saved a Sick City'. *Fortune* 27 March:106–110.

Marschall, D., ed. 1979. *The Battle of Cleveland: Public Interest Challenges Corporate Power*. Washington, DC: Conference on Alternative State and Local Policies.

McGuire, Patrick. 1986. 'The Control of Power: The Political Economy of Electric Utility Development in the US, 1870–1930'. Unpublished doctoral dissertation, SUNY-Stony Brook.

Metcalf, Lee, and Reinemer, Vic. 1967. *Overcharge*. New York: David McKay.

Mollenkopf, John H. 1977. 'The Crisis of the Public Sector in America's Cities', in Alcaly and Mermelstein, *The Fiscal Crisis of American Cities*.

Molotch, Harvey. 1976. 'The City as a Growth Machine'. *American Journal of Sociology* 8(2):309–32.

Monkkonen, Eric H. 1984. 'The Politics of Municipal Indebtedness and Default, 1850–1936', in Terrence J. McDonald and Sally K. Ward, eds, *The Politics of Urban Fiscal Crisis*. Beverly Hills: Sage.

Moody's Municipal and Government Manual. 1979.

Morgan, Richard. 1979. 'The Bargain Consumers Can't Afford', in Lee Stephenson and George Zachar, eds, *Accidents Will Happen: The Case Against Nuclear Power*. New York: Harper & Row.

Munson, Richard. 1979. 'The Price Is Too High', in Robert Engler, ed., *America's Future*. New York: Pantheon.

New York Times. 1978–82. Various issues, as noted.

Newfield, Jack. 1983. 'Redline Fever', in Mark Green, ed., *The Big Business Reader*. New York: The Pilgrim Press.

Norton, R. D., and Rees, J. 1979. 'The Product Cycle and the Spatial Decentralization of American Manufacturing'. *Regional Studies* 13:141–51.

O'Connor, James. 1973. *The Fiscal Crisis of the State*. New York: St. Martin's.

Olson, McKinley. 1976. *Unacceptable Risk: The Nuclear Power Conspiracy*. New York: Bantam Books.

President's Commission for a National Agenda for the Eighties. 1980. *Urban America in the Eighties*. Washington DC: US Government Printing Office .

Ratcliff, Richard E. 1980a. 'Capitalist Class Structure and the Decline of Older Industrial Cities'. *The Insurgent Sociologist* 9(2–3):60–74.

Ratcliff, Richard E. 1980b. 'Banks and the Command of Capital Flows: An Analysis of Capitalist Class Structure and Mortgage Disinvestment in a Metropolitan Area', in Maurice Zeitlin (ed.), *Classes, Class Conflict, and the State*. Cambridge, Mass.: Winthrop.

Ratcliff, Richard E., Oehler, K., and Gallops, M. 1979. 'Networks of Financial Power: An Analysis of the Impact of the Internal Structure of the Capitalist Class on the Lending Behavior of Banks'. Paper presented at the annual meeting of the American Sociological Association, Boston.

Rifkin, Jeremy, and Barber, Randy. 1978. *The North Will Rise Again: Pensions, Politics and Power in the 1980s*. Washington, DC: People's Business Commission.

Rudolph, Richard, and Ridley, Scott. 1986. *Power Struggle*. New York: Harper & Row.

Schultze, Charles L., Fried, Edward R., Rinlin, Alice M., Teeters, Nancy H., and Reischauer, Robert D. 1977. 'Fiscal Problems of Cities', in Alcaly and Mermelstein, *The Fiscal Crisis of American Cities*.

Smith, Michael P. 1980. *The City and Social Theory*. Oxford: Basil Blackwell.

Stillman, Don. 1983. 'The Devastating Impact of Plant Relocations', in Green, *The Big Business Reader*.

Swanstrom, Todd. 1985. *The Crisis of Growth Politics*. Philadelphia: Temple University Press.

Swanstrom, Todd. 1986. 'Urban Populism, Fiscal Crisis, and the New Political

Economy', in M. Gottdiener, ed., *Cities in Stress*. Beverly Hills: Sage.

Swanstrom, Todd. 1988. 'On the Power of Finance Capital over Cities: A Rejoinder to the Political Economic Power of Finance Capital and Urban Fiscal Crises: Cleveland's Default, 1978'. *Journal of Urban Affairs* 10(3):241–48.

Tabb, William K. 1982. *The Long Default: New York City and the Urban Fiscal Crisis*. New York: Monthly Review.

Tabb, William K. 1984. 'The New York City Fiscal Crisis', in William K. Tabb and Larry Sawers, eds, *Marxism and the Metropolis: New Perspectives in the Urban Political Economy*, 2d edn. New York: Oxford.

US Congress: House of Representatives. 1979a. 'The Role of Commercial Banks in the Finances of the City of Cleveland'. Staff study by the Subcommittee on Financial Institutions Supervision, Regulation and Insurance of the Committee on Banking, Finance and Urban Affairs. Ninety-sixth Congress, first session.

US Congress: House of Representatives1979b. 'Role of Commercial Banks in the Financing of the Debt of the City of Cleveland'. Hearing before the subcommittee on Financial Institutions Supervision, Regulation and Insurance of the Committee on Banking, Finance and Urban Affairs. Ninety-sixth Congress, first session.

US Congress: Senate. 1975. 'Home Mortgage Disclosure Act of 1975'. Hearings before the Committee on Banking, Housing and Urban Affairs. Ninety-fourth Congress, first session.

US Congress: Senate. 1980. 'Home Mortgage Disclosure Amendments of 1980'. Hearings before the Committee on Banking, Housing and Urban Affairs. Ninety-sixth Congress, second session.

Wasserman, Harvey. 1979. *Energy Wars: Reports From the Front*. Westport, Ct.: Lawrence Hill.

Whelan, E.P. 1975. 'Mayor Ralph J. Perk and the Politics of Decay'. *Cleveland Magazine* (September).

Whitt, J. Allen. 1979. 'Toward a Class-Dialectial Model of Power'. *American Sociological Review* 44(1):81–99.

Whitt, J. Allen. 1980. 'Can Capitalists Organize Themselves?' in G. William Domhoff, ed., *Power Structure Research*. Beverly Hills: Sage.

Whitt, J. Allen. 1982. *Urban Elites and Mass Transportation: The Dialectics of Power*. Princeton: Princeton University Press.

Yago, Glenn, Korman, Hyman, Wu, Sen-Yuan, and Schwartz, Michael. 1984. 'Investment and Disinvestment in New York, 1960–80'. *The Annals of the American Academy of Political and Social Science* 475(Sept.): 23–38.

Young, Louise. 1973. *Power over People*. New York: Oxford University Press.

Acknowledgements

Earlier versions of this paper were presented at the 1987 annual meeting of the American Sociological Association, Chicago; and published in *The Journal of Urban Affairs*, vo. 10, no. 3, 1988. The author wishes to thank Michael Schwartz, J. Allen Whitt, Patrick McGuire, Nancy Kleniewski, Laura Whistle Cates and several anonymous reviewers for their help and assistance. They are not singly or collectively responsible for any inconsistencies herein.

8

Chicago: The Legacy of Harold Washington

David Moberg

Chicago, for many decades home turf of the nation's strongest Democratic Party political machine and still the most racially segregated big city in the United States, has rarely been friendly territory for 'progressive' or reform local politics. Union, socialist, Black and community movements have fought pitched battles here – from the Pullman Strike and Haymarket in the late nineteenth century to Martin Luther King's open housing campaign and the 1968 Democratic convention antiwar demonstrations – but with more losses than wins to count.

Local left electoral politics have been even less productive. The politics of ethnicity and race, as well as personal and group patronage, have long triumphed over the politics of either class or efficient, honest public management. But in 1983 Harold Washington, a strongly liberal congressman who had broken with the old machine, confounded the odds. In a dramatic underdog campaign that galvanized the Black community and forged an alliance with Hispanics and liberal whites, he became the city's first Black mayor and the first reformer in five decades. But the legacy of those machine years dies hard.

Washington inspired a self-conscious 'movement'-style politics that won at the ballot box, but in many ways his was a personal victory. With his sudden death from a heart attack in 1987, the coalition he put together began to fall apart. Yet despite his short, troubled tenure in office, Washington left behind a strengthened, although minority, reform movement. He also changed the framework of local politics in ways that are not likely to be completely reversed. His victory inspired Chicago-based Jesse Jackson (as it pushed Jackson off his stage as pre-eminent local Black leader) and set in motion his Rainbow Coalition presidential drives (even though Washington at first was cool towards Jackson's candidacy).

There are two distinct – sometimes complementary, sometimes contradictory – keys to unlocking the meaning of Washington's victories and policies: race and reform. Washington tapped the growing force of independent (that is, anti-machine) and protest politics within the Black community, inspired a new level of voter registration and participation, and united a fragmented Black electorate. But he probably could not have succeeded in doing that, and certainly could not have forged the crucial political coalition with whites and Hispanics, if he had not also been a clear partisan of reform.

Yet Washington often was, and still is, seen primarily through the prism of race. In running and governing as a reformer, Washington embraced part of the older meaning of reform – fighting political patronage, corruption, inefficiency, favoritism and closed government – but he also gave reform new meanings, including participatory political and economic democracy. Washington's victory can be attributed in part to his reform of a machine politics that had gradually excluded and disillusioned the Black vote.

The 'machine' has long shaped Chicago political culture. After Republican Big Bill Thompson effectively launched the modern electoral machine during the 1920s, Mayor Anton Cermak inaugurated the nearly half-century rule of the Democratic machine in the early Depression era. Ultimately supporters – and beneficiaries – of Franklin Roosevelt's New Deal, the machine politicians at the local level emphasized a politics of patronage through local ward organizations that effectively used government favors to reinforce their political operations. Their army of political workers and contributors, who owed jobs and contracts to their city government patrons, took care of individual citizens' petty needs and cultivated their support. At times the machine allied with organized crime (and often indulged in its own independent corruption), later uniting with both conservative labor unions and the city's business elite.

Blacks, who arrived in Chicago in large numbers as World War I cut off the supply of central European immigrants, voted Republican, a Civil War legacy, and were mainstays of Thompson's machine. With Roosevelt's victory, Blacks moved strongly towards the Democrats nationally, somewhat less so locally. But Thompson's Depression-era Democratic successors,

Cermak and the corrupt Ed Kelly, did bring Blacks into the machine. The Black politicians who dominated their communities for decades to come were servile lackeys of their white machine bosses, but often corrupt petty tyrants within their own bailiwicks. In the 1940s Martin Kennelly, a supposed reformer, was brought in as mayor, then abandoned by the party bosses; he fought back against the machine by playing on white racism and the image of Black machine politicians as vice kingpins. But Richard J. Daley, the eventual boss of all bosses, defeated Kennelly with very heavy Black support.

After he was threatened in 1959 by a white ethnic vote for a Democrat-turned-Republican, Daley increasingly catered to the racial fears and hates of whites, especially lower middle-class and working-class voters of central and eastern European ancestry. He reinforced the policies of deliberate racial segregation that his predecessors, particularly Kennelly, had adopted.

Black voters remained fairly loyal to the machine, even at a time when there was a growing independent, or reform, movement among professional and middle-class whites in wards along the shore of Lake Michigan. Poor Black wards yielded reliable, machine-controlled votes, secured with low-level patronage and intimidation, but there was relatively low political participation. Middle-class Black wards began to show signs of more activity and independence in the 1960s. After state's attorney's police killed two Black Panthers in their apartment in 1969, the first big Black political earthquake shook city politics: Daley's reslated state's attorney was defeated.

Political scientist Milton Rakove, a Daley supporter, compared Daley's rule to the totalitarian regime of a Stalinist state, complete with political police ('the Red squad') that spied on and disrupted any political opposition. Many middle-class whites objected to Daley's closed government, the corruption of his political cronies, his abuse of civil liberties and his failure to deal with many serious urban problems. But Daley won over the business elite and building trades with his ambitious programs of urban renewal, highway construction and taxpayer-subsidized development of the central city ('the Loop') office area that had been stagnant.

Daley systematically promoted residential segregation and discriminated against Blacks in schools (where Blacks were crowded in makeshift facilities to avoid integration with nearby white schools), public housing (which was concentrated in

Black areas and mismanaged, creating isolated ghettos of very poor Blacks), police, parks, city services and nearly every other facet of city life, including political representation. Daley guaranteed that federal poverty funds were channeled through city agencies with minimum feasible participation of the poor, using the new flow of money to create political dependency. Daley tolerated, at times even encouraged, police brutality towards Blacks (for example, issuing his famous 'shoot to kill' order during the 1968 Black riots after Martin Luther King's assassination).

Near the end of his 21-year tenure in office in 1976, the city was beginning to show some financial strains, even though it was healthier than many other big cities. But Daley succeeded financially in part because of his ability to bring in federal government aid. In his single-minded devotion to the downtown, he neglected the diverse, important manufacturing base of the city's economy. City money was squandered on maintaining patronage rather than providing critical services.

In his last election, Daley won handily but trailed the combined votes of a Black state senator and white liberal reformer in fourteen Black wards. Yet when State Senator Harold Washington challenged Daley's successor in 1977, he won only five middle-class Black wards. But an irate Black electorate was largely responsible for the 1979 upset victory of a machine maverick, Jane Byrne. When as mayor Byrne subsequently turned to the 'evil cabal' of machine hacks she'd previously denounced and later reduced Black representation, especially on the board of the predominantly Black school district, Chicago's African Americans became irate. There was a grass-roots community drive to run a Black candidate against her, and Harold Washington, by then a member of Congress, was the overwhelming favorite. But Washington demanded that the insurgent groups dramatically boost Black registration before he would run.

The registration drive laid the foundations of a spirited but poorly organized grass-roots electoral movement and convinced Washington that he could run a serious race. About 52 percent of registered votes were white, 40 percent Black and most of the remainder Hispanic, about two-thirds of them Puerto Rican and one-third Mexican. Washington's first task was to unite Blacks and convince them that he was a real contender. He recounted the years of Black support for white politicians and the abuse they had received in return, then declared, 'It's our turn' to try to run the city. This was not a typical ethnic appeal for votes, but a protest against years of discrimination and injustices and an assertion against both Black and white disbelief that a Black could govern the city. His bravura performances in three televised debates were crucial in establishing him as knowledgeable and competent.

Washington also explicitly ran against machine politics and patronage. He called for fairness in government, an openness that would bring in all those who had been excluded, and a commitment to the classic, neglected populist issues of jobs, affordable housing and education. In Black communities, Washington's campaign took on the religiously tinged liberation rhetoric of the civil rights movement. In white neighborhoods, he was more likely to touch on traditional reform issues, civil liberties (including women's and, to a lesser degree, gay rights), and varied left issues, such as the nuclear freeze.

Washington would have had little chance of winning despite the Black voter registration drive if there hadn't been a split in the machine. Byrne was vulnerable after an erratic, often vindictive term in office. Polls in late 1982 suggested that Cook County State's Attorney Richard M. Daley, son of the late boss, would easily defeat her. Most observers counted Washington out as a marginal player, and some prominent white lakefront liberal leaders endorsed Daley, who had a slim claim as a reformer. But Byrne ran a strong campaign, and Daley, a bumbling, wooden speaker, sank in popularity. Washington attracted a small sliver of the white liberal-left, a few Hispanics and a growing segment of Blacks. Daley and Byrne were reluctant to attack Washington openly, since they hoped to win over Blacks. But in the final weeks Washington's support among Blacks rose, then surged as Byrne's campaign increasingly argued that Daley couldn't win and urged whites to support her to stop Washington.

With about 6 percent of whites, about 12 percent of the small number of Hispanic voters, and 85 percent of Blacks, Washington won the Democratic primary. Byrne and Daley had split the white vote nearly evenly, allowing Black enthusiasm for Washington to carry the day. It was a stunning blow, and Byrne momentarily considered a write-in campaign. But eventually Washington faced only Bernard Epton, a moderate Republican former state legislator.

Under most circumstances in heavily Democratic Chicago, the election conclusion would have been clear. But many white

Democratic committeemen broke with Washington, endorsing Epton or remaining neutral and in effect supporting Epton. There was an ugly, fearful racist reaction to Washington, who was little known to whites – except for inflammatory accounts of his past misdemeanors (not filing his income tax returns for four years, not representing legal clients on some minor matters). Washington failed to act as quickly and dramatically as he should have to win over or neutralize whites in the working-class ethnic wards. He probably counted on the Democratic loyalties of the committeemen (along with the unions) to deliver those votes. But as an outspoken critic of the machine, he had alienated most of the party regulars, who would have been cool towards him even if he hadn't been Black.

Washington's campaign stumbled, and the improbable Epton prairie fire took off, with race overwhelmingly the issue, both overtly or covertly (as in the campaign slogan, 'Vote for Epton – Before It's Too Late'). The Epton surge was also fueled by the press reports and grapevine rumors that questioned Washington's character. In the end, the most virulent character and race attacks, including leaflets accusing Washington of having been arrested as a child molester and a hateful demonstration against Washington and Vice-President Walter Mondale outside a white Catholic church on Palm Sunday, may have backfired. Washington appealed to liberal guilt and discomfort with such blatant racism and also continued to appeal to whites on reform issues.

Ultimately, the Black community coalesced. Hispanics stuck by their Democratic traditions (and unlike older leaders oriented to the machine and coalition with white ethnics, many new young Hispanic political leaders strongly identified with Washington's reformism and coalition with Blacks). Enough white liberals (especially Jews) and a few gut-loyal Democrats from ethnic wards joined the small white primary core. Much of the Democratic Party leadership may have deserted him, but Washington won in part because of Democratic traditions. The turnout was generally high (73 percent of Blacks and 67 percent of whites). According to exit polls, Washington got virtually all Black votes, somewhere between 11 and 18 percent of whites, and about 75 percent of the small Hispanic vote.

During his first three years in office, Washington fought unending 'council wars' with a hostile, obstructionist 29 to 21 majority of the mainly white old guard in the City Council. The 29, as they were known, blocked appointments and legislation, and Washington governed largely by using his veto, which could be sustained. Washington's own bloc consisted of a few self-conscious reformers, both Black and white, and a bloc of machine-oriented Blacks. Some of those Black politicos would have been happy simply to reslice the patronage pie but were forced to go along with Washington's reforms because of his immense popularity. In the spring of 1986, after a court-ordered remap of discriminatory ward boundaries, Washington finally took control of the council by the narrowest of margins as voters elected two Blacks and two reform-minded Latinos.

Without such protracted opposition, Washington might have accomplished more in office. But even so he managed to establish a new political paradigm for Chicago, combining elements of classic managerial reform with an attempt to forge new grass-roots involvement in government. In so doing, he transformed several fundamental relationships among people and institutions in the city, often building on changes already under way.

First, he forged new political relationships. Second, he reorganized city government and created a new relationship of government to the neighborhoods and the city as a whole. Third, he tentatively established a new relationship between government and business. Fourth, he fashioned a new neighborhood-oriented populism. Fifth, and most problematical, he began to change race relationships.

Politics

Washington had grown up within the machine, but he had always shown streaks of independence that eventually led to a break with it. Although always concerned with Black political power, he also developed close ties with labor and varied liberal organizations as an award-winning state legislator and later a congressman. Although a tough political pragmatist, he was also an intellectual who read widely and had long been sympathetic to liberal and left ideas.

But Washington differed strongly from some of his supporters in the Black community. Even if African Americans were his base, and the one he had to consolidate first, Washington believed deeply in coalitions. Black nationalists as well as simple machine hacks objected that he should be concerned above all with Blacks. But Washington defined his goal as 'fairness', a principle that permitted redress of past injustices on matters from garbage collection to police treatment but did not single out favors for Blacks. 'Fairness works' became his motto for Chicago, which had, under Daley, smugly and inaccurately called itself 'the city that works'.

Washington's strategy was simple political necessity in a city where Blacks are not the majority, a necessity that eluded some of his backers. But his pledge of fairness won over many Hispanics and white liberals. In the process, the center of gravity of the reform movement shifted from the white middle class to the Black community. That shift meant that redistribution of resources, as well as honesty and efficiency, became a central reform goal.

Government

The machine had been losing ground politically since Daley's death, but city government hadn't changed: it was still irrationally organized, inefficient, opaque to the average citizen, unresponsive and filled with unproductive dead-wood employees as well as stifled talent. Most employees still owed their jobs to political connections, even though a series of court decisions – one that restricted political firing came just before Washington took office – had curbed patronage abuses.

Washington embraced the antipatronage mandate, even though he chafed at his ability to replace only about 900 of 40,000 employees, leaving much of the city's bureaucracy in the hands of political enemies and incompetents. He might have bought off much of his council opposition with a few patronage perks. As one of the leaders of 'the 29' said later, Washington 'didn't realize how cheap many members of the City Council come, nickels and dimes in the overall picture. He could have co-opted me easily.' But Washington's principle and some mistakes in negotiations with the council and racial pressure on white council members all helped to consolidate his opposition. Sharp conflict with the machine also kept up grass-roots pressure on Washington's less-than-enthusiastic Black City Council supporters, who ideologically were closer to machine politics than to Washington's reformism.

Washington inherited both a city government whose financial health had declined rapidly as a result of mismanagement and a slumping local economy. He raised taxes nearly as much as Byrne had (relying mainly on higher property taxes and generally losing efforts to increase state income tax aid to the city or to introduce new business taxes). But Washington was also forced to begin imposing efficiency and austerity measures on city operations. There was little chance to provide jobs directly for Blacks, except in top policy jobs, but the city's bond rating started rising after several years of decline. Washington cut the number of city jobs about 10 percent (reducing the bloated garbage truck crews in part through the introduction of new technology), computerized many operations, and put more contracts out for competitive bidding.

But he also set new guidelines for affirmative action in hiring and contracts, redressing past discrimination and giving a boost to the Black middle class (but little help to the poor majority). In the end, his desire to placate constituents who wanted to keep or get jobs compromised his drive for efficiency. But he raised standards of honesty and performance, embodied in part in a new ethics ordinance, even though some of his supporters and aides were trapped by an FBI undercover agent trying to bribe officials to get contracts.

As part of the move from patronage and towards more rational government, Washington eased the way for unions to organize the vast majority of previously unorganized city workers. He negotiated formal contracts and grievance procedures with them, replacing the politically advantageous informal handshake agreements that Daley had long maintained with the craft unions. Washington agreed to only modest pay increases but took the first steps towards more equitable pay and promotion opportunities for women.

Finally, unlike his predecessors, Washington made government more open to the public. He made municipal records readily available, encouraged debate, and solicited – and usually followed – community group advice on many matters, such as the allocation of federal community development block grants.

Chicago's government hardly became a model of honesty, efficiency and responsiveness during Harold Washington's term in office, but he helped to set new standards of professionalism and fairness that ultimately helped poorer citizens even more than the middle class that usually promotes such values.

Business

Most business leaders viewed Washington with fear or suspicion at first. The feeling was often mutual. But eventually most businesses, except for some of the big real estate developers, reached some accommodation with him. A few actually changed how they viewed the city, accepting some responsibility for its social and economic welfare.

Washington began shifting city government's economic support from big business and downtown hotel and office construction, which were on a self-sustaining boom, toward small businesses in the Chicago's neighborhoods, including long-neglected manufacturers. He began, ever so slightly compared to Boston or San Francisco, to exact fees from downtown developments to subsidize projectss elsewhere in the city. His Planning Department moved a little away from the local tradition of 'anything goes' in approving real estate developments and began demanding a few public amenities. He proposed an ordinance (enacted after his death) to protect manufacturing districts from displacement by encroaching condominium conversions and shopping malls.

The city began taking action to fight plant closings (threatening one company with a lawsuit, setting up an early warning system, helping to negotiate strategies to save other plants). It helped, in cooperation with one local utility, to finance home energy conservation for low-income citizens. And Washington announced plans to bargain hard with Commonwealth Edison over renewal of its franchise to provide electricity to Chicago, commissioning studies on the possibility of municipal ownership.

In the past, like most cities, Chicago had offered tax breaks and other advantages to businesses to induce them to build, stay put or expand, hoping there might be some public payoff (and usually exacting private payoffs for the machine). Washington had some success in turning that relationship around, getting private investors, banks and corporations to put their money into projects that served a clear public good. Often the city would assume the primary risk, then line up private financing for the remainder of the project, such as the rehabilitation of an apartment building for low-income residents.

Although Washington was sucked into public support of dubious new stadium projects, he tried to minimize both municipal financial contributions and displacement of communities. His strict standards of financial accountability and reluctance to commit lavish public subsidies ultimately doomed a misguided business-led drive for a world's fair.

Increasingly, his administration tried to systematize its economic development activity, giving job training graduates a first chance at jobs in city-subsidized businesses, linking capital spending to economic development, and using city purchasing power to bolster local small businesses.

Washington barely initiated most of these changes, but the signposts of change were clear: fewer blank-check handouts to business, more insistence on business cooperation with government on publicly defined goals, more emphasis on job creation and manufacturing, and more neighborhood involvement in deciding and implementing economic policy.

Neighborhoods

From his 1983 campaign onwards, Washington's emphasis on neighborhoods became a metaphor for greater grass-roots democratic participation and city attention to the needs of its residents more than those of downtown business.

Washington poured money into street, sidewalk and basic infrastructure repair, spreading the money evenly throughout the neighborhoods. He distributed routine city services fairly, from garbage pickup to park amenities, a dramatic break with the past. He saw a chance for bootstrap revival of aging parts of Chicago where others saw only decline, and he channeled public and private money into housing rehabilitation, energy conservation and revival of both neighborhood shopping districts and manufacturing. He supported neighborhood groups fighting landfills and pushing for recycling.

Community groups had proliferated throughout Chicago over several decades. Initially they formed on the model of organizer Saul Alinksy as alternatives to the machine that fought city hall on local issues but not elections. Increasingly many groups formed to take action where city government was doing nothing: education reform, environment, local economic development, manufacturing revival.

Washington not only identified with the neighborhood-oriented programs of these groups but saw them as alternatives to the traditional machine's ward organizations as means of delivering city services and developing links with city hall, even if most would never actively work in elections. But they also embodied Washington's goal of participatory democracy, a concept from the 1960s that he continued to take seriously. Ironically, even though he stimulated much independent electoral activity, he never forged a strong political organization. He apparently believed his own half-joking pledges to stay in office twenty years, like Mayor Daley, and figured he could keep his forces together with his own charismatic personality.

Race Relations

Most Blacks felt that race relations improved during the Washington years, although white ethnics apparently felt the opposite. But Washington after his death was remembered fondly as a good mayor even by many of the whites who had never voted for him. He at least laid to rest the wild urban fears of many whites that a Black mayor would mean instant urban nightmares. But despite his well-received, frequent forays into white neighborhoods, Washington never managed to persuade most whites that he was their mayor. Partly he was victim of the 'council wars', which kept implicit racial conflict alive, but partly he failed politically. He was always extremely sensitive to the need to maintain his political base in the Black community, even though he could have taken it for granted. He was a proud man who thought his record deserved support, and who did not feel like courting the opinion of whites who had often been such implacable foes. Washington was disappointed that in his 1987 race he received about the same percentage of white votes as he did in the 1983 general election, even losing some 'lakefront liberal' middle-class wards in the 1987 general election to his city council arch nemesis, the clever but widely disliked Ed Vrdolyak.

But after he won, Washington found his power sufficiently consolidated that he could begin to strike deals with some of the white machine politicians, especially in the slating of a multiracial ticket for county-wide offices. He insisted on being treated as an equal, if not stronger, partner, and it appeared that white machine politicians were prepared to live with him, even if they didn't like it.

Washington's administration in the end did little to improve the lot of the poorest Blacks in Chicago, except to reduce police brutality under a Black police superintendent. Although Washington eventually passed school reform measures, he did little to improve the abominable conditions he had inherited in public housing or public health. He often moved too slowly on even the important new measures he took. Although hampered by deep cuts in federal aid, he led the fight for a new federal urban policy and took some important steps in using city resources more effectively. But between political opposition and financial constraint, Washington would have been limited in what he could do, even if he had not been cautious in breaking new ground.

Washington died at the peak of his power, just before Thanksgiving 1987, and his accomplishments were immediately put in jeopardy. Scheming to succeed him, the white machine aldermen were able to strike a deal with the machine-oriented Blacks on the City Council. This new, conservative coalition installed soft-spoken Alderman Eugene Sawyer as mayor against the first choice of Washington's staunchest followers, Alderman Tim Evans. Sawyer tried to pursue many of Washington's ideas, but because of the way he had gained power, he had to repudiate Washington's allies (who were, ironically, the best supporters of his legislation in the council) and grant favors to the white and Black machine bloc.

Black political leadership remained deeply divided. Even though Evans initially had the support of most Black voters, he lacked Washington's political savvy or vision, and was unable to establish a claim as the alternative mayor. Meanwhile, the Black community increasingly addressed politics as a racial issue, leaving white and Hispanic allies feeling more and more excluded. Then Sawyer vacillated about firing a Black aide who had made hare-brained, anti-Semitic (and anti-Christian, anti-Washington, anti-Jesse Jackson) conspiracy lectures to Louis Farrakhan's Nation of Islam. To make matters worse, many Black leaders seemed to apologize for the aide or resist his firing. Then a couple weeks later, a group of Black aldermen seized an unflattering picture of Harold Washington from the walls of the school of the Art Institute, dismaying liberal civil libertarians.

Increasingly, Black leadership was not only divided but oblivious to the need to maintain a coalition (which some never had wanted in any case). In a special election in early 1989, Sawyer refused to drop out of the primary, and Evans refused to back Sawyer, as he declared his independent candidacy on a new Harold Washington Party ticket. Unenthusiastic about either candidate, Blacks failed to turn out as they had in 1983 and 1987. Sawyer was completely abandoned by the white machine leaders who had put him in power; they shifted allegiance to Cook County State's Attorney Richard M. Daley. With Black voter turnout down and white turnout up, Daley first rolled over Sawyer in the primary, and then Evans and Vrdolyak (the latter the surprise Republican nominee) in the general election.

In an extremely well-crafted campaign, Daley tried to appear as a candidate above the fray (even though he had worked against Washington quietly but consistently). He stressed the need for better education (but as on most issues had few proposals), and projected the image of an efficient manager who would be a liberal reformer, despite his machine heritage. He won an enthusiastic white ethnic vote, but he also swept Hispanic wards and took all but a tiny hard core of the white left. He had effectively peeled off most of the coalition partners Washington had aligned with Blacks, leaving Blacks an isolated numerical and political minority.

Daley did not repudiate Washington's initiatives. But having quickly raised $6 million, mainly in big contributions (many of $100,000 or more) from developers, law firms and other businesses, Daley is likely to cater to their needs. Yet he realizes that some of Washington's agenda is politically popular. He will not, could not and probably does not even want to revive the old machine. The 'new machine' depends more on big money and business, less on the neighborhood ward heeler who works by day on the garbage truck. Business wants managerial efficiency, but it does not want Washington-style participatory democracy.

Washington managed to juggle the politics of Black mobilization and coalition-building, even though he could have – and should have – done more to win white working-class and middle-class voters to his reform programs. In some ways, he was midwife to changes in politics and government that were already building against the continued resistance of the old machine. He defined new directions for the city, as his neighborhood populism breathed life into an old, abused cliché about Chicago as 'the city of neighborhoods'. In many ways he forged a synthesis of the different waves of reform challenge to the machine – the early middle-class reformers who wanted efficiency, the 1960s reformers who wanted fairer political representation, and Blacks who wanted equity (to use political scientist William Grimshaw's distinctions).

Washington's mix of populist economics, redistribution of resources, efficient government and a more public-spirited relationship between government and business could provide a model for other cities. In an era of tattered central city economies and skimpy federal aid, mayors face huge problems with little power or money to solve them. Some of the framework Washington established for city government may remain intact, but Richard M. Daley is likely to pursue a more subservient relationship to business and to downplay grass-roots participation in government, opting for a narrower model of simple efficiency and 'good management', with patronage now at a grander level of business and professional rewards for supporters.

Washington's victory was partly a result of decades of cumulative effort, part fluke and part personal triumph. The great tragedies of his too-short administration were his failure to act swiftly and forcefully in many areas that would have most helped the poorest Blacks and his failure to bring large numbers of working-class whites into the reform coalition. Without the mobilization of Blacks in rebellion against the machine, he could never have won or accomplished what he did. Without a broader alliance, many of the gains he made are now in jeopardy.

PART III

The Sunbelt

9

Black Political Power on Trial in Alabama

Frances M. Beal

The struggle of the African American people for justice and equality has traveled a long and rocky road, particularly in the southern states that make up the Old Confederacy. Alabama is an excellent case in point. The route to Black political rights there has been blocked not only by individual racists, but has also been cluttered by federal agencies and local police agencies at the service of the bourgeoisie. The people's forces have registered their victories nonetheless, and none was sweeter than the triumph registered in the 1984–86 Alabama voter fraud trials in which Black activists turned back a concerted effort by Ronald Reagan's Justice Department to deny African Americans the political empowerment that the racists have been unable to prevent at the ballot box.

In 1984, the US Attorney's office in Alabama brought 210 charges of vote fraud against eight voting rights activists, seven of whom were African Americans. After an extensive investigation and the expenditure of millions of dollars, the Justice Department had very little to show for its efforts: of all the defendants, only one was found guilty, and on only four counts following court pressure on an all-white jury. Even his convictions were reversed on appeal. Despite the enormous power of the federal government, these activists were able to mount a successful defense that combined a political as well as legal strategy. At a time when the people's movements are suffering one defeat after another, it is useful to look back and analyze the ingredients that made up this recipe for victory.

The struggle for Black voting rights in the South – particularly in the Alabama Black Belt – has sharpened to take on national significance over the past few years.

The Black Belt takes its name from the vein of dark, rich soil that stretches from Florida to Texas. Mansions and plantations as well as wooden shacks and dilapidated houses dot the vast landscape along Highway 80 in western Alabama. These contrasts reflect what Southern rural politics are all about: the seemingly never-ending war between the haves (almost exclusively white) and the have-nots (mainly African American). On one level, this fight to defend voting rights and Black empowerment in areas of Black majority represents one of the major fronts in the struggle for democratic rights in the US. On another level, the struggle for empowerment has led inevitably to basic contradictions between capital and labor. On the surface, this contention is manifested as a polarization between Black and white; at a deeper level, it is a struggle to raise the conditions of life of an especially oppressed sector of the US working class. Thus, in microcosm, the Alabama Black Belt shows a number of class and social forces at play, all of which highlight the dynamics of the struggle against racism and its link to working-class politics as a whole.

The Black Belt struggle also provides a classic verification of the analysis of the spontaneous struggle against racism that views the Black Liberation Movement as composed of competing political tendencies struggling for the domination of its strategy in the common struggle against racism. In particular, the Black Belt struggle epitomizes the contention between a moderate, accommodationist wing against a more radical resistance wing. The struggle is all the more significant in that the progressives hold the political initiative and have not only successfully challenged the bourgeois racist status quo, but the hat-in-hand politics of the moderate Black leadership.

The successes achieved in Alabama also provide invaluable lessons in using the electoral and legislative arenas as key terrain in the class struggle and the fight to dismantle the political and ideological hegemony of the cross-class alliance of whites that has historically held sway. The lessons are particularly sharp, given the fact that this struggle unfolded in a region where the white working class has often turned its back on its Black class brothers and sisters in favor of a self-destructive unity with the hegemonic white bourgeoisie. Politically, this battle has provided further verification that the struggle for democratic rights is far from over and will in all likelihood constitute a battleground of antiracist struggle for some time.

Alabama Roots

The South as a region is arguably the most politically, economically and socially backward area of the United States. It is aptly named the Bible Belt, a stronghold of fundamentalist Christianity and reactionary social movements and culture. Progressive movements are very weak, and the labor movement has never been able to make much headway. This weakness reflects the hegemony of the politics and organized power of the system of white supremacy, built on the disenfranchisement of African Americans, who constitute a large proportion of the working class.

The political economy of the region has accelerated the level of oppression. National farm policies that favor corporate agriculture have resulted in a massive decline in the number of farms, particularly among Blacks. Consequently, millions of former farmers and rural workers have been thrown into the lower strata of the working class and into the reserve army of labor that now swell the populations of the South's major urban centers – Atlanta, New Orleans, Baton Rouge, Mobile. Others languish in the depressed rural areas with little hope of building more prosperous lives in the future. Because of this intersection of racial and class oppression, African Americans have also provided the principal impetus for progressive change in the region, whether struggling for Black political rights or defending the interests of the most exploited sector of the working class as a whole.

As in the rest of the South, the demographics of the African American population play a key role in Alabama politics. African Americans currently compose 30 percent of the state's population and 25 percent of its voters, giving them potentially strategic influence in the politics of the state. They are concentrated in the cities of Birmingham, Montgomery and Mobile. Although only about 15 percent of the state's African Americans live in the Black Belt of western Alabama, these ten rural counties have from 60 percent to 70 percent majority-Black populations and provide an invaluable laboratory that concentrates the political lessons regarding the fight for voting rights and empowerment.

Alabama's history has been characterized by thoroughly reactionary politics locally, statewide and nationally. The state's conservative 'Boll Weevil' Democrats support a bellicose foreign policy and have been key partners in the Reagan/Bush alliance. White supremacists have ruled the roost for many years, and race hatred politics has been the norm. Alabama was the scene of adamant opposition to the Civil Rights Movement from both fascist groups like the Ku Klux Klan and from the State apparatus itself.

At the same time, Alabama was one of the strongest fronts of the Civil Rights Movement, and many veterans still active have backgrounds of twenty-five to fifty years in the struggle for Black equality in the political and economic life of the state. The Black Belt, with its overwhelming majority of Blacks, has been a scene of constant conflict between Blacks and the white oligarchy. Since the 1965 Voting Rights Act was passed, the local bourgeoisie and its political representatives have used a myriad of tricks to derail the Black advance toward empowerment. Nevertheless, dogged persistence has won a modicum of Black power in the form of some important electoral gains on the county level and in the state legislature. Since 1982 three of the Black Belt counties have attained majority-Black governments, taken control of school boards, and elected Blacks to the State Assembly and Senate. Currently, half the Black Belt counties have achieved Black rule, and the state now has thirty Black mayors.

These gains were achieved despite the most vicious opposition from the bourgeoisie and from whites of all classes. Roadblocks of very sort were thrown up to oppose the implementation of the 1964 Civil Rights Act and the 1965 Voting rights Act. White children were sent to all-white 'Christian' academies to avoid desegregation, Blacks were forced to register time and again through 'reidentification' schemes, and intimidation, harassment and corruption were the norm. Some concessions were nonetheless wrenched from the white supremacists in the wake of the successful registration and concentrated voting patterns of African Americans.

As a result, the liberal bourgeoisie, operating through the Democratic Party, was forced to ally itself with some accommodationist Blacks in order to deflect the struggle for Black empowerment. A concrete expression of this process was the about-face of former Governor George Wallace, who actively sought the support of African Americans during his 1982 reelection campaign after standing at the courthouse door to prevent Blacks from registering to vote in 1964.

Black Politics in Alabama

African Americans have been organized statewide in the Alabama Democratic Conference (ADC) for the past nineteen years. The ADC is the official Black Caucus of the Alabama Democratic Party and has been led by Montgomery City Councilman Joe Reed for all that time. President of the teacher's union, Reed also sits on the boards of many of the state's Black educational institutions. Under Reed, the ADC had largely controlled the direction and scope of Black politics in the state.

As the state's principal accomodationist leader, Reed has pursued a strategy of supporting the most liberal whites but not rocking the boat. The ADC has sought accomodations with the corporate power structure in return for a piece of the action. Over the years, Reed has established himself as the broker of the Black vote in exchange for personal political and economic patronage. He has also run the ADC as his own personal fiefdom, with his use of high-handed and undemocratic procedures giving rise to discontent not only among progressive African Americans, but among those who demand an organization that allows them to participate democratically.

The resistance forces in Alabama, mostly but not exclusively concentrated in the Black Belt, were forged in the struggles of the 1960s with tactics of direct action, mobilization of the masses, and confrontation with the state apparatus. This struggle was particularly intense in the Black Belt, where African Americans compose the vast majority of the population. Using the tactics and organizational know-how of the 1960s, the resistance forces organized a number of civic groups to help people in each county. These formations became the foundation for political organization and political machines with a direct ideological link to the 1960 ideals of 'pay attention to the least of us', combined with adamant opposition from the white oligarchy in the Black Belt.

A painstaking door-to-door level of organization to take advantage of every opening was put in place by the civil rights veterans, resulting in some political gains and the election of county officers, school board members and state representatives. Using the weapon provided by the Voting Rights Act to consolidate political power, Greene, Sumter and Perry counties had attained Black governments by 1982 and opened the road for similar achievements in the other seven majority-Black counties.

But the road to political empowerment was strewn with opportunist Black political forces who were ever ready to accommodate themselves to the principal racial and economic interests of Alabama's ruling elite. In this context, the progressives had to contend with the backward forces in the ADC, and the political battles between the two came to a boiling point in the mid-1980s. Some examples should serve to clarify this polarization:

1. ADC's endorsement of George Wallace – the 1960s symbol of racist reaction in Alabama – in the 1982 gubernatorial race rather than a more liberal candidate irritated not only progressives, but antiracist democratic forces who remember Wallace's long career as a defender of white supremacy.

2. ADC gave only luke-warm support to a plan to divide Alabama counties into electoral districts to replace the former county-wide election process, which tended to minimize the African American vote. Redrawing electoral boundaries would have the most impact in the Black Belt counties, but because the leadership there is solidly progressive, Joe Reed was unethusiastic about a plan that would enhance his opponents' political power.

3. Over the years, the ADC had developed an authoritarian streak. Reed was fond of saying, 'You don't have to agree with me, you have to obey me.' His authoritarianism came under fire when Reed strongarmed the ADC's endorsement of Walter Mondale rather than Jesse Jackson in the 1984 Democratic presidential primary by manipulating procedural rules. This infuriated not only the progressives in the ADC, but also others who began to view Reed's tyranny as a fetter on their participation in the political process. Jackson's overwhelming 1984 Alabama victory – despite ADC's endorsement of Mondale – highlighted Reed's waning influence and the statewide strength of the progressive forces.

4. The last straw, however, was the obvious ADC collusion in the FBI investigation of voting rights activists in the Black Belt. When ADC could no longer control Black voters at the polls, it tried to maintain itself by collaborating with white reactionaries.

Jesse Jackson's Campaigns

The victorious Jackson primary campaign in Alabama had a number of consequences for the bourgeoisie, the conservative Black leadership and the progressive African American forces: that drama is still being played out today.

The bourgeoisie, both locally and nationally, was shaken by this signal that the progressive politics of peace and justice had gained a foothold in Alabama. Their consternation was rooted in the fact that progressive politics was positioning itself to challenge bourgeois politics on its own terrain – the electoral arena within the Democratic Party. Clearly this would have a dramatic progressive impact on national and statewide politics if it could consolidate its gains. In particular, the rise of progressive voices in the heart of Dixie threatened the Republican strategy of pulling the South into its electoral camp.

Particular concern about the reelection hopes of arch-reactionary Senator Jeremiah Denton (Rep., Ala.) was expressed in Republican councils. Denton had been elected by a slim margin on Reagan's coattails in 1980. His hopes of returning to Washington after the 1986 senatorial race were threatened by a galvanized, registered and voting African American population.[1]

Locally and statewide, some of the same concerns prevailed. African American legislators in the state, particularly those from the Black Belt, like Sen. Hank Sanders and Rep. Lucius Black, had been challenging cozy corporate perks that legislators had historically dished out to themselves. Local white oligarchies were frightened that five of the ten Black Belt counties had Black governments and school boards. The Black population was poised to capture the other Black Belt counties in upcoming elections.

The ADC's Joe Reed was frightened at the erosion of his power as the number one broker of the Black vote, since the challenge to ADC came from Black elected officials in the Black Belt who were not under his domination. The Jackson victory indicated that the ADC had lost substantial credibility among African Americans, who were looking to the new progressive Black politicians. It quickly became obvious that the ADC would not be able to regain its lost preeminence in Black politics on its own. Most important, from the point of view of the bourgeoisie and its Black flunkies, however, was that Jackson's statewide victory suggested that the progressive momentum could no longer be confined to the Black Belt, but was spreading throughout the state

Prior to Jackson's 1984 victory, the progressives had been organized under the umbrella of the Campaign for a New South (CFNS). CFNS had pulled together the various civic organizations in the Black Belt, initially as the electoral machine to elect Hank Sanders as the first Black state senator from the area since Reconstruction. This network, along with the political machine of State Sen. Michael Figures of Mobile, provided the organizational scaffolding for the successful Jackson campaign in Alabama.[2]

The success of the three-month effort on behalf of Jackson strongly suggested that there were now sufficient progressive elements throughout the state to begin to think about establishing a statewide political apparatus to challenge the ADC in an organized and sustained manner. This was the first time since the demise of the National Alabama Democratic Party that the material basis for a statewide progressive organization-politics existed.[3]

The Voting Fraud Investigation

In the fall of 1984, the US Department of Justice launched a far-reaching FBI criminal investigation of alleged voting fraud by key leaders in the Black Belt – a classic example of manipulating the criminal justice system in the service of reactionary political objectives; namely, to remove African American leaders from office and to create an atmosphere of intimidation so that Blacks would fear exercising their right to vote.

In particular, progressives had learned to make use of the absentee ballot, which formerly had been manipulated by the minority white ruling class to maintain political control in many of the Black Belt counties. Over the years, however, voting rights activists had learned all the mechanisms of absentee ballot voting and made provisions so that all who were entitled could have access to the voting booth through this means. Absentee ballots had become critical to the rural, impoverished area of the Black Belt. A high unemployment rate has forced many African Americans to seek work elsewhere; others attend school outside the county; still others are elderly and infirm and cannot vote unless by absentee ballot. Given the small populations of these counties, many a local election was won on the basis of the absentee ballot. The difference was that now voting rights activists had mastered the rules of the absentee ballot game.

The FBI investigation featured scores of agents spreading out around the Black Belt, interrogating hundreds of people about how they had voted in the September 1984 primary. FBI agents raided community offices and conducted nighttime interrogations. They loaded dozens of elderly Black witnesses onto buses and carried them to testify before federal grand juries miles away. Often the buses were accompanied by automobile escorts of Alabama State Troopers, whose claim to national fame includes a history of beating civil rights workers with truncheons and fire hoses just twenty-five years ago. Upon arrival at their destination, witnesses were photographed, fingerprinted and required to give handwriting samples.

Eventually, only eight Black voting rights leaders were brought to trial, but the chilling effect on rural Black voters was obvious. The eight were charged with everything from mail fraud, conspiracy to commit voting fraud, and voting more than once to giving false information to an election official. Of 210 charges, only 4 were eventually made to stick, and then only after a shameful elimination of all Blacks from the jury by the prosecution and only after the trial judge sent back the all-white jury several times.[4]

These tactics were designed to tie Black leaders up in judicial fights so that the political war that was raging could be fought under conditions more advantageous for the bourgeoisie and the local white racists. A particularly insidious aspect of this case was the attempt by the Justice Department and local media to portray the incident as a 'Black-on-Black' fight by recruiting local ADC members to bring charges – a blatantly partisan effort to remove the ADC's progressive political opponents from the upcoming electoral contests by throwing them in jail.

This strategy ultimately failed on both the judicial and the political fronts. In the ensuing primary elections, despite oodles of money and backing from corporate sources, the ADC members who had been put up to oppose the progressives were routed at the polls. At the same time, the federal investigation and its gestapo-like tactics did have a chilling effect on the use of the absentee ballot. Only half as many African American voters chose to use the absentee ballot in 1986 as in 1984. Yet in the final analysis, the Justice Department, the white racists and their Black collaborators faced a resounding defeat. No substantial decline in voter turnout was registered, and in some counties, even more turned out than ever before.

The Progressive Strategy for Victory

The strategy for this victory against an impressive array of reactionary forces combined a vigorous legal defense with an aggressive political offensive that called upon the support and solidarity of the national antiracist community.

Legal defense

A prestigious legal defense team was pulled together by Hank Sanders, a partner in the principal civil rights law firm in Selma. The local attorneys were assisted by the national civil rights legal apparatus – for example, the Center for Constitutional Rights, the NAACP Legal Defense Fund, the National Lawyers Guild, the Southern Poverty Law Center and individual civil rights attorneys from elsewhere in Alabama and around the country.

In the courtroom, the defense team was able to demolish the government's case by exposing the vindictive nature of the prosecutions. The organizational foundation for the legal defense was provided by the Selma-based firm of Chestnut, Sanders, Sanders and Turner. The financial resources were provided by the establishment of the Black Belt Defense Committee, which did a national fundraising campaign. In addition, the legal team went on the offensive and filed cases against the Alabama prosecutors charging them with selective prosecution. They also managed to call for and get a congressional hearing on the role of the FBI in the Alabama persecution cases, in which the progressives were able to expose the underlying political bases for the attack on Black voting rights activists.

National political defense

Local activists called upon and were able to obtain substantial support from the national civil rights community and from some key Black elected officials. This part of the strategy really took off after the first round of trials, in which the Perry County Three – Albert Turner, Evelyn Turner and Spencer

Hogue, Jr. – were acquitted on all charges. A key element in building this support was provided by State Sen. Clarence Mitchell (Dem., Md.) who at that time was the chair of the National Black Caucus of State Legislators.

The defense strategists were also able to generate enough media attention to make the government's nefarious political objectives a public issue. Public speaking events and fundraising activities around the country added to the sense of a national fightback. Important individuals made trips to the Black Belt to show their support, including Jesse Jackson, Andrew Young and Julian Bond.

The national contact who supplied the most organizational muscle, however, was Rev. Ben Chavis, executive director of the United Church of Christ's Commission for Racial Justice. The CRJ launched a series of Freedom Rides to turn the nation's attention to what was unfolding in the Alabama Black Belt. Under the auspices of the Alabama New South Coalition, a Freedom Spring 1986 was launched to bring antiracist activists to the Black Belt to help register voters and dissipate the residue of fear that the FBI investigation and indictments had left in their wake.

Local political defense

With the recognition that 'we could win the judicial battle, but lose the political war', the Alabama activists launched a vigorous campaign to maintain the political advances already achieved, even while paying close attention to the legal defense in the courtroom. 'I'll Vote On' became the rallying cry against the intimidation tactics, and people pledged themselves to an even greater effort to see that political power was not nullified by fear.

The Alabama New South Coalition

In January 1986, the progressives, along with some important middle forces, formed the Alabama New South Coalition (ANSC).[5] The ANSC became the statewide expression of progressive politics whose possibility was highlighted by the successful Jackson candidacy. The organization was established to challenge ADC's hegemony, and, more broadly, to provide a voice for antiracist politics and progressive politics more broadly. Its heart was the Sanders, Figures and Arrington political machines. Arrington's unity with the former Jackson supporters in particular provided a powerful base upon which to build the new organization. Unlike the ADC, the ANSC has a democratically elected leadership and operating procedures. It has launched a number of projects, including a youth leadership training program, and has become a much-sought-after group when political endorsements are needed.

The ANSC proceeded to endorse a number of local and statewide candidates and in the main routed the ADC collaborators at the polls. There are now a number of political forces associated with the ANSC who range from moderates to progressives. The ANSC could thus change the political equation in Alabama in the years to come. When Jackson's 1988 campaign took off, the activists grouped in the ANSC once again stepped forward and produced an overwhelming victory for the politics of peace and justice in Alabama.

It is also noteworthy that the ANSC is not restricted to African Americans and has in fact attracted a small number of whites to its ranks. To date, however, racial polarization is such that not many whites have been able to break with the white ruling class, and only the most progressive have been able to see their political future with the fledgling organization.

The Alabama struggle to defend the political gains made over the past two decades provides a heartening example of what people can achieve once they are organized. At a time when progressives throughout the country have been taking a beating at the hands of reactionaries on the Supreme Court and in Congress, it is a breath of fresh air to look at one of the people's victories.

Notes

1. It was a joyous moment on election night in November 1986 when Black Belt activists sent Denton down to defeat. Denton had a slight lead over his Democratic opponent Howell Heflin when all the votes had been counted except those from the majority-Black counties. Blacks flexed their political muscle by giving overwhelming support to Heflin and ridding not only Alabama but the entire nation of a neofascist senator.

2. Richard Arrington, the first Black mayor of Birmingham, owed some political debts to the Mondale campaign. Although he did not support Jackson in 1984, he distanced himself from the ADC and mended political fences with the progressives. In Jackson's 1988 presidential bid, Arrington supported Jackson, as did most Black elected officials in the state, conservative and progressive.

3. In the wake of the Voting Rights Act of 1965, Alabama Democrats placed one roadblock after another in the way of Black political participation in the state. Despite several challenges to the all-white convention delegations, Blacks made little progress. The NADP was a third-party effort launched in the 1970s in an attempt to circumvent racist maneuvering in the regular Democratic Party. Although the effort ultimately failed, it gained a certain momentum for a time and attracted a number of African American supporters.

4. Of thirty-seven counts, only four against Greene County leader Spiver Gordon finally stuck after the trial judge pressured the all-white jury for a conviction. All four counts were later overturned on appeal.

5. Immediately following the 1984 electoral season, the Alabama progressives were more or less prepared to form an official arm of the National Rainbow Coalition (NRC). But given the organizational weaknesses of the NRC, the Alabama Rainbow network did not have any reason to continue as such. While the Rainbow was on hold, the political battles in Alabama were not. Given the intense political conflicts raging, the progressives just could not wait for Jackson to get his act together before they moved to coalesce and regroup on a statewide basis.

10

Phoenix Rising: Explosive Growth in the Sun Belt

Tom Good

> Whoever stayed in Mahagonny
> Had to have five dollars a day
> And if he lived it up more than the others
> He needed some extra maybe
> But in those days they all stayed.
> They lost either way
> ...But they got something out of it.
> —Bertolt Brecht

Bertolt Brecht would have understood Phoenix, Arizona. It bears a striking resemblance to the City of Mahagonny. Rapacious developers and get-rich-quick bunko artists abound. It is a city that does not disguise its purpose – the quest for profits. For most workers in the service-dominated economy this means long hours in low-wage, non-union jobs in fast food chains, auto parts and department stores or, for better wages, in dangerous construction work, high-tech and burn-out jobs in the troubled health-care industry.[1] Most people are from out-of-state and would gladly move elsewhere. The local folk wisdom acknowledges the absence of hometown pride. It is every man for himself. One local citizen described the community ethic as, 'I got mine, piss on you.'[2]

The unsolved 2 June 1976 car-bomb murder of *Arizona Republic* investigative reporter Don Bolles in downtown Phoenix is a permanent reminder of the sleazy underworld of Arizona politics and business. Get rich and get out, just as in the old mining camps. Historian Patricia Nelson Limerick has accurately observed, 'Mining set a mood that has never disappeared from the West.'[3]

There is, of course, another way of looking at it, as the Valley National Bank summarizes: 'Rapid growth always creates opportunity. These numbers seem to indicate that a society such as the one that has grown in Phoenix tends to attract entrepreneurial types who seek to take advantage of these opportunities. In the process they create jobs and more growth. The bulk of these firms created have been small and entrepreneurial in nature.'[4]

Corporate developers have transformed Phoenix. In 1940 some 65,000 people lived in the city, some having arrived from the East with lung trouble in search of healthful desert air. By 1960 the population had grown to 439,000, and in 1988 over 2 million people resided in sprawling, polluted Maricopa County (those with lung problems were advised to stay away). According to the US Census Bureau, between 1980 and 1987 Phoenix was the fastest growing metropolitan area in the country. Over 3 million are expected to live in the city by the year 2000.[5] Tucson, Arizona's second largest metropolitan area with a population of 395,000 in 1987, is expected to increase its population by 50 percent by the end of century.[6] Arizona will grow faster than any other state with a projected population of 5.3 million by 2010.[7]

A Developer's Paradise

By the late 1980s the entire county appeared to be under construction. New highrises sprouted along Central Avenue in Phoenix. With its postmodernist plazas, open spaces destined to be forever empty of pedestrians, and glass towers blocking the view of the surrounding mountains, the 'Valley of the Sun' was acquiring the familiar skyline of late twentieth-century America. As Tucson's muckraking *City Magazine*, edited by naturalist Charles Bowden, put it in an article on the developer Charles Keating, Jr.: 'It is morning in Phoenix, but the time that counts, the basic time, is that of money. Somewhere, always, the markets are open and moving and it is the time for action, for making plays.'[8]

The players include Democratic US Senator Dennis DeConcini, who acknowledged during the 1988 campaign that his family had purchased land along the path of the Central Arizona Project canal for $400,000 and then sold it to the US government for $1.4 million. He denies any wrongdoing.[9] The senator easily won reelection to a third term, defeating an unpopular, far-right Republican.

Phoenix is a developer's paradise, business for the sake of business in a right-wing political atmosphere of unrestrained growth. And the tidal wave of the Pacific Rim boom is 'heading this way', according to Eric Anderson, chief executive of Mountain West Research.[10] Los Angeles will become the world city of the twenty-first century, and the second-tier cities near Los Angeles will benefit as well, Anderson explained recently to a meeting of executives.[11] The *Phoenix Gazette* reporter then noted, 'Southern California's weaknesses – congestion, bureaucracy, commuting costs, high land, utility, labor and building costs – are strengths for Arizona, where zoning cases don't take nearly as long.'[12] In 1986, only 4.3 percent of manufacturing labor was unionized in Arizona, compared with 23.9 percent in California.[13]

Local planning in Phoenix is a fraud, as a drive down any major street will confirm. If you have the money you can build anything, anywhere. One European speculator told the City Council that he wanted to construct the world's tallest building in downtown Phoenix. The edifice would have been directly in the flight path of nearby Sky Harbor International airport, the nation's fastest growing airport.[14] Only threats from the Federal Aviation Administration to close the airport stopped the project. Not to be outdone, a local architect wants to design a laser light downtown that would project a beam miles into the sky. Despite the obvious degrading of the night sky – light pollution from Phoenix is already visible as far away as the California border – Mayor Terry Goddard was reported as enthusiastic.[15]

Citizens in the path of the new projects might just as well stand in front of a speeding dirt-hauler. 'Skeptical and bitter. That best describes Sunnyslope residents' reaction to the new plans for the city's much maligned redevelopment project at Central and Dunlap avenues. "I'll tell you something now, this whole area has been maimed. I just wish you'd get the hell out", said one man to Councilman Paul Johnson.'[16]

The new Phoenix of the corporate planners and architects is a lifeless city in the middle of nowhere, like Brasília. Its streets are congested corridors of frustration, hostility and carnage; its sidewalks are deserted. The giant shopping malls constructed as alternatives to the anarchic life of a real city are claustrophobic environments with piped-in junk music and teams of security guards always on patrol. The construction fever has given rise to a new phenomenon – dead malls. There are so many that some have simply been bypassed by consumers, leaving their corridors empty and their shops deserted. It is not surprising that *Psychology Today* magazine recently rated Phoenix one of the worst cities in which to live in terms of personal mental health.[17]

Downtown Phoenix is stone dead, the habitat of the dreaded 'transients' (the number of homeless increased from 6,000 in 1986 to 9,000 in 1988). Ambitious development schemes for the area promise revitalization, but it is questionable whether large numbers of people will ever have any reason to venture downtown. It will be difficult to overcome its reputation as a place to be avoided. Most people in the outlying areas are probably only dimly aware of its existence, and many, in fact, may never have been there. Van Buren Street, which runs through downtown, is infamous for prostitution and drugs.

The Mexican neighborhoods begin just south of downtown. Anglo attitudes toward this area are reflected in the fact that a local TV news team was offered bullet-proof vests by management when they were sent to the community to film a documentary there. The documentary angered local residents, who demanded an apology from station KPNX for what they considered a negative portrayal of their neighborhood.[18] One scene objected to by residents featured a close-up of a cockroach, an insect found in nearly every home and business throughout Phoenix, regardless of income or life-style. As one *New Times* wit observed, cockroaches even have their own listing in the 'Government' section of the phone book, under 'Roaches in Sewers'.

Despite the problems in downtown Phoenix, the developers are optimistic:

> Stores that once abandoned downtown can come back – and stimulate more downtown development – said a developer who saw it happen in San Diego. Ernest Hahn, founder and chairman of the board of The Hahn Company, a west coast shopping center developer, spoke to a Phoenix audience last week about the success of San Diego's Horton Plaza. The talk was sponsored by the Phoenix Community Alliance, the group that conceived Phoenix's Superblock, a project it hopes will rejuvenate our downtown as Horton did San Diego.[19]

In order to 'heal the scars' of the new eight-lane Papago Freeway that runs through central Phoenix, a vast deck or park above the freeway is under construction. 'A half-mile civic parkland of trees, fountains, shops and eateries is taking shape, literally suspended above an eight-lane freeway by steel cords and concrete columns. What makes the Deck and its accompanying park extraordinary is the scale – a 29-acre hanging garden where visitors will be oblivious to the 197,000 cars passing underneath each day.'[20]

Part of the city's new central library will also rest on top of the deck; this is considered an engineering challenge, one that will cost the taxpayers $95 million. One engineer compared the project to building a highrise on its side. The deck will be supported by 1,200 cement columns.[21] Landscaping and the possibility of water leaking onto the traffic below are 'one of the few details' that worry designers. A 'Japanese tea garden' is also planned for the deck. The *Phoenix Gazette* writer described this future paradise: 'Imagine stepping off the Third Avenue bridge above the Papago freeway into a half-mile maze of gardens, fountains and pathways. Tired? Rest at a park bench or catch a bit of shade under a tree grove. Hungry? Pick up a hot dog or snow cone at a food stand near Central Avenue. Bored? Catch a show at the amphitheater or select a book from the 300,000 square-foot Phoenix Public Library.'[22]

In April 1988, voters approved a record $1 billion bond package that included funds for the new library. Other 'cultural improvements' encompass expanding the Phoenix Art Museum, restoring an old downtown theater and 'a small downpayment', $46.7 million for affordable public housing. The bond proposal, which also included funds for sewers and street improvements, was drafted by 'everyday citizens' according to the political literature published by the Phoenix Citizen's Bond Committee. One of Mayor Goddard's main arguments over the past few years has been that quality-of-life issues are crucial in the effort to attract major corporations to Phoenix. Goddard has also urged developers to be careful lest they spark anti-growth initiatives such as those that have been passed in California.

In a speech before the nonprofit Urban Land Institute Goddard 'criticized some developers for opposing new fees designed to make outlying developments pay for extension of basic services, such as streets, sewers, police protection and parks'.[23] In one such 'good-old-boy' deal, the state Transportation Board backed a developer's proposal to have the state pay

$22 million toward improving a road that leads to a new 'dream community'.[24] Goddard also criticized developers for proposing projects that conflict with the 'General Plan' of placing business developments in the 'village cores'. He warned against 'environmental degradation' and predicted that Phoenix could end up like Southern California in five to twenty years.

Gateway to Environmental Disaster

Meanwhile developers are bullish, if not euphoric. 'The crossroads of five expressways – some completed and others still on the drawing board – will be one of the Valley's chief centers of construction, commerce, entertainment and employment by 1991', according to one developer.[25] One local newspaper gushed at the prospect: 'Art Cunningham, vice-president of Sunbelt Holdings Inc., developer of Phoenix Gateway Center at the core of the megachange, envisions the three-square-mile tract as a bustling business center. ... Graham calls the location of the freeways in the Gateway area a "win-win situation."' Don McGowan, a spokesman for a group of developers and businessmen known as the Gateway Association, put it more frankly: 'The Gateway megachange is a tool for developers.'[26]

The resulting mess – horrible traffic, perpetual clouds of dust and diesel fumes, round-the-clock noise – is frequently described as 'nightmarish' by the local Phoenix newspapers. 'Dust. Bright lights. Roaring engines. Sleepless nights. That is what those living near the Squaw Peak Freeway can look forward to for the next 18 months.'[27] The newspapers portray this condition as unavoidable, like the heat in July. It's just the way things are. Scientists suggest that Phoenix is becoming an artificial 'heat island' with temperatures rising every year due to urban growth, but this is also regarded as just a fact of life.

Phoenix is, indeed, an urban island in the vast Sonoran desert.[28] Perhaps the best way to understand its relationship to the natural world is to visit the Desert Botanical Garden located next to the zoo. The garden is one of the last surviving refuges of desert vegetation in the Phoenix area. Since 1987, giant new power lines have been erected on its east side, new car dealerships have arisen to the north, and the nearby highway is being widened. Jet and helicopter noise bombards the entire area. Here it is easy to see that Phoenix has consumed the desert in its midst. It is now poised to spread like a cancer across the surrounding landscape. Maricopa County extends seventy-five miles to the west to the awesome Eagletail Mountains. Billboards advertising McDonalds are already up along Interstate 10, adjacent to the majestic range. Signs indicate that nearby land is for sale.

The remote Sonoran desert is also becoming a battleground in the drug-smuggling war. The state is now a key port-of-entry for cocaine. Some experts believe that nearly $9 billion worth of the drug is brought into the state each year.[29] Nearly 10,000 pounds of cocaine were confiscated by law enforcement agencies in 1988. Some of the drugs are brought in along remote desert roads or flow into isolated desert airstrips. Low-flying Drug Enforcement Agency and military aircraft criss-cross the remote desert hunting the outlaws of the cartel.

In Phoenix and Tucson, the drug inflow has not, as yet, resulted in an epidemic of gang warfare similar to that in Los Angeles. However, gang killings do occur and there are rumours that L.A. gangs are attempting to gain a foothold in the state.

The border is also the arena in which the brutal struggle for survival of countless Mexican migratory workers takes place. The Mexican nationals cross the border clandestinely in the knowledge that farm labor jobs await them on the giant corporate-owned Arizona ranches. Many do not survive the treacherous desert crossing.[30]

Arizona's geographical position as a border state with Mexico casts a shadow of moral turpitude over its conspicuous consumption. The Mexican border towns of San Luis, Nogales and Agua Prieta provide a shocking contrast to the prosperity on the US side. (The films *The Border* and *Touch of Evil* come to mind.) In Nogales even fresh water is difficult to obtain. The crowds look as if they belonged in some bygone decade. The Indians who squat on the street and beg are grim testimony to disasters in other regions of the country (conditions for Native Americans in Arizona aren't much better). The absence of social services or medical care cannot be effectively compensated for by the charity of well-meaning people from the US. New industry provides jobs but also draws in greater numbers of people, burdening an infrastructure that is already in a state of near collapse.

The famous mountain parks of Phoenix, considered sacrosanct by many citizens, are being traded to developers despite referendums that supposedly guaranteed their preservation.[31] In one infamous trade, upheld by the Arizona Supreme Court, Gosnell Builders acquired land in the South Mountain Preserve for a golf course. Since then, they have constructed a road in the preserve despite orders against any such action from the park's administration. The road destroyed a revegetation project that Mountaineers Inc., a volunteer group, had taken three years to complete.[32] The Mountain Preserves receive very heavy use and have also been the frequent target of vandals.

Even worse, land trades by the Bureau of Land Management (BLM) are encouraging the city to consume the surrounding desert. In one recent BLM land swap a developer acquired fifty-five square miles for a projected new community of 500,000 residents in the desert, thirty-eight miles west of Phoenix. The original buyer, Seven West properties of H.B. Bell Investments, Inc., sold the newly acquired land later the same day in a $14 million profit-taking scheme, according to the *Arizona Republic*, a charge denied by the developers.[33] Dean Bibles, Arizona director of the Bureau of Land Management, was quoted as saying, 'I am not convinced a large amount of money was made by Seven West on yesterday's transaction.'[34]

One far-sighted developer termed his new project on the far west side of Phoenix 'a suburb of Los Angeles'. And, as one *Phoenix Gazette* writer described it, the desert is about to 'bloom with construction plans'.[35] Desert plants can survive on a limited amount of water but if the desert is to 'bloom' with new developments a great deal of water will be required, as the British developers who bought land from Seven West suggest.

There are three schools of thought regarding the water requirements of Phoenix. The first can be easily dismissed, or so it might seem. It is the conventional wisdom of the city, of its citizens, government and developers. Water is simply taken for granted. There will always be enough water, even for unlimited expansion. Government may occasionally issue a mild rebuke to business leaders but without serious intent. Homeowners and apartment dwellers have their swimming pools, developers confidently build their artificial lakes, and government buildings have acres of green lawns. In fact, the conventional wisdom regarding the water supply has some truth in it. Cities and industries consume only 8 percent of Arizona's water. The largest consumer of the state's water is agribusiness, which uses nearly 89 percent.[36]

About half the state's farm acreage is in cotton. Alfalfa hay makes up another 16 percent and grain 24 percent. Most of the cotton is exported to Asia, and two-thirds of the hay is exported to California. But agriculture contributes barely 2 percent to the state's personal income.[37] These facts are used by Frank Welsh, a professional civil engineer, to support the thesis advanced in *How to Create a Water Crisis* that Arizona's water projects are largely pork barrel subsidies for agriculture. In 1988, the US Congress approved $3 billion for Arizona water and power projects. Welsh maintains that the aquifer under Phoenix presents a convincing case for the present and future abundance of Phoenix water. However, some experts believe Arizona may be entering a prolonged dry spell.[38]

Wet and dry spells tend to run in cycles of seven to ten years. Since 1978 Arizona has been in a wet cycle. According to Howard Alexander of the Salt River Project (SRP), there has been less groundwater pumping during the current wet spell. In 1987 the SRP pumped 55,000 acre-feet of groundwater. During 1977, a dry year, the utility 'pumped more than 200,000 acre-feet.'[39] Clearly, a new dry spell would place greater demands on the aquifer.

The precious groundwater has also been at the mercy of corporate giants like Goodyear Tire and Rubber, which has allowed industrial solvents to seep into the aquifer in the Litchfield Park-Avondale area since the Second World War.[40] The Motorola Corporation has also been responsible for polluting groundwater in the Phoenix area.

Besides failing to emphasize groundwater pollution, Welsh also supports former Governor Babbitt's proposal to disperse the state's urban population to smaller communities, particularly those along the Colorado river in western Arizona. He seems oblivious to the environmental consequences of such a large-scale population shift. For example, if Yuma were to become another Phoenix, the nearby Kofa Wildlife Refuge would be transformed into an urban park like the Saguaro National Monument in Tucson which, 'once sat in the middle of nowhere and now sits on the edge of Tucson'.[41] Last year 1.5 million vehicles drove through the park; only 5 percent stopped.

Perhaps the most logical way to look at Phoenix is in historical terms, recognizing it as typical of other desert civilizations. Phoenix is the direct descendent of the Hohokam Indian civilization, desert farmers who thrived until the climate changed or the salinity of the soil increased. As Marc Reisner, author of *Cadillac Desert*, explains, those who say the future is unlimited fail to see that the cities in the Southwest are only beachheads in the desert: 'Such a surfeit of ambition stems, of course, from the remarkable record of success we have had in reclaiming the American desert. But the same could have been said about any number of desert civilizations throughout history – Assyria, Carthage, Mesopotamia; the Inca, the Aztec, the Hohokam – before they collapsed.'[42]

From the air one gets a clearer idea of the nature of Arizona's 'hydraulic civilization'. Looking down from 20,000 feet, the Arizona Project canal is a vast scar across the landscape. Patches of agricultural green are evidence of the desert's destruction. The Palo Verde Nuclear Generating Station, the largest in the US, belches steam into the desert air from its three reactors. Headlines such as 'Effects of Fire at Palo Verde Plant Uncertain', and 'Subpoenas Issued in Safety Probe', hardly inspire confidence.[43] Increasingly, on the way from Phoenix to L.A. smog is visible along the entire route. Where Phoenix ends and L.A. begins in the brown soup below may soon be a topic of conversation for air travelers. According to the Sierra Club, 'The forefront of our automobile-dominated megalopolis will now be a good 48 miles from downtown Phoenix and only 92 miles from Southern California as the (fleeing) crow flies.'[47] There are reports that the new West Side developments are being built on land saturated with pesticides and other hazardous chemicals.[48]

General health concerns among the public in Phoenix, the city with the nation's highest carbon monoxide levels, are on the increase. Bottled water is a very popular commodity in local supermarkets. Zero Population Growth recently gave Phoenix its lowest rating in four categories (air quality, hazardous wastes, water, and sewage) compared with 192 other US cities.[49]

On 17 May 1988 state health officials finally confirmed a cluster of childhood leukemia cases in the Maryvale district of west Phoenix, in addition to higher death rates among senior citizens and an above-average rate for deaths due to birth defects.[50] From 1970 to 1986, leukemia deaths in the Maryvale area were twice the national average. Alarmed local residents who attempted to enlist the help of state officials were dismissed as cranks until the gadfly local newsweekly *New Times* broke the story. Homeowners attempting to flee the area face the fact that home values have dropped 10 percent since the health crisis was disclosed. Dr. Timothy Flood of the Arizona health department tried to reassure the frightened and angry residents: 'There is nothing in the data we see that indicates anyone should move from west Phoenix.'[51] At several tumultuous meetings state officials faced the local residents, one of whom commented, 'I hope the crowd brings ropes to lynch every one of them.'[52] The state is still investigating possible causes of the cancer cluster, which range from a nearby oil storage depot to everyday exhaust emissions from heavily congested streets. The City of Phoenix Planning Committee document lists one of the goals of the Maryvale 'village: 'Establish more control over industrial pollution.'[53]

The first summer of the Greenhouse Effect saw the highest daily average temperatures ever recorded in Phoenix for the month of July. Across the border in Sonora, Mexico temperatures are 4 degrees higher than on the Arizona side due to the destruction of desert vegetation by cattle ranchers, according to the University of Arizona Arid Lands Office and the Arizona State University Laboratory of Climatology.[54] The state has the highest skin cancer rates in the nation and worldwide is second only to Queensland, Australia. In the future, increased levels of ultraviolet radiation caused by ozone depletion in the atmosphere may have a devastating effect on desert vegetation and wildlife.

One local resident who suggested that Phoenix should consider a slow-growth initiative offered his own weather forecast for the year 2000 in a letter to the *Phoenix Gazette*: 'Good morning, Phoenix. Today's outlook is for sunny skies with an afternoon high of 123 degrees along with a humidity reading of 4 percent. The overnight low will taper off to a balmy 98 degrees. Freeway drive speed during rush hour is estimated to be 11 miles per hour. Have a nice day.'[55]

Phoenix expanded so quickly that the area became a large metropolitan center before it had a freeway system. Traffic that is routed onto freeways in cities like Los Angeles runs on city surface streets in Phoenix. The local demand for freeways mounted, until a 231-mile system funded by a sales tax increase was approved by voters in October 1985. It was widely believed that freeways would ease the traffic problem in Phoenix. But the facts contradict this local wishful thinking. It is expected that the new freeways will be heavily congested soon after the ceremonial ribbons are cut.[56] A voluntary program of 'no drive days' is the latest fanciful proposal to solve the traffic mess. Nearly all local arterial streets are being scheduled for lane expansion. At times it seems as if the city is being paved over.

In 1988 the issue of mass public transportation seemed for the first time to become a real public issue. Maricopa County has established a Regional Public Transportation Authority (RPTA) that will have some real clout if voters approve a half-cent sales tax to pay for the $8.4 billion, 103-mile elevated light-rail system in the 28 March 1989 election.[57] The proposal has received the strong support of Mayor Goddard, who has emphasized its economic advantages. In a speech before Valley Partnership, a group of two hundred developers, lawyers and bankers dedicated to improving the image of developers, the mayor cited the fact that property values have increased by $1 billion along the right-of-way of the Atlanta transit system. 'When people come to look for investments here, they take the freeways for granted. The question is, "When is the mass transit system coming in?"'[58] Some homeowners are already protesting the proposed route of an elevated rapid transit line, claiming that it will result in the removal of too many homes.

Local transportation policy has already had a dreadful impact on the health and well-being of the community. The freeways promise only more growth and congestion. The state has even refused to buy out homes rendered unlivable by noise, dust and exhaust fumes.[59] But the proposed public transit system is perhaps an even greater disaster in the making. It promises to raise property values, wiping out affordable housing in its path, and initiating new rounds of speculation and development.

In the absence of any effective opposition, the developers dominate Phoenix politics. Even affluent homeowner associations fight losing battles against the schemes of the neighborhood wreckers. When so-called compromises are worked out they are abandoned as soon as the neighborhood defenders leave the City Council chambers. This is exemplified in the case of the development known as 'The Esplanade', located on East Camelback Road, the key affluent commercial corridor in Phoenix. Three years ago the City Council set limits on the project after a long battle between residents and Canadian developer J. Fife Symington III. In a recent meeting the council set aside these limits, agreeing to a request from Symington to expand the project's area by 13 percent.[60] Symington's development originally included offices, shops, a hotel and apartments,

2.4 million-square feet on twenty-two acres. After protests, his proposal was reduced to a hotel and apartments. The latest expansion proposal involves a three-level glass-enclosed mall. One of the representatives of the Bartlett Estates Homeowners Association is Dino DeConcini, brother of Senator Dennis DeConcini. In such a political climate owners of more modest homes are simply bulldozed away.

While the homeowners were busy battling the Esplanade, developers submitted a proposal for an even more massive project nearby at 16th Street and Camelback Road. The project would include four 12-story office towers, an eighty-unit condominium tower, and a seven-story hotel. The intersection of 16th and Camelback presently handles more than 100,000 cars daily, making it one of the busiest in the city. The new development would reportedly add 23,000 additional cars to the intersection. Twenty-two single family homes are presently located on the proposed site in addition to various business establishments.[61]

Voters have struck back at developers on two recent occasions. On 6 November 1985 they affirmed the integrity of the Phoenix Mountain Preserves in a ballot initiative that fixed permanent boundaries for the park. The proposition won 80.5 percent of the vote. Citizens also soundly defeated the proposed $3 billion dollar development of the Salt River bed, the Rio Salado Project, by a 2 to 1 margin on 4 November 1987. The ballot box, however, does not seem to be an effective barricade in the path of the bulldozers. The City of Tempe has its own plans to develop the Salt River, and the Mountain Preserves are still being carved up.

Nevertheless, the defeat of the financing for Rio Salado was a significant blow against the corporate profiteers, who had hoped to pay for their schemes with property tax revenues. Mayor Goddard chastised the voters for their decision. The Rio Salado opposition was led by a small but vocal group, the Concerned Citizens against the Rio Salado Project. The victory was particularly noteworthy because the project's supporters and financial contributors included the Phoenix 40, Merabank, First Interstate Bank, Mountain Bell, Arizona Bank, Charles Keating, Jr., American Greyhound Corporation, Valley National Bank, and the Phoenix Newspapers, Inc. Still, proponents claimed that the project actually received only lukewarm support from potential corporate backers.

Perhaps the most successful effort against state development schemes took place in 1976. A broad coalition made up of environmentalists, Indians and recreationists came together to oppose the construction of Orme Dam on the Salt River above Phoenix. The dam would have benefited agribusiness while flooding two-thirds of the Fort McDowell Indian Reservation and destroying a popular stretch of the Salt River used by thousands every summer for tubing. Citizens Concerned about the Project (CCAP) was the main opposition organization, whose members included civil libertarians from the ACLU, Gray Panthers, Sierra Club activists, Democrats, Republicans, Indians, construction workers and the Catholic Diocese of Phoenix. Members leafleted shopping centers and the Salt River recreation area. The *Arizona Republic* supported construction of the dam, but the newspaper's effort could not compete with the broad base of opposition that threatened legal action to stop the dam. More recently, Cliff Dam, proposed for the Verde River, was also defeated by environmentalists.

As Patricia Nelson Limerick has explained in her book *The Legacy of Conquest*, the history of the West is largely the story of land speculation: 'If Hollywood wanted to capture the emotional center of Western history, its movies would be about real estate. John Wayne would have been neither a gunfighter nor a sheriff, but a surveyor, speculator or claims lawyer. The showdowns would occur in the land office or the courtroom; weapons would be deeds and lawsuits, not six-guns. ...'[62] Today's dominant business civilization has strong roots in the past. When Governor Bruce Babbitt called out the state police and the National Guard to break the copper miners' strike in 1983–84, in one of the most violent episodes in recent state history, there was ample precedent – the use of force in Bisbee in 1917 against striking copper miners. When President Reagan signed legislation in 1988 closing the Phoenix Indian School, and selling the property to a Florida developer in a land-swap deal, the outrage certainly had equally strong historical precedent.

Perhaps without precedent, though, was the passage of a ballot initiative in 1988 declaring English the state's official language. The measure passed by only a 2 percent margin, and was opposed by liberals and conservatives alike. The proposition has fueled political activism in the normally conservative Mexican community (in Arizona most Spanish-speaking people refer to themselves as Mexicans). On 12 April 1987 over 2,000 Spanish-speaking residents of Phoenix marched to protest the

English-only petition drive.[63]

Disregarding the grievances of Blacks, Mexicans, Native Americans and miners, the dominant business civilization rolls on at a mighty pace. Consumer values, expectations of economic gain, 'family values', religion and patriotism are the foundation of the shopping mall culture. Former geographic zones of opposition, such as the counterculture district of Tempe, are being redeveloped. TV news consists of 'happy talk' and civic boosterism. One of the only non–rock 'n' roll radio stations, KJZZ, a public radio station formerly devoted to jazz, recently changed its format to 'new age' music. A small independent cinema devoted to retrospectives of directors such as Godard and Fassbinder closed its doors after only three months. The movie theater, designed by its Yugoslavian architect-founder, was one of the only genuine alternative spaces in the community.

Inside the shopping mall it is difficult even to imagine another way of life. Donald Worster describes the feeling: 'The private interior is invaded by hucksters and planners. Material life alone flourishes, and for the manipulated mass man that seems to be enough. ...'[64] To the surprise of radical critics and the powers that be, the 'manipulated mass' can on occasion break up quickly into angry groups of protestors when neighborhoods are threatened or the health of children is at stake. Yet the ability of the system to sustain itself through cultural hegemony and false consciousness should not be underestimated.

The Mecham Recall Campaign

Doubtless the most sensational episode of recent Arizona populism followed in the wake of the election of Republican Evan Mecham as governor in 1986. The catalyst for the opposition movement was Mecham's cancellation of a state holiday honoring the birthday of Dr. Martin Luther King, Jr. Mecham came from the far right of the Republican Party, a Mormon outsider who was regarded with suspicion by the Goldwater wing of the party. Mecham's election to the govenorship was widely believed to have been the result of a split in the Democratic vote between Carolyn Warner, the official Democratic candidate, and Bill Schultz, who ran as an independent. Mecham won 40 percent of the vote, Warner 34 percent, and Schultz 26 percent. In the weeks following his election, Mecham incensed the Black community by repeatedly making racist remarks, and shocked just about everyone else with his bumbling and crudity by denouncing gays, declaring that a woman's place was in the home, and declaring that the US was a Christian nation in a speech before a Jewish group.

On 19 January 1987, opponents of Mecham, including Black leaders and union activists, were able to organize a march of 15,000 people in downtown Phoenix that received national news coverage. A recall movement began to take shape. Business leaders increasingly felt that Mecham was damaging the state's image and could hurt business in the long run. They were also alarmed by the number of organizations that agreed not to hold conventions in Arizona. Meanwhile, the *Arizona Republic* ran a story claiming serious improprieties in the financing of Mecham's campaign for governor. The story eventually resulted in Mecham's indictment on 8 January 1988, and initiation of impeachment proceedings against him that forced his removal before a recall election could be held. Thus, from its beginnings as broad-based movement against racism, initiated by Black community leaders, the anti-Mecham struggle became a single-issue recall effort – one that quickly fell apart once Mecham left office.

Community Control?

The City of Phoenix Village Planning Committee document states, '... continued citizen participation in planning is the basis for experiencing a sense of control over one's environment and for gaining a sense of community.' These are utopian goals within the present social system. 'Control' and 'community' are absent from daily life in the Phoenix metropolis. Obviously, 'planning' in Phoenix is done by developers, not average citizens. 'Control' and 'community' in themselves are democratic values. A different Phoenix will emerge only if the citizenry can be united in continued opposition to the systemic power of the developers and their political allies.

Independently, Blacks, Mexicans, labor activists, Native Americans, environmentalists and neighborhood defenders have acted politically, sometimes with dramatic results. But the dream of unity has been materialized only once, and then only temporarily, in the campaign that ousted Ev Mecham.

It is impossible to predict the ultimate economic consequences of the speculation and profit-taking occurring in Phoenix and other cities. However, one conclusion can be drawn. The final chapter of the history of the American West has been written. In the coming decades the tale of the West will be the history of the giant urban centers of capitalism or, more specifically, of the Pacific Rim.

Notes

1. *Arizona Progress*, published by Valley National Bank (August–September, 1988), vol. 43 no. 6, p. 2. Metro Phoenix employment distribution, 1987: manufacturing, 14.9%; mining, 0.1%; construction, 7.6%; goods producing, 22.6%; transportation, communications, public utilities, 5.4%; trade, 25.3%; finance, insurance and real estate, 8.2%; services, 25.4%; government, 13.1%.
2. Gene E. Keefover, 'Blinded by the Blight', *New Times*, 16–22 November 1988.
3. Patricia Nelson Limerick, *The Legacy of Conquest: The Unbroken Past of the American West*, New York 1988, p. 100.
4. 'Dynamic Growth Pattern Persists in the Phoenix Metro Area', *Arizona Progress*, vol. 41, no. 2, p. 2.
5. Ibid., p. 1.
6. 'Tucson: A New Look at the Old Pueblo', *Arizona Progress*, , vol. 43, no. 1, p. 1.
7. Sean Griffin, 'Boom: Census Pegs Arizona No.1 in Growth', *Phoenix Gazette*, 19 November 1988.
8. Charles Bowden and Richard S. Vonier, 'Charlie', *City Magazine*, August 1988, p. 25.
9. Michael Murphy, 'DeConcini Alters Story on Land Sale', *Phoenix Gazette*, 21 October 1988.
10. Joe Costanza, 'State Economy Expects to Profit from L.A. Growth', *Phoenix Gazette*, 26 September 1988.
11. Ibid.
12. Ibid.
13. *Arizona Progress* (August–September, 1988), vol. 43, no. 6.
14. Ken Western, 'Terminal 4, "Skybreaking" Held', *The Arizona Republic*, 20 October 1988.
15. Ray Schultze, 'Laser Centerpiece Envisioned Downtown', *Phoenix Gazette*, 9 May 1988.
16. Susan Herold, 'Sunnyslope Residents Blast Renewal Plan', *Phoenix Gazette*, 9 May 1988.
17. Barbara Yost, 'Survey: People Crazy to Live in Phoenix', *Phoenix Gazette*, 13 October 1988.
18. Steve Cheseborough, 'TV Crew Offered Flak Jackets, S. Phoenix Residents Cite Bias', *Phoenix Gazette*, 26 September 1988.
19. Steve Cheseborough, 'Developer: San Diego a Model for Phoenix', *Phoenix Gazette*, 25 March 1988.
20. Susan Herold, 'On Deck', *Phoenix Gazette*, 9 August 1988.

21. Ibid.
22. Ray Schultze, 'Step Ahead: Officials Laud Bond Approval', *Phoenix Gazette*, 20 April 1988.
23. Ray Schultze, 'Builder Issued Challenge', *Phoenix Gazette*, 10 September 1988.
24. Susan Herold, 'Road Plan Backed: Allocation Delayed', *Phoenix Gazette*, 22 October 1988.
25. Kim Sertich, 'Megachange Seen as Business Hub of 90's', *Phoenix Gazette*, 30 March 1988.
26. Ibid.
27. Susan Herold, '24-Hour Construction Schedule for Freeway Stirs Anger', *Phoenix Gazette*, 30 March 1988.
28. John Alcock, *Sonoran Desert Spring*, Chicago 1985.
29. Scott Craven, 'Investments Help Launder Drug Cash', *Phoenix Gazette*, 19 November 1988.
30. Ted Conover, *Coyotes: A Journey Through the Secret World of America's Illegal Aliens*, New York 1987.
31. Andy Van De Voorde, 'Welcome to Gosnell Park', *New Times*, 25–31 May 1988.
32. Clare Gramer, 'Cosnell's "Insensitive" Work Angers Officials', *Phoenix Gazette*, 26 September 1988.
33. Peter Reich and Kim Sertich, 'Land Swap Nets Developers Huge Parcel', *Phoenix Gazette*, 9 June 1988.
34. Barbara Rose, 'BLM Swap No Bonanza, Trader Says', *The Arizona Republic*, 10 June 1988.
35. Reich and Sertich, 'Land Swap'.
36. Ibid.
37. Mike Padgett, 'Preparing for Boom in Desert', *Phoenix Gazette*, 31 May 1988.
38. Frank Welsh, *How to Create a Water Crisis*, Boulder 1985, p. 44.
39. Clay Thompson, 'Arizona's Desert's "Wet" Spell Might Be Coming to an End', *Phoenix Gazette*, 22 July 1988.
40. Ibid.
41. Sean Griffin, 'Goodyear Ordered to Clean Up Tainted Water', *Phoenix Gazette*, 7 September 1988.
42. Clay Thompson, 'Parks Threatened by Urban Sprawl', *Phoenix Gazette*, 7 September 1988.
43. Marc Reisner, *Cadillac Desert: The American West and Its Disappearing Water*, New York 1987, p. 6.
44. Donald Worster, *Rivers of Empire: Water, Aridity and the Growth of the American West*, New York 1985, p. 48.
45. Scott Craven, 'Effects of Fire at Palo Verde Plant Uncertain', *Phoenix Gazette*, 7 July 1988; Victor Dricks, 'Too Many Worker Errors at Palo Verde Unit 2, NRC Says', *Phoenix Gazette*, 1 April 1988; Victor Dricks, '7 Reactor Workers to Testify: Subpoenas Issued in Safety Probe', *Phoenix Gazette*, 1 November 1988.
46. Fareed Abouhaidar, 'Tonopah Succumbs to Growth', *Canyon Echo*, July–August 1988.
47. Kathleen Stanton, 'The Damage Is Done: Yesterday's Industrial Contamination Becomes Today's Redevelopment Nightmare', *New Times*, 28 September 28–4 October 1988.
48. Charles Kelley, 'Phoenix Ranks Worst on Environmental Ills', *The Arizona Republic*, 20 October 1988.

49. Victor Dricks, 'Leukemia Cluster Confirmed', *Phoenix Gazette*, 17 May 1988.

50. Ibid.

51. City of Phoenix, *Village Planning Committee Document*.

52. Tom Spratt, 'Both Sides of Border Make Contribution to Global Warming Trend', *Phoenix Gazette*, 23 November 1988.

53. Bruce G. Levitta, 'And Have a Nice Day', *Phoenix Gazette*, 27 June 1988.

54. *Arizona Progress*, (March–April, 1988), vol. 43, no. 3.

55. Rebecca Mong, 'Phoenix or Bused', *Metro Phoenix*, May 1988, pp. 36–40.

56. Steve Cheseborough, 'Mass Transit's Benefits Extolled by Goddard', *Phoenix Gazette*, 1 July 1988.

57. Susan Herold, 'Residents Near Freeways Told Not to Expect Buyouts', *Phoenix Gazette*, 22 April 1988.

58. Ray Schultze, 'Esplanade Expansion Approved', *Phoenix Gazette*, 15 September 1988.

61. Susan Herold, 'Massive Project Proposed', *Phoenix Gazette*, 27 September 1988.

59. Sammy S. Jenkins, Sr., *Mecham: Arizona's Fighting Governor*, Albuquerque 1988.

60. Limerick, *Legacy*, p. 55.

61. Venita Hawthorne James, 'Union Sues DPS in Alleged Plot to Break '83 Strike in Morenci', *The Arizona Republic*, 20 May 1987.

62. Sean Griffin, 'Reagan OKs Land Swap – Indian School to Close in '90', *Phoenix Gazette*, 19 November 1988.

63. Kimberly Mattingly, 'English Only Drive Protested', *Phoenix Gazette*, 12 April 1987.

64. Worster, *Rivers of Empire*, p. 58.

11

The Battle of East L.A.

David R. Diaz

At city hall, another committee meeting is in session, but Richard Alatorre's seat is empty. This apparent boredom with the mechanics of government has become his norm. Arguably California's most powerful Chicano politician, he eventually arrives but exhibits a marked air of disinterest and will leave early. This level of 'public service' is his standard practice in the labyrinth of city hall. He ignores most of a debate over the potential expenditure of hundreds of millions of dollars for affordable housing and economic development that could directly benefit his constituents and Chicanos throughout the city.

Alatorre's nonchalant, almost contemptuous approach to political power is indicative of the leadership vacuum within the Latino political hierarchy in California and a major reason why the media-touted 'Hispanic Decade' of the 1980s became a shallow PR fad. The fragmentation and self-interested distraction of the Chicano political hierarchy has inhibited any meaningful movement toward confronting the political economy of the region's crime, drug and gang crises. In particular, city and county tax redistribution policies, engineered through urban redevelopment programs, should be inviting targets for any conscientious elected official. The anomaly of minority politics in Los Angeles is that both the Chicano and Black political leaderships have become docile pawns of global capital. The progressive political agendas that formed the basis for minority political mobilization in the late 1960s have been replaced by an emphasis on ingratiation with the Democratic Party and acceptance of remedial 'advancement'.

Historically, the financial power of the Democrats has effectively blunted major grass-roots efforts to wrest power from the Chicano hierarchy. Both major parties have used satellite minority power blocs as a way of preventing the development of a cohesive minority community political agenda. However, because of feuds within the leadership, growing regional economic class inequities, and the corruption endemic to American politics, popular movements have significantly increased their political leverage. This populist uprising has laid the basis for a new era of progressive politics on L.A.'s Eastside. Mobilization at the grass-roots has entered a phase of direct confrontation with the hierarchy over control of the political agenda. Within the next two to four years the Eastside will experience another period of struggle between populist groups and an increasingly conservative Chicano political elite.

The Evolution of Modern Chicano Politics in Los Angeles

In a different era, the Chicano political leadership in Los Angeles was both activist and populist. Chicano politics in the city developed as a reaction to a racist oligarchy. In the mid-1940s the Zoot Suit riots served as both a political outburst and a cultural rallying point within the Chicano *barrios*. The media never reported what happened to the numerous sailors who were trapped by their arrogant zeal in Chicano neighborhoods and lived to regret their 'social' transgressions. The media hysteria surrounding the Zoot Suit riots worked to unite Chicanos, setting the stage for the first steps in progressive organizing. When the Chicano World War II veterans returned to the Eastside, they were forced to hear the stories of this confrontation with US occupation forces from their younger brothers and cousins. Police repression and discrimination did not have eyes that recognized service to one's country as being of any importance. Chicano vets began to organize under the same conditions as Black vets. The G.I. Forum was created by returning Chicano veterans to win civil rights and increase employment opportunities.

This movement and the community's continuing resistance to a conventional, all-American racist ideology formed the foundation of Ed Roybal's work in electoral politics in the late 1940s. After an initial unsuccessful bid, he was elected to the Los Angeles City Council in 1949: an enormous barrier to political progress had been breached. Any political pioneering by the current group of elected Chicanos in Los Angeles pales in comparison to Roybal's achievement.

Assured that the Chicano community would support his political agenda, Roybal became the standard-bearer for Chicanos throughout Southern California. He lost some battles but won the war with the racist political establishment. He maintained his council seat throughout the 1950s, and in 1962 became the first Chicano from California elected to the House of Representatives. No Chicano/Chicana would again sit on the City Council until the mid-1980s, and the next Chicano elected to Congress from the area took office in the early 1980s.

The Chicano political structure in the region is still based on Roybal's success. Grace Davis, Mayor Tom Bradley's principal liaison to the city's Latinos, was an early Roybal campaign worker. Councilman Richard Alatorre's sister worked in Roybal's office, a factor that must have influenced his career in electoral politics. Art Torres married into the politically prominent Nava family, who were Roybal loyalists. Congressman Estaban Torres and Henry Lacayo's political organizing and influence in the AFL-CIO coincided with Roybal's political opening. No Chicano was elected in the Eastside without Roybal's blessing for over twenty years. TELACU, the scandal-plagued community-based organization (CBO), benefitted directly from his congressional clout, as did most CBOs in the Eastside area. Every important Chicano elected official in the area can trace a linkage to Ed Roybal. He recently reasserted his political power within the third generation of Chicano/Chicana elected officials by supporting a political novice for a California State Assembly seat: his daughter Lucille.

But the factors that allowed Roybal to win have apparently been forgotten by both the right and the left. His early campaigns articulated conventional populist themes. Housing, representation, employment and, of course, the struggle against racism were the rallying points of the council's only progressive member. Community organizing was the only strategy open to him in challenging a power elite that used any means to degrade and defeat him. In blunting these attacks, the community was unwavering in its support. Clearly, progressive populism is the political thread that has guided Chicano politics from the 1950s through the 1980s. These lessons provide both the motivation and direction for the new, urgent pursuit of a progressive urban program. Developing within the Chicano community is a renewed sense of the form and content of the leadership necessary to implement alliances that can assume legitimate community control of the political system. More similar to the spirit of the past than the present, a movement in opposition to the established hierarchy will necessarily borrow from tactics effectively used in the 1950s and refined in the mid-1960s.

Community Political Mobilization in the 1960s

On the Eastside, police abuse, racial discrimination and poor quality education were the main issues at the grass-roots level during the civil rights era. Two other factors influenced the development of political consciousness in this period: the United Farm Workers Union organizing drive and indigenous protests against the Catholic Church. The school district's arbitrary rules against speaking Spanish, overt degradation of Chicano students, and denial of any form of recourse to protest these conditions became the basis for the single most important political mobilization since Roybal's election to the Los Angeles City Council.

In the 1967–68 academic year, high school students throughout the area supported a series of walkouts to protest unequal educational opportunity. The protest rocked the foundation of the region's power elite. Lasting an entire spring, the walkouts resulted in numerous arrests and generated national media attention. Community support was widespread. Parents, teachers, and students rallied behind the students' demands for education reform. The school district's initial response was predictable – massive police repression to intimidate the teenagers. But the student resistance movement refused to cower. Students continued to conduct marches and rallies, joined by parents and community leaders, to force the school district to address their demands for improved and culturally relevant education. These walkouts trained a generation of radical activists and regenerated community organizing efforts.

At this juncture, all Chicano politicians were 'progressive', advocating an agenda of economic, social and political redistribution. The radical student movement, in an attempt to wrest control of the growing politicization of the Chicano movement, developed a series of anti–Vietnam War protest marches. The first march, in the summer of 1970, was the largest political protest mobilization that had occurred on the Eastside. The rally was frustrated, however, by an all-out assault by a massive police force. Tragically, the leading Latino journalist in the country, Ruben Salazar, was shot by the police while sitting in a restaurant a half-mile from the rally site. The police were exonerated after a media-invoked inquiry, an expected if unpopular decision from the police commission. Three other protest marches followed in the ensuing months, all ending in violent street clashes with the police.

Media coverage of the anti-Vietnam protests, the increasingly successful organizing efforts of the La Raza Unida Party, and the student walkouts forced the traditional Democratic Party leadership to develop a mainstream Latino political strategy. This policy of political containment, basically unchanged to the present, has been to limit the election of Chicanos to overwhelmingly Chicano districts. However, this concession was not accepted by progressive forces. In particular, initial support for the La Raza Unida Party clearly indicated the long-term potential for progressive mobilization in the Eastside. The next political focus became the struggle to incorporate the Eastside into a Chicano city. The region's power structure worked feverishly to prevent this consolidation of Chicano political strength from occurring. After two ballot initiatives failed, this strategy and along with it the most radical elements of the Chicano movement lost their political base.

The Mainstreaming of Chicano Politics

The state and federal government response to the spectre of a permanent radical Chicano opposition was the rapid acceleration of programs to create an 'instant' Chicano middle class. Three factors were essential to this strategy: a compliant Chicano political leadership, increased opportunities for higher education, and a massive federal buyout of moderate and conservative elements through the Model Cities Program. Both the political containment strategy and the effort to develop a Chicano middle class succeeded. Three Chicanos were elected to the state legislature by the early 1970s, providing the Democratic Party with a tangible gesture of progress. The combination of college programs for minorities and War on Poverty give-aways mollified the demands of nominally activist middle-class Chicanos. Band-aid politics succeeded in exagerating expectations of upward mobility for the middle class and blunting much of the cultural nationalist fervor generated in the late

1960s. The stage had been set for the consolidation of a Chicano political hierarchy alienated from its political base, the Chicano community.

Representation in the state legislature shifted the direction of political activity from demands for social justice to enhancing the stature of Chicanos within the system. Community mobilization networks were subtly restructured into a campaign base for emerging Chicano officeholders. Between 1974 and 1982, Chicano representation at the state level gradually increased. In return for control over disbursal of massive federal poverty program funding, this hierarchy began to advocate a 'status quo' agenda within the Democratic Party framework. Control of federal funds gave the politicians the only major source of power at the community level. Through the introduction of social progress entwined with the rapid development of community-based organizations, political discipline and corruption blunted any attempts to build a progressive counterweight to the newly established political order.

This semblance of integration gave rise to an unprecedented national media campaign endorsed by virtually all Chicano elected officials. In late 1978, numerous magazines and newspapers began proclaiming the 1980s as the 'Decade of the Hispanic', promoting the view that major political, and economic advances would be achieved solely on the basis of an increasing Latino population. Despite retrenchment in college support programs for minorities, steady decline in the level of funding for CBOs, and an acceleration in the net loss of manufacturing jobs, the Chicano political hierarchy acted as a public relations arm of this media campaign. The campaign for the 'Decade of the Hispanic' was thus a shallow attempt to divert attention from the economic and political realities facing a grossly underrepresented minority group. By enhancing this positive image, the purportedly liberal leadership abstained from debating the serious problems of underdevelopment within the larger community.

At the grass-roots level, an Alinskyite organizing effort was initiated on the Eastside through the stewardship of the Catholic Church and the Industrial Areas Foundation. Within two years, the United Neighborhood Organizations (UNO) was being proclaimed a national success story for organizing efforts in minority communities. The Church promoted the idea that limited opposition was healthy and could achieve modest goals. UNO received a favorable response from the political establishment for two reasons: the organization did not participate in electoral politics, and it adopted a single-issue strategy that inherently could not address the deterioration of the Eastside in a comprehensive way. This bark-but-don't-bite approach allowed the politicos to avoid the risk of actually pursuing a progressive reform agenda. In fact, the UNO leadership has directly aligned itself with the Chicano political hierarchy despite the organization's charter.

Political Fragmentation Within the Leadership

The campaign for the 'Hispanic Decade' had the unintended effect of enflaming latent political rivalries within the Chicano leadership. Believing their own press notices, which projected an increase in Hispanic political power, they began a battle for control of the future direction of Chicano political aspirations. Two events, one exposing the limits of control over federal grants and the other, a political race between two competing factions, indicated serious schisms within the Chicano hierarchy. This fractionalization eventually led to the revival of strong independent community groups to counter a leadership that had lost touch with its constituency and had failed to address basic community issues.

Traditionally, the political hierarchy had created a system of patronage within the Eastside's numerous CBOs, bartering federal and local grants for unwavering political support. The battle to oust the executive director of the East Los Angeles Health Task Force by a progressive majority on the organization's board of directors was the first serious revolt against control of CBOs by politicos. The Task Force was a notoriously corrupt organization that had always received the financial and bureaucratic blessings of the political hierarchy. Under fire, the executive director was able to obtain the full support of the entire leadership, despite clear evidence of improper activities. The hierarchy quickly realized that this revolt called their authority into question and that controlled corruption was preferable to a CBO reform movement that would threaten their Eastside political base. They responded with a rearguard action to reinstate the executive director. The political hierarchy lost the battle for continued control of the Task Force, but won the war by exerting tighter control over directorships among the numerous CBOs disbursing federal funds.

The other event, a contest for a seat in the state legislature between Gloria Molina and Richard Polanco, forced the rupture within the leadership into the open. Instead of settling on the traditional behind-the-scenes consensus candidate, two factions embarked on what has become a series of electoral battles. In this race, a Chicana challenged the conventional view that a woman could not win a contest in a male-dominated cultural enclave. State Senator Art Torres and Congressman Roybal supported Molina. Alatorre's camp provided the finances necessary for Richard Polanco, a mid-level Democratic Party functionary. The race was close, with Molina becoming the first Chicana to sit in the California state legislature. Most observers believe that the revelation of Polanco's failure to pay child support was the key to Molina's victory. The result of this bitter contest was an irrevocable split within the hierarchy.

During this era a further expansion of power and influence in the Democratic Party occurred. Two Chicanos were elected to congress, the first from the area since Roybal's 1962 campaign. In the State Assembly, Richard Alatorre led the state Democratic Party in carrying through a partisan plan to redraw California's legislative districts. This highly political job is an important stepping-stone toward a major party leadership role. State Senator Art Torres served as state chairman for Senator Walter Mondale's unsuccessful presidential bid in 1984. In a high-profile state, this was also an important move into the central circles of party politics for a minority politician.

However, the serious underrepresentation of Chicanos in government belies this perception of 'advancement'. The Los Angeles City Council and county Board of Supervisors did not have a single Chicano member. The lack of adequate political access allowed popular movements to move into the void this situation presented at the local level.

Popular Opposition Emerges

The splintered Chicano hierarchy in Los Angeles, the center of international and national economic restructuring, lacked the ability to respond cohesively to the crisis impacting the Eastside. Incapable of developing initiatives to encourage labor-intensive industrial development or the construction of affordable housing, or to link redevelopment policy with the gang and drug situation, Chicano politicians have seen their influence erode. Forced by economic and political circumstance, neighborhood organizations have generated effective strategies to defend their sense of community autonomy. A series of recall campaigns against the controversial councilman Art Snyder spurred different neighborhoods to develop local progressive movements. Snyder, who had tightly held his Eastside council seat for over ten years, was an embarassing symbol of the hierarchy's political impotence.

At the center of the recall efforts was a moderate Democrat, Steve Rodriguez, who posed the first serious challenge to the hegemony of the Chicano political hierarchy. Instead of proceeding through the normal network of office visits to obtain approval for the recall campaign, Rodriguez and his supporters bypassed the entire Chicano establishment. The tremendous level of grass-roots support and the momentum that the recall campaigns created were a clear threat to entrenched Democratic Party interests. The hierarchy had lost control of the local political agenda and was rapidly losing its position of dominance on the Eastside. Snyder, after escaping recall by less than twenty votes through sleight-of-hand maneuvering in the city clerk's office, was forced into a second recall campaign by the Rodriguez support network.

The Chicano leadership was forced into a contradictory position. They decided to support a candidate to run against Rodriguez if the recall succeeded to make sure that he did not take the seat against them. However, the leadership steadfastly refused to support the recall effort. The second recall also failed, although the candidate supported by the leadership was embarrassed by Rodriguez in the actual vote for a new council member.

Through these campaigns, the progressive support network realized what effect a community-based strategy could have on the established leadership. The politicos themselves recognized this threat and moved to defuse it. The hierarchy cut a deal with Snyder: it would not openly oppose him in the second recall campaign in exchange for Snyder's support for Alatorre as his successor. Tiring of the constant political battles, Snyder accepted the arrangement and resigned from office, paving the way for Alatorre to take his seat on the council.

The net result for the progressive movement was that after almost five years of organizing and struggle, the Chicano leadership had weathered the political storm. The only alternative was to maintain the existing base network on a local scale to continue opposition to development intrusion into community affairs.

Popular Movements in Chicano *Barrios*

In the last four years grass-roots organizing has begun to reshape the political structure of the Eastside. The Neighborhood Action Committee (NAC) mounted a campaign against the linkage of the last section of the Los Angeles freeway system in order to protect their community from complete destruction. With limited political support, NAC, in an alliance with the upper-middle-class city of South Pasadena, has maintained its resistance to the project for the last four years. This struggle has been expanded into a comprehensive analysis of the housing situation and transportation issues in the area. The organization has networked with citywide coalitions challenging city redevelopment and economic development policies.

For example, the Mothers of ELA (East Los Angeles) was formed in 1984 to stop construction of a new state prison close to residential neighborhoods. The Eastside has traditionally served as the region's infrastructure dumping ground. Many *barrios* have been destroyed or suffered major dislocation from freeways, toxic dumps and jail construction. Despite little outside support, their campaign has achieved stunning success in confronting the power of the governor's office. Initially, the group copied the strategy of the Argentine Madres de los Desaparecedos, conducting nightly candlelight marches from their homes to the proposed prison site. In media-crazed Los Angeles, this tactic was a brilliant use of symbolic protest that received widespread coverage for a number of months. The Mothers developed a network of local community groups to oppose the governor's proposal, sought technical expertise in land use and environmental planning, analyzed state prison expansion plans, and packed every important public hearing with their supporters. After four years of planning, the state is no closer to building the proposed prison than it was at the beginning, when the funds were initially allocated. The Mothers of ELA have also begun to broaden their political agenda. They are active in opposing a trash incineration project in a city close to the Eastside and the newly proposed expansion of the Los Angeles County Jail. Like NAC, this group began with a local issue and has widened its focus to include city and region-wide issues. The housing crisis and economic restructuring in the region will eventually lead these and other community-based movements into broad-based networks that focus on a number of regional growth issues.

Two other important examples in the region provide a strategic framework from which to draw in developing effective coalitions and pursuing a populist urban platform. These organizations, the Westside Homeowners and Tenants Association (WHTA) and El Centro de Accion Social (El Centro), confronted imposing political hurdles in struggles to combat the imposition of housing and economic programs on their communities. Their resistance and politically astute strategies are the most prominent success stories in the region's Chicano communities in the past decade.

The Westside Homeowners and Tenants Association, based in San Bernardino, formed in 1978 to oppose the city and the redevelopment agency from taking complete control over land use policy in their community. The multi-ethnic group generated a strong protest movement in defense of community self-determination. With no political support and scant resources the WHTA developed a strategy based on creating alternative community plans and legal challenges to the city's attempt to domineer their neighborhoods. The group halted the initial redevelopment efforts, and after seven years of struggle the city acquiesced to community election of a planning oversight committee, an election in which the organization won an overwhelming victory. As a result, the city essentially abdicated its authority to WHTA on housing and economic development issues in minority areas of the city.

Based in Pasadena, El Centro was the only Chicano community organization in a historically right-wing city. After the Chicano community suffered from urban renewal and freeway construction during the 1960s and early 1970s, the group began to oppose city-sponsored redevelopment proposals in the Chicano community. The city's initial response was to ignore El Centro's alternative proposals. The organization quickly recognized the narrowness of a strategy based solely on opposing redevelopment project within their neighborhoods. El Centro then adopted a five-point strategy: 1) strong community opposition to any redevelopment proposal in the *barrio*; 2) an all-out offensive against the city's entire urban development program and use of federal funds in minority areas; 3) development of technical and legal expertise in state and federal planning and environmental regulations; 4) networking with the Black community, historic preservationists and neighborhood associations; and 5) publication of critiques of every significant city-sponsored development project for a two-year period. The strategy had a dual purpose: to expose the city's failure to adhere to existing regulations and to forstall the political pressures that the city would exert on the community in response to its opposition to redevelopment.

The city had never faced a direct and concerted challenge over land use policy from the minority community. Initially, the conservative city council simply ignored El Centro's public opposition. During this critical juncture the organization generated four important critiques of various city-sponsored projects. El Centro's main goal was to prevent intrusive condominium development in the *barrio* at all costs. After three years of intense struggle, the city, the redevelopment agency and the developer, a subsidiary of a regional bank, abandoned the project in 1981. This was the first significant victory over land use policy for Pasadena's minority communities and the most important minority struggle since the school integration battles of the 1960s. Because of the controversy sparked by El Centro, the federal government denied approval of three major development projects and forced the city to reform its entire administration of federal urban development programs. El Centro's strategy provided significant support to the growing neighborhood association reform movement that defeated the entrenched conservative hierarchy and took control over city government in 1982.

In Los Angeles, the Redevelopment Agency is attempting to greatly expand its power and influence, the shortage of affordable housing has reached crisis stage, and the city has no economic development programs to benefit the city's working class. Labor-intensive manufacturing, the real solution to the drug and crime chaos, is overshadowed by expensive favors to facilitate the plans of international capital. In addition, other regional government bodies are in the process of implementing a series of crucial environmental regulations in a forum strikingly devoid of minority representation. Air quality, waste management, transportation policy and growth management are major concerns that directly affect the future development of affordable housing and blue-collar manufacturing jobs. Community groups need to assume aggressive public roles on these issues. If they do so, they can gain some influence over the political agenda on urban policy – in contrast to the passivity exhibited by the Chicano hierarchy.

Conclusion

The lesson of the last fifteen years in Los Angeles is that politicians of color do not automatically act in the interests of their communities. In this city, politicos have remained captives of an international cartel whose wealth is based on the exploitation of low-wage workers. Ironically, Chicanos had initially elected leaders willing to challenge this same establishment. But the community and even many conservative and liberal Chicanos have lost confidence in a Chicano political establishment that allows itself to remain politically fragmented and structurally incapable of pursuing a populist agenda in defense of its constituency. Progressives in Los Angeles must therefore assume leadership in the land use and social justice battles currently raging. Numerous forces expressing different levels of class interests are converging to challenge global capital's hegemony over political institutions. The evolution of the growth control movement into a nominally anti-establishment force, the fragmentation of the Democrats, and the crisis of environmental regulation coinciding with the underdevelopment of minority communities have created an unprecedented opportunity for Chicanos to align themselves with other groups in progressive citywide alliances.

Directly correlated to issue-oriented political mobilization is direct action in the electoral arena. Constant lobbying, media exposure and negative voting patterns will force grass-roots groups into direct confrontation with elected officials. By pursuing a such a citywide strategy, progressives can break down the seemingly impenetrable walls of the City Council.

The key to a successful strategy is the realization that political isolation in pursuit of self-determination is a road to political oblivion. Chicano groups need to maintain strategic networking with various oppositional forces, along with the ability to obtain political concessions that directly benefit the interests of the working classes in the regional economy. The Black community's strategy in defeating the LANCER trash incineration project and the strong voter support generated by the Rainbow Coalition for Jesse Jackson in the Eastside in the 1988 Democratic primary are the most recent examples of strategic relationships linking a broad spectrum of organizations and communities.

The needs of the working class and middle class do not have to be perceived as mutually exclusive in advanced capitalism. Opposition to environmental pollution and the widespread clamor for regulation of growth can be used to create political tension with the potential to force capital to restructure the regional economy. Progressives can take action on a wide range of urban problems to exploit the leadership vacuum in Los Angeles politics while consolidating the direction of political activism into the next decade. Through tactically astute negotiations, the issues of affordable housing, urban redevelopment, labor-intensive economic development and health care can become the focuses of a broad-based political movement.

The lack of Chicano leadership involvement in the Redevelopment Agency reform movement is typical of these new political openings. While grass-roots organizations have mounted a highly effective campaign to cripple the power of the agency, the hierarchy has failed to generate any semblance of a cohesive platform on the issue. As a result, Chicano progressives have been able to outmanuever the leadership. The immobility of the hierarchy in the face of these battles over major public issues has led to a conjuncture favoring renewal of the populism that created the Chicano movement in the 1950s. By developing alternative urban policies, minority populist movements are gradually setting the stage for the necessary evolution into an electoral base that can topple a fragmented and inept political hierarchy.

PART IV

Canada and Mexico

12

The Montreal Citizens' Movement: The Realpolitik of the 1990s?

Susan Ruddick

Until the mid-1970s, Montreal shared the role of Canada's dominant metropole with its rival Toronto, serving as a national headquarters for (Canadian) anglophone finance capital, a gateway to the largest inland water transportation system in the world, the Great Lakes, and acting as regional headquarters for a poorly integrated and underdeveloped hinterland, the province of Québec.

In the past two decades, worldwide economic restructuring has all but stripped Montreal of its national preeminence, relegating it to a regional status, while Toronto has risen to the ranks of 'world city'.[1] This process, however, was not the simple product of economic competition between the two cities, with Montreal the loser. The 'new regionalism' of Montreal was actively supported by the francophone bourgeoisie and petty bourgeoisie, who struggled for ascendancy in the city and the province. They did so by riding a wave of labor militancy and general unrest, which in the early 1970s triggered a rash of strikes including, in 1972, the largest general strike of public service workers on the continent. This militance in turn sparked the formation of radical, separatist and nationalist movements including the provincial level Parti Québécois, the armed liberation movement Le Front de Libération de Québec, as well as the municipal-level Front d'Action Politique and Montreal Citizens' Movement. The rising Parti Québécois favored a new regionalism through policies that downplayed the national role of Montreal and that assessed, correctly, that an economy reoriented to local, regional and European markets, would inevitably be more francophone.

Montreal, as the largest city in the province, became a crucial venue for these struggles, as both provincial and national parties sought, at different junctures, to affect the local political process. Here the local realm has indeed inflected the outcomes of global economic restructuring, not by helping to incarnate another 'world city',[2] but rather by supporting the simultaneous emergence of a new kind of global 'second city'. Montreal's central role is not that of regional arm to a nationally dominant Toronto, which in the past two decades has usurped Montreal's former position as host to Canadian corporate headquarters. Rather, the city is an *international* hinterland, the locus of a refracted regionalism: a dumping ground for British, Italian and Belgian real estate investment in the mid-1970s and for French and American finance capital, and American industrial branch plants (once automobile, now para-military). Local businesses now compete not in national, but international, markets. This regional reorientation was first managed under the Parti Civique, whose boss Jean Drapeau transformed Montreal's central business district (CBD) into an attractive locus for foreign real estate, commercial and finance capital by introducing infrastructural improvements tied to the hosting of Expo '67 and later the Olympic Games. Regionalism has been more recently orchestrated by the Montreal Citizens' Movement. The MCM's fifteen-year history as champion of the deteriorated inner city and critic of the autocratic style of the Drapeau regime made it better able to sustain CBD expansion through a central tenet of this current growth strategy: economic revitalization of the inner city, which (ostensibly) in a spirit of citizens participation and local input promises to remake the inner city as a new residence for the CBD labor market and incubator for local industry.

The unequivocal popularity of the Montreal Citizens' Movement – swept to power in 1986, in a city election that won it 55 out of 58 municipal districts – has given rise to conflicting interpretations about its current role. Born in 1974 out of the ashes of Le Front d'Action Politique – a self-declared socialist alternative to Drapeau's political machine of the period – the Montreal Citizens' Movement seemed for many activists to create the potential for development of a new political space within the city, a stepping stone to the realization of popular mobilization through the formation of neighborhood councils; for some, perhaps, even rekindling the dream of creating a Red Bologna on the North American continent. Indeed, after three years in power, the Montreal Citizens' Movement has made substantial changes to both the political and planning processes within the city. It has formed five commissions that, with citizen input, study questions of economic development, housing and transportation, cultural development, community welfare, and administration and finance. In June 1988 it initiated the largest public consultation in the history of the province of Québec around the planning and development of the downtown area, drawing briefs from 165 organizations. For the first time in the city's history, the administration demanded and secured major concessions from real estate developers, involving allocation of funds from redevelopment to pay for both relocation and rental subsidies to displaced tenants. And it promises in the future a variant of the 'neighborhood councils', 'comitées d'arrondissement', which will allow citizens to have direct input into the city's local development policies. But the MCM government has seriously diluted the original program of the party, moving from a stance of social mobilization and citizen empowerment to one of beneficent service delivery.[3]

Proponents of the new regime are fond of contrasting its approach and achievements with that of its predecessor: the MCM's public hearings versus the secrecy of the Parti Civique; the focus on needs of the inner city versus Drapeau's penchant for grandiose and costly extravaganzas; a new professionalism versus the 'small shopkeeper's approach' of the previous regime. Other analysts such as Léonard and Léveillée go so far as to suggest that economic restructuring has *required* a democratization of municipal politics, arguing that in the early 1980s the programs of the Parti Civique and the MCM began to converge, as a new emphasis on local redevelopment called for institutions encouraging input of businesses and citizens. Although a more accurate picture, this analysis lends an air of inevitability to the transition, downplaying both the differences between the Drapeau and Doré regimes, and, more importantly, to the possible current and future incarnations of the MCM.

Shaking the Foundations – Economic Restructuring and the Unmaking of the Drapeau Regime

The fall of the Drapeau regime can be largely attributed to the success of his growth strategies for the city, which ironically undercut the very foundations of his political and social base.

The Parti Civique, headed by Drapeau, was largely responsible for achieving the city's economic restructuring – transforming it from a traditional industrial town dependent on heavy manufacturing to a commercial and office center. While this indeed was a lesson for the old regime, it should also be a signal to the left within the MCM, which has failed to capture, or perhaps even to identify, their new political constituency – the mass of clerical and white-collar workers that fuels the transformation. In some cases this myopia has taken the form of a strong attachment to the 'old style' working class; in others it derives from a failure to see the new forms as they are constituted in the city of Montreal, leaning instead towards the drama of 'world city' politics in a curious form of boosterism that *overcounts* the underclass – the homeless, the undocumented workers, the youth gangs, the sweatshop workers – produced in the course of restructuring. In addition, supporters of the MCM often fail to see that the current form of participatory democracy has emerged in part because it is simply better suited to the exigencies of contemporary restructuring, as the form and style of Drapeau's political machine was suited to growth strategies of a previous era.

Between the mid-1960s and late 1970s Drapeau reorganized the city's core to stimulate growth of financial and commercial capital, laying the foundation for the formation of oppositional groups that were to become the basis of a new urban regime. By the 1980s, however, a much more delicate surgery on inner-city neighborhoods was needed to assist the expansion of the central business district, and to transform surrounding low-income and working-class neighborhoods into residential enclaves for the CBD's new labor force. To do this, the Drapeau regime needed a new political style and a new institutional framework that could incorporate its traditional base of support and elements of a new social base critical to this process.

Transcending the inner city: Expo '67, the Olympic Games and the politics of exclusion

Economic restructuring in the postwar era lessened Montreal's importance as a financial and corporate headquarters while expanding that of Toronto. With a hinterland dominated by American-owned and resource-based industries, and local industries dependent on their proximity to New England for a market for both goods and components,[4] Montreal was particularly vulnerable to transformations in the US economy, which from the postwar period on weakened its industrial base. The stagnation of New England's economy, a suburban exodus of Montreal's industries and shifts in US regional growth from the northeast to the southwest devastated the industrial base in Montreal's inner city and reduced the city's attractiveness as a location for corporate headquarters. Between 1960 and 1970 unemployment more than doubled, fluctuating between 8 percent and 13 percent for the next fifteen years.[5] Traditional sectors of industry – textiles, and garments – were later vulnerable to the exodus to countries with cheap labor such as India, Hong Kong, South Korea and Taiwan.

The grandiose projects of the Drapeau era were in part designed to transcend a metropolitan rivalry between Montreal and Toronto that had begun to lay bare a more fundamental antagonism: that between a predominantly francophone working class and an anglophone bourgeoisie. For the French working class, rivalry with Toronto or Ontario did not obfuscate class politics through focus on place, but rather invoked it. The average francophone earned 19 percent less than his or her anglophone counterpart in Toronto; francophones constituted 80 percent of the provincial population but owned 20 percent of the industry. With 27 percent percent of the nation's labor force, Québec was home to 37 percent of its unemployed.[6] For the francophone petty bourgeoisie, anglophone business and industry constituted a roadblock to upward mobility, as francophones were systematically passed over for upper management positions. Young lower class francophones suffered the indignity of having to pass English language tests in order work alongside French neighbors in low-level jobs in Anglo companies.

In Montreal and across Québec, class and ethnic politics were reinforced by geography. On the island of Montreal, upper- and middle-class anglophones, who made up only 20 percent of the city's population, rarely ventured east of Boulevard St. Laurent. Culturally, the francophone and anglophone communities remained two solitudes – with the francophone population contained in the eastern sector of the city and in the eastern regions of the nation.

Faced with an angry and organized working class and a resistant intelligentsia, with the latter beginning to venture into municipal politics, Drapeau had to be cautious in developing a growth strategy for the city. Explicit competition with Toronto or Ontario tended to incite class antagonisms rather than to build consensus.[7]

The centerpiece of Drapeau's urban redevelopment strategies therefore set Montreal apart from most North American cities. Through a program of immense spectacle Drapeau intended to elevate the city to international stature. He orchestrated a series of attractions and festivals, including a World's Fair in 1967, the creation of a major league baseball team, popular concerts, public exhibits, the construction of a modern concert hall, Place des Arts, and, for the grand finale, the Olympic Games of 1976.[8]

Too often considered a testimony to the man's flamboyance, extravagance and excess, these grandiose schemes were a conscious political strategy to unify disparate and conflicting ethnic and sectoral interests around an economic restructuring of the city.

Emphasizing the city's tourist, financial and commercial role within the wider region of central Canada, and ignoring the decline of its industrial base, Drapeau avoided any direct confrontation with Toronto's hegemony as a manufacturing center. Drapeau's response was economic liberation of Québec through state intervention, a forerunner of the 'Quiet Revolution' that intended to redress its underdevelopment relative to Ontario, through regional economic planning and modernization of the provincial economy with such schemes as a massive hydroelectric industry and a revamped educational system. The strategy he pursued posed neither a direct economic challenge to Toronto, nor to Canadian federalism. Both the Metro line and the international spectacles that gave it legitimation were indeed, as the vice-president of the MCM Abe Limonchick later put it, 'a monument to the Quiet Revolution'.[9]

'Expo' and 'the Games' created the consensus for introduction and expansion of a public transit system that bore no relation to the needs of the working class for better transportation to their workplaces, but instead drew them to a rejuvenated anglophone central business district and its newly constructed department stores, now rivalling suburban malls, and a secondary francophone business district to the east. This bipolar strategy gained support from warring, geographically disparate French and English business interests historically divided into two municipal Chambers of Commerce – one, the Board of Trade, representing mostly nonfrancophone monopoly capital and larger commerical and industrial interests, and the other Le Chambre du Commerce, representing smaller francophone commercial and industrial capital.[10]

The grandiose flavour and international stature of Drapeau's schemes insulated them from any direct, effective opposition from the low-income and working-class communities that bore the economic brunt of their implementation.

The beauty, dynamism and international prestige of the city itself, for the average Montrealer – part of a francophone working class and petty bourgeoisie that constituted about 60 percent of the community – answered long-frustrated aspirations within a predominantly English Canada. Like the mayor himself, these megaprojects symbolized talent, *savoir-faire*, and the possibility of validation by developing an identity distinct from that of English Canada and recognized on an international scale. Symbolically, Drapeau's projects *transcended the shabbiness of 'les quartiers grises' without actually having to confront it*. Unlike the detailed social programs offered by the opposition, Expo and the Games found wide acceptance. As one critic of the regime noted at the time: 'social and economic programs ... generate opposition, [and] create dissatisfaction among the very people they intend to aid, because they always deliver less than they promise.' Drapeau himself correctly assessed that the contributions of the administration would be measured 'not in terms of [their benefit to] the people, but rather the prestige they accorded the city.'[11]

The style of the Drapeau government was consensus democracy: the leader determined the direction of the party and presented it to the people as a symbol with which they could identify. The grand schemes of Drapeau were well-suited to this style, although, as the Malouf Commission revealed in its enquiry into overspending for the Olympics, the mayor had so much power that a coordinator to oversee the cost mangement and construction of stadiums and housing for the Games was never appointed. Drapeau retained absolute control.

Unable to stop the decline of Montreal vis-à-vis Toronto, these extravaganzas made the city vulnerable to massive debt burdens – $1 billion for the Games alone. By the late 1970s, this growth strategy was no longer acceptable to a debt-ridden federal government and was an easy target of criticism from the newly elected Parti Québécois.

Transforming the inner city: PIQA, PAQ and the politics of incorporation

Blinded by its own boosterism, the Montreal municipal government by the late 1970s and early 1980s was at last forced to address fundamental weaknesses in the city's economy. These included a declining manufacturing base, persistently high levels of unemployment, the flight of corporate headquarters from the city – a fifteen-year trend exacerbated by provincial language laws – and competition with its suburban corona for the financial and commercial headquarters that remained.[12]

The result was a shift away from grandiose projects to what one theorist has called a new 'localism' that focused attention on rebuilding the inner city. The principal characteristic of this new localism was that 'it would rely essentially on economic forces already within the city or the Montreal metropolitan area'.[13] This reorientation was strongly supported by the French business community, which became increasingly implicated in growth strategies for the city. The programs focused primarily on local incubator industries intended to serve international markets, avoiding competition with established industries in Toronto and leaving aside for the moment the question of the flight of corporate headquarters to the rival city. As with other regional development strategies, the new localism sought less to internationalize the city than to create a local elite with an international role – or, more candidly, to establish an alliance between the local elite and foreign capital.[14]

The program of 'new localism' was a three-pronged attack on the inner city which sought to revitalize the housing stock and cultural/commercial life of the inner city with trendy restaurants and boutiques, making the area more attractive to a new suburban middle class, generating funds for the city's coffers through increased tax revenues, and sustaining the CBD's role as a financial and commerical headquarters by enabling its labor force to live in close proximity to the downtown. As will be seen later, however, the Parti Civique was unable to make the shift to this new growth strategy – in part because it was too strongly associated with an older institutional form and political style associated with grand projects such as the Olympic Games, but also because it directed these new growth strategies towards its old social base, ignoring for the most part the new socio-demographic composition of the city.

Twelve Years Inside the MCM: The Birth of Janus?

The MCM replaced the Parti Civique because it was able to bring together diverse elements of a new social base, which were important to new growth strategies within the city. The strategies of the Parti Civique had required the inner city only as a throughway for major transportation arteries. Community opposition to such schemes did not have the same impact as it did on subsequent growth strategies, which tried to recast the inner city as a 'liveable place' for professionals from the suburbs. Geographically peripheral, the inner-city working-class opposition under the Drapeau regime was dealt with through a politics of exclusion, leaving repression and legitimation largely to upper tiers of government.

Under the Doré regime, the MCM has incorporated this opposition, a new stratum of paraprofessionals and white-collar workers, as well as parts of Drapeau's constitutency, into a broader social base through institutions of public representation and participation, more fitting to the delicate surgery of inner-city revitalization that characterizes a central aspect of development during the 1980s. The stability of the Doré regime cannot be taken for granted, however. It has been tenuously maintained through the twelve-year history of the party, expressed both in struggles over its internal structure and party program.[15] The MCM has been transformed from a political *movement* whose rallying slogan was 'Les Salaires aux Pouvoirs', to a moderate, technocratic political *party*, whose self-characterization is 'Une Entreprise de Service Publique à la Population' – the outcome of a protracted and often bitter struggle among three currents within the party: moderate, social democratic and socialist.

From political movement to political party: 1970 – 1974

The first stage in this series of transformations was its destruction as a radical movement, Le Front d'Action Politique (FRAP), and resurrection as the more populist Rassemblement des Citoyens de Montreal, or Montreal Citizens' Movement. According to Marcel Sevigny, party militant of both FRAP and the MCM, the birth of the MCM

> marked an historical rupture with FRAP. ... It was born and developed as if FRAP never existed ... without the militants who participated in its founding having a clear vision of all its aspects, and above all a

common vision. It did not follow a historical trajectory, but was dropped, like a parachute, into the political arena of Montreal. So it appears, many 'errors' marking FRAP's history were rewritten.[16]

Compared with its predecessor, Le Front d'Action Politique, the MCM was clearly reformist in program and structure, even in its early phases. The original brain child of the Conseil des Syndicats Nationaux (CSN), FRAP in its earliest form was like a second front for the union movement, which was grappling with industrial decline and erosion of its base in the city's deteriorating manufacturing sector.[17] The movement was met half-way by neighborhood citizen groups, who wanted to transcend the limits of neighborhood action through the formation of an umbrella organization. This period marked an all too brief bridging of the gap between workplace and neighborhood organization.

Although FRAP has been characterized as a party of intellectuals who only idealized the labor movement and neighborhood groups it sought to represent,[18] it nevertheless established formal links between popular groups, the unions and the student movement through its CAPs. The legacy of FRAP's activity remains in those neighborhoods that most strongly supported the CAPs. Under the Doré regime, these constitute the strongest sources of critical support or even outright opposition to the MCM from left of center.

The strongest blow to FRAP's political program came on the eve of the 1970 election. Faced with the defection of twelve municipal council members – many from inner-city districts where FRAP was based – Drapeau launched a venomous attack on FRAP, linking it to the armed terrorist organization Le Front de Liberation de Québec (FLQ). In spite of the wide support for the FLQ, and the fact that FRAP only formally endorsed the objectives of the FLQ while rejecting its terrorist tactics, Drapeau's linking of the two organizations was enough to damage FRAP at the polls and to destroy the new and fragile alliances that the organization was establishing with community groups.[19]

The vacuum created by the exodus of community organizations from FRAP was filled by members of the left of the Parti Québécois, who quit provincial politics for the neighborhoods as the PQ began to turn away from a socialist platform towards a more strictly nationalist orientation.[20] Further radicalization of FRAP's objectives, and the growing domination of its ranks by union organizers and militant socialists at the expense of community organizers, led to a gradual detachment of the organization from the neighborhoods and to a focus on workplace issues and the study of Marxism.

In 1973 the remaining militants, now concentrated in three municipal districts, tried to revive the electoral challenge to the Drapeau regime, proposing that the regional arm of the CSN form a political party to challenge the Parti Civique the following year. Abandoning municipal politics in favour of building of a provincewide movement, the CSN left this task to two warring factions – the old members of FRAP, who favored the formation of a workers' party, and a more moderate electoral current, linked to the Parti Québécois.[21]

It was the moderates who came to dominate, supported in part by the PQ machine. But the politically ascendant Parti Québécois kept an arms-length relationship to the local party, lending organizational support without formal endorsement. Well-served by the development of a radical movement in Montreal, the PQ was wary of associating itself too quickly with an organization that might repeat, as PQ leader René Levesque put it, 'the gaucheries of FRAP'.[22] The MCM owed its later success in part to the strength of the Parti Québécois political machine, which lent it experience, networks and contacts that came ultimately to influence the orientation of the party.

The last gasp: the organized left within the MCM: 1974–1978

The MCM was born out of the ashes of FRAP. But this birth marked a pronounced shift in the nature of political opposition in four major areas: 1) the development of a party program; 2) the relationship of the party to unions and community organizations; 3) involvement in workplace issues; and 4) a focus on electoralism or mobilization. At the outset, this shift signaled the victory of the moderate and social democratic elements within the party over the socialist current. Conflict was institutionally contained as members tended to gravitate towards activities most nearly akin to their own political philosophy. The left tended to dominate the executive committee and ancillary committees, which in the eyes of one long-term party member led them to overestimate the degree of power and influence that they had within the party;[23] the social democrats and liberal reformists tended to be better represented among elected officials and the party's municipal council. The ensuing division of labor inevitably played itself out in conflicts over whether the party's program and energies were to be directed towards social mobilization and education, or rather towards developing its electoral appeal.

Following the electoral defeat of 1970, FRAP party members had focused their energies on clarifying party ideology and politcal program – a task that led to bitter internal divisions within the party. The Montreal Citizens' Movement, by contrast, thrived in the very chaos of its conception and the lack of clarity in its political program, strategies and even in its name, as it attempted to suture together three ultimately irreconcilable positions within the party. It bathed in a confusion of vocabulary, modus operandi and institutional form that would sustain rather than shatter what might, and indeed did, become a fragile alliance.

While many militants still considered it the socialist alternative to the Drapeau regime, because of their experience of the devastating defeat of FRAP, and a concern 'not to scare the people', they worked to develop both party name and program and repressed internal differences without resolving them. The party name, 'Rassemblement des Citoyens de Montreal/ Montreal Citizens' Movement', satisfied both those who had wanted a workers' party organizationally linked to the unions and those who sought a coalition of progressive forces, but it conflated the distinction between members responsible for a clearly defined program and citizens at large, who were linked to the party in sporadic strategic alliances.[24]

The party program, 'Une Ville Pour Nous', espoused a radical analysis of the city's urban problems for those able to infer it, such as Abe Limonchik, an MCM militant and executive committee president. But the document remained, nevertheless, limited to examining municipal problems and proposing administrative reforms. More important, there was no clear consensus on what the official party program actually was, with different members referring to the diluted electoral document, or the pronouncements of successive executive committees, according to their own political persuasion.[25]

A second distinction between to the MCM and FRAP was the nature of the links between the party, the unions and neighborhood organizations. In spite of party rhetoric, the MCM was formed without official links to either. In part, this dissociation was mutual. The unions abandoned the municipal sphere in favour of building a movement at the provincial level, rallying around the national question.[26] Community groups dependent on government funds drew back from formal support for fear of reprisal. Independent groups feared they would be 'drowned in illusory adventures, offered without cessation by reformers'.[27]

One of the founding principals of FRAP had been to unite 'les quartiers ouvriers' and 'les quartiers populaires' into a single movement privileging neither the workplace nor consumption issues. However, conscious of its scarce resources, the left within the MCM abandoned this objective in 1976 and began to focus its energies on housing as the single most important political issue. Even before this time, however, support for union struggles was symbolic rather than substantial, often tabled for further study to special committees, a practice that cut short debate at the heart of the party and established a bureaucratic norm of functioning.[28]

In spite of attempts to redirect its energies towards mobilization, the left continually ran up against its own structural organization oriented towards achieving electoral victory, which both diluted party policy and diverted party energy. This focus was at odds with its programmatic objective of creating a society based on neighborhood units of self-management ultimately defined by neighborhood councils.[29] The left-dominated executive committee attempted to refine party energies around mobilization as a central priorty, beginning in the first postelection congress in November 1975. Calling for a socialist analysis of the urban crisis, it stressed the role of neighborhood councils as a means to link 'political program, militant practice, and social structure'.[30] But the contemporary conception of neighborhood councils was substantially different from the current one, the former to be created through citizen mobilization around specific political struggles – 'never ... another level of government within the capitalist society [but] rather ... an alternative to the present state at all levels ... [one which] must never be imposed from above by legislative act or party dictate'.[31]

For militant party member Marc Raboy, the program established by a left-dominated executive committee signalled 'an irreversible move to the left in the MCM's political evolution.' But in retrospect, this burst of activity within the MCM was more like a supernova, prelude to the final demise of the left. The period between 1976 and 1978 marked a watershed in the history of the MCM. Perhaps buoyed by the provincial victory of the Parti Québécois, a left-oriented executive committee sought to radicalize the municipal party's objectives, issuing programmatic statements about the need for urban socialism and outlining the ways and means that the party would achieve this objective. What resulted was a bitter struggle between the left and moderate reformists, waged largely through the press, as the moderate faction charged the MCM with beginning to act 'more like a party and less like a coalition'.[32]

The final divisive issue was not over local program, but the attempt of two leaders of the moderates to engage simultaneously in provincial-level politics. Not only did this action violate a party dictum intended to prevent 'springboarding'; it raised the studiously avoided question of party members' position on the national question. In spring 1978, a few months before the municipal elections, two leading liberals from the MCM formed their own party, the Municipal Action Group (MAG), to run against both the MCM and the Parti Civique. Their campaign was backed by the federal Liberal Party – which feared the emergence of a radical municipal party – with election coffers three times that of the MCM. MAG began a slick, professional media campaign that eclipsed the style of the MCM, with the latter's emphasis on community links and a low-key mayoralty candidate who acted rather as party spokesperson than party leader.[33]

In the election, the Municipal Action Group had a devastating impact on the MCM, splitting the vote in several of its strongholds and reducing its elected candidates from eighteen in 1974 to one in 1978. Among the lessons learned by the MCM in this bitter struggle was that a party that did not develop its public image through radio, television and the daily press severely limited its chances of electoral success in a city.[34] Battered and embittered, many MCM members refocused their energy on other arenas, including cooperative housing, legal aid offices and medicare clinics.

Les jeunes des smarts: the MCM re-formed, 1982–1986

The ensuing lull in party activity was broken in 1982 by a 'third wave' of Parti Québécois members entering the municipal party. Elected to power in 1976, the Parti Québécois had proven itself by 1982, with the exception of the referendum and radical position on language, to be very much an extension of the Quiet Revolution. Moreover, its early sympathic stance towards the union movement, with emphasis on health and reform of the labor code, had given way to attacks on the Common Front alliance of public and para-public sector workers and introduction of anti-union Bill 45.

A key player in this movement to municipal-level politics was subsequent mayoralty candidate Jean Doré, former press secretary to PQ leader René Levesque. Doré typified a new political attitude among these members, dubbed by the Parti Québécois as the 'syndrome des jeunes de smarts', which signalled a shift towards a more technocratic service orientation. Once again ex-Parti Québécois members made significant changes to the style and substance of the party, reshuffling the balance of power that had held together different elements of the party's social base, and molding it into a new configuration better able than the Drapeau regime to undertake transformation of the inner city.

This new political configuration within the Montral Citizens' Movement, indicated a process of momentary convergence between the MCM and Parti Civique as they struggled to incorporate within their ranks an as yet undefined, unaligned social base. For the MCM the task was to maintain ties with inner-city communities while wooing both business and a new stratum of paraprofessionals and white-collar workers.

This task was made easier by a growing dissatisfaction of the business community with the Drapeau regime and its inability to forestall the city's economic decline, heightened by the debt burden left behind by the Olympic Games.[35] The MCM capitalized on this mood, casting itself as the progressive, efficient, professional alternative and pressing for public consultations and participation in the city planning process. Most important, however, it dropped earlier plans to orchestrate community redevelopment, subordinating itself to private sector initiatives and emphasizing subsidies and incentives as a key strategy.[36]

Next, it broadened its social base geographically, demographically and ideologically, relaxing criteria and procedures of selection for potential municipal council candidates. The result was a rapid increase in party membership, including ex-council members of the Parti Civique, which skyrocketed from a base of 3,500 to 6,000 members in 1985 to 22,000 by the election year of 1986.[37]

Like the Parti Civique, the MCM drew its members from the

ranks of the professional-managerial-technical stratum, but it drew from the ranks of the newer professions, such as computer programmers, consultants and newer small- and middle-sized businesses, and it cast itself as a new, efficient, upscale city management,[38] widening its appeal among both the new petty bourgeoisie and clerical workers.

With the expertise of ex-Parti Québécois campaign organizers, the MCM marketed as its new candidate for mayor Jean Doré, a choice acceptable to labor, citizens' groups and to the Parti Québécois. Making full use of the media, highlighted in events like giving blood, and more recently stripping away 'the folksy markings of his old MCM image with a chic new veneer' Doré espoused the life-style of the new petty bourgeoisie. One not-so-sympathetic journalist has written: 'He moved from his Plateau Mont Royal flat to a downtown condominium. A limousine has replaced his bicycle as a means of getting to work. He windsurfs and works out on rowing machines at the YMCA.'[39]

Ironically, in many ways Doré mimicked the strategy of Drapeau. Drapeau's charisma among the lower class and working-class elements of his constituency was enhanced by the fact that he never moved from his modest working-class home, and answered all letters sent to him at City Hall personally and by hand. Dore's shift in life-style is more than the old theme of being seduced by the trappings of power – it is the specific style of this power that is important, reflecting the social base to which it appeals.

The final piece in the puzzle of the Doré regime – the incorporation of the MCM's old social base – has come about partly out of the success of Drapeau's early attempts at revitalization. This drove many of the more militant community groups to strengthen their alliance with the MCM, and in 1986, to re-enter electoral politics. One long-time militant – now public relations officer for the MCM – has asserted that this was not a happy decision, but rather a short-term and tactical alliance on behalf of these groups, who feared that another term of the Drapeau regime would spell the final expulsion of traditional working-class and welfare populations from the inner city.[40]

Day for Night: The MCM in Power

> *'Il n'y avait pas besoins d'élire le RCM pour faire ce type de reforme. Ce que nous avons c'est un gouvernment de consultants.'*
>
> —M. Rotrand, Municipal Councillor, Snowdon

> *'The adminstration carries out its election promises, but I haven't the slightest idea of where it is going and can't count on it to be social democratic.'*
>
> —Sam Boskey, Municipal Council member, MCM party member since 1974, expelled 1988

Following its campaign promise of 1986, the victorious Montreal Citizens' Movement presented a General Plan for the Central Area, some 1,570 hectares of downtown Montreal. With its breezy title 'Faites Votre Ville!' (Build Your City!), the document enjoined Montrealers to participate in a public hearing in June 1988. This was to be the largest public consultation ever to take place in Québec, with some 165 briefs presented from business associations, community groups, academic institutions and labor organizations.

There is little controversial in its treatment of the Central Business District and core of the Central Area: the worst damage had already been done under the Drapeau regime. The real battle lies in the 'revitalization' of 'les quartiers gris' – the base of MCM activity for almost two decades – and their relationship to the CBD. Their choice of the Central Business District and Central Area as a starting point for planning is a telling commentary on the transformation of the party. Even the boundaries are significant, bisecting two of the older working-class districts, to the southeast and southwest, and redefining them as part of the Central Area – subordinated at the outset to the imperatives of CBD expansion. Here lie the major fissures in the MCM's coalition and here the social, spatial and institutional suturing of antagonistic social bases must take place if the MCM's strategy is to succeed.

This may not prove an easy task. Within the first few months of taking power, the Executive Committee was confronted with a delegation of the city's biggest developers. They hinted that the new administration should go slowly or the delegation would trigger a wave of disinvestment and cautioned against using urban redevelopment as a source of revenues for social programs.[41] On the other hand, as has become evident in the struggles over the General Plan and downtown redevelopment schemes, the administration cannot afford to ignore its old social base completely.

The General Plan has become the focus for a qualitatively new politics of place. It differs from that of the early Drapeau regime, not only in its new institutional forms of participation but also in the architectural style, images and objects around which a new sense of community is being constituted.

Under Drapeau, the massive, uni-functional, modern structures of Expo '67, the Place des Arts, and the Olympic Games characterized the architecture of redevelopment. Form dominated over function, international image over pragmatism. The design of the Olympic Stadium – the 'Big O' – included a retractable roof so complicated, expensive and unwieldy that it wasn't constructed for over a decade. The Olympic Village, 1,800 dormitory units designed with little thought for the needs of Montreal's low-income families, quoted its counterpart in a resort of Southern France so exactly that it was unusable, without substantial modification, during Montreal's winter months.

Geared to brief, orgiastic, mass participation in spectator events, these monuments reinforced the passive and symbolic participation of the city's working class and welfare recipients in decisions about the nature of urban redevelopment and in cultural and recreational pursuits. High admission prices precluded their participation, high budgets drained funds and green space from much needed recreational and community services in low-income neighborhoods, dropping Montreal to ninety-fifth place among Québec municipalities in municipal funds allocated to popular parks, recreational and cultural infrastructure, and last among large North American cities in its ratio of green space to inhabitants. Perhaps the biggest irony was the establishment of a municipal lottery to meet the $1 billion Olympic debt: low-wage earners, its major participants, now purchased the dream of winning the lottery to pay for the fantasy of hosting the Olympic Games.[42]

Under Doré, the festival has become the daily life in the inner city, with communities revitalized – supposedly – to meet two decades of working-class dreams and demands, and the upscale life-styles of the new petty bourgeoisie. But the new harmony of social mix, the new vitality of social diversity is a chimera – the incongruous blend of life spaces of professionals, clerical workers, a traditional petty bourgeoisie of shopkeepers and property owners, and increasingly beleaguered welfare recipients and the traditional working class.

Revitalization cannot take place without this mix. Unlike Boston or San Francisco, Montreal has a small professional-managerial stratum, its growth limited by the regionalization of Montreal's economy; low use of ancillary services by corporate headquarters; linguistic and licensing barriers to provincial expansion; and an international focus that is francophone in emphasis. Its role is in many ways a symbolic one – not that of tastemakers but rather placemakers who through their residence in the downtown lend it a status and prestige it could not have achieved twenty years ago. For the 12 percent of the workforce that is unemployed, and for the low-paid textile workers, clerical workers and service workers in hospitals, schools and institutions who dominate the labor force,[43] the presence of the professional-managerial stratum and the status it accords the downtown can hardly justify the eleven-fold increase in housing costs as rental units are transformed into condos and co-ownerships.[44] Yuppie gentrification of downtown Montreal is a myth; the reality is the displacement of low-income residents by slightly better-off 'pseudo-yuppies' who simultaneously aspire to and decry a life-style they can ill afford.

In this era of urban restructuring, social polarization is the watchword of North American world cities – its architecture expressed in the citadel/ghetto relationship of buildings like Hotel Bonventure of Los Angeles to a nearby wasteland of homeless people.[45] But in second cities such as Montreal, potential fissures are papered over through the innocuous evocation of the 'lively street' and the residential 'Faubourg' – a kind of new-town in-town – both of which the Montreal planning committee hopes to gaily insert into depressed communities surrounding the Central Business District. This is not a landscape of violent opposites, but of minute partitionings, by sleight-of-hand reproducing a logic of social and spatial segregation – once writ large between suburb and inner city – in the intricate and confined space of 'les quartiers grises'. The new infrastructure of parks, cultural facilities and neighborhood improvements long demanded by local working-class and welfare residents will do little to enhance their life, appended rather to the high-rent 'Faubourgs' and boutique-lined streets that are part and parcel of revitalization. Stephen Schecter, long-time local activist and urban theorist has commented:

> It is difficult to conceive of this social mix, when the social fabric of the neighborhood is already crushed, and the dominant image of the citizen à la mode, publicized and sought for everywhere, is a robust solitary individual, on his way up, doing his jogging, saving with his retirement plan, and eating out in restaurants whose tables are covered in ice pink and green tablecloths.

This incarnation of inner-city vitality, which in the General Plan transforms the city into a storefront and its residents into consumers, has not gone uncontested, but it dominates the nostalgic images of Montreal resurrected by both the left and the Parti Civique. The image nurtured by activists and organizers of the 1970s was the romantic revival of the history of working-class neighborhoods. Developed to counter Drapeau's calumny – which cast 'les quartiers grises' as outmoded, dangerous, dirty and obsolete, thus justifying gentrification – this image was made concrete in community museums, through oral histories and by retrieval of personal artifacts, tools and photos of residents whose families had lived in the areas for generations. It recaptured the vibrancy of day-to-day life from the turn of the century to the heyday of the 1950s.

These forms of cultural and artistic expression receive scant attention in the cultural agenda of the new General Plan. Like the social base they allude to, their image can scarcely be sustained, because the lifeblood of these neighborhoods has been drained through plant closings and shutdowns and the ravages of Drapeau's revitalization schemes. However noble, this backward-looking image has in some ways been the fallacy of the left, failing to capture a new social, economic and political reality emerging in these communities.

The alternative image, hastily adopted by the Drapeau regime in the early 1980s, also invoked the past, but it was a past devoid of production. Masterminded by Yvon Lamarre, president of the municipal Executive Committee, owner of a major hardware store and council representative from a traditional Parti Civique stronghold, St. Henri, this image responded to the growing discontent among the traditional base of the Parti Civique, the small shopkeepers, small businesses and property owners who felt ill served by the megaprojects of the Drapeau regime. The image recalled the golden age of small businesses and shops. In the words of one contemporary city bureaucrat,

> [M. Lamarre] wants to recapture the lively spirit of the neighborhoods ... to retrieve in every neighborhood the spirit of forty years ago. Analogous to the little village where you find a commerical street, a church, a library, shops, specialty stores, eventually a cultural center, and even a sports center.[46]

The image, however, was decidedly outdated, invoking a past rather than celebrating a future, with little appeal for the new petty bourgeoisie, professional-technical-managerial types, or the mass of low-paid clerical workers who dominated the downtown. Moreover, the method of intervention and style of consultation required to transform the inner city was also alien to the administration and its traditional social base. As Leonard and Leveille noted, this new style was 'probably considered premature by the very interests that stood to benefit', local merchants and small businesses. Some merchants even launched public campaigns to undermine them.[47]

The triumphant image of the inner city, portrayed by the MCM administration in its General Plan, is one that sings harmony to the melody of the Central Business District, with its supporting role as residence for the CBD labour force, shopping venue, tourist attraction and cultural venue for the new avant garde. Leisure needs are satisfied by a string of parks along boutique-filled streets where busy shoppers can rest between spending bouts; culture is the high culture of the Place des Arts or the Latin Quarter.

The MCM does not ignore the needs of its traditional social base. The General Plan plan calls for subsidized and low-income housing for low-paid workers, the homeless, single parents and large families, as well as orientation of some amenities to their social, recreational and cultural needs. But these objectives are a counterpoint, almost overwhelmed by the main theme of the document, and the means to achieve them are unspecified. Moreover, the current administration has shown itself willing to implement redistributive programs only under duress. For many community groups, the concept of a 'social mix' in the central area is simply lip service: a means of destroying the social integrity of their communities by justifying the construction of luxury housing enclaves. 'We will believe in this social mix when there are subsidized housing units in Westmount and on L'Ile des Soeurs', has been their response.[48]

The community response: 'faites votre ville – mais pas avec notre quartier'

Given the limited size of the professional-technical-managerial stratum in Montreal, the administration may need subsidies to attract middle-class suburbanites to central-city housing. However, it has already been forced to divert funds to the less lucrative subsidy of dwellings for welfare recipients, pensioners and low-income workers. The strength of now atrophied working-class and low-income communities lies in their adept alliances with heritage and environmental groups, and their strategic location in the path of CBD expansion. Bounded to the north by the mountain and already gentrified communities, and blocked to the south by the St. Lawrence River, the most logical path of CBD expansion is southwest and southeast, through Centre Sud and Pointe St. Charles. Drawing on networks established through two decades of organization and militance, these communities are already challenging 'revitalization' schemes geared to downtown expansion. They are developing their own concept of revitalization, specifying in concrete terms the form of residential, industrial and commercial redevelopment they want in their communities.

Flanking the southwest of the CBD, Pointe St. Charles has for decades been cut off from the downtown by the Lachine Canal, limiting access to its stock of turn-of-the-century row housing, and slowing gentrification. Until the mid-1980s it remained an enclave for a low-income population of 14,055, 40 percent of whom were single-parent families. The canal itself, extending for miles southwest from the CBD, is currently highly sought after by real estate developers who envision along its banks the transformation of aging industrial buildings into deluxe condominiums for the downtown labor force.

The first wave of gentrification began in the early 1980s, stimulated by Drapeau's creation of PIQA – Program d' Intervention dans les Quartiers Anciens. Masquerading as a response to two decades of demands for renovated housing, the PIQA program had a devastating impact on the community. Beginning in May 1981, armies of inspectors went door to door in the area, demanding extensive renovations and offering a partial subsidy by the city – which would be recouped in four years through increased property taxes. By 1984, 39 percent of the orginal population had been forced to leave the area as rents quadrupled and rental units dropped from 95 percent to 75 percent of the total housing stock. Properties changed hands rapidly as speculators consolidated holdings block by block for renovation or demolition. But the pace was not fast enough for the administration. In 1982 it began redevelop municipal holdings in the heart of the community, directly opposite some of its most militant community organizations.

Community organizations and the MCM, then in opposition, responded with a new range of strategies that now, ironically, form part of the arsenal against the current MCM administration. The first counter-response from the Pointe was a series of strategies borrowed from administration boosterism. It began to publicize the area as a distinct and vital community which would be destroyed by municipal intervention, adopting as community mascot a watchdog whose image appeared on buttons and a community flag; forming a community baseball team that played against local reporters on the very lot the city sought to redevelop; and holding local festivals to celebrate community spirit. But public pressure was not enough. In 1984 the lot fell to a condo project whose style mimicked in miniature the bland suburbia of outlying municipalities. In a neighborhood where rents averaged $160 per month, these units were priced at a minimum of $48,000 with average monthly payments of $720. However, perhaps because of the bad publicity, the units sold slowly.

Centre Sud, on the southeastern flank of the CBD, offers an even juicier plum for redevelopment. Devastated by fifteen years of government interventions that ripped the community apart with a major expressway and commercial and office projects such as Radio Canada, and Complex des Jardins, the community lost 35 percent of its low-income population between 1971 and 1986 – mostly families – who were replaced by a younger, better educated and better paid population. According to the Urban Development Institute of Québec, which includes among its members international developers such as Trizec, Cadillac Fairview, and Marathon (a subsidiary of Canadian Pacific Rail), and five of the ten major Canadian banks, Centre Sud is the most viable area for downtown expansion, stimulating downtown growth by linking three disparate poles of office, finance and tourism, bounded by the western limits of the CBD and the eastern limits of Old Montreal.

In both Centre Sud and Pointe St. Charles, community organizations have produced counter-plans – alternative visions of revitalization that have challenged both Drapeau and the

Doré regimes. The two planning documents – 'Des Choix pour la Pointe' and 'Faites Votre Villes – Mais Pas avec Notre Quartier' – mark the beginning of an intense struggle over every patch of land in the community.

This battle is not a chiaroscuro of exchange value versus use value – the former championed by the municipal administration and the latter defended by the community. It is cast in the muddy greys of linkage politics. On the one hand, the administration has done its best to evade or ignore many of the more controversial demands laid out in these counter-plans, particularly those which block the development of luxury housing enclaves – the 'Faubourgs' of Centre Sud and the vacant industrial buildings which border the Lachine Canal – which will reap huge revenues in property tax. On the other hand, it does promise 500 units of social housing for Pointe St. Charles and subsidized units for Centre Sud.

In addition, the issue of industrial redevelopment – a point of agreement between the General Plan and the counterplans – is already creating fissures within the ranks of community groups and within the MCM coalition as well. For both the administration and some community groups, 'incubator industries' – high-tech services, research laboratories, data banks and the like – are the key to economic revitalization. For the former they are the answer to declining employment in heavy manufacturing. For the latter, including the Chambre de Commerce, they are a stimulus to local business interests and a potential door to international markets.

Within community groups, the issue is enlarging the rift between militant community organziations such as FRAPRU and and liberal professional community groups like the YMCAs and CLSCs. More militant community groups argue that incubator industries are a backdoor to CBD expansion, a Trojan horse for the Pointe and other low-income communities whose low levels of education preclude them from such employment. In the coalition of business interests the conflict is emerging between industrial and real estate concerns. Real estate interests such as the IDU argue that 'the maintenance of secondary industries can only be looked upon as a transitional land use, [as they] represent a serious underuse of land at a time when new housing sites are required. Their presence impedes the expansion of the downtown core.'[49]

How will the MCM sustain the current coalition? So far, it has relegated radical politics to the symbolic realm, with public events like the naming of Mandela Park, and made redistributive concessions only under duress, the latter largely to low-income housing – the forte of community organizations. In the less-tread terrain of economic development, however, it has sided with federal Conservative policy, hoping to transform Montreal into a Cape Canaveral of the north through aerospace and high-tech federal contracts.

This strategy has widened the fissures between the administration and its rank and file in disagreements over the federal drug patent bill, C-22; the Free Trade Agreement between the United States and Canada; and the inclusion of military- and nuclear-related industry in municipal industrial development policy. In each instance, the MCM administration acted in support of these policies, either without prior consultation of its rank and file and in clear contradiction of their position, or worse, leaning heavily on council members in an attempt to get them to change their position. Party policy has been disregarded as the administration hides behind the letter of the MCM electoral platform, hairsplitting distinctions between the military, nuclear and nuclear weapons industries in order to assist Vickers secure a contract for nuclear submarines. In the case of the Free Trade Agreement, which the MCM's Economic Development Commission sees as a threat to both social programs and Montreal's service economy, the party has been reluctant to mobilize against the administration for fear of embarrassing it.[50]

Residential redevelopment is another matter. The administration's tendency to support developers' schemes has on two occasions forced it up against its old allies. Overdale – fourteen Victorian residences that constitute a last enclave of low-income housing within the CBD – has become a watchword for the growing rift between the administration and community and heritage groups. In an area already so devasted by urban redevelopment that it has been nicknamed 'Montreal's Beirut', developers planned to demolish this block and build a $120 million condo project – which would bring the city an estimated $3 million to $5 million in taxes per year. Acting surprisingly like the Drapeau regime it replaced, the administration sponsored a slideshow by developers that contrasted existing delapidated buildings with the proposed project. This tactic sparked an alliance between tenants, heritage groups and housing activists, forcing the administration to propose a replacement project. But their 'solution' more than doubles the rent for all tenants except roomers and provides for relocation rather than *in situ* maintenance.

The conflict was noteworthy because of the adeptness of tenants and housing activists in forming alliances with other groups, and the willingness of heritage groups to defend social as much as architectural heritage. This theme has also been a rallying cry for ethnic groups such as the Chinatown Development Consultative Committee, which argues that the revitalization of Chinatown will transform a once-vital neighborhood into a 'two-dimensional plan with restaurants as stock characters – i.e., a sort of cartoon existence for the area'. This tactical proficiency of community groups is also evident in the struggle against condominium conversion of Lachine Canal's vacant industrial buildings. Here, drawing support from both heritage and environmental groups, neighboring communities are calling for a moratorium on residential development. They propose instead the creation of public parks and industrial museums, which, they argue, would keep the area more accessible to the general public.[51]

Aside from the occasional genuflection to social policy, the MCM intends to diffuse most conflicts through processes of public consultation and citizen participation. To this end, it has established its five commissions on economic development, housing and transportation, culture, community welfare, and administration and finance; introduced a policy of public consultation on important issues through public hearings; and proposed Comités Conseil d'Arrondissements (CCAs), amalgams of neighboring district councils that can provide input on development issues, zoning changes and the like.

This strategy is itself causing problems for the administration. With the relative influence of different municipal interests unspecified, with no formal structures of representation or voting procedures, both community groups and business interests are becoming disgruntled with these procedures, deeming public consultation a piecemeal process – a waste of time with no assurances of having any impact. Having raised expectations around the possibility of public consultation, the administration risks dashing them by holding power too tightly within the ranks of the Executive Committee.[52]

Moreover, the strength of this coalition depends largely on the success of the administration's growth strategy. Even if it is able to stimulate economic and industrial development through the attraction of military contracts or the 'take-off' of incubator industries, the administration is vulnerable to opposition alliances around inner-city revitalization programs. The question remains whether community groups will be able to block attempts at 'revitalization' and force housing subsidies away from projects for the new middle class and to lower income groups, and moreover, if they succeed, what impact this will have both on municipal revenues and on the growth of the CBD, which needs housing nearby to compete with suburban growth poles.

But even if the administration fails, its opposition may dissolve into a cacophony of voices, rather than crystallize into a social force. The current strength and audacity of the administration are exemplified in its recent expulsions, the first in party history, of three long-term MCM militants. This was not for some transgression of fundamental party doctrine, as was the case with MAG members in the mid-1970s – but rather for their attempts to defend founding tenets of the party against its current conservatism. They criticize the administration for abandoning the political goals of the party in favor of technocratic management, centralization of power in the hands of the Executive Committee, and the disappearance of a pluralist atmosphere within the caucus. Their expulsion brings to four the number of long-time members who have left the party in the past year, with others threatening to follow.

The history of the left as an important force within the MCM appears to have come to a close, sustained only at the district level by individual council members such as Marcel Sevigny in Pointe St. Charles, who has for the moment been able to carve out a limited political space for his community. Whether the left can build a viable opposition outside the MCM, an idea scarcely entertained only two years ago, depends not only on its ability to sway the allegiance of a range of political subjects – among them antinuclear groups, environmentalists, women and conservationists, but also on its ability to create a new political culture and to project a new image of citizen and city that rises above that of consumer in a shoppers' paradise.

Conclusion

The specificity of Montreal's political transformations relative to those in other North American cities lies in its constant dialogue with larger political projects at the provincial and national levels in a struggle over separatism, which at critical junctures changed the course of the local political scene. To this extent it is not possible to understand local political events in Montreal except in their relationship to larger shifts at regional and national levels. The regional move towards separatism, which coalesced when a francophone working class and emerging petty bourgeoisie were forced to bear the brunt of a declining Fordist economy, inflected local political struggles as both the provincial Parti Québécois and the federal Liberal Party sought to create a municipal climate sympathetic to their different agendas. In the current conjuncture, this situation has become more diffuse as the municipality, now an international hinterland rather than a subregion of the Canadian anglophone economy, attributes a certain 'cachet' to the current round of internationalization. Unlike American cities, Montreal finds the prospect of domination by foreign capital preferable to the continued supremacy of a homegrown anglophone bourgeoisie.

The commonality of Montreal's political and economic transformations with those of other North American cities lies in the importance of infusing growth strategies with a sense of celebration of social life – a basis for consensus among the general populace. What we learn from Montreal's history, however, is that not just any celebration will do. The success of the growth machine under the Drapeau and Doré regimes derives from their having chosen, by accident or design, symbols that speak directly to the aspirations of the classes that stand to benefit the least from them. Drapeau's Expo '67 and the Olympic Games had to transcend daily life in the inner city; 'Faites Votre Ville', the General Plan of inner-city revitalization, had to invoke this daily life. Ironically, in the latter instance it is the left that has provided many of the social and cultural symbols and identified the critical terrain that has become the sustenance of the new regime. However, the vibrancy of inner-city life, once proclaimed in street festivals and gatherings of all shapes and colors, has been reduced to the quintessential act of consumption. The panoply of alternative images of the city – of nuclear-free zones, of safe streets for women, of recreation and culture that speaks directly to the daily life of the last remnants of a Fordist working class and the new armies of clerical and garment workers who occupy the city's core – has been relegated to the amphitheater of public hearings or remained stillborn in committees. It remains the task of the left to resurrect them.

Notes

This article is dedicated to the memory of John Bradbury.

1. John Friedmann and Goetz Wolff, 'World City Formation: An Agenda for Research and Action', *IJURR*, vol. 6, 1982, pp. 309–44.
2. For more on local processes in world cities, see Roger Keil, 'Political Dimension of Urban Restructuring: Los Angeles', Paper for AAG, 1988.
3. For an elaboration of this typology, see Susan Fainstein and Norman Fainstein, 'Regime Strategies, Communal Resistance and Economic Forces', pp. 245–82, in Fainstein and Fainstein, eds, *Restructuring the City*, New York 1983.
4. Benoit Benko, *Analyse du Système Urbain Québécois et le Rôle de Montréal*, Ecole des Hautes Etudes en Sciences Sociales, Paris 1982, pp. 82–148.
5. Office de Planification et de Développement du Québec, 'Equisse de la Région de Montréal', pp. 31–59, in *Les Cahiers de l'ACFAS*, no. 43, 1986; *Le Systeme Politique de Montréal*, ACFAS, Montreal, 1986, pp. 40–41.
6. 'Equisse de la Région', p. 40.
7. Compare Kevin Cox and Andrew Mair 1988, 'Locality and Community in the Politics of Local Economic Development', *Annals of AAG*, vol. 78, no. 2, 1988, pp. 307–25.
8. Marcel Adam, *La Démocratie à Montréal ou le Vaisseau Dort*, Montreal 1972, pp. 55ff.
9. Abe Limonchik, 'The Colonization of the Urban Economy', *Our Generation*, vol. 12, no. 2, Fall 1977.
10. Jean Drapeau, 'Vous Parles', p. 105, in Adam, *La Démocratie*, p. 57.
11. Adam, *La Démocratie*, p. 57, 59.
12. Léonard et Léveillée, *Montreal After Drapeau*, Montreal 1986, p. 49; Chambre de Commerce, 1970, in Benko, *Analyse du Système Urbain*; and Commission Malouf in *AFCAS*, pp. 481–99.
13. Léveillée and Léonard, 'The Montreal Citizens Movement Comes to Power', *IJURR*, 1988, p. 571.
14. Benko, *Analyse du Système Urbain*, p. 267.
15. McGraw in Jacques Godbout and Jean-Pierre Collin, *Les Organismes Populaires en Milieu Urbain: Contre-Pouvoir ou Nouvelle Practique Professionelle?* Montreal 1977, p. 71.
16. Marcel Sévigny, 1978, 'Bilan du RCM', Travail présenté à Jean Godin. POL 4840 - Système politique Montréalais. Université du Québec à Montréal. Session automne 1978, pp. 8, 12.
17. Godbout and Collin, *Organismes Populaires*, p. 229.
18. Jacques Léveillée, interview, June 1988, Montreal.
19. Milner and Milner, *The Decolonization of Québec*, Toronto 1973, p. 204; Godbout and Collin, *Les Organismes Populaires*, p. 203.
20. Marcel Sévigny, interview, June 1988, Montreal.
21. Sévigny, 'Bilan du RCM', pp. 4, 9.
22. Ibid., pp. 6, 14.
23. 'Mobilisation', in Godbout and Collin, *Organismes Populaires*, p. 235; also Sévigny, 'Bilan du RCM'.
24. Executive Committee, Montreal Citizens' Movement, 1975, 'Unofficial Translation', 15 September 1977, p. 19, 21–22.
25. Limonchik, 'The Colonization of the Urban Economy', *Our Generation*, vol. 12, no. 2, Fall 1977, p. 19; Godbout and Collin, *Organismes Populaires*, p. 233; Executive Committee, Montreal Citizens' Movement, 1975, 'Unofficial

Translation', pp. 21–22.

26. Sévigny, interview.

27. Sévigny, 'Bilan du RCM', pp. 16–17; 'Mobilisation', in Godbout and Collin, *Organismes Populaires*, p. 235.

28. Between 1975 and 1977 the city was affected by five major strikes, including that of the Common Front in 1976. Sévigny, 'Bilan du RCM', p. 72.

29. Sévigny, 'Bilan du RCM', p. 8.

30. M. Raboy, 'The Future of Montreal and the MCM', *Our Generation*, 1978, p. 12.

31. Raboy, 'Future of Montreal', p. 12.

32. See Beer, 'Inside the Montreal Citizens' Movement', *City Magazine*, vol. 3, no. 3, 1978, p. 15.

33. L. Quesnel-Ouellet, 'Les Partis Politiques Locaux au Québec', in *Cahiers de l'ACFAS*, pp. 317–46.

34. Sylvain du Cas, interview, June 1988, Montreal.

35. Malouf Commission, in *Cahiers de L'ACFAS*, pp. 481–49.

36. Léonard and Léveilllée, p. 576.

37. Sam Boskey, interview, June 1988.

38. Léonard and Léveillée, *Montreal After Drapeau*, p. 48.

39. I. Peritz. *Gazette*, 7 Nov. 1987.

40. Suzanne Laferrière, Public Relations, Municipal Administration, interview, Montreal, 13 June 1988.

41. Laferrière, interview; L'Institut de Développement Urbain du Québec, *Memoir on the Planning Statement for the Central Area*, Montreal 1988, p. 48.

42. Montreal Citizens' Movement Programme 1974, 'Unofficial Translation', pp. 29, 19.

43. G. Bourassa, 'Les Montréalais et la Démocratie' in *Les Cahiers de l'ACFAS*, no. 43, 1986, *Le Système Politique*, p. 294; Pierre Lamonde and Mario Polèse, *Le Déplacement des Activités Economiques dans la Region Métropolitaine de Montréal de 1971 à 1981*, Montreal 1985, p. 82.

44. Pierre Marquis, 'Comment on Vend le Plateau Mont Royal', *Actes du Colloque Organisé par le Frapru*, 1987, p. 4.

45. Mike Davis, 'Urban Rennaissance and the Spirit of Post-Modernism', *New Left Review* 151, p. 110.

46. Léveillée, 'Pouvoir et Politique à Montréal Renouveau dans les Modalités d'Exercice du Pouvoir Urbain', *Cahiers de Recherche Sociologique*, p. 9.

47. 'Mobilisation', in Godbout and Collin, pp. 229–31.

48. Comité de Logement Centre Sud, 'Faites Votre Ville – Mais Pas Avec Notre Quartier', unpublished paper. Westmount and Ile des Souers are two of the most prestigious neighborhoods in the city.

49. Robert Pilon and Jean-Pierre Wilsey, 'Le Développement Economique: Le Cheval de Troie du Mouvement Populaire', *Revoltes*, Winter 1988, p. 11; L'-Institut de Développement, *Memoir*, p. 17.

50. Sam Boskey, interview, June 1988. Boskey is a former Municipal Council member and founding member of MCM; Lewis Harris, 'MCM Cosies Up to Conservatives', *Gazette*, 15 Oct. 1988.

51. Sam Boskey, interview; Le Frapru Frappe, *Encore!*, no. 18, September 1987; Pierre Gaudreau, interview, *FRAPRU*, June 1988; Micheal Fish, *Brief Submitted to the Comité Consultative on the Subject of the Downtown Master Plan*; La Clinique Communautaire de Pointe Saint-Charles, *Une Population à Respecter*, pp. 49–55.

52. L'Institut de Développement, *Memoir*, p. 48.

13

Social Democracy on the Frontier: The Case of the Yukon

Jonathan Pierce

The success of neoconservatism in North America and Europe has been uneven. In Canada, a country with historic economic, political and cultural ties to both Britain and the United States, one could have expected a rightist attack on the welfare state similar to those launched by Thatcher and Reagan. The replacement of the left-leaning Liberal government by the Conservatives in 1984 seemed to provide the conditions for such an onslaught. However, neoconservatism has not yet won many victories in Canada. While a slow erosion of many programs that underpin the welfare state has taken place, medicare, old-age pensions and other social programs remain a 'sacred trust' and are all but untouchable.

In spite of the reelection of the Conservative government with a significantly reduced majority in the fall of 1988, opposition to the Free Trade Agreement with the United States is significant enough to restrict government plans for continental economic integration. Since the election, business lobby groups have again raised the banner of neoconservative restructuring under the guise of deficit reduction and the need for means-testing to replace universal accessibility to social programs. Whether a neoconservative agenda will be adopted by the Mulroney government in its second term is still an open question.

Since 1984, the New Democratic Party (NDP), a European-style Social Democratic party, has been on a roller-coaster ride in public opinion, even leading the public opinion polls. On election day, the New Democrats won more seats than ever before but still placed a distant third. During this same period, the last NDP provincial government was defeated in Manitoba, and the party failed to make significant gains in any other province save one. That exception was the Yukon, where the NDP took over the territorial government from the Conservatives in 1985 and was elected to a second term in 1988. A New Democrat also won a by-election in 1987 for the Yukon's one federal member of Parliament, replacing a Conservative who had been Deputy Prime Minister; he easily won reelection in 1988. In Canada, then, if neoconservatism has not won great battles, neither has the left made a breakthrough. It is, perhaps, a more polarized country than before the Reagan-Thatcher era, but still one of traditional moderation. In spite of its lack of electoral success (see Table 1), the NDP has remained influential in making public policy and is certainly one the major factors limiting the rise of neoconservatism.

Table 1
Canada: Federal Elections

Year	*Liberals*	*Conservatives*	*NDP*
1972	37.3%	34%	17.2%
1974	42.4	34.9	15.2
1979	39.8	35.6	17.8
1980	44.1	32.3	19.7
1984	27.8	49.7	18.7
1988	32	43.1	20.2

But while social democracy is indeed influential in Canada at the federal level, the NDP has been unable to move beyond third-party status. Various commentators and intellectuals on the left argue than Canada is going through a transition from a US-style two-party, nonideological political system to a British-style system in which two parties clearly represent two sides of the political spectrum. As the election campaign began in the fall of 1988, NDP leader Ed Broadbent even predicted the disappearance of the Liberal Party. This did not happen, but perhaps Broadbent's prediction was merely premature.

To understand Canadian politics on the national level, one must also understand regional politics. Since the 1930s, there has been a growing right–left polarization that started in western Canada and has gradually moved eastward. Over the past two decades, NDP governments have been elected in all the western provinces except Alberta, and at one point Liberals has been all but eliminated from elective office at both the federal and provincial levels in the west. However, the past few years have seen not only a resurgence of the center in western

Canada, but a failure by the left to make gains in central or eastern Canada. It is therefore timely to question the unequivocal status of the polarization thesis.

This article examines one region, the Yukon, not only the latest, but the last, regional jurisdiction in Canada to elect a Social Democratic government. Why did this region go against national trends? How could the political culture in a region that, like Texas or Alaska, is popularly known as a refuge of unbridled individualism, abruptly change its political stripes?

The Yukon Territory lies north of 60° and borders on Alaska in the United States and British Columbia and the Northwest Territories within Canada. It is one of the least peopled regions in the world, with a population of around 29,000, of whom approximately one-third are Native. While having a tradition of limited representative government since the turn of the century, only in the past thirty years have significant gains been made in establishing self-government.

Known throughout the world as the home of the Klondike gold rush, the Yukon has nevertheless remained on the fringe of Canadian settlement and development. From the end of the short-lived gold rush at the turn of the century until the Second World War, the Yukon was all but forgotten, except in the popular mythology created by the poems and stories of Robert Service and Jack London. A few thousand people, half of whom were Native, worked the Yukon's mines and goldfields or pursued traditional subsistence activities such as hunting, fishing and trapping.

Occupation by US armed forces during the Second World War drew the Yukon into the twentieth century, as all of Northern Canada gained in strategic importance. In the decades following the war, the introduction of the programs of the modern welfare state had contradictory results when applied to the North, particularly for Native people. Subsistence hunters and gatherers were redefined as unemployed, and nomadic people had to be settled, if only to facilitate 'proper' administration. Natives were settled in small communities and provided with inadequate housing and little hope of employment in the wage economy. While increased medical care raised the general state of health, alcoholism and lack of purpose became endemic.

Denied rights that other Canadians took for granted (status Indians in Canada did not gain the right to vote until the late 1950s; Yukon Indians could not drink alcohol legally until 1968), by the late 1960s Yukon Indians had swept away the last obstacles to equal political rights. In doing so, they gained a strong voice expressed through community and territorial organizations and began to demand certain collective rights, including the right to have their Aboriginal title to the Yukon established in a treaty with the federal government. But increased participation in mainstream politics has not led to increased participation in the market economy, and many Natives remain dependent on welfare programs.

The postwar Yukon economy developed in a similar fashion to the truncated economies of the northern and more remote provinces, characterized by the paramount reliance on renewable and nonrenewable resource-based industries. The basis of the market economy in the Yukon remained mineral extraction. By the 1960s, the industry had expanded from precious metals (gold and silver) to base metals (lead, zinc and copper). This diversification was made possible by heavy public investment in infrastructure. Roads and other methods of transportation, communications systems, subsidies, and the provision of the full array of government services available in the south provided the conditions necessary for opening new mines in the North. The value of mineral production grew from $60 million in the first half of the 1950s to over $1.2 billion in 1976–80. All of the mineral production, except for a handful of gold nuggets, was exported in raw form to Japanese, American, European, or southern Canadian mills.

Industrial development was not without cost. Prices rose with the rapidly improving standard of living and left many people, particularly Natives, far behind. Most of the jobs in the mines went to outsiders. Traditional Native economic pursuits declined until, by the 1970s, these activities were popularly thought to be unimportant.

Where the Yukon departed from the experience of the provincial North was in the growth of the government and service sectors. The number of federal government employees increased from 200 in 1946 to over 2,000 by 1964, and expenditures increased fourfold between 1954 and 1966. Currently, 4,200 government jobs comprise 33 percent of the workforce. The remoteness of the Yukon from any major metropolitan center has resulted in the growth of a relatively healthy service sector. Both the government and service sectors have been centered in Whitehorse, the territorial capital, which has grown at a rapid rate and today claims some two-thirds of the Yukon population.

Although tourism has increased rapidly in the last two decades, the goal of a more diversified Yukon economy remains far from realization. In the late 1970s, a plan to build a natural gas pipeline along the Alaska Highway corridor provoked significant opposition to the forces favoring industrial development. A coalition of Native organizations, environmentalists, social democrats, and others argued before two successive federal inquiries that the negative impacts of this project would outweigh the benefits. The dream of industrial development leading social development in the North was seriously questioned throughout Canada for the first time.

In the mid-1970s the Council for Yukon Indians (CYI) could claim, with some justification, that Indians formed the majority of the permanent population. It is true that some Yukoners could trace their family roots back to the turn of the century, but they were rather few in number. Employees in both the government and the mining sectors were highly transient, on average staying for only a couple of years. Mining camps and government enclaves were isolated from the broader community, particularly from the Native population. But by the late 1970s, this too was changing. As government services were increasingly provided by the territorial government, the relative size of the federal presence decreased. Through preferential hiring practices, superior pay and benefits, and with fewer opportunities to move to jobs in other governments, many territorial employees became permanent residents. Whitehorse itself has become a modern city with most of the services and facilities one would expect in a much larger center.

Throughout the 1960s and 1970s, two parallel and sometimes confrontational positions marked Yukon politics. Yukoners, particularly white Yukoners, had for years argued for increased political autonomy from Ottawa. The federal government, on the other hand, was slow to turn over the reins of government, and the federally appointed commissioner retained ultimate legislative authority. Ottawa was not against the territorial government providing many of the services it provided, but the dream of a treasure house of Northern riches was still alive enough for the 'national' interest to dictate that it retain ownership of Northern resources.

The tension between Yukoners and the federal government was further complicated by land claims negotiations with Yukon Indians. Forced by judicial decisions to accept that the federal government had an obligation to clear Aboriginal title to the territory, something that had taken place in most of the rest of Canada in the preceding centuries, Ottawa embarked on a long and tortuous path of conducting direct negotiations with CYI. The Yukon territorial government (YTG), leading the fight for responsible administration, used the land claims process to further its own objectives. Political confrontation between CYI and the Yukon Territorial Government, and between the YTG and Ottawa, became the order of the day.

By the late 1970s, Canadian politics had polarized, with the decline of popular support for the Liberal Party – particularly in the western provinces – and the rise of the Conservative and New Democratic parties. The Yukon, in spite of heavy federal presence, was part of this polarization. The Territorial Council (later called the Legislative Assembly), the elected legislative body of the territorial government, had for years operated on the basis of informal party alliances. Although many candidates did not run under party banners, political allegiances were often visible. In the early 1970s, right-wing Liberals deserted to the Conservatives.

By 1978 the alliance of traditional Conservatives and former Liberals was formalized with the formation of the Yukon Territorial Progressive Conservative Party. A battle for the leadership of the Progressive Conservatives developed between Erik Nielsen, the Yukon Member of Parliament, who represented the old guard, and Hilda Watson, a former Liberal. Watson won the leadership but lost her seat at the general election in the fall of 1978. However, on a platform opposing land claims and favoring constitutional and economic development, her party won eleven of sixteen seats and assumed power. Chris Pearson, another former Liberal, became leader and held that post until 1985. The Liberal Party formed the official opposition with two seats, and the New Democratic Party was reduced to one seat, which was won by Tony Penikett, a newcomer to the legislature.

This first administration of the Territorial Conservatives was rocked by successive scandals, but it pursued its agenda with some determination. While serious land claims negotiations did not resume for two years, a major victory for the forces supporting responsible government came in 1980. In 1979 the Trudeau Liberals were replaced by Joe Clark and his short-lived Conservative government. Clark had promised provincehood to the Yukon during his first term of office and the growing influence of Erik Nielsen in the federal cabinet led to a letter of instruction to the Yukon Commissioner that effectively removed the Commissioner from participation in the territory's Executive Committee and reduced his role to that of a provincial Lieutenant-Governor. After eighty years, responsible government was a reality in the Yukon, but the federal government still retained control of most land and resources.

Although Trudeau was returned to power in 1980, his government remained unpopular in the Yukon. The cost to the territorial Liberals was high. In the early fall of 1981, the NDP won a by-election and was joined in the Legislative Assembly by an independent member to become the official opposition. Opposition to the territorial Conservatives then coalesced around the NDP.

The Yukon had been spared the initial impact of the 1981 recession, but within the first few months of 1982, every mine was shut down. Over three years into a four-year mandate, the Pearson government decided to call an election before the worst effects were realized. Under the slogan 'Land for all Yukoners', the Conservatives entered the election confident that once again opposition to land claims and federal control of land would ensure victory.

But the election was by no means a sure thing. With a good organization, well-known candidates, and a well-developed coalition of oppositional forces, the NDP came very close to winning. In the last week of the campaign under a new slogan, 'Stay Free, Vote PC', Conservative electioneering degenerated into racist attacks in local newspapers against Indian candidates running on the NDP slate and McCarthyite warnings about the dangers of creeping socialism. On election day, the Pearson government returned to office with a reduced majority, holding nine seats, while the NDP doubled the number of its representatives to six. The Liberals were shut out.

The second Pearson administration was troubled by internal squabbles, more confrontation with Yukon Indian organizations and the Liberal federal government, and the worst economic recession since the Second World War. In its final days, it simply drifted, lacking any sense of purpose. And by 1984, the original Conservative agenda was, in a sense, complete. An imminent land claims settlement had reluctant Conservative support, the Trudeau Liberals had been replaced in Ottawa by the Conservatives, and the long-serving Yukon MP, Erik Nielsen, had become federal Prime Minister Brian Mulroney's second-in-command. Ottawa-bashing was now out of the question for

Conservatives, even though it became increasingly evident that the new government was not going to move quickly on matters of further devolution of responsibilities to the Yukon government, including the control of land and resources.

In early 1985, Pearson retired and was replaced as leader by Willard Phelps, the chief land claims negotiator for the Yukon government. Attempting to capitalize on the federal Conservative victory of the previous summer and the momentum the party had gained during the leadership contest, Phelps quickly called an election. With a party membership of over 2,000 and with the Mulroney government still in its honeymoon with the electorate, Conservative strategy was to take a higher road than the previous campaign and to make few promises.

While the NDP organization had not improved substantially since the 1982 election (in fact, membership had fallen to less than 300 when the election was called), the experience had improved party effectiveness. More people, particularly the Native community, saw the NDP as a viable alternative. The laissez-faire economic policy of the Conservative government had in particular not endeared it to either people working in the mining industry, still in deep recession, or to many business people. Faced with seemingly overwhelmingly odds, the NDP developed a three-pronged strategy: to address the issues of the economy directly; to concentrate on seats where the Conservatives were most vulnerable; and to take advantage of the popularity of the NDP leader, Tony Penikett.

On the eve of the election, Conservative strategists were confidently predicting that they would win twelve to thirteen seats. They were stunned as both leaders went on live national television on election night; the NDP led with seven seats, followed by the Conservatives with six and the resurgent Liberals with two. The outcome would hinge on Old Crow, a small, isolated Indian community in the northern Yukon. When the results finally came in after midnight via a ham radio operator in Alaska, the NDP had won!

Assuming power was understandably more difficult than winning the election. Not only were the Tories reluctant to relinquish what they felt was all but their birthright, but the appointment of Sam Johnson as Speaker of the Legislative Assembly (the first Native to hold such a position) meant that the Penikett government would have to meet the Assembly in a minority position. A temporary arrangement with the Liberals provided the necessary votes; however, the situation was far from satisfactory. Two by-elections provided opportunities for the New Democrats to establish a clear majority. The first came with the death of a former Conservative minister in a highway accident, but the NDP lost. The second came when the Liberal leader was charged and convicted of dealing cocaine. (The Yukon remains true to some of its mythology.) Danny Joe, a former chief of the Selkirk Indian band, won for the NDP, and what many had thought might be a temporary regime turned into a full-term government.

An objective assessment of the success of the Penikett government in its first term is perhaps impossible, but some successes are evident. On assuming office, the new government undertook a broad-based economic planning exercise, Yukon 2000, consulting all sectors of the population. Yukon 2000 has focused attention on the fragile and dependent nature of the Yukon economy and the need for diversification, greater self-sufficiency, and attention to small- and medium-scale developments. In addition, Indian subsistence activity has been broadly accepted as worthwhile economic endeavor, and linkages have been made to other productive activity that a purely market economy cannot value, such as household work and volunteerism.

Beyond planning, the government has intervened directly in the economy. The Yukon Development Corporation, under public ownership, was established and took over the largest forestry operation and the power utility. Cypress-Anvil, the

Table 2
Yukon Economic Indicators, 1985–88

	1985	*1986*	*1987*	*1988*
Population	25,158	26,668	27,953	29,183[a]
Employment	10,554	10,991	11,567	13,802[a]
Unemployment	15%	n.a.	12.8%	10%[a]
Mineral production (000's)	$56,807	$162,340	$439,859	$437,900[b]
Gov't expenditures (000's)	$372,707	$425,700	$433,000	$476,000[b,c]
GDP growth	6.6%	19.9%	10–11%	8–10%

a. End of September 1988. b. Forecast. c. Fiscal year basis.
Source: Government of Yukon, *Yukon Economic Review and Outlook, 1987–1988*; 'Yukon Economic Development Perspective Outlook, 1981–1985, Summary and Recommendations', 'Yukon Economic Forecast, January 1989', and *Statistical Review*, Third Quarter 1988.

Yukon's largest mine, was reopened under private ownership with a number of concessions and subsidies from both the federal and territorial governments in return for various commitments to enhance the economic benefits to the local economy; other new and smaller mines have since opened. Local hire and local purchase policies have concentrated the benefits of government expenditures in the local economy. In the past three years, the general health of the economy, as measured in conventional terms, has been greatly improved (see Table 2). Annual growth has led Canada with an average of over 10 percent, and over 3,000 jobs have been created.

The new government has not concentrated exclusively on economic development. Of the greatest significance, CYI, YTG, and the federal government agreed in late 1988 in principle to settle Indian land claims that would see Yukon Indians receive $257 million over fifteen years, 41,000 square kilometers of land (much of which would remain under Aboriginal title), and guaranteed participation in various government institutions.

Various municipal programs offered by the territorial government were extended to Indian bands, and some pilot projects allowing Indian management of certain social and welfare programs have been undertaken. Attempts by the former administration to withdraw from social housing have been reversed. A Human Rights Commission has been established. Native people have become increasingly involved in the business of government.

Table 3
Yukon: Federal Elections

Year	*Liberals*	*Conservatives*	*NDP*
1972	32.2%	53%	11.6%
1974	33.5	47.1	19.5
1979	30.1	44.6	25.3
1980	39.6	40.6	19.8
1984	21.7	56.8	16.1
1987	32.3	27.2	35.6
1988	12	35	51.1

The NDP government has grown in popularity. Audrey McLaughlin won a federal by-election for the NDP in 1987, replacing Erik Nielsen, who had held the seat since the late 1950s. In the general election in November 1988, she was reelected with 51 percent of the popular vote (see Table 3), even leading polls in areas that were thought to be Tory strongholds. (McLaughlin was chosen in November 1989 as leader of the federal NDP to replace Ed Broadbent.)

In early 1989, Penikett called a territorial general election. When the ballots were counted on 20 February, the NDP had been returned to power for another term. The party retained a majority with nine seats, the Conservatives picked up one for a total of seven, and the Liberals were once more left wandering in the desert. But this tells only part of the story. In one constituency, Watson Lake, the Conservatives won by three votes; the election is now under court challenge. The NDP made significant gains in seats won by small margins in 1985, while overall, it won a plurality of votes for the first time (see Table 4).

Table 4
Yukon: Territorial Elections, 1978–89

	1978	*1982*	*1985*	*1989*
Independents	13.5%	3.8%	4.3%	0%
Liberals	28.5	15	7.6	11.1
Conservatives	37.1	45.8	46.9	43.9
NDP	20.9	35.4	41.1	45

Does the experience of the NDP in the Yukon have lessons that can be applied in other places? Does this example support the argument that Canada is becoming increasingly polarized? The answer to both questions must be a qualified yes. Several factors provided the conditions for the NDP's success.

1. The growing stability of settlement throughout the past two decades has encouraged a sense of community in the Yukon. Individual isolation is more apparent in southern urban centers than in the North. As community values have grown, strident individualism has decreased, and the notion that the rights of the community are greater in many respects than the rights of any one individual has more currency.

2. Economic development in the North has in large part been led by government intervention. The notion that a 'freer market' would lead to enhanced economic development was finally put to rest during the 1982 recession. As the largest employer, government also provides a stabilizing function during economic downturns.

3. The strength of the NDP resides in the rural areas (those areas outside Whitehorse). In the 1989 election, the NDP retained six of the nine rural seats, and their ratio of the popular vote in the rural Yukon rose to 50 percent. As is often the case, rural and remote areas have felt left behind or not given adequate consideration by government. This would seem to apply to local regions throughout Canada.

4. A precondition for the NDP success was the decline of the Liberal Party. But its disintegration in the Yukon was not caused just by political polarization. Regions on the periphery seem to elect local parties that counter those in Ottawa. As well, a third party always runs the risk of being caught in the squeeze between the two major parties. In this sense, while the polarization theory seems to have some legitimacy, it alone does not adequately explain electoral politics in Canada.

5. The maturity of the NDP and party strategy distinguished it from the other parties. Social democratic parties throughout the western world are not highly trusted for their economic policies. Therefore, it was important for the NDP to address economic issues squarely and not just concentrate on the social policy areas that are seen as the social democratic strong suit. A successful electoral strategy should concentrate on areas of strength; coalitions should be developed with oppositional groups and party resources mainly directed to those constituencies where success is most likely. (All of these latter points should have been considered by the federal NDP during the last election.)

With a relatively stable and healthy economy provided in good part by government intervention, the NDP government's attention is now focused on social issues like childcare, family support and education. The economic focus is shifting towards sustainable development and the linkages between the environment and the economy. One of the biggest challenges facing the government in its next term will be to establish a constitutional development process to define the Yukon's relationship with the rest of Canada and to dovetail this with the finalization of the Indian land claims settlement. The challenges that face social democracy in the Yukon are many and profound. But the left can take some heart that a light is burning brightly in the Canadian North.

References

Two general histories of the Yukon have been recently published: Catharine McClellan, *Part of the Land, Part of the Water: A History of the Yukon Indians*. Vancouver 1987; and Ken S. Coates and William R. Morrison, *Land of the Midnight Sun: A History of the Yukon*. Edmonton 1988. See also my thesis, 'Indian Land Claims in the Yukon, 1968–1984: Aboriginal Rights as Human Rights', Carleton University 1987.

14

The Battle for New Tenochtitlan

John Ross

I

On the fourth night following the Mexican presidential election of 6 July 1988, ballot boxes from the nation's 53,000 polling places were consolidated in three hundred federal electoral district headquarters where local boards were to confirm the still-contested preliminary results. Although the Federal Electoral Commission's own computers had suspiciously crashed minutes after the polls closed, the word on the street in this nation of 83 million was that Cuauhtémoc Cárdenas had won. The 54-year-old son of Mexico's most beloved president and candidate of the first real coalition that the splintered Mexican left has been able to anneal since his father presided over the country in the 1930s, Cárdenas had defeated Carlos Salinas de Gortari. Salinas de Gortari, moreover, had been handpicked by outgoing president Miguel de la Madrid to be the tenth straight winner for the ruling Party of the Institutional Revolution (PRI), which has now held power longer than any other political machine on the western side of the planet.

That Sunday night, down at Mexico City's District Five in the historic center of the city a half-block from the Zócalo – the great Plaza of the Constitution and the political heart of the nation – Cárdenas supporters were fearful that the election was being stolen out from under them. '*Pinche rateros!*' grumbled Mario Becerra, organizer for one old Mexico City's groups of *damnificados* (displaced survivors of the 1985 earthquake), as he glared up at a smokey second-floor enclave where the tabulations were taking place in the moonless dark of 4 am. 'We pasted them good for once', Becerra growled as he huddled over the red coals of a Tacuba Street bonfire, 'but these fucking thieves are out to steal the vote back for "El Pelón"' ['the Bald One', Salinas's nickname]. Becerra already knew that Cuauhtémoc Cárdenas had won District Five, because he had tramped from polling place to polling place on the night of 6 July to add up the results posted outside on handwritten cardboard signs.

Since the cataclysmic earthquakes on 19 and 20 September cut a murderous swath through the old center of Mexico City, Becerra has become something of a fixture in the fifty-square-block neighborhood south of the Zócalo, an area built on the site of the original Mexico City: the man-made island of Tenochtitlan and the focal point of Aztec civilization. A founding member of the Popular Union of New Tenochtitlan, a still active *damnificado* group, Becerra and his neighbors combined forces with fifty-one other such groupings that sprang up from the rubble of the tragedy and melded together in the Sole Coordinating Body of Damnificados (CUD). Together they pressured a reluctant De la Madrid government into expropriating blocks of badly damaged buildings in earthquake-devastated working-class neighborhoods. The enormous energy generated by these groups eventually forced the PRI, fearful of losing its grip on these downtown *colonias*, into putting together the most effective housing program ever carried out in Latin America. Nonetheless, despite producing 45,000 units of fair-quality replacement housing over an eighteen-month period and maintaining the *damnificados* in their neighborhoods, the PRI failed to hold Mexico City on 6 July. Indeed, Cuauhtémoc Cárdenas took thirty-seven out of the city's forty electoral districts, 57 percent of the vote compared to Salinas's feeble 27 percent, despite the PRI's mighty efforts to steal the election back.

Eduardo Miranda is a 52-year-old barber and block captain (Jefe de Manzana – literally 'chief of the apple') on the second block of Regina Street, one of a warren of cluttered alleys south of the Zócalo. When the quake hit he was dangling his feet over the side of his bed searching for his shoes. Nieves, his hard-working wife of thirty years, was out in the kitchen getting the three boys off to school and boiling sauces for the lunchtime crowd. Suddenly, at 7:19 a.m., the world began to rattle violently for three long minutes, lacing the walls of the century-old apartment building (*vecindad*) with gaping cracks through which sunlight shone, lowering the roof a good foot, and changing the lives of tenants forever. 'Nothing was ever the same after those three minutes', Nieves remembered. The earthquake changed her life and the life of the nation as well.

Because Lalo Miranda runs a living-room barbershop and Nieves a dining-room restaurant, their apartment is the nerve center of 39 Regina Street. Within minutes, Miranda was inventorying the building's nine other apartments and four storefronts, and although the structure seemed in imminent danger of collapse, the damage hadn't killed or seriously injured any of his immediate neighbors. Elsewhere, the story was tragically different. Down the block, a four-story building full of garment sweatshops, a neighborhood industry, fell onto a bank as the morning shift was settling in. To this day, no one knows how many seamstresses were trapped in the rubble. Two blocks west on the central avenue named after Lázaro Cárdenas, one of the most popular working-class breakfast spots in the city fell apart, killing perhaps three hundred customers. The Juárez and General hospitals a mile south had both fallen in, burying several thousand patients, doctors, and other employees, including five hundred babies. Down at the end of Republic of Chile Street, thousands more were lost in the wreckage of the thirteen-story Nuevo León Building in Tlatelolco, once Latin America's most ambitious housing complex: 71 out of 120 high-rise apartment structures were severely damaged. In the Zócalo itself, the whole back of the Federal District building collapsed, a graphic illustration of the erosion of state power that the PRI was to suffer in the wake of the great quake.

The 8.1 earthquake on 19 September and the 7.5 aftershock on the 20th, collectively known as *el Sismo*, tore apart 800 buildings in the center of the city and seriously damaged 6,000 more. Although the PRI-run government continues to insist on a count of 8,000 dead or missing, popular belief and western intelligence sources reported by the *Washington Post* place the number at between 30,000 and 35,000. The number who suffered complete or partial loss of their homes and belongings has been calculated at close to 1 million. Seven hundred thousand workers lost their workplaces. Mexico City's financial and tourist centers were devastated, and its telephone system has never recovered. Total losses mounted to over $5 billion.

For the next two days, Lalo Miranda walked the twisted streets of his neighborhood with a shovel. He pitched in with volunteer brigades trying to pull survivors from the wreckage, argued with the military and the police when the troops forcefully removed the rescuers from the ruins, and demanded that the Cuauhtémoc Delegation (one of the sixteen geographic areas of Mexico City) restore severed gas and electrical lines to the neighborhoods before government buildings were served. He comforted families now living on the median strip of Izazaga Boulevard, and began to piece together the fabric of the old neighborhood with friends like Mario Becerra by planning the first meetings of what eventually became the Popular Union of New Tenochtitlan.

The amazing days that followed the quake taught the neighbors of New Tenochtitlan some lessons that have not been forgotten. One was that the PRI government, far from being invincible, was incapable of responding to the needs of the people when calamity struck. Miranda had watched the bureaucrats fleeing the Zócalo buildings in utter panic. Now the deserted offices offered mute testimony to the PRI government's naked instinct to first save its own skin and then maybe try and rescue the citizens of the republic. 'We began to do many things for ourselves that before *el Sismo* we left up to the PRI government', Miranda quietly recalled.

During the first days, the *vecinos* were joined by impromptu brigades formed by tens of thousands of volunteers – often politically conscious young people who helped to rescue neighbors, count the dead, feed the living, direct traffic, deliver babies, and encourage the victims to take charge of their own lives. When the government finally shook off paralysis three days after the earthquake, it made the blindly predictable mistake of trying to retake the neighborhoods by force, keeping away rescuers who had worked for ninety-six hours straight to free their *compañeros* from the rubble piles and sealing off one block from the next so that the living could not even leave their own streets to find food or meet with each other to compare experiences. Wholesale looting of corpses and apartments by troops and police did not do much to soothe indignation: one apartment building south of Garibaldi Square where mariachi musicians had lived was stripped bare, even the instruments taken; fingers were chopped off corpses for their rings.

But the lessons learned best by the people of New Tenochtitlan and their neighbors all over the city was that the government, which had responded so erratically to the tragedy, was in truth deathly afraid of the neighborhoods' new-found moral authority. Miranda recalls a march in early October in which 15,000 angry *damnificados* walked right up to the gates of Los

Pinos, the presidential palace out in Chapultepec Park. He is still amazed that his neighbors were able to come so close to De la Madrid's heavily guarded executive mansion. That day, 12 October, Eduardo Miranda was elected to a commission to meet with De la Madrid face-to-face to demand the expropriation of the buildings that landlords were already abandoning. 'We knew we had power after that', Miranda reflected. He was later appointed to a neighborhood expropriation commission, which went door-to-door twice in October to declare as public property 10,000 badly damaged privately owned buildings.

As *damnificado* groups sprang up by the dozen in the ruins of the city, observers began to puzzle out where they had all come from. One irony of the quake was that it had touched neighborhoods with long histories of organizing themselves for survival. In some, the organizing vehicle was the remnants of the local PRI committee that the ruling party had used only to fill the Zócalo whenever a president needed a great crowd to affirm his authority over the nation. In others, where government neglect was a long-standing tradition, the opposition quickly gained a firm foothold. Long before 19 September, left political parties had opened fronts in inner-city neighborhoods and the volunteer brigades that played such a vital role in bringing together the *damnificado* groups were often formed from their ranks. The Revolutionary Workers Party (PRT), a group with Trotskyist roots, played a major role in the formation of the Popular Union of New Tenochtitlan, mostly because it had been organizing workers at the Agrarian Reform Ministry on nearby Bolívar Street in pre-earthquake days. In addition, PRT convert Dr. Cuauhtémoc Abarca, long a catalyst in the Tlatelolco housing complex, became the leader of the CUD, the epitome of *damnificado* organization. PRT student brigades were led by energetic young *políticos* like Carlos Imaz and Antonio Santos, who later graduated to direct university students in the first strike at the Autonomous University since the 1968 student massacre – an act that had silenced campus rebellion in Mexico for a generation.

In neighborhoods where the PRI still held sway, counter-organizations developed organically. Down in Tepito, the thieves' kitchen market *colonia* under the fallen Tlatelolco towers whose tough reputation is demonstrated by the enormous number of hungry young boxers who come off its mean streets, *ambulantes* or street vendors had been organized for decades to hawk their contraband imports (*fayuca*). Commercial and family dealings organized each building for its own survival, explained Gustavo Esteva, who runs a maverick Mexico City community organizing think tank that was active in promoting nongovernment aid after the quake. 'One person lends another some money. He in turn lends a bit of that to a cousin who needs cash. Then the original lender needs the money back and more neighbors and their cousins are brought into the arrangement. Pretty soon, whether you knew it or not, you have an organization.'

During the winter of 1986, badly shaken by its loss of credibility and mindful of a damaged international reputation (clouded by charges of thievery in international aid distribution) the PRI and the government it runs finally began to clear away the rubble. Two hundred thousand *damnificados* were temporarily herded into 300 improvised encampments as rows of tin-shed *campamentos* blossomed all over the city. As the initial shock ebbed, the deprivations of daily living and the common chord of the tragedy tended to bring the neighbors and their organizations even closer together. Demonstrations became daily events as the *damnificados* demanded a greater voice in the design and location of replacement housing. Miranda's building on Regina Street was officially declared a historical monument, one of 179 such structures in the inner city and a designation the tenants took seriously. Day after day during the World Bank–financed reconstruction they would stroll over from their nearby *campamento* to argue with architects and construction workers over the dimensions of rooms and the accuracy of the renovation, a process that so intrigued Miranda's middle son that he is now studying architecture. To the government's credit, it did not ship the *damnificados* off to Quintana Roo on the Belize border (one of the initial plans). The Popular Habitational Rehabilitation (RHP) program run by the Housing and Urban Development Secretariat (SEDUE) under current Mexico City regent Manuel Camacho Solís and a savvy troubleshooting aide, Manuel Aguilera (now Camacho Solís's secretary general), understood that long-time inner-city dwellers could not peacefully be moved to Quintana Roo let alone the shanty-town misery belt that surrounds the capital and that, moreover, involvement of the tenants in rebuilding the center of the city was essential to winning the disaffected back to the ruling party.

But the government's response had a darker side. *Damnificado* groups that realigned themselves with the PRI were given new housing first. 'The PRI sent brigades and threatened us even before we were in the camps. They said that unless we joined the PRI, the building would be torn down and never rebuilt', Miranda recalled. On frigid winter nights in the camps, *damnificados* who supported the PRI got portable heaters while the New Tenochtitlan refugees were given one thin blanket each. And at Christmas time, three months after *el Sismo*, the PRI came round with chickens for the *damnificados* who were still huddling in the street or the ruins of their apartments. 'They sent photographers to take our pictures for the papers, which made us feel like we were being used', Becerra remembered. To the PRI's consternation, the *damnificados* refused both the chickens and the publicity, dining instead on chorizo amidst the rubble on the corner of Isabel la Católica and Nezhualcoyotl, Colonia Centro, Nuevo Tenochtitlan. 'It was a humble meal but it was very fraternal', Becerra recalled fondly.

Despite the array of perks given the neo-PRIstas, the opposition groups survived the long months in the camps intact. The PRI's best chance to win back popular loyalties came as the government was able to rehouse 70 percent of the *damnificados* within a year and half of the earthquake. As of the summer of 1989, two years after the RHP went out of business, 5,000 *damnificados* still remained in a handful of *campamentos*, but 48,000 families were back in apartments far superior to the ones abandoned in the quake. For many, the frustrations caused by *el Sismo* began to fade. Today, militants like Dr. Abarca readily concede that the RHP program muted the *damnificado* movement and forced activists to seek out other issues.

'If this movement is going to survive, we have to turn our attention from those who became *damnificados* because of the earthquake to those who are *damnificados* because of life', Magdalena Trejo, the moving force in the Calle Gómez neighborhood, told a US reporter at the founding convention of the Asamblea de Barrios (Assembly of Neighborhoods) in April 1987.

II

According to Mexico's administrative map, no such entity as Mexico City exists. What the world knows as the capital of Mexico is, in reality, the Federal District, a 920-square-mile enclave divided administratively into sixteen delegations, some of which are quite rural. But it is the large urban stain known as the 'metropolitan area' that dominates the floor of the 7,600-foot-high Valley of Mexico and is popularly considered to be the capitol of the country.

Despite its lack of administrative recognition, Mexico City is a crushing reality for 19 million harried citizens, the most densely populated urban area in the world – a populace that is now the size of Peru and that will grow to 28 million by the turn of the century. Moreover, Mexico City is surrounded on all sides by sprawling cardboard-shack and cinderblock encampments of squatters from the impoverished Indian countryside; they expand the 'metropolitan area' by an acre and a half a day. Some of these 'lost cities' have grown to unmanageable dimensions themselves. After thirty years of quasi-legal existence, the rutted moonscape of Nezhualcoyotol, once the royal seat of the fabled Mexican coyote poet-king, now has 3.5 million souls (a population that rivals Los Angeles) living within its ill-defined borders on what was the bed of Lake Texcoco east of the airport and Chalco, a devastated swatch of uncultivatable ground further south labeled Death Valley by demographers, holds another 2 million. Indeed, Mexico City's eastern suburbs now contain 10 million people, more than the rest of the city. Even in Aztec times, when Tenochtitlan occupied only ten square miles and the population peaked at 80,000, the Valley of Mexico had difficulty supporting so many people. Now, with 700,000 poor people arriving from the countryside each year (equivalent to the population of San Francisco) and a birthrate generating another 900,000 a year (40 percent of all Mexican births), the plain truth is that Mexico City can no longer be supported by its hinterland.

Nor can other geographies continue to support this urban monster. 'Mexico City' now consumes 45 percent of the food produced in the center and south of the country. Its water needs have long exhausted all available sources in surrounding Mexico state, and now a billion gallons a day are pumped in at an absurd cost from the Lerna River 100 kilometers away, a process that is drying up Lake Chapala, outside Guadalajara, 500 miles north. The water is undrinkable anyway. Estimates are that by 1992, even that source will be tapped out and water will have to be pumped in from a more distant river system, a process that will require the construction of six 1,000-megawatt powerplants at a cost that would equal 20 percent of the nation's $108 billion foreign debt.

On the other end of the water flow, every day 11,000 tons of raw sewage pour back out of these mountains towards Tula in Hidalgo state, the once proud home of the Toltec civilization, now a festering eyesore and the site of what ecologists call the most poisonous dam in the country whose black waters now irrigate – and infect – tens of thousands of acres of farmland. But much of Mexico City's effluvia is never flushed down the drain. Indeed, the homes of 2.6 million people, about 17 percent of the population, are not hooked up to any sort of drainage system; it is said that on any given day, 20,000 tons of dried fecal matter litter the capital of the country.

In the thirty-odd years since Carlos Fuentes published a first novel about 'Mexico City' entitled in English *Where the Air Is Clear*, the capital has become unlivable most of the year. During the winter, thermal inversions seal the poisons produced by 140,000 industrial plants and 3 million badly tuned vehicles unequipped with emission control equipment, leaving the citizens retching and gasping for breath. Whereas living in Mexico City in the 1970s was equivalent to smoking two packs of unfiltered cigarettes a day, that rate is now up to three. In 1988, pollution registered over the life-threatening threshold of 200 points for a total of sixty-six days, double the number for 1987, a winter when birds like Canadian starlings fell dead from the sky by the thousands. In the spring, huge dust storms pepper the city with fine particles of bacteria-laden earth and gastrointestinal diseases ravage the 'lost cities'. During the brief rainy season, acid rain, laced with 6.2 million tons of toxic contaminants drench city streets and peel the hair off uncovered heads. Seventy percent of the births recorded here now register dangerous levels of lead in blood samples, and some doctors think a million kids have suffered irreversible brain damage as a result. One hundred thousand deaths annually are attributed to respiratory problems that arise from trying to live in this unlivable place.

'We *chilangos* [what Mexico City homeboys call themselves] are committing collective suicide', mutters Alfonso Cipres Villareal, director of the Mexican Ecology Movement.

The promise of employment to a perpetually disemployed rural population has always been Mexico City's magnet, but these days, the capital is doing an increasingly poor job of providing it to a burgeoning population. National unemployment stood at a semi-official 16 percent in 1988 with at least a million new jobs needed to accommodate restless youth each year – there is a shortfall of about 900,000 jobs in the area. Last year, 2.5 million residents of Mexico City, most of them under twenty-five (Mexico's median age is now sixteen) did not have any visible means of support.

As the rural unemployed pour into the capital, some are absorbed into the construction industry as *peones*, laborers, at the minimum wage ($3.10 a day). During the rebuilding process after the earthquake, tens of thousands of poor Indians from the south were trucked up to the capital by private construction firms to pad out lucrative contracts. One irony of the successful rehousing drive is that many of the newly unemployed *peones* stayed on, adding to the swelling stream of unemployed, underhoused emigres trying to scratch out a living on the city's increasingly unproductive surface.

After seven years of economic austerity, perhaps a sixth of the city's residents now depend on street vending to eat each day. Because so many people are now selling on the streets, turf wars are common and the *ambulantes*, whose long-standing ties to the PRI have been a traditional source of bodies for government rallies, are now being courted by the Cardenist opposition. Indeed, the PRI has organized a goon squad of street heavies from the enormous La Merced market who regularly confront Cardenist *ambulantes* in battles that sometimes spill right onto the floor of the nation's Chamber of Deputies.

Selling on the street is not limited by age. About 150,000 children are said to be working – and living – on Mexico City streets, a third of them addicted to the use of industrial solvents to ease the pains of hunger. One result: Mexico City now has one of the highest adolescent suicide rates in the world. Deteriorating mental health in the capital of the country puts about a million diagnosable schizophrenics on the streets, according to estimates of the Mexican Psychiatric Institute.

Increased crime is another result of chronic unemployment. Half the crimes committed here are not reported to the police – and no wonder; about 45 percent of the crimes committed in Mexico City, according to the Federal District's special district attorney, now involve the police. Police protection is just one of a myriad of services available only in corrupted form in Mexico City. The public transportation system, which now provides 19 million daily rides, is far outstripped by need. One final indignity that residents of the noisiest, most polluted, most corrupt, and most crowded city on the planet suffer: the absence of democratic representation in city government.

III

Mexico City's 6 million registered voters do not get to vote for their municipal officers – the regent (mayor), whose title unaccountably carried over from colonial days, is appointed by the president. Salinas's selection of former PRI secretary-general Manuel Camacho Solís, the boy wonder who rescued the ruling party once with his earthquake rehousing program, underscores the importance the PRI attaches to the loss of the capital in the 1988 elections. Other cosmetic measures designed to mask the lack of democracy here include a new Federal District Assembly convened during the fall of 1988 for the first time; however, it enjoys only consultative powers. Despite the lambasting the PRI received in July, the party manipulated itself into a majority of the sixty-six seats, an arrangement that caused riots at the assembly doors in September by furious constituents of what is now being called the 'popular urban movement' – the new focal point of the *damnificados*.

One of the premier pushers at the great bronze doors of the assembly's recently refurbished chambers was a yellow-masked, scarlet-caped gentleman who dubs himself 'Superbarrio Gómez' and is rapidly becoming a civic legend. Superbarrio (really a suit with three different militants donning it, depending on the occasion) is the creation of another assembly, the Asamblea de Barrios, a group that increasingly sets the pace for the popular urban movement.

Formed in April 1987 from inner-city *damnificado* groups by youth elements of the moribund Popular Socialist Party (PPS, part of the Cardenist coalition), the Asamblea claims a constituency of 30,000, 23 percent of them 'solicitors of housing' and was the first organization to realign the focus of neighborhood organizing once it became evident that the government would rehouse citizens 'damned' by the earthquake. 'The capital had a huge housing deficit before *el sismo*, and land speculation since then has made the problem much graver', reasons Marcos Rascón, the burly roughhouse leader of the Asamblea. He calculates that the metropolitan area needs at least 171,000 new units annually, a full million by the year 2,000. Virtually no new residential housing was built in Mexico City in 1988.

Using the housing crunch as a springboard to reach those 'damned by life', the Asamblea challenged big landholders, fighting the federal district government for legislation to control soaring rents, and confronting the police over evictions. In the center of the city where the apartment squeeze is worst, landlords hire goon squads to throw tenants' possessions into the street while the police back them up. Sixteen such evictions occur daily, often with Asamblistas on hand to put the furniture back.

To accompany this pugnacious stance, Rascón and his *compañeros* invented Superbarrio Gómez, a figure who draws on the underclass's long-time love affair with the dubious spectacle of professional wrestling. One of Superbarrio's first performances was a wrestling match against an eye-patched malevolent dubbed 'Super Landlord', scheduled for the Zócalo on a Saturday afternoon when thousands of Asamblea members had pitched a tent city in the courtyard of the Metropolitan Cathedral. The sudden appearance of motorcycle police who confiscated the 'ring' only added to the hilarity of the situation – one of the Asamblea's great talents is to make people laugh even as it directs the Federal District government's feet to one embarrassing fire after another. Subsequent adventures of Superbarrio Gomez, most often played these days by a pudgy Argentina Street *ambulante*, have included being the first masked man to enter the nation's congress (police tried to block his passage), a near-unmasking by an enraged Jalisco state governor, who is now the nation's attorney general, and a recent wild and wooly tour to California during which la Migra (the INS), allegedly on instructions from the Mexican consul in Los Angeles, arrested Superbarrio for several hours while they checked out his lack of papers. Invited by the American Friends Service Committee, Superbarrio had been denied permission to enter the United States because he could not establish financial resources, and, like so many of his countrymen, crossed into California illegally. Now Superbarrio's adventures have become so notorious that Hollywood mogul Sidney Pollack and Chicano director Luis Valdez are talking up a movie, in which, it is rumored, Dustin Hoffman and Robert De Niro will be asked to play.

Another of Superbarrio's superexploits: a tongue-in-cheek run at the nation's presidency in an effort to shame the disunited Mexican left into supporting the candidacy of Cuauhtémoc Cárdenas. Once a modicum of unity had been forged, Superbarrio, much like socialist candidate Heberto Castillo, withdrew from the race and became Cárdenas's constant champion at the myriad marches and rallies both before and after the election. Cárdenas himself reciprocated by actually writing in Superbarrio's name as *his* presidential choice on 6 July, paying tribute to all of Mexico City's Superbarrios. In a very real sense, Cuauhtémoc Cárdenas's landslide victory in the capital can be attributed to the many Superbarrios who are the rank-and-file of the popular urban movement. 'On 19 September 1985, after the earthquake, we rescued our neighbors', declares Rascón, 'on 6 July we rescued our nation. ...

IV

In March 1989, three years after the earthquake and with the tumult of the stunning presidential elections behind it, Mexico City's popular urban movement is marching down diverse avenues. For the Asamblea de Barrios, attaining 'Anáhuac' (the Mexican name for a region of which Tenochtitlan was only one city-state), the conversion of the Federal District into Mexico's thirty-second state is now the most pressing task. Demonstrations regularly mark the afternoons on the Zócalo outside Federal District offices – at this writing, the Asamblea has just completed five days of marches demanding the resignation of Camacho Solis as an unelected – and therefore unconstitutional – executive officer. The Asamblea's deep immersion in this past summer's political waters has turned its attentions towards democratizing the most undemocratic metropolis in the world, where 19 million citizens are constitutionally barred from voting for their own city's officials.

If the Asamblea is about democratizing the more central areas of the Federal District, CONAMUP (National Coordinating Body of the Urban Popular Movement), a loose federation of many squatter groups, is trying to alter political equations in the outskirts. Tirelessly working in the marginalized *colonias* – the ones precariously perched on the sides of the eroded hills twenty miles from the Zócalo, the 'last arrivals' – CONAMUP is an outgrowth of the brigades of young left students who went into the urban slums after the 1968 student movement had been crushed by the government in a bloody massacre of some 337 students at the Tlaltelolco housing complex. Following a stretch of frustrated guerilla activity in the southern mountains and northern cities (fifteen micro-guerilla focos operated in Mexico from 1965 to 1974), handfuls of hardcore survivors began working in the *colonias* of smaller cities throughout the country – cities of 100,000 to 400,000 are the fastest growing population centers. In Mexico City, one CONAMUP stronghold in San Miguel Teotongo in the desolate Iztapalapa delegation on the southeastern fringe of the capital where the Union of Colonos even fielded a candidate for Congress on 6 July, an atypical strophe for CONAMUP-style organization. For years, CONAMUP militants have condemned elections as a trap laid by the state to absorb organizing energies, citing self-reliance and community defense as far more pressing priorities, a position that has separated this group from other popular movements and organizations. Now CONAMUPistas are looking for convergence, ways to line up with less radical groups in the Federal District's metropolitan area in an effort to combat the natural isolation of the far-flung *colonias* in which they work and a position influenced by last July's left electoral coalition, according to Pedro Moctezuma, the CONAMUP candidate in San Miguel Teotongo.

CONAMUP's coalition tendencies are not limited to Mexico City – or even Mexico itself. In the fall of 1987, the organization played a prominent role in pulling together a caravan of *damnificados* that drove a circuitous route to New York City to mark the United Nations' designation of The Year of the Homeless. Joining with Latin American housing organizations that had met in Managua in February 1986, and invited by the New York–based October 6th Coalition of squatters and homeless, CONAMUP women led an energetic march on the UN, chanting the familiar slogan of Mexico City's *damnificados*: Lucha! Lucha! Lucha!/No deja de luchar/por vivienda digna/barrata y popular! (Struggle! Struggle! Struggle! Don't ever stop struggling for a decent, low-cost and proletarian home!)

Back downtown in Mexico City, the Union of Neighbors and 19 September Damnificados (UV y D-19) concentrates on culture. After *el Sismo*, the organization became particularly concerned about 'earthquake syndrome' kids – children traumatized by the catastrophe who shut out the world in self-defense. Art and theater became healing tools for playwright Mario Enrique Martinez, the guiding spirit of the Teatro Zopilote, who still lives in the Roma, where the group is rooted. The Roma, a middle-class neighborhood located adjacent to the fashionable Zona Rosa, was devastated by the quake but did not qualify for many aid programs because its residents were not poor enough, so it turned to its own resources, doing rummage sales and dances and drumming up aid from European philanthropists to revive its pre-*Sismo* semblance. Today the UV y D-19 puts its money into the neighborhood Frida Kahlo gallery, a weekly film club, dance and theater groups, a ceramics workshop, a neighborhood philharmonic and a sewing cooperative.

The Seamstresses Union of 19 September (usually referred to simply as the Las Costureras), owns an indelible chapter of the *damnificado* legend. In the aftermath of el Sismo, sweatshop owners, determined to rescue their inventories and machinery, hired crews to dig their possessions out of the rubble even while many garment workers were still trapped under collapsed buildings. Eight hundred sweatshops were destroyed in the quake, and many bosses just packed up and left town with PRI-run garment worker unions never lifting a finger to stop the runaways or help the survivors recover unpaid wages. Working with a determined group of union sisters, Evangelina Corona, a serene, white-haired dynamo who might pass for Mexico's Mother Jones, began pulling the threads together. In the first weeks after the catastrophe, when access to Mexico's ruling circles was magically opened by the new-found moral aura of the *damnificados*, Las Costureras were granted recognition as a legal bargaining agent by President De la Madrid. However, this government connection went cold when the women began actively signing up shops that the PRI-run unions had not bothered to organize. By the first May Day after the earthquake, heavily armed police were beating the seamstresses when they tried to join the PRI labor movement's annual tribute to the President, a confrontation that has since become a yearly scuffle.

For a while, Las Costureras were a favored project for international lefties, particularly radical feminists who, with a cadenced regularity, tramped through the union's compound out in San Antonio Abad on the site of a collapsed eleven-story building that had housed many sweatshops. But as *el Sismo* fades from memory, the union has fallen on hard times, losing contracts to PRI thugs, who, armed with baseball bats, invade shop elections with impunity. On 19 September 1988, after an early morning street mass to commemorate the third anniversary of the deaths of a thousand union sisters, Mexico City's Preventative Police beat the seamstresses to the ground with batons when Corona tried to lead them to the offices of the Secretary of Interior to protest the ruling party's union goons.

Prospects for the Popular Union of New Tenochtitlan are

equally mixed. The presidential election forced a split in the union with those living north of the Zócalo (originally organized by the Mexican Socialist Party) supporting Cárdenas, and those south of the Zócalo remaining loyal to Rosario Ibarra de Piedra, the candidate of the Revolutionary Workers Party, which had been instrumental in founding the union three years earlier. The rift was temporarily healed when Ibarra, a red-headed whirlwind of social justice advocacy, joined forces with Cárdenas to challenge the presidential vote fraud. Sadly, despite years of organizing in the neighborhood, Ibarra's vote totals here on Tenochtitlan were dismal, and nationally the party lost all its Congressional seats plus its electoral registration, a loss that cuts considerable political ground from under the Popular Union. Now New Tenochtitlan has turned to organizing solicitors of land, negotiating for lots in the south of the city, far from the Zócalo, which members can buy into. Some of Mario Becerra's attentions are currently tied to organizing *ambulantes*, many of them blind, who have recently pulled away from the PRI. His friend, Eduardo Miranda, furious over police *razzias* (raids) on neighborhood youth, organizes trips to the PRI-controlled delegation to complain. Both have spent a lot of energy urging neighbors to demand rent freezes in the popular rehabilitation housing – RHP units have jumped from 28,000 to 71,000 pesos a month since April 1987. 'Our goals really haven't changed much in the last few years', reflects Becerra, 'we are still fighting for a decent living space and a decent life.'

The ruling party's response to the deep wounds the urban movement has inflicted on PRI domination of Mexico City's myriad neighborhoods has vacillated wildly from homicidal violence to copycat protest marches to rewriting history. Sometimes the reaction is soft – a gentle but wholesale eviction of squatters in a Lomas del Seminario shantytown pitched on an environmentally sensitive hillside in the south of the city was quietly applauded by the PRI ecology clique. More often than not, the glove comes off – for example, when *ambulante* mobs under PRI control brutally beat inner-city Indians protesting a Columbus Day celebration on Reforma Boulevard this past October. And sometimes the PRI even tries to emulate the opposition: the head of the Mexico City PRI, Jesús Salazar Toledano, led marches against pollution and delays in Tlaltelolco reconstruction before he was forced from office after a few months of such unprecedented mixing with the rabble. Another

PRI gambit has been what prominent media critic Raul Trejo Delarbe called 'the process of dememorization' – rewriting history to make the PRI government the hero of the *damnificado* struggle, a practice now echoed in speeches by government functionaries each 19 September. A steady stream of personal testimony by such chroniclers of the urban movement as Elena Poniatowska, Carlos Monsiváis, and Cristina Pacheco has overwhelmed government efforts to corrupt the community's sense of its own history.

But the PRI's best card in trying to wrest power back from the people remains the regency and the city government it holds hostage from elections. As mayor, Camacho Solís and his secretary general, Manuel Aguilera, fence agilely with an urban movement they have come to know well since 19 September 1985.

Before dawn on Wednesday, 6 July 1988, Eduardo Miranda slipped into his shoes and padded down Regina Street to stand watch outside the polling place at number 57. 'I wanted to make sure they didn't try anything before people started to vote', he says – in Mexico, ballot boxes often come 'pregnant' with mysteriously cast ballots. All that day and most of the night, Miranda watched first the voters, then the vote counters, and finally, the vote count itself, which, in the end, admitted that Cuauhtémoc Cárdenas had won the first three blocks of Regina Street, 198 to 172 over El Pelón. Convinced that his poll watching had kept the election honest, at least on his block, Miranda drifted off to sleep early on the morning of the seventh, even as the PRI was boisterously announcing that it had won a landslide victory everywhere in the country. The next morning and the next seven mornings after that, the Federal Electoral Commission and Mexico's PRI-paid media did its damndest to substantiate the ruling party's claim but its efforts were ineffective against public incredulity. 'This is like Alice in Wonderland', marveled Miranda at the PRI government's rockheaded efforts to explain the stupendous electoral fraud. 'They have never understood that *el Sismo* changed everything here', he observed.

Three years after the great quake, what Miranda understands and what the PRI still doesn't: when the tectonic plates start grinding and the earth starts shaking, when the sky turns upside down and buildings fall on you, the shape of things gets skewed. The neighborhood looks big, and the government small. At such moments, the prospect of altering balances shines just like the sunlight right through the damaged walls at 39 Regina Street. This is what happened fourteen years ago in Nicaragua when Somoza looted the international earthquake aid and bolstered the Sandinistas' fortunes in the cities at a crucial stage in the struggle. In El Salvador, the 1986 quake allowed the FMLN to creep back into the capital. Ecuador's 1988 earthquake finished Febres Cordero, Ronald Reagan's favorite Latin American demagogue. Peru's tremendous earthquake in 1969 brought the mountain people down to the sea, a process whose impact echoes loudly every night in shantytowns of Lima. Just how badly the destruction of downtown Mexico City in September 1985 damaged the longest running political dictatorship in the western world is still being measured – but one matter is certain: Mexico has never been the same since.

Contributors

FRANCES BEAL is a long-time activist in the Black liberation movement and was formerly an editor of *The Black Scholar*. She currently writes about Black politics for *Crossroads* magazine and other publications.

ELLEN DAVID-FRIEDMAN is a member and former chairperson of the Vermont Rainbow Coalition.

BARBARA DAY covers New York City politics for the *Guardian* (New York).

DAVID R. DIAZ is an urban planner and environmental activist who has long been active in East L.A. and the San Gabriel Valley. He is currently engaged in a major comparative study of growth control politics in Southern California.

MAURICIO GASTÓN was active as an urban planner/theorist/activist in Boston's Roxbury and Jamaica Plain neighborhoods. While at the University of Massachusetts at Boston he worked with Marie Kennedy on the research from which 'Roxbury: Capital Investment or Community Development?' was drawn. He died in 1987.

DAVITA SILFEN GLASBERG teaches sociology at the University of Connecticut-Storrs.

TOM GOOD is a writer and activist who lives in Phoenix, Arizona.

MARIE KENNEDY is a long-time community and labor activist in the Boston area. She currently teaches in the community planning program at the University of Massachusetts at Boston.

STAUGHTON LYND is a historian and labor lawyer active in Youngstown.

DAVID MOBERG is an editor of *In These Times*.

GUS NEWPORT is a veteran of the civil rights movement and has long worked in community development programs. He was mayor of Berkeley, California from 1979 to 1987, and is currently executive director of the Dudley Street Neighborhood Initiative in Boston and a vice-president of the World Peace Council.

JONATHAN PIERCE traveled to mining camps and fishing villages as one of the organizers of the NDP's victory in the Yukon. He is now completing his dissertation at Carleton University in Ottawa.

JOHN ROSS lives in Mexico City. He covers Mexican politics for the San Francisco *Bay Guardian* and the *San Francisco Examiner*.

SUSAN RUDDICK is a long-time activist in Montreal citizen politics. She is now at UCLA, where she is completing a dissertation on homeless youth.

CHRIS TILLY is an editor of *Dollars and Sense*. He currently teaches at the University of Lowell in Massachusetts.

DICK WALKER teaches in the Geography Department of the University of California, Berkeley, where he studies urban development and the political economy of California.